HIDDEN SOURCES

Family History in Unlikely Places

HIDDEN SOURCES

Family History in Unlikely Places

Laura Szucs Pfeiffer

Ancestry

Library of Congress Cataloging-in-Publication Data

Pfeiffer, Laura Szucs, 1967-
     Hidden sources : family history in unlikely places / Laura Szucs Pfeiffer.
       p. cm.
     Includes bibliographical references and index.
     ISBN 0-916489-86-8
      1. Genealogy--Sources. 2. United States--Genealogy--Sources. I. Title.

CS14 .P48 1999
929'.1'072073--dc21

99-0550690

Published by Ancestry® Publishing, an
imprint of MyFamily.com, Inc.

P.O. Box 990
Orem, Utah 84059
www.ancestry.com

First Printing 2000
10 9 8 7 6 5 4 3 2 1

Printed in the United States of America

Acknowledgments

There are many people to whom I owe thanks for sharing knowledge, support, and guidance throughout this project.

First and foremost, my mother, who has nurtured my interest in preserving family history for as long as I can remember. She also provided the encouragement to write this book and shared her expertise to help make this work a solid reference piece. Sandra Luebking graciously reviewed my earliest drafts and provided many helpful suggestions. Thanks also to Raymond S. Wright, III, Ph.D., AG, for reading this manuscript and contributing the foreword for the book. I would also like to thank my sister, Juliana Smith, for her ideas and for answering my many questions pertaining to Internet research. Another individual who deserves my gratitude is Rev. Charles Banet, who was among the first to encourage my work in the field of family history.

I'm very thankful to my family and friends for supporting me during what seemed like a never-ending project. My daughters, Caroline and Anna, and my husband, Dan, put up with me and the endless stacks of books and papers that managed to take over every flat surface in our home. My sisters, father, husband, and friends all kept me on track by regularly asking, "Aren't you finished with that book yet?"

Others who have generously helped in the project include: Brian Andersson; Judy Barnby; Kelley Blake, National Archives-Mid-Atlantic Region; James Otto Bombach; Peter Bunce, National Archives-Great Lakes Region; Kent Carter, National Archives-Southwest Region; John Celardo, National Archives-Mid-Atlantic Region; Dr. John Daly, Illinois State Archives; Raymond Dennis; Donn Devine; Thomas J. Fleming; Scott Forsyth, National Archives-Great Lakes Region; Gerry Curtin Ganley; E. Wade Hone; Roger Joslyn; Linda Lamberty; Kory Meyerink; Gary Mokotoff; Dr. Robert Morris, National Archives-Northeast Region; Joan Murray; Sunny Nash; James Neagles; James Owens, National Archives-New England Region; Dr. Robert Plowman, National Archives-Mid-Atlantic Region; Connie Potter, National Archives-Washington, D.C.; Jayare Roberts; John Scroggins; Joseph Silinonte; Marian Smith, Immigration and Naturalization Service; John Stitz; John Sullivan; Linda Herrick Swisher; Rick Tapio; and Phil Willner. My colleagues at Ancestry.com also deserve special mention for their help and encouragement, especially Paul Allen, Jennifer Browning, André Brummer, David Farnsworth, Jake Gehring, Janet Haniak, Suzanne Russo, Heather Stratford, Dan Taggart, Rebekah Thorstenson, John Tolman, Jennifer Utley, Megan Vandre, and Matthew Wright.

—Laura Szucs Pfeiffer

Contents

List of Illustrations

Foreword

Show me the record. Just give me the facts. Where can I find my family? Most of the millions of Americans searching for ancestors have no interest in thick methods manuals or how-to books. They would not describe themselves as genealogists or even family historians. Most Americans just want to learn when ancestors were born, married, or died and where these events happened. They are curious about forebears' lives: how they earned a living, what they looked like, and what their world looked like. They do not want to read a book about how to do it. Persons studying the origins of their family prefer to have someone tell them what to do. Or they want to look up a short entry in something like a dictionary of genealogy that will explain in a paragraph or two where to look for the information they want. Until now, no book filled this need.

Expert researchers know that thousands of agencies and organizations created records about the persons within their jurisdictions or about potential customers or members. Regardless of the ravages of war, nature, and man, so many records have been created since the Middle Ages ended that everyone should be recorded in a surviving record somewhere. The key to reconstructing lives is understanding where the records are. First, records created by family and neighborhood are examined. Next, researchers scour the city and county or township in which ancestors lived for any record local agencies kept. Before leaving this level, old directories and newspapers are studied to identify local businesses, churches, societies, cooperatives, unions, and any other institutions that sought members or customers. One soon learns that city, town, and county offices preserve records, as do local libraries and historical and genealog-ical societies. Businesses, hospitals, churches, and other associations also preserve older records or turn them over to archives, historical societies, or libraries. State archives and libraries provide access to countless records stored there because of their historical or legal value. Rooting through inventories, finding aids, and catalogs will help researchers learn about state records that preserve the names and life events of people from the past. The government of the United States has been counting and recording the people within its boundaries for over two centuries. The executive, legislative, and judicial branches of the U.S. government have all kept records about our ancestors. We just need the patience to find them. Fortunately, *Hidden Sources* has identified many of the personal, local, state, regional, and national records everyone interested in their heritage will need as they reconstruct family histories.

The information in *Hidden Sources* can be found in other publications, but few persons searching for ancestors would know their titles or how to find them. If they did search for books detailing the thousands of sources available, they would discover that these books comprise a small library of sources with thousands of pages to sort through in search of records that may provide researchers with ancestral facts. In *Hidden Sources* the average researcher will find many little-known sources that probably contain information about their ancestors' lives. Rather than lengthy descriptions of records, readers will discover short explanations that help them determine immediately whether or not a given record may contain the information they need. The author provides clues to the location of these little-used records and a list of books with further information about the records. For those that enjoy using the Internet in their research, the author provides URLs (Web site addresses on the Internet) that will take them to sites with further information about these hidden sources.

Most of the manuals and encyclopedic works that mention the records detailed in *Hidden Sources* do not provide examples of the documents themselves. A great strength of this volume is the unusually large number of illustrations. The captions for these illustrations provide essential facts about the content and use of the documents the captions describe.

Where do people look for more information—or for missing information—once a search for birth, marriage, and death records has ended? Where would they look if federal census data is incomplete or missing for their family? *Hidden Sources'* real strength is that it provides those interested in learning about their family a *vade mecum* they can take with them into clerks' offices, libraries, historical societies and genealogical societies and which is filled with facts about the records the researcher needs. If clerks or archivists are unsure of a researcher's request, the person can show them an example from *Hidden Sources*. No other book is as easily used nor as filled with information about so many unique sources of information.

This work fills a void in the literature of family history and genealogy. Americans searching for facts about their ancestors would normally use several hefty reference books to find the clues contained in this compact volume. It is the first handy research aid capable of providing the details researchers need in order to find information in sources that are often overlooked.

—Raymond S. Wright III, Ph.D., AG
Professor of Family History
Brigham Young University

Introduction

As the title suggests, *Hidden Sources: Family History in Unlikely Place*s is a collection of records and sources that have been identified and described with the family historian in mind. There is no doubt, however, that writers, journalists, historians, and anyone else with an interest in the past can benefit as well from the fascinating selection of research topics in this volume.

Everyone is connected to the past through family relationships. Yet, proof of these connections, and an adequate understanding of the places and times in which our predecessors lived, can be hard to find. Generally, family history research will lead us in many directions—often wasting our time and money. But with a proper guide to sources, it is usually possible not only to identify people who died long ago, but to discover things more meaningful than just their names and the dates of their births and deaths. If we know where to look, we may be fortunate enough to get a glimpse of their everyday lives, to capture their personalities, and to comprehend the traits and values they have handed down to us through the generations. In this country, there are enormous quantities of rich historical materials from which to draw. Every state has documentation on millions of Americans—the famous as well as the unnoticed. The primary goal of this work is to shed a light on a wide range of sources that are frequently overlooked, even by experienced researchers.

One of the main objectives of family historians is to prove the existence of an individual or family, and then to prove a relationship to that individual or family. The basic rules of genealogy are to begin with yourself and work backward in time, and to make a record of each source of information you use as you go along. It is not acceptable or wise to simply adopt information from something just because it has been printed, or just because someone said it was so. Original records are the core of good research. Over the years, however, billions of records that were rich in historical information have been lost in fires and floods, and enormous numbers of them have been tossed in the trash bin because they were no longer deemed valuable. As "official" registrations of vital records become unavailable, the biographical information in a hidden historical source assumes greater importance. Because so many information sources have been lost over time, it often becomes necessary to use alternative sources to locate and document facts about individuals and families. This book is loaded with alternative sources that reflect the lives of famous and ordinary people.

Chances are, anyone who picks up this work will have some degree of experience in researching family history, and will probably have used the more traditional records. These traditional records include such things as home sources, vital records (recordings of births, marriages, and deaths), cemetery records, printed local and family histories, and census records. While it may come as a surprise to some readers that the author has included a number of traditional records in *Hidden Sources*, it is the non-traditional use of the records that earned them a place here.

Once a researcher feels that traditional avenues have been exhausted, there is a vast array of lesser-known sources that should be considered, and that kind of fascinating material dominates this work. In this volume over a hundred hidden sources are described and generously illustrated. Each section provides information on where the category of records can be found, and where applicable, addresses (URLs) for "Internet Sites of Interest" are provided. Readers seeking more information are referred to a "Selected Readings" section that appears at the end of each subject description.

In my estimation, there is no better way to understand an information source than to actually be able to see it and study it. With that in mind, this volume has page after page of wonderful illustrations of the sources described. Because of the age and fragile condition of some of the documents, it was hard to capture a clear copy, but the images presented here surely provide an idea of the format of records, and demonstrate the potential of a source to advance or enhance a research project.

Beyond identifying individuals and proving relationships, most family historians want to have a deeper understanding of their ancestors' lives. As one family historian put it, a collection of names, dates, and places, however well proven and documented, are as dull as a telephone book. In order to better understand our ancestors, we have to know more about them. Records of adoptions and apprenticeships, autobiographies, unusual death records, farm records, coroner's inquests, court records, guardianship records, homestead records, immigrant letters, licenses, marriage dispensations, midwives' records, neighborhood collections, passport applications, school records and all the others in this book have the potential of giving insight into the lives and times of ancestors.

In compiling this work, the author drew from "Lesser-Used Sources," a presentation I have given at a number of national and local genealogical conferences. From that presentation, she has taken the topics I discussed, researched each one thoroughly, and treated each one in a separate section. Becoming absorbed in the subject matter, she found new sources I had missed and turned it all into a solid reference work.

Understandably, this book could not be an all-encompassing encyclopedia on the subject of hidden family history sources, and it is expected that some readers will find that some of their favorite obscure sources have been left out. There is such a vast array of research material available that it would take more than a lifetime to catalog it all. Some sources were intentionally omitted because, while they exist, they are next to impossible to access. Additionally, the author depended on sources with which she or I had actually used, not wanting to present any information we did not fully research. Readers who know of potential hidden sources that may have been overlooked in this volume are encouraged to send recommendations to the author in care of Ancestry.com, P.O. Box 990, Orem, UT 84059.

Most of those who have gone before us have left traces of their lives somewhere, and fortunately documentation on millions of Americans from all walks of life still exists. *Hidden Sources* points to an exciting assortment of material that represents a great cross-section of the American experience. For some, the topics discussed here will bring brand new discoveries. For others, the book promises fresh insights into overlooked or forgotten storehouses of information. Hopefully, *Hidden Sources* will spark creative research ideas and open up new ways for every reader to learn more about his or her past. The great thing about family history research is that in sifting through the evidence of our past, we usually discover a great deal about ourselves as well.

—Loretto D. Szucs
Vice President of Publishing
Ancestry.com

HIDDEN SOURCES

Family History in Unlikely Places

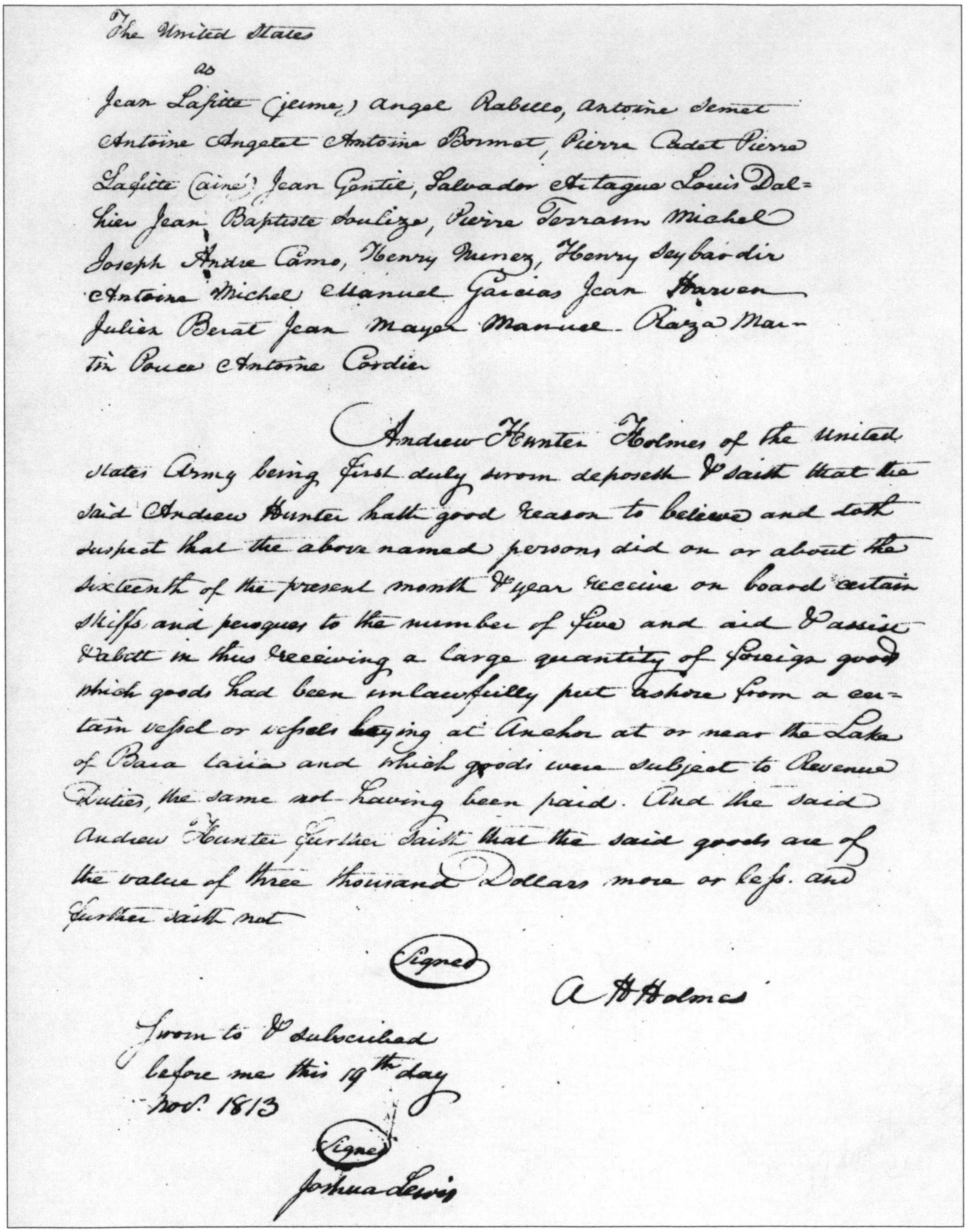

The United States
vs
Jean Lafitte (jeune) Angel Rabello, Antoine demet
Antoine Angetet Antoine Bormet, Pierre Cadet Pierre
Lafitte (ainé) Jean Gentil, Salvador Aitagua Louis Dal=
lier Jean Baptiste Souliza, Pierre Terraim Michel
Joseph Andre Camo, Henry Munez, Henry Seybardir
Antoine Michel Manuel Garcias Jean Harven
Julien Berat Jean Mayor Manuel Raza Mar-
tin Ponce Antoine Cordier

Andrew Hunter Holmes of the United States Army being first duly sworn deposeth & saith that the said Andrew Hunter hath good reason to believe and doth suspect that the above named persons did on or about the sixteenth of the present month & year receive on board certain skiffs and perogues to the number of five and aid & assist & abett in thus receiving a large quantity of foreign goods which goods had been unlawfully put ashore from a certain vessel or vessels laying at Anchor at or near the Lake of Barataria and which goods were subject to Revenue Duties, the same not having been paid. And the said Andrew Hunter further saith that the said goods are of the value of three thousand Dollars more or less. and further saith not

(Signed)
A H Holmes

Sworn to & subscribed
before me this 19th day
Nov. 1813

(Signed)
Joshua Lewis

Figure 1

A page from an 1813 admiralty case in which privateer and freebooter Jean Lafitte, his brother Pierre, and others are charged with aiding and abetting a criminal act "in thus receiving a large quantity of foreign goods which goods had been unlawfully put ashore from a certain vessel or vessels laying at Anchor near the Lake of Berataria and which goods were subject to Revenue Duties, the same not having been paid." The original record, which is at the National Archives - Southwest Region (Fort Worth), is similar to millions of admiralty documents that can be found at the Fort Worth region and in other regions of the National Archives.

Admiralty Court Records

It is a common misconception that admiralty court records are limited to cases pertaining to seamen and the vessels that traveled the high seas. While a court with admiralty powers regularly oversaw such matters as seamen's wages, smuggling, piracy, prize (the confiscation of enemy ships and their cargo during wartime), shipwrecks, salvage, insurance, freight and passenger

Legal records pertaining to people that lived along the shoreline of any navigable waterway of the United States, including lakes, rivers, and canals, are likely to be found in admiralty courts.

contracts, bottomry (using a ship as collateral), and contracts between merchants and mariners, they also had civil and criminal jurisdiction over all persons having any relation to maritime transactions, including shipbuilders and dockworkers.

Legal records pertaining to individuals who lived along the shoreline of any navigable waterway of the United States, including lakes, rivers, and canals, are likely to be found in admiralty courts. In addition to dockets and case files, a researcher may find evidence such as ship registers, licenses, crew lists, manifests, passenger lists, seamen's contracts, logbooks, and other correspondence carried by ships.

Records from American admiralty courts, as well as some English records obtained during the American Revolution, can be found in most branches of the National Archives. Pre-colonial records can sometimes be found in England as well.

See also *Maritime Records.*

Selected Readings:

Andrews, Charles M. *The Colonial Period of American History: England's Commercial and Colonial Policy.* vol. 4. New Haven: Yale University Press, 1938.

Eakle, Arlene H. "Research in Court Records." *The Source: A Guidebook of American Genealogy.* Rev. ed. Salt Lake City: Ancestry, 1997.

Szucs, Loretto Dennis, and Sandra Hargreaves Luebking. *The Archives: A Guide to the National Archives Field Branches.* Salt Lake City: Ancestry, 1988.

Towle, Dorothy S. *Records of the Vice-Admiralty Court of Rhode Island: 1716-1752.* Washington, D.C.: American Historical Association Committee on Legal History, 1939.

Ubbelhide, Carl. *The Vice-Admiralty Courts and the American Revolution.* Chapel Hill: University of North Carolina Press, 1960.

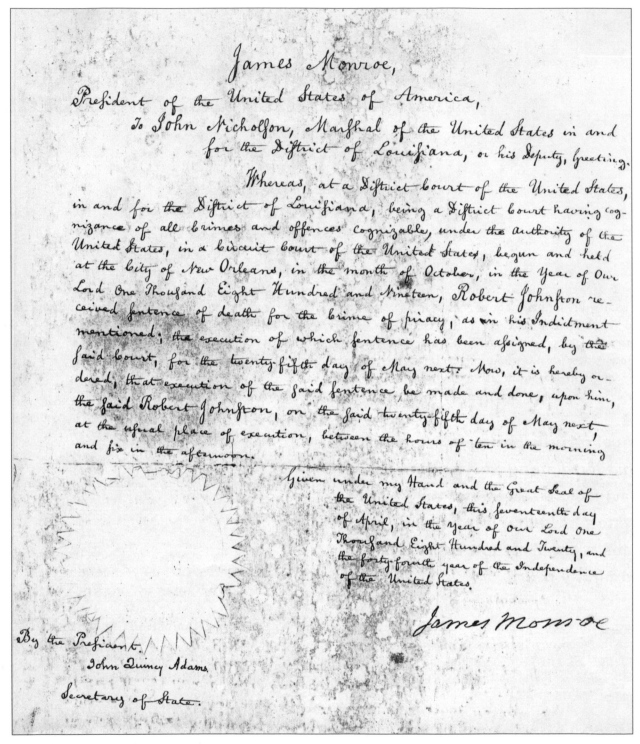

Figure 2

A page from *U.S. v. Dasfargus, et. al*, U.S. District Court at New Orleans, in which pirates sentenced to hang appealed to the President of the United States for pardons. President James Monroe denied their appeals. The original case is at the National Archives - Southwest Region, Fort Worth.

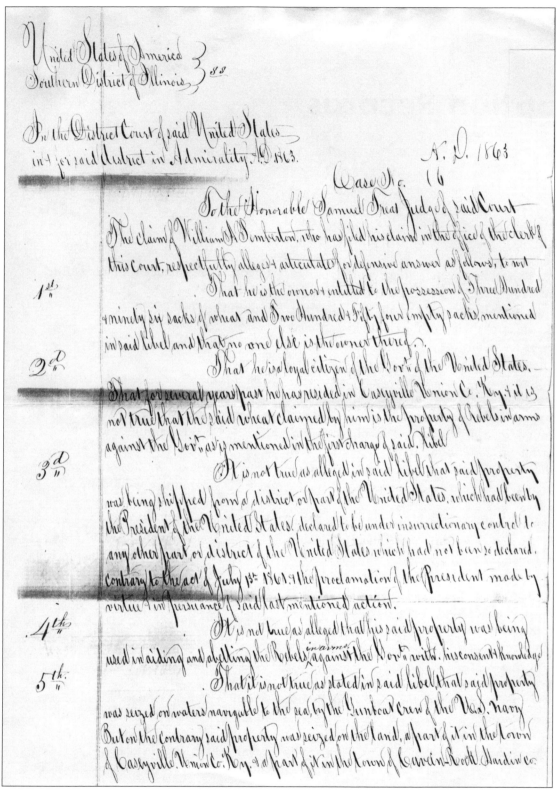

Figure 3

An 1863 admiralty case concerning the claim of William Pemberton, that he was wrongly accused of aiding and abetting "the Rebels in arms" along the Mississippi River. The original file is in the National Archives - Great Lakes Region, Chicago.

Adoption Records

Generally, adoptions result from court processes. State statutes vary in the amount of information required, but records typically contain the name, residence, and age or birth date of the child to be adopted; the names of the biological parents; and the names of the adopting parents. The consent of the biological parents, along with their sworn and signed statements relinquishing their rights to the child, and the final decree are also found in case files. Very old case files may still be found in courthouses and archives in some states, but for privacy considerations, recent and even the oldest adoption files are sealed and inaccessible without a court order in many other states.

While original birth certificates are most desirable to begin the research procedure, most adopted children today have amended birth certificates with the adoptive parents' names listed. Many states have reunion registries that help to connect birth parents and adoptees (over the age of eighteen or twenty-one) who are seeking each other. Reunions are allowed if all the involved parties agree.

The following are a few of the organizations that provide information and support for those seeking birth parents and those who have been adopted.

Adoptee Liberty Movement Association
P.O. Box 727
Radio City Station
New York, NY 10101-2727

American Adoption Congress
1000 Connecticut Avenue NW
Washington, DC 20036

International Soundex Reunion Registry
P.O. Box 2312
Carson City, NV 87111

Selected Readings:

Askin, Jayne. *Search*. Phoenix, Ariz.: Oryx Press, 1998.

Culligan, Joseph J. *Adoption Searches Made Easier*. Miami, Fla.: FJA, Inc., 1996.

Rillera, Mary Jo. *The Adoption Searchbook*. Westminster, Calif.: Pure, Inc., 1991.

Strauss, Jean A. *Birthright: The Guide to Search and Reunion for Adoptees, Birthparents, and Adoptive Parents*. New York: Penguin, 1994.

Tillman, Norma Mott. *How to Find Almost Anyone, Anywhere*. Nashville, Tenn.: Rutledge Hill Press, 1998.

Internet Sites of Interest:

ADOPT: Assistance Information Support
http://www.adopting.org/ffcwnr.html

Adoptee Searcher's Handbook
http://www.ouareau.com/adoptee/index.html

Adoption Reunion Research
http://womenshealth.miningco.com/library/bladopt.htm

BirthQuest
http://www.birthquest.org/

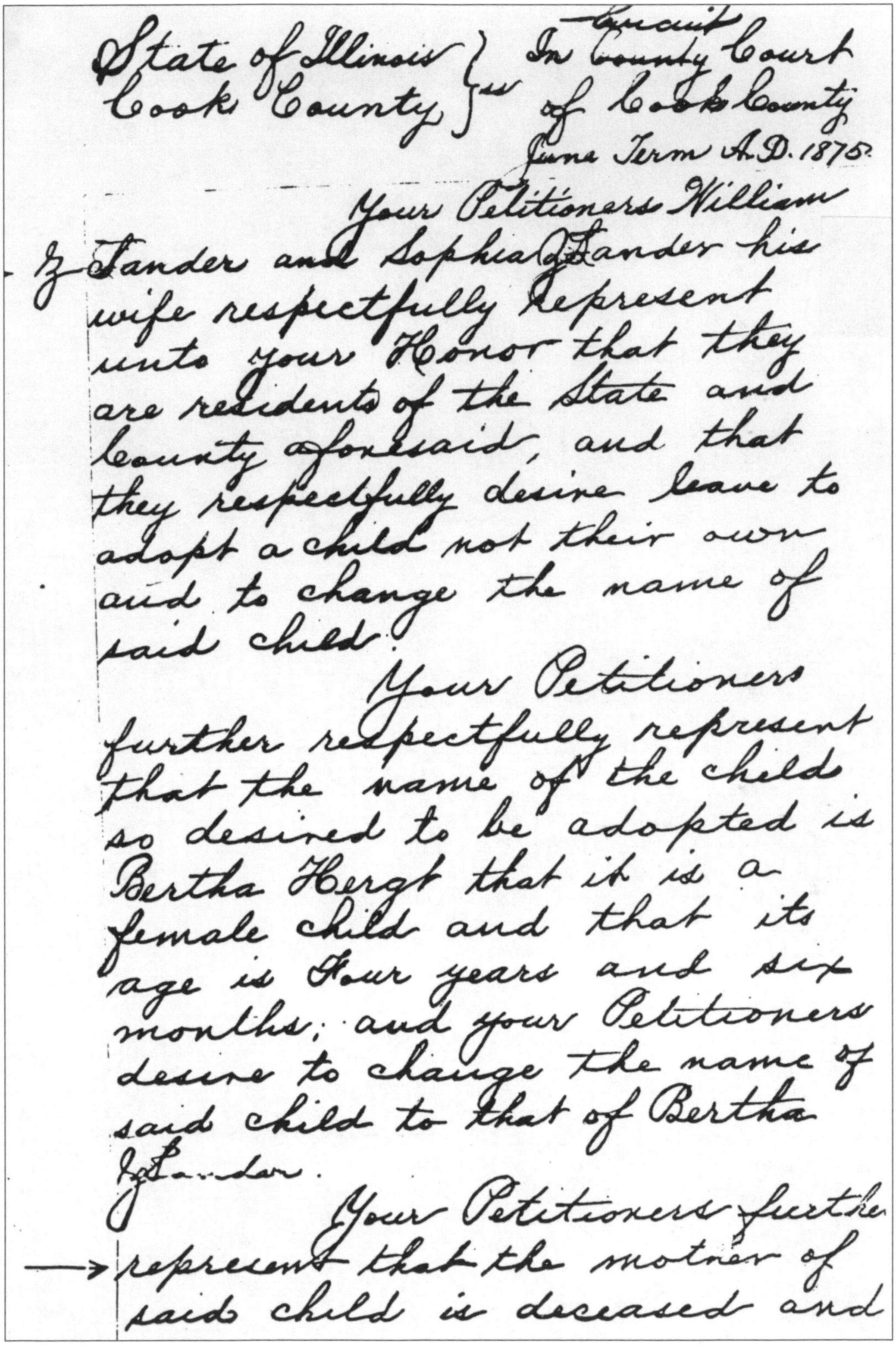
State of Illinois } ss In ~~County~~ Circuit Court
Cook County } of Cook County
June Term A.D. 1875.

Your Petitioners William Z Zander and Sophia Zander his wife respectfully represent unto your Honor that they are residents of the State and County aforesaid, and that they respectfully desire leave to adopt a child not their own and to change the name of said child.

Your Petitioners further respectfully represent that the name of the child so desired to be adopted is Bertha Hergt that it is a female child and that its age is Four years and six months; and your Petitioners desire to change the name of said child to that of Bertha Zander.

Your Petitioners further represent that the mother of said child is deceased and

Figure 4

While adoption records have been sealed off from public view in almost every state, that was not always the case. This court document is that of child Bertha Hergt, adopted by William and Bertha Zander in 1875. Note the initial misspelling of the name that was probably corrected after the document was recorded. This example points to the importance of considering alternative spellings when records are not found where they were expected to be.

ORPHAN COURT RECORDS OF COOK COUNTY
(Copied by June B. Barekman, Chicago)

Adopting Parents	Child	Docket	File Date
1883			
Rudoph Junghaus	Sarah Ann Callahan	43500	Jan. 8
William Patterson	George William Patterson	43791	Feb. 6
Frank J. Limbach	Clarrissa M. Harnish	43931	Feb. 15
Harry A. Haynes	Mary Alice Burbie	44256	Mar. 20
Joseph Dinek	Louise Venn	44966	June 5
William G. Godman			
William Walter Quinn	Edward Garner Quinn	45121	June 21
Christian Tofe	Helga Jennette Christine Sharblad	45502	Aug. 6
George W. Sheldon	Parmilla Albertson Pray	46531	Nov. 7
Charles P. Libby	Anne Hughes	46584	Nov. 24
1884			
Herod P. Garrison	Edna Blossom Brown	46946	Jan. 2
Herman E. Schnabel	Herman E. Bayer	47056	Jan. 11
John V. Jones	Alba Almira Young	47330	Feb. 7
Henry Dartsch	Thelka Louise Maisch	47458	Feb. 19
Willis M. Sherman	Honora Shea	47683	Mar. 7
Charles Tessman	August Manz	47836	Mar. 20
Fredrick J. Buck	Anna Imagine Buck	47841	Mar. 21
Edwin Austin	Nellie Katz	48076	Apr. 12
William Sues	Lillie Fretsch	48237	Apr. 29
Edward G. Clark	Georgianna Olivette Clark	48580	May 29
Leonard St. John and Mortimer McClintock	Francis Louise	48811	June 19
Charles Hageman	Laura Hageman	49201	July 26
John Rhode	Edna Smith	50234	Sept 26
William M. Brewer	Eva Aurilia Brewer	50348	Oct. 16
Henrick Buls	Bertha Laioerboch	50456	Nov. 5
Thomas J. Hodgson	Laura A. White	50507	Nov. 10
1885			
Giovanni Giannini	Matteo Arbisone	51443	Jan. 29
Fred Goulding	Lillian Malan	51708	Feb. 19
Leo D. Meyer	Leopold Sternberger	51916	Mar. 11
Edward Uren	Joseph Hund	52015	Mar. 21
Bernard Hackbush	Carrie Jachinson	52016	Mar. 21
Milton Weston	Mattie Mitchell	52024	Mar. 23
Charles N. Black	Carrie E. Bishop	52105	Mar. 31
Henry Willman	Anna Catherine Jachinson	52344	Apr. 23
Peter Schlapp	Marie Schlapp	52697	May 28
John & Jean Childs	Mary Werhart Whyte	52875	June 12
William G. Lewis	Laura Josephine Williams	52995	June 24
James Bell	Edith McMurty	53209	June 27
William J. Hoffman	Ada Telyea	53091	July 1
Jacob Winkler	unnamed child	53162	July 8

Figure 5

In some cases, adoption records have been indexed and preserved by genealogical and historical societies. Such is the case with this page of Orphan Court Records of Cook County (Illinois) that appeared in the *Chicago Genealogist*, vol. 2 no.3 (Spring 1970), pgs. 68-75.

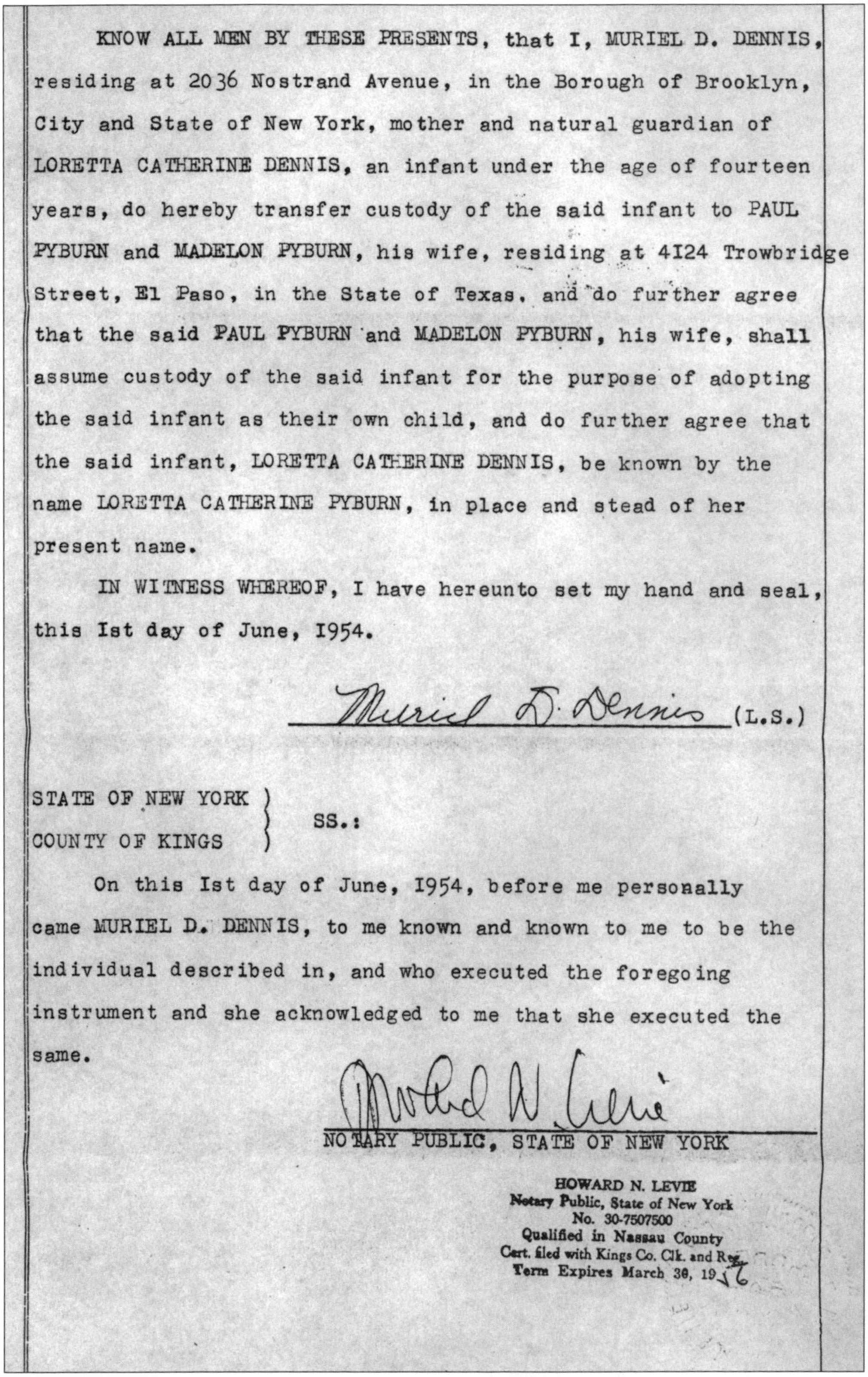

KNOW ALL MEN BY THESE PRESENTS, that I, MURIEL D. DENNIS, residing at 2036 Nostrand Avenue, in the Borough of Brooklyn, City and State of New York, mother and natural guardian of LORETTA CATHERINE DENNIS, an infant under the age of fourteen years, do hereby transfer custody of the said infant to PAUL PYBURN and MADELON PYBURN, his wife, residing at 4124 Trowbridge Street, El Paso, in the State of Texas, and do further agree that the said PAUL PYBURN and MADELON PYBURN, his wife, shall assume custody of the said infant for the purpose of adopting the said infant as their own child, and do further agree that the said infant, LORETTA CATHERINE DENNIS, be known by the name LORETTA CATHERINE PYBURN, in place and stead of her present name.

IN WITNESS WHEREOF, I have hereunto set my hand and seal, this Ist day of June, 1954.

Muriel D. Dennis (L.S.)

STATE OF NEW YORK }
COUNTY OF KINGS } SS.:

On this Ist day of June, 1954, before me personally came MURIEL D. DENNIS, to me known and known to me to be the individual described in, and who executed the foregoing instrument and she acknowledged to me that she executed the same.

NOTARY PUBLIC, STATE OF NEW YORK

HOWARD N. LEVIE
Notary Public, State of New York
No. 30-7507500
Qualified in Nassau County
Cert. filed with Kings Co. Clk. and Reg.
Term Expires March 30, 1956

Figure 6

One of the most difficult record types to find are adoption records. In some cases, however, a researcher may be lucky enough to find a record in the home, as was the case with this adoption affadavit.

Agricultural Schedules of the Census, 1840-80

Agricultural schedules have a variety of uses but are little known and rarely used. This set of records can be used to fill gaps when land and tax records are missing or incomplete; distinguish between people with the same names; document land holdings of ancestors with suitable follow-up in deeds, mortgages, tax rolls, and probate inventories; verify and document black sharecroppers and white overseers who may not appear in other records; and identify free black men and their property holdings, while tracing their movements and economic growth.

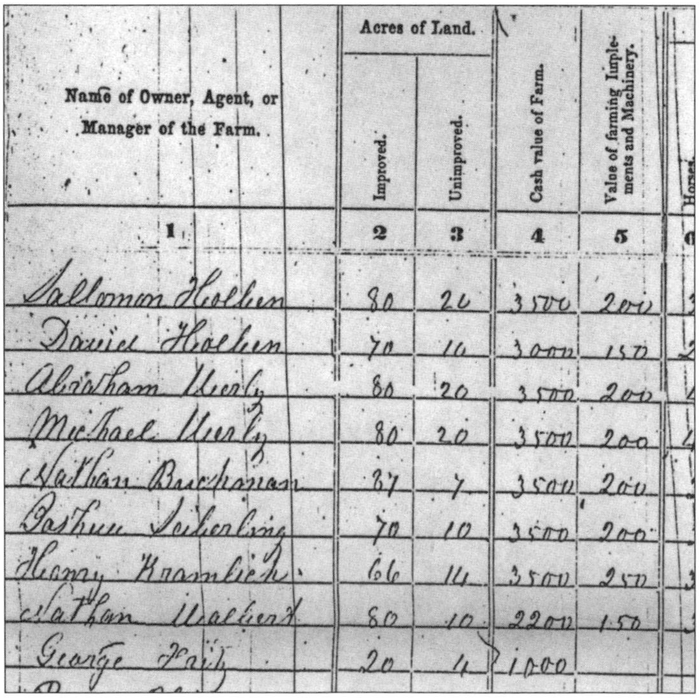

The schedules for 1890 were destroyed by fire, and those for 1900 and 1910 were destroyed by congressional order. The remaining schedules were deposited among a variety of state and university archives by the National Archives and Records Service. Most are not indexed, and most had not been microfilmed until recently, when the National Archives asked that copies be returned for historical research.

Selected Readings:

Davidson, Katherine H., and Charlotte M. Ashby, comps., *Preliminary Inventory of the Records of the Bureau of the Census*, Preliminary Inventory 161. Washington, D.C.: National Archives and Records Service, 1964.

Meyerink, Kory L., ed. *Printed Sources: A Guide to Published Genealogical Records*. Salt Lake City: Ancestry, 1998.

Szucs, Loretto Dennis, and Sandra Hargreaves Luebking, eds. *The Source: A Guidebook of American Genealogy*. Rev. ed. Salt Lake City: Ancestry, 1997.

Internet Sites of Interest:

Ancestry.com
http://www.ancestry.com

National Archives and Records Administration
http://www.nara.gov/publications/microfilm/census/census.html

Figure 7
Detail of agricultural schedule for Lehigh County, Pennsylvania.

SCHEDULE 4.—Productions of Agriculture in _Meisenburg Township_ enumerated by me, on the _Twentyeith_ day of _August_

Name of Owner, Agent, or Manager of the Farm.	Acres of Land.		Cash value of Farm.	Value of farming implements and Machinery.	Live Stock, June 1st, 1850.								Wheat, bushels of.	Rye, bushels of.	Indian Corn, bushels of.	Oats, bushels of.	Rice, lbs. of.
	Improved.	Unimproved.			Horses.	Asses and Mules.	Milch Cows.	Working Oxen.	Other Cattle.	Sheep.	Swine.	Value of Live Stock.					
1	2	3	4	5	6	7	8	9	10	11	12	13	14	15	16	17	18
Sollomon Hollen	80	20	3500	200	3		3		3	4	8	325	12	150	100	20	
David Hollen	70	10	3000	150	2		4		3	3	5	300	18	250	40		
Abraham Mierly	80	20	3500	200	4		5		10	3	13	400	40	275	50	25	
Michael Mierly	80	20	3500	200	4		5		4	3	12	350	40	275	40	25	
Nathan Buchman	87	7	3500	200	3		5		2	6	9	370	110	200	50	40	
Bashure Seiberling	70	10	3500	200			3		1		8	355	50	250	100	160	
Henry Kramlich	66	14	3500	250	3		4			6	7	390		150	50	40	
Nathan Walbert	80	10	2200	150	3		4		3	1	3	250	20	200	75	20	
George Frail	20	4	1000				2				1	35	5	50	30	10	
Paul Bleiler	130	40	6000	200	2		4		1		4	190	150	350	200	30	
Nicole Heis	15	5	1200	50	1		2		1	2	3	80		40	20		
Michael Heis	60	20	3000	200	2		4		4	3	7	300	30	200	100	80	
Peter Rabinold	78	12	3000	250	3		4			2	3	290	100	250	40	75	
Henry Weis	14	18	3000	250	2		4		3	3	4	165	10	200	100	60	
Nathan Xander	60	9	1500	100	2		3		2	3	6	150	10	100	50	40	
David Sechler	55	25	2200	100	2		5		1		6	200	100	100	100	80	
Dennis Bachman	90	18	3500	150	3		2		2	5	1	250	50	150	100	50	
Nicholas Mierly	50	60	3000	100	2		5		1		4	205		150	50	20	
Abraham Frey	40	6	1300		3		3			4	3	70	10	40	30	15	
Daniel Greenawalt	70	40	3000	150	2		5		5	3	6	270	70	70	100	60	
Charles Greenawalt	75	35	5000	200	2		6		3	6	6	300	65	160	150	70	
John Grim	105	15	3500	200	2		2		2	3	3	205	100	200	150	100	
Elijah Old	57	10	2500	100	3		3			3	1	155	20	50	30	12	
Thomas Grim	85	25	3500	150	3		4		4	6	10	300	30	150	150	30	
William Sheafer	53	7	1000	100	2		2		1	2	2	140	30	80	40	15	
Henry Mierly	50	20	2000	100	2		2				7	150		100	40		
Henry Frail	14	1	900	50	1		2				4	115	8	25	15	20	
Betsy Frail	22	3	1200				2				2	40		45	15	16	
Charles Frail	19	3	1000	50	1		2			1	4	80	10	40	20	25	
David Reiss	133	40	10000	350	6		7		4	6	5	645	300	350	200	50	
Daniel Ebert	25		1100	50	1		3				3	105	14	70	50		
Abraham Mierly	87	8	3000	200	2		5		4	5	9	275	15	200	80	65	
Jacob Mierly	85	15	3000	200	3		5										

Figure 8

A page from the 1850 Agricultural Census Schedule for Meisenburg Township, Lehigh County, Pennsylvania.

Alien Registration Records

Alien registration records provide a rich source of personal information for several million individuals who were required to register during various periods of American history. In 1798, the Quasi War with France prompted an act that called for the registration of alien enemies—defined as all male citizens, age fourteen and older, of a nation formally at war with the United States.

For the period from 1802 to 1828, all aliens were required to register with local courts of record, with the War of 1812 again placing special emphasis on the reg-

istration of alien enemies. All British subjects had to report to the U.S. Marshal in their state or territory their name, age, length of residence in the United States, names of members of their family, place of residence, occupation, and whether they had applied for naturalization.

Under the 1929 Alien Registration Act, aliens were again required to register their current residence and place of employment annually with the federal government. This act also required aliens to carry an identification card with them to be considered legal aliens. Any alien with-

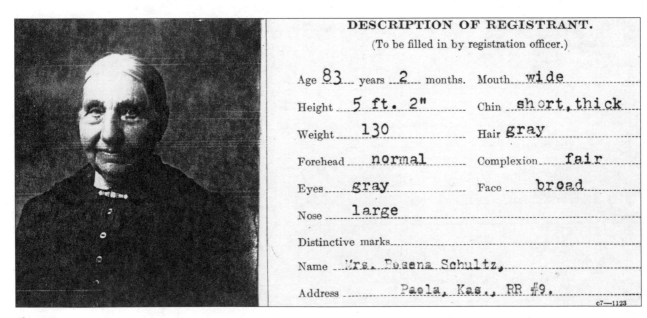

DESCRIPTION OF REGISTRANT.
(To be filled in by registration officer.)

Age **83** years **2** months. Mouth **wide**

Height **5 ft. 2"** Chin **short, thick**

Weight **130** Hair **gray**

Forehead **normal** Complexion **fair**

Eyes **gray** Face **broad**

Nose **large**

Distinctive marks

Name **Mrs. Rosena Schultz,**

Address **Paola, Kas., RR #9.**

c7—1123

Figure 9
Rosena Schultz registered as an enemy alien during WWI. The above is from enemy alien registration affidavits, 1917-18, Attorneys and Marshals records at the National Archives - Central Plains Region, Kansas City.

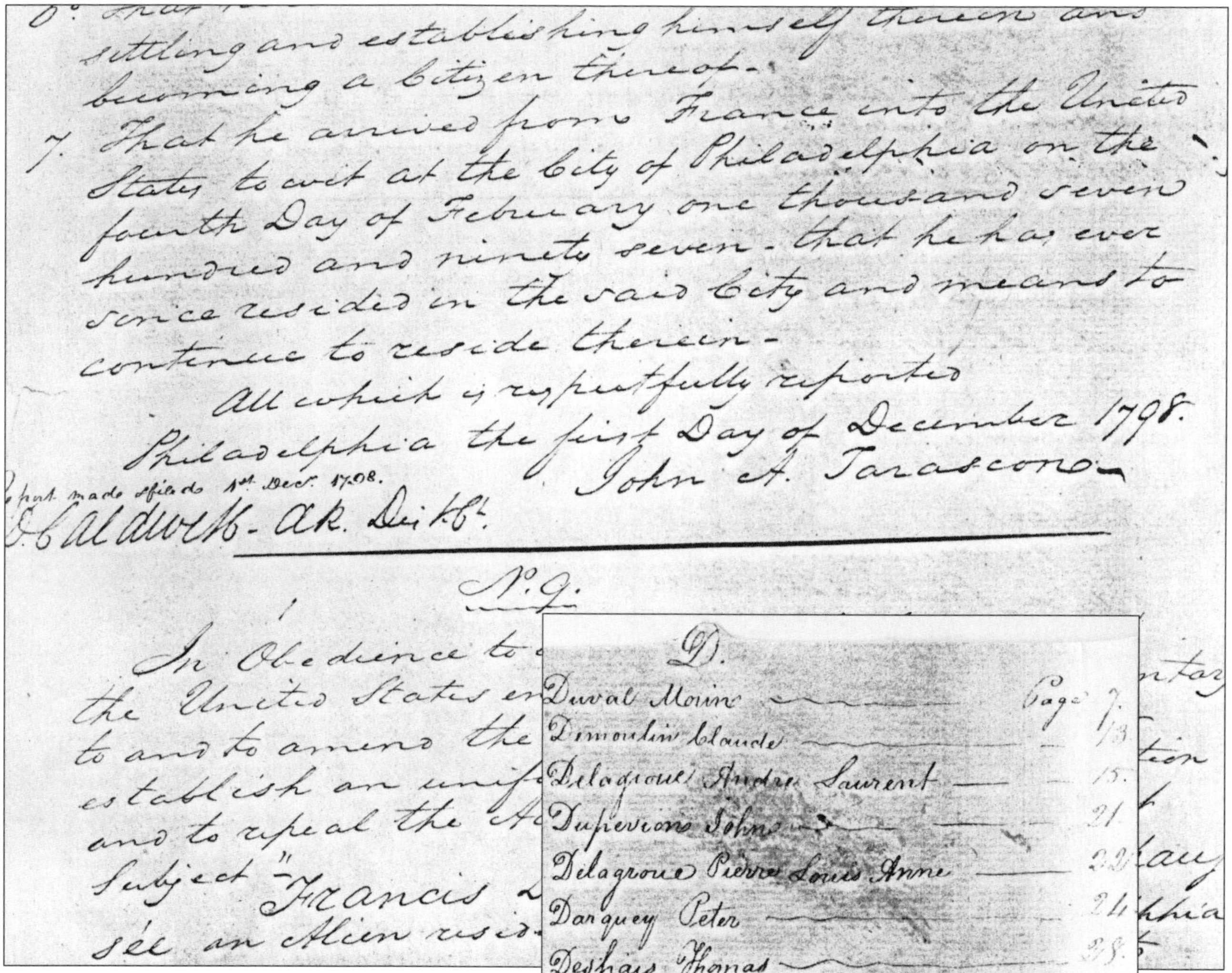

settling and establishing himself therein and
becoming a Citizen thereof.
7. That he arrived from France into the United
States to wit at the City of Philadelphia on the
fourth Day of February one thousand seven
hundred and ninety seven. that he has ever
since resided in the said City and means to
continue to reside therein.
All which is respectfully reported
Philadelphia the first Day of December 1798.
John A. Tarascon
Report made & filed 1st Decr. 1798.
J. Caldwell - Ck. Dist Ct.
No. 9.
In Obedience to
the United States en
to and to amend the
establish an unif
and to repeal the A
subject "Francis
see an Alien resid

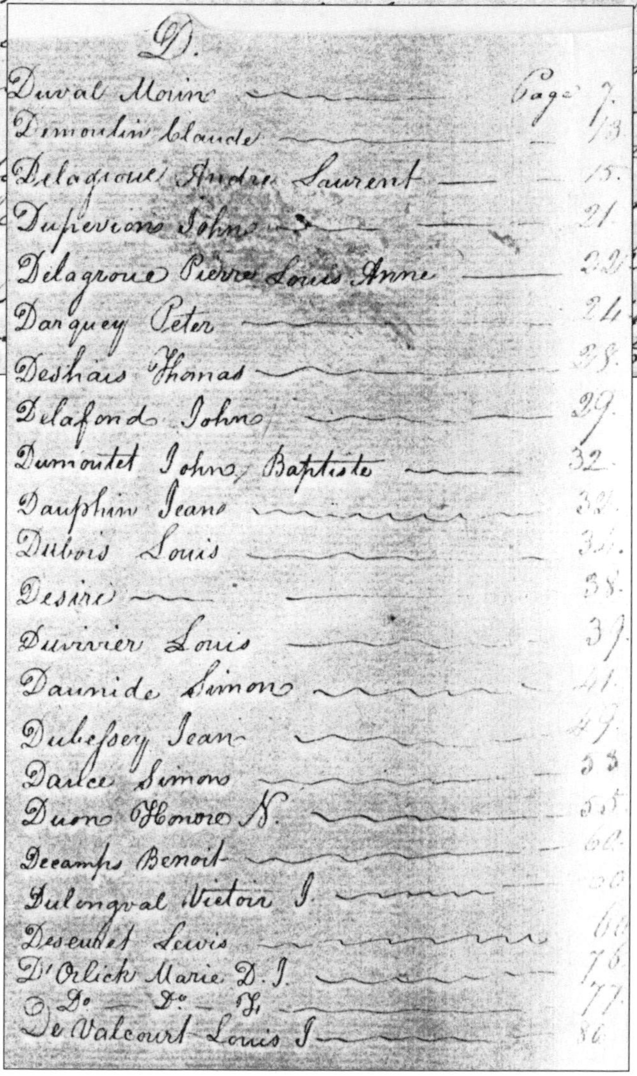

D.

Duval Moine	Page 7
Dimoulin Claude	13
Delagroue Andre Laurent	15
Dupievion John	21
Delagroue Pierre Louis Anne	22
Darquey Peter	24
Deshais Thomas	28
Delafond John	29
Dumoutet John Baptiste	32
Dauphin Jean	[illegible]
Dubois Louis	[illegible]
Desire	38
Duvivier Louis	[illegible]
Daunide Simon	41
Dubessey Jean	47
Darlee Simons	53
Duron Honore N.	55
Decamps Benoit	60
Delongval Victoir J.	[illegible]
Deseubet Lewis	[illegible]
D'Orlick Marie D. J.	76
Do Do G.	77
De Valcourt Louis J.	86

Figure 10

1798 French Alien Registration (top) and Index from the Immigration and Naturalization Service records (right) held at the National Archives - Mid-Atlantic Region, Philadelphia.

out one could be deported without a hearing. These forms of identification, which include immigrant identification cards, certificates of lawful entry, certificates of arrival, and alien registration cards, are often found among home sources.

The threat of World War II was the impetus for the Alien Registration Program that began in July 1940. Pursuant to the Alien Registration Act (also known as the Smith Act), every alien resident living in the United States had to register at a local post office. Aliens entering the United States had to register as they applied for admission. Alien registration requirements applied to all aliens over the age of fourteen, regardless of nationality and regardless of immigration status. As part of the registration process, aliens were fingerprinted and asked to fill out a two-page form. Each set of forms was numbered with an alien registration number and then forwarded to the Immigration and Naturalization Service (INS) for statistical coding, indexing, and filing.

Registers of Aliens, 1798 to 1812, for the U.S. District Court for the Eastern District of Pennsylvania, recording primarily those French immigrants who registered with the Clerk of the Court during the Quasi War with France, are located at the National Archives in Philadelphia. Many of the registrations for the period from 1802 to 1828 are indexed in P. William Filby and Mary K. Meyer's *Passenger and Immigration Lists Index*. The National Archives - Central Plains Region in Kansas City, Missouri has a collection of German Alien Registrations from World War I. Registry files from the 1929 Alien Registration Act and the 1940 Alien Registration Act are in the custody of the INS and are subject to the Freedom of Information/Privacy Act.

Selected Readings:

Filby, P. William, and Mary K. Meyer. *Passenger and Immigration Lists Index*. Detroit: Gale Research Co., 1981– (including supplements).

Guide to Genealogical Research in the National Archives. Washington, D.C.: National Archives Trust Fund Board, 1985.

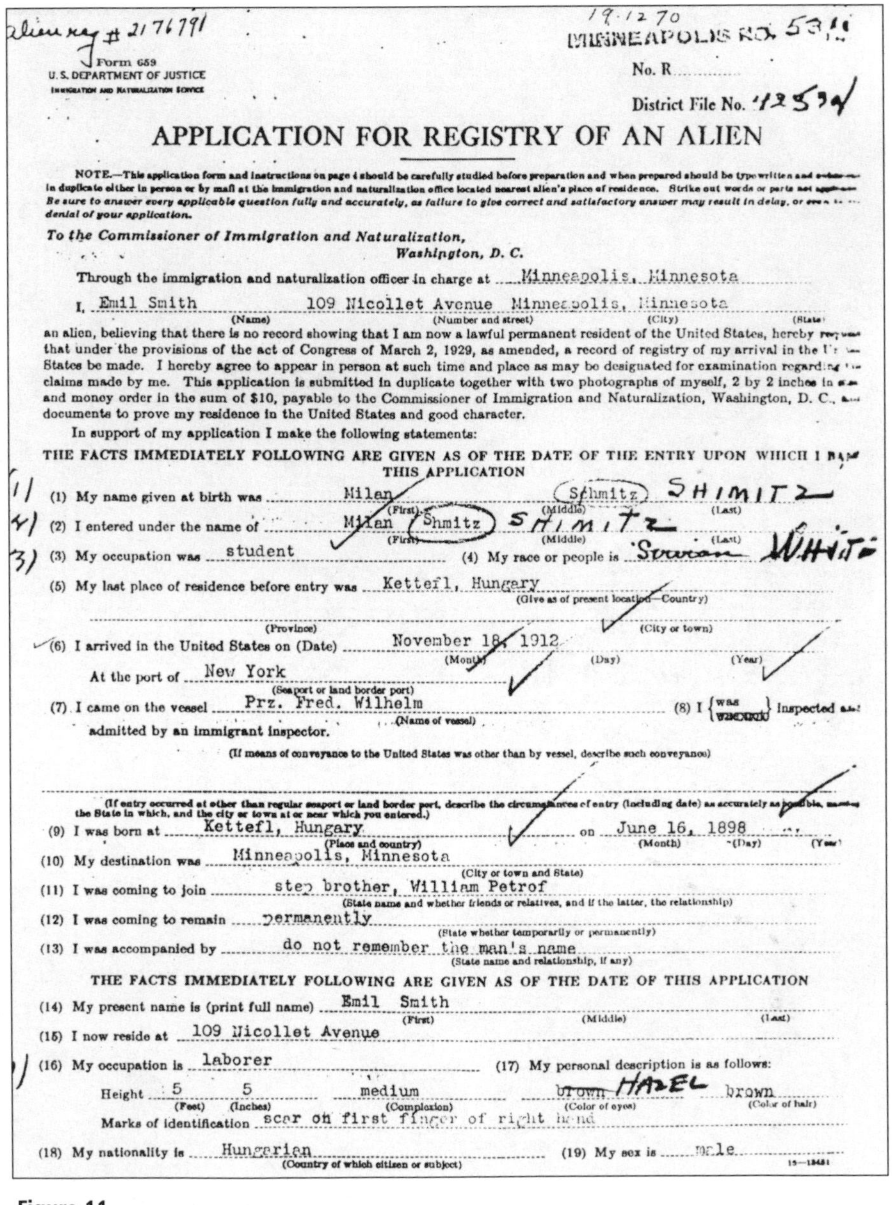
alien reg # 2176791

19.12.70

MINNEAPOLIS NO. 53

Form 659
U.S. DEPARTMENT OF JUSTICE
IMMIGRATION AND NATURALIZATION SERVICE

No. R..........

District File No. 12594

APPLICATION FOR REGISTRY OF AN ALIEN

NOTE.—This application form and instructions on page 4 should be carefully studied before preparation and when prepared should be typewritten and submitted in duplicate either in person or by mail at the immigration and naturalization office located nearest alien's place of residence. Strike out words or parts not applicable. *Be sure to answer every applicable question fully and accurately, as failure to give correct and satisfactory answer may result in delay, or even ... denial of your application.*

To the Commissioner of Immigration and Naturalization, Washington, D. C.

Through the immigration and naturalization officer in charge at Minneapolis, Minnesota

I, Emil Smith (Name) 109 Nicollet Avenue (Number and street) Minneapolis, (City) Minnesota (State)

an alien, believing that there is no record showing that I am now a lawful permanent resident of the United States, hereby request that under the provisions of the act of Congress of March 2, 1929, as amended, a record of registry of my arrival in the United States be made. I hereby agree to appear in person at such time and place as may be designated for examination regarding the claims made by me. This application is submitted in duplicate together with two photographs of myself, 2 by 2 inches in size and money order in the sum of $10, payable to the Commissioner of Immigration and Naturalization, Washington, D. C., and documents to prove my residence in the United States and good character.

In support of my application I make the following statements:

THE FACTS IMMEDIATELY FOLLOWING ARE GIVEN AS OF THE DATE OF THE ENTRY UPON WHICH I BASE THIS APPLICATION

(1) My name given at birth was Milan (First) Schmitz (Middle) SHIMITZ (Last)

(2) I entered under the name of Milan (First) Shmitz SHIMITZ (Middle) (Last)

(3) My occupation was student (4) My race or people is Slovakian WHITE

(5) My last place of residence before entry was Kettefl, Hungary (Give as of present location—Country) (Province) (City or town)

(6) I arrived in the United States on (Date) November 18, 1912 (Month) (Day) (Year)

At the port of New York (Seaport or land border port)

(7) I came on the vessel Prz. Fred. Wilhelm (Name of vessel) (8) I {was} inspected and admitted by an immigrant inspector.

(If means of conveyance to the United States was other than by vessel, describe such conveyance)

(If entry occurred at other than regular seaport or land border port, describe the circumstances of entry (including date) as accurately as possible, naming the State in which, and the city or town at or near which you entered.)

(9) I was born at Kettefl, Hungary (Place and country) on June 16, 1898 (Month) (Day) (Year)

(10) My destination was Minneapolis, Minnesota (City or town and State)

(11) I was coming to join step brother, William Petrof (State name and whether friends or relatives, and if the latter, the relationship)

(12) I was coming to remain permanently (State whether temporarily or permanently)

(13) I was accompanied by do not remember the man's name (State name and relationship, if any)

THE FACTS IMMEDIATELY FOLLOWING ARE GIVEN AS OF THE DATE OF THIS APPLICATION

(14) My present name is (print full name) Emil Smith (First) (Middle) (Last)

(15) I now reside at 109 Nicollet Avenue

(16) My occupation is laborer (17) My personal description is as follows:

Height 5 (Feet) 5 (Inches) medium (Complexion) ~~brown~~ HAZEL (Color of eyes) brown (Color of hair)

Marks of identification scar on first finger of right hand

(18) My nationality is Hungarian (Country of which citizen or subject) (19) My sex is male

15—13481

Figure 11

The initial page of the Application for Registry of an Alien filed by Emil Smith (Shimitz) in 1941. This record is from the files of the Naturalization and Immigration Service, Washington D.C.

Scott, Kenneth. *British Aliens in the United States During the War of 1812.* Baltimore: Genealogical Publishing, 1979.

Szucs, Loretto Dennis. *They Became Americans: Finding Naturalization Records and Ethnic Origins.* Salt Lake City: Ancestry, 1998.

Internet Sites of Interest:

National Archives and Records Administration
http://www.nara.gov/

Genealogical Searchable Database - NAIL
http://www.nara.gov/genealogy/genindex.html

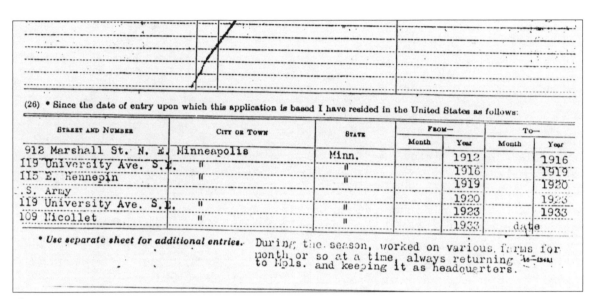

(26) * Since the date of entry upon which this application is based I have resided in the United States as follows:

STREET AND NUMBER	CITY OR TOWN	STATE	FROM— Month	FROM— Year	TO— Month	TO— Year
912 Marshall St. N. E.	Minneapolis	Minn.		1912		1916
119 University Ave. S. E.	"	"		1916		1919
115 E. Hennepin	"	"		1919		1920
.S. Army				1920		1923
119 University Ave. S. E.	"	"		1923		1933
109 Nicollet	"	"		1933		date

* *Use separate sheet for additional entries.* During the season, worked on various farms for month or so at a time, always returning .... to Mpls. and keeping it as headquarters.

Figure 12
Detail of page two of the Application for Registry of an Alien filed by Emil Smith.

NOTE CAREFULLY.—This application must be sworn to before an officer of the Immigration and Naturalization Se......

(Application not to be signed on this page until applicant appears before an officer of the Immigration and Natural...... Service for a hearing on the application.)

I, **EMIL SMITH** ...., do swear (affirm) that I know the contents of ...... application for registry subscribed by me, that the same are true to the best of my knowledge, except as to matters th...... stated to be alleged upon information and belief, and that as to those matters I believe them to be true, and that correct...... numbered (*1*) to (*4*) were made by me or at my request, and that this application was signed by me with my ...... true name: So help me God.

Emil Smith
(Complete and true signature of applicant)

Subscribed and sworn to before me by the above-named applicant at .....**MINNEAPOLIS, MINNESOTA.**

this ....**18th**........ day of ....**NOVEMBER**........, Anno Domini 19 **41**

Royall H. Storey
ROYALL H. STOREY
Immigrant Inspector designated
Naturalization Examiner.
(Title of officer)

PHOTOGRAPHS.—You are required to send with this application two photographs of yourself taken within 30 d...... the date of this application. These photographs must be 2 by 2 inches in size, and the distance from top of head to p...... chin should be approximately 1¼ inches. They must not be pasted on cards or mounted in any other way, must be on thin ...... have a light background, and clearly show a front view of your face without hat. Snapshots, group or full-length portraits ...... not be accepted. Both of these photographs must be signed by you on the margin and not on the face or the clothing......

Figure 13
Detail of page three of the Application for Registry of an Alien filed by Emil Smith.

Almshouse Records

During the early 1800s, many states enacted legislation concerning the care of the poor and the needy. Persons who were unable to provide for themselves were provided with overseers by town or county officials or were admitted to a tax-supported almshouse. Such almshouses were required, by law, to maintain registers.

These registers may offer insight into what life was like in an almshouse. The registers may also provide genealogy-rich material, including dates of admission and discharge and the name, sex, age, color, occupation, residence, birthplace, education, literacy, and personal habits (temperate or not) of each inmate.

Many registers have been turned over to county clerks and are stored in courthouses, while others are in state and local archives. In some cases, if management of the property was taken over by a private organization, records may exist at the original location.

Selected Readings:

Benton, Josiah Henry. *Warning Out in New England.* 1911. Reprint. Bowie, Md.: Heritage Books, 1992.

"Chautauqua County Home and Infirmary. Poor House for Chautauqua County, New York." FGS *Forum* 3 (4) (Fall 1992). Journals abstracted by the Chautauqua County Genealogical Society, P.O. Box 404, Fredonia, NY 14063.

Katz, Michael B. *In the Shadow of the Poorhouse: A Social History of Welfare in America.* New York: Basic Books, 1986.

Lainhart, Ann S. "Records of the Poor in Pre-Twentieth-Century New England." *New England Historical and Genealogical Register* 146 (January 1992): 80–85.

Warren, Paula Stuart, and James W. Warren. *Ramsey County Minnesota Relief Records, 1862–1868.* St. Paul, Minn.: Warren Research and Publishing, 1990.

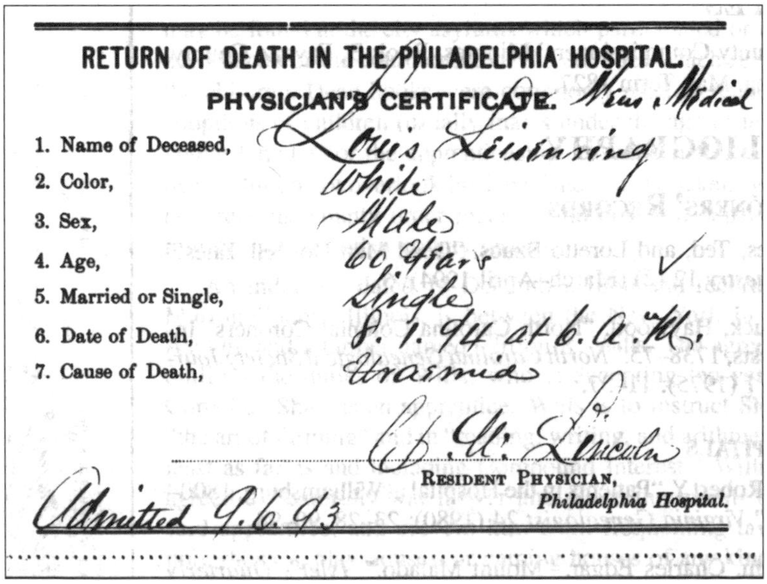
RETURN OF DEATH IN THE PHILADELPHIA HOSPITAL.

PHYSICIAN'S CERTIFICATE.

1. Name of Deceased, Louis Leisenring
2. Color, White
3. Sex, Male
4. Age, 60 Years
5. Married or Single, Single
6. Date of Death, 8.1.94 at 6. a.m.
7. Cause of Death, Uraemia

C. W. Lincoln

RESIDENT PHYSICIAN, Philadelphia Hospital.

Admitted 9.6.93

Figure 14
Death certificate, Almshouse Hospital, Bureau of Charities, Philadelphia County, Pennsylvania.

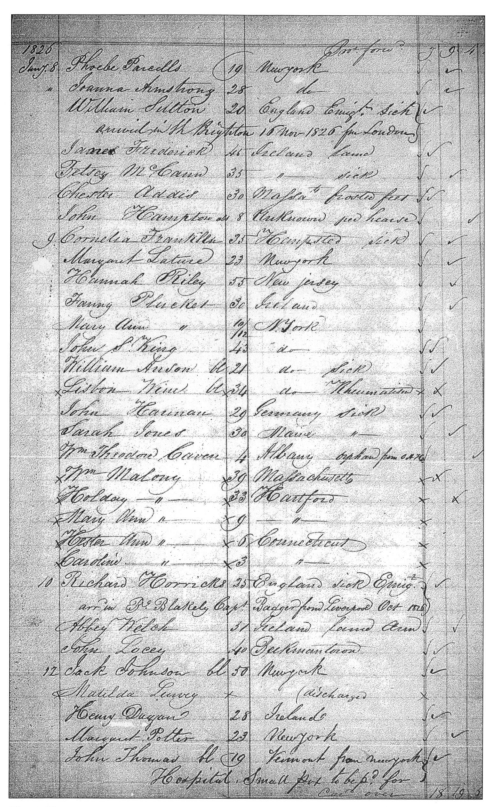

Figure 15

Almshouse admissions registers for New York City can be found at the Municipal Archives in New York City and are available on microfilm at the Family History Library and its centers. This example shows the date of admissions and the individual's name and age, as well as notes that often include previous residence.

American Genealogical-Biographical Index

The *American Genealogical-Biographical Index* (*AGBI*) (Middletown, Conn.: Godfrey Memorial Library, 1952–) is an every-name collective index containing entries for more than 6 million individuals. Sometimes referred to as the Rider Index for its creator, the *AGBI* project was started in 1942 with a primary emphasis on family histories produced before 1900. With additional sources, including town and county histories, genealogical dictionaries, biographies, published vital records, published revolutionary war

Alphabetically arranged by surname, each AGBI entry contains the subject's complete name, birth year, state of residence, and a citation to the source indexed.

records, the 1790 Census, and the *Boston Evening Transcript* genealogical column, the index is near completion with 197 volumes.

Alphabetically arranged by surname, each entry contains the subject's complete name, birth year, state of residence, and a citation to the source indexed. In some cases, a brief biographical statement is provided as well.

The *AGBI*, historically limited in availability due to its size and cost (fewer than two hundred libraries subscribe to the index), is now available on microfilm at the Family History Library and was recently made available on the Internet to subscribers of Ancestry.com's Web site located at <www.ancestry.com>. The sources cited in the index can be located at the Godfrey Memorial Library in Middletown, Connecticut, where the project began. The Family History Library has most of the sources; they are available on microfilm through its Family History Centers. Libraries with major family history collections are likely to hold many of the sources as well.

Selected Readings:

Meyerink, Kory L. "Genealogy's Best-Kept Secret." *Ancestry* 17 (2) (March/April 1999): p. 36.

_____, ed. *Printed Sources: A Guide to Published Genealogical Records*. Salt Lake City: Ancestry, 1998.

Internet Sites of Interest:

Ancestry.com
http://www.ancestry.com

Godfrey Memorial Library
http://www.godfrey.org/

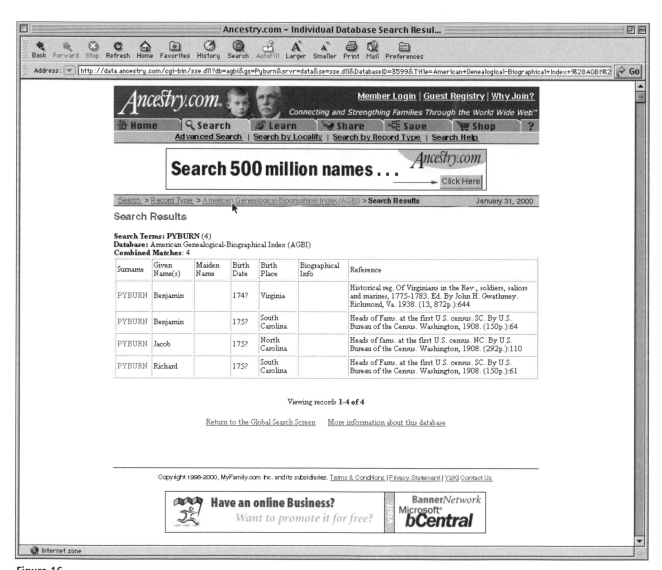

Figure 16

The results of a search conducted through Ancestry.com's *AGBI* database.

American Medical Association

The American Medical Association has collected information on the personal and professional backgrounds of more than 350,000 doctors who have practiced in the United States. Some of the records date back to the early 1800s and continue through the year 1969, although the records kept prior to 1907 do not contain as much information as the later files.

These records are now in the possession of the National Genealogical Society in Arlington, Virginia. Persons wishing to inquire about the records and search fees should write to The National Genealogical Society, 4527 17th Street North, Arlington, VA 22207. The Genealogical Society of Utah has made arrangements to microfilm the collection and will make it available at the Family History Library and its Family History Centers.

Selected Readings:

Directory of Deceased American Physicians: 1804–1929. 2 vols. Chicago: American Medical Association, 1992.

Meyerink, Kory L., and Johni Cerny. "Research in Business, Employment, and Institutional Records." *The Source: A Guidebook of American Genealogy.* Rev. ed. Salt Lake City: Ancestry, 1997.

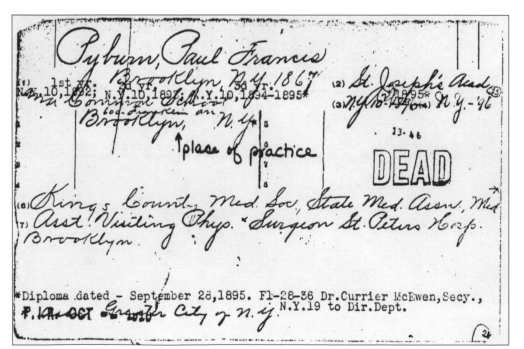

Figure 17

A copy (with notes) of an original card from the AMA file of deceased physicians. Line 1 includes the year and place of birth, line 2 shows the high school attended, line 3 gives the medical school code and year of graduation, line 4 provides the year and state in which the license was attained, line 6 lists medical association memberships, and line 7 provides information on hospital affiliations.

American State Papers

A part of the U.S. Serial Set, the *American State Papers: Documents, Legislative and Executive, of the Congress of the United States* consists of thirty-eight separately indexed volumes containing documents recorded by the U.S. Congress from 1789 to 1837. The documents are arranged by category, or "class," and by date. With its references to more than 80,000 Americans, Class 8, Public Lands holds the greatest interest to family historians. The eight volumes that make up Class 8 contain records of private land claims presented before federal agencies, most of them pertaining to grants, purchases, or settlements that took place before the United States acquired sovereignty over the land.

The *American State Papers* can be found in most state libraries and has been microfilmed by the National Archives and the Family History Library. Facilitating the use of the collection are publications that include Phillip W. McMullin *Grassroots of America: A Computerized Index to the American State Papers: Land Grants and Claims (1789-1837)* Salt Lake City: Gendex Corp., 1972, Reprint. Greenville, S.C.: Southern Historical Press, 1994. (An index of names that appear in the eight volumes of Public Lands, and various compilations focusing on specific geographic regions.)

Other classes in the collection are foreign relations, Indian affairs, finance, commerce and navigation, military affairs, naval affairs, post office department, claims, and miscellaneous.

See also *U.S. Government Documents, Deeds, Homestead Records, Land Grants and Patents, Territorial Records,* and *U.S. Serial Set.*

Selected Readings:

American State Papers: Documents, Legislative and Executive of the Congress of the United States (1789-1838). 38 vols. Washington: Gales and Seaton, 1833-34, 1859-61. Various editors.

Boyd, Anne Morris. *United States Public Government Publications.* New York: The H.W. Wilson Col, 1949. 3rd ed. rev. by Rae Elizabeth Rips.

Checklist of United States Public Documents, 1789-1909. Vol. 1: Lists of Congressional and Departmental Publications. Washington: U.S. Government Printing Office, 1911. 3rd ed. New York: Reprint by Kraus Reprint Corp. 1962.

CIS US Serial Set Index: Part 1 American State papers and the 15th-34th Congresses, 1789-1857. Washington: Congressional Information Service, Inc., 1975. (A supplement to the *American State Papers* indexes)

McMullin, Phillip W. *Grassroots of America.* Salt Lake City: Gendex Corp., 1972. (Index to land grants and land claims in Classes 8 and 9 of the *American State Papers*)

Stathis, Stephen W. "The Evolution of Government Printing and Publishing in America." *Government Publications Review.* Vol. 7A, pp. 377-390. Pergamon Press Ltd., 1980.

Applications, Appointment Papers, and Commissions

Biographical information in the form of applications, appointments, and commissions can be found in a number of record groups in the National Archives. While agency names and responsibilities over the years have shifted, the usefulness of some of these records should not be overlooked.

Records of appointment, commission, and personnel include copies of commissioners issued, original commissions that were never delivered, and copies of letters, appointments, and promotions. Commissions signed by the president but not delivered are arranged for the years 1812 through 1902. The information found in the registers of commission include the name of the officer, rank, date of commission, and remarks. Registers of appointments include name, rank, residence, organization, and date of appointment. The National Archives has three volumes of registers of commissioned officers:

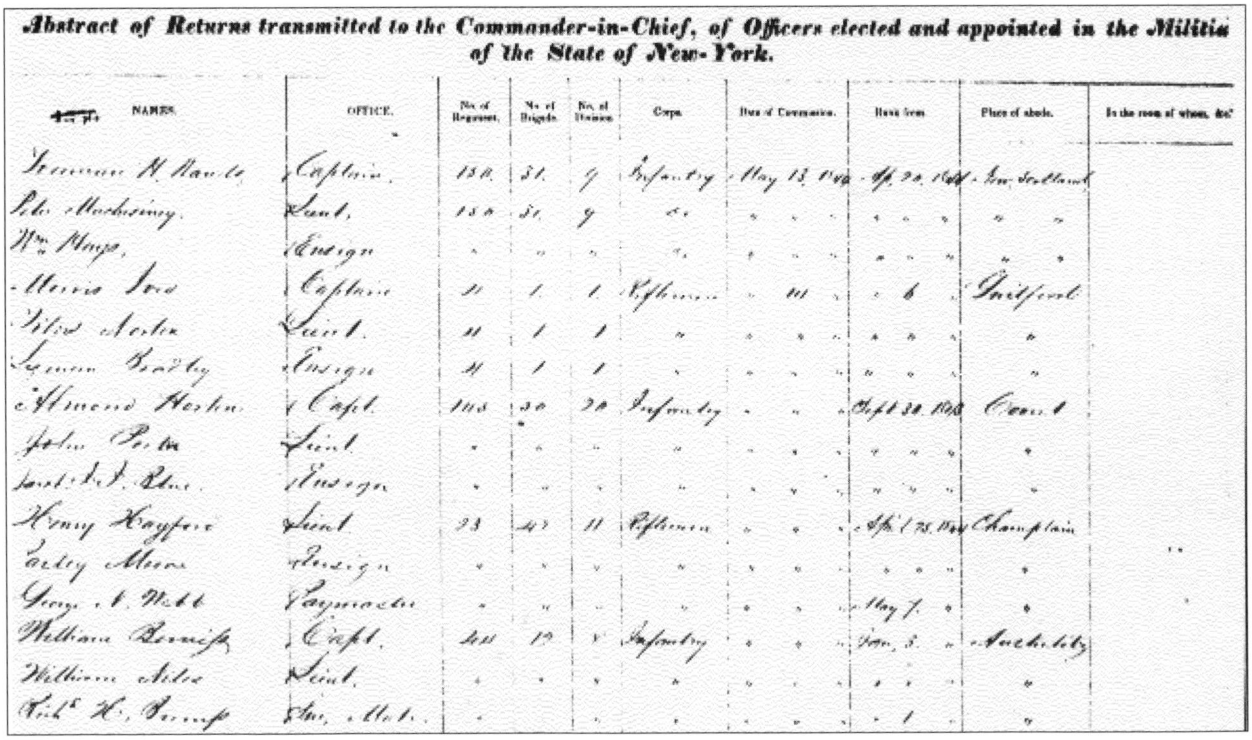
Abstract of Returns transmitted to the Commander-in-Chief, of Officers elected and appointed in the Militia of the State of New-York.

NAMES.	OFFICE.	No. of Regiment.	No. of Brigade.	No. of Division.	Corps.	Date of Commission.	Rank from	Place of abode.	In the room of whom, &c.

Figure 18

A list of Officers Elected and Appointed in the Militia of the State of New York - Revolutionary War. (Courtesy of the National Archives) vol. 1 covers the period 1799 through 1860; vol. 2, 1861 through 1900; vol. 3, 1901 through 1915. There is an additional volume containing a roster of officers, 1783 to 1826, that is arranged by initial letter of the surname. Also available at the National Archives is a set of alphabetically arranged records created in 1816, when every officer was required to furnish his place of birth and a 1917 set of registration cards containing information relating to individuals who were qualified for appointment as officers in time of war. The cards give name, address, occupation, date of birth, race, qualification, previous military training, and other data.

The National Archives also has an alphabetical card index, prepared by the United States Office of the Adjutant General, of each officer appointed to the Confederate army. The cards give information about the appointment and the officer's subsequent military history, including promotions.

DEPARTMENT OF THE INTERIOR

Established in March 1849, the Department of the Interior took powers previously held by the Secretary of War over the Commissioner of Indian Affairs, the Secretary of the Treasury over the General Land Office, the Secretaries of War and the Navy over the Commissioner of Pensions, the Secretary of State over the Commissioner of Patents, and the President over the Commissioner of Public Buildings. Additionally, the Secretary of the Interior held jurisdiction over census taking, marshals and court officers, federal buildings and grounds throughout the United States, and charitable and penal institutions in the District of Columbia.

Appointment papers concerning positions under the direct control of the Office of the Secretary of the Interior and filled by presidential appointment include letters of application and recommendation, petitions, oaths of office, bonds, and reports from the Commissioner of Indian Affairs or the General Land Office. A collection of Interior Department appointment papers for the period 1849-1907 has been microfilmed by the National Archives and can be found in several of the National Archives regional offices. The files are arranged by office or position, and thereunder filed alphabetically by name of applicant or incumbent, and thereunder by the date the document was received in the Appointments Division.

Selected Readings:

Genealogical & Biographical Research: A Select Catalog of National Archives Microfilm Publications. Washington, D.C: National Archives Trust Fund, 1983. (See pages 14-18, for a listing of the contents for each roll.)

Guide to Genealogical Research in the National Archives. Washington, D.C.: National Archives Trust Fund Board, 1985.

Heitman, Francis B. *Historical Register of Officers of the Continental Army During the War of the Revolution.* 1914, With Addenda by Robert H. Kelby, 1932. Baltimore: Genealogical Publishing Co., 1973.

Matchette, Robert B. comp. *Guide to Federal Records in the National Archives of the United States.* 3 vols. Washington, D.C: National Archives and Records Administration, 1998.

Neagles, James C. *U.S. Military Records: A Guide to Federal and State Sources, Colonial America to the Present.* Salt Lake City: Ancestry, 1994.

Szucs, Loretto Dennis, and Sandra Hargreaves Luebking. *The Archives: A Guide to the National Archives Field Branches.* Salt Lake City: Ancestry, 1998.

Apprenticeship Agreements

Apprenticeships, a practice carried over from England, indentured young men and women to skilled craftsmen by way of a written agreement to learn a trade. In many cases, the apprentice was an orphan that was bound out by a county court until the age of twenty-one (eighteen for young women). The indenture agreement may contain information such as the apprentice's name, his parents' or guardians' names, the length of the indenture term, the trade to be learned, and whether the apprentice would be taught to read or allowed to attend school.

Because many apprenticeships were the result of a court appointment, records are often found at the local, county, and state levels of courts. State archives and historical societies may have collections on microfilm.

Selected Readings:

Coldham, Peter Wilson. *Child Apprentices in America, From Christ's Hospital, London, 1617–1778.* Baltimore: Genealogical Publishing Co., 1990.

Gill, Harold B. Jr. *Apprentices of Virginia 1623–1800.* Salt Lake City: Ancestry, 1989.

Meyerink, Kory L., and Johni Cerny. "Research in Business, Employment, and Institutional Records." *The Source: A Guidebook of American Genealogy.* Rev. ed. Salt Lake City: Ancestry, 1997.

Pennsylvania German Society. *Record of Indentures of Individuals Bound Out as Apprentices, etc.,[in] Philadelphia, 1771 to 1773.* Baltimore: Genealogical Publishing Co., 1973.

Ritter, Kathy. *Apprentices of Connecticut 1637–1900.* Salt Lake City: Ancestry, 1986.

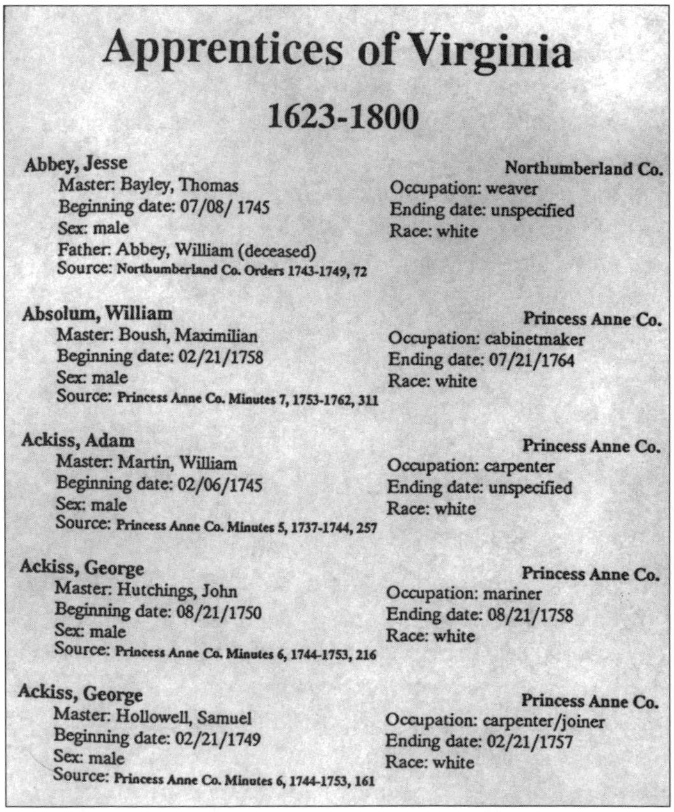

Apprentices of Virginia

1623-1800

Abbey, Jesse — Northumberland Co.
Master: Bayley, Thomas — Occupation: weaver
Beginning date: 07/08/ 1745 — Ending date: unspecified
Sex: male — Race: white
Father: Abbey, William (deceased)
Source: Northumberland Co. Orders 1743-1749, 72

Absolum, William — Princess Anne Co.
Master: Boush, Maximilian — Occupation: cabinetmaker
Beginning date: 02/21/1758 — Ending date: 07/21/1764
Sex: male — Race: white
Source: Princess Anne Co. Minutes 7, 1753-1762, 311

Ackiss, Adam — Princess Anne Co.
Master: Martin, William — Occupation: carpenter
Beginning date: 02/06/1745 — Ending date: unspecified
Sex: male — Race: white
Source: Princess Anne Co. Minutes 5, 1737-1744, 257

Ackiss, George — Princess Anne Co.
Master: Hutchings, John — Occupation: mariner
Beginning date: 08/21/1750 — Ending date: 08/21/1758
Sex: male — Race: white
Source: Princess Anne Co. Minutes 6, 1744-1753, 216

Ackiss, George — Princess Anne Co.
Master: Hollowell, Samuel — Occupation: carpenter/joiner
Beginning date: 02/21/1749 — Ending date: 02/21/1757
Sex: male — Race: white
Source: Princess Anne Co. Minutes 6, 1744-1753, 161

Figure 19

An example of the entries found in Harold B. Gill, Jr. *Apprentices of Virginia, 1623-1800* (Ancestry, 1989). This resource was compiled from various record sources.

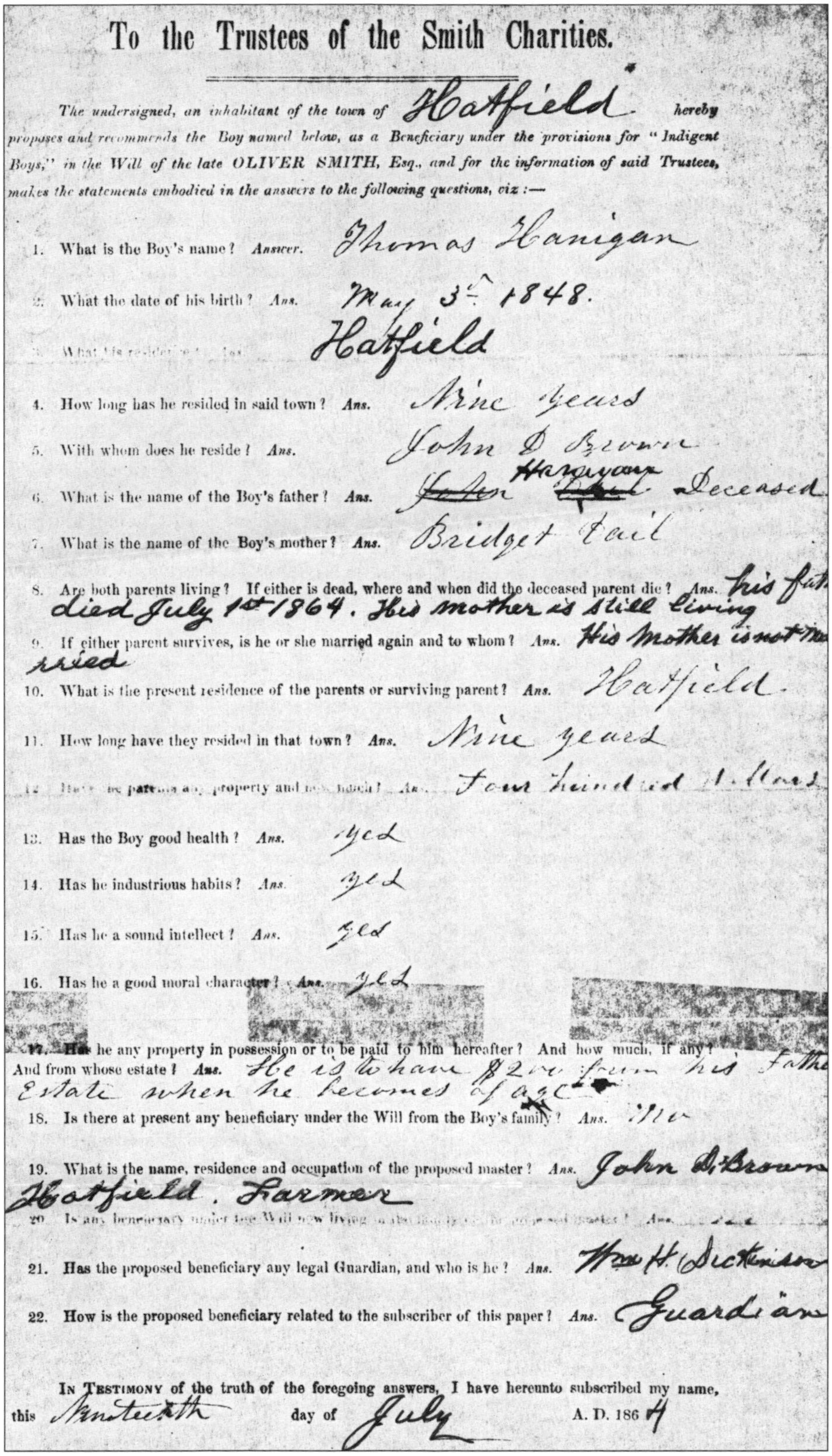

To the Trustees of the Smith Charities.

The undersigned, an inhabitant of the town of Hatfield *hereby proposes and recommends the Boy named below, as a Beneficiary under the provisions for "Indigent Boys," in the Will of the late OLIVER SMITH, Esq., and for the information of said Trustees, makes the statements embodied in the answers to the following questions, viz :—*

1. What is the Boy's name? *Answer.* Thomas Hanigan
2. What the date of his birth? *Ans.* May 3rd 1848.
3. What is his residence? *Ans.* Hatfield
4. How long has he resided in said town? *Ans.* Nine years
5. With whom does he reside? *Ans.* John D Brown
6. What is the name of the Boy's father? *Ans.* ~~John~~ Hanigan ~~[illegible]~~ Deceased
7. What is the name of the Boy's mother? *Ans.* Bridget Gail
8. Are both parents living? If either is dead, where and when did the deceased parent die? *Ans.* his father died July 1st 1864. His mother is still living
9. If either parent survives, is he or she married again and to whom? *Ans.* His Mother is not married
10. What is the present residence of the parents or surviving parent? *Ans.* Hatfield.
11. How long have they resided in that town? *Ans.* Nine years
12. Have the parents any property and how much? *Ans.* Four hundred dollars
13. Has the Boy good health? *Ans.* yes
14. Has he industrious habits? *Ans.* yes
15. Has he a sound intellect? *Ans.* yes
16. Has he a good moral character? *Ans.* yes
17. Has he any property in possession or to be paid to him hereafter? And how much, if any? And from whose estate? *Ans.* He is to have $200 from his fathers Estate when he becomes of age
18. Is there at present any beneficiary under the Will from the Boy's family? *Ans.* No
19. What is the name, residence and occupation of the proposed master? *Ans.* John D. Brown Hatfield. Farmer
20. Is any beneficiary under the Will now living with the proposed master? *Ans.* [illegible]
21. Has the proposed beneficiary any legal Guardian, and who is he? *Ans.* Wm H. Dickinson
22. How is the proposed beneficiary related to the subscriber of this paper? *Ans.* Guardian

In Testimony of the truth of the foregoing answers, I have hereunto subscribed my name, this Nineteenth day of July A. D. 1864

Figure 20

An 1864 record proposing an apprenticeship for Thomas Hanigan of Hatfield, Massachusetts to John D. Brown, a farmer. Note the difference in the information contained in this agreement versus the apprenticeship agreement for the same individual in Figure 21. One contains valuable information about his parents, while the other provides specific information about the arrangement.

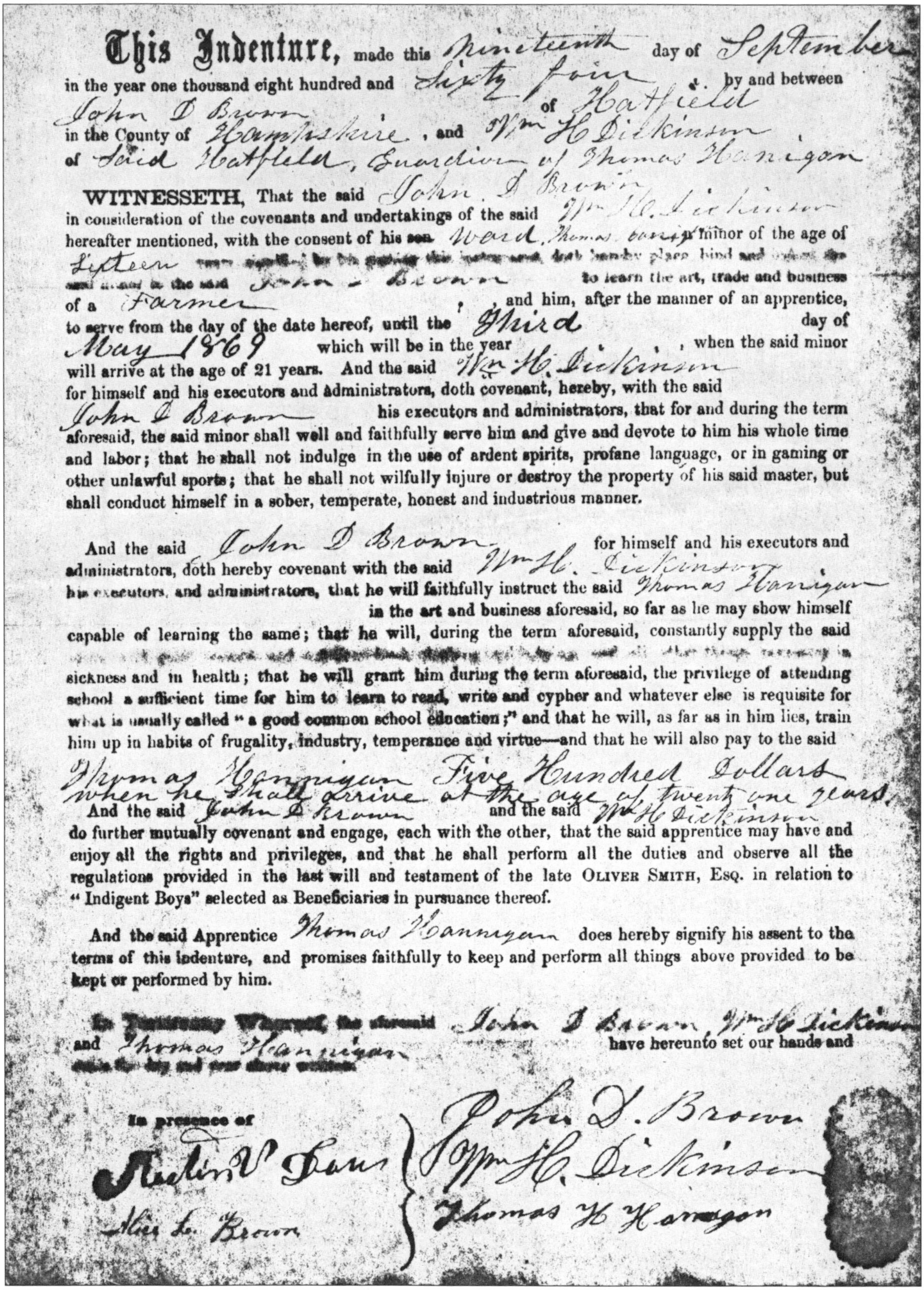

Figure 21

The 1864 agreement outlining the details of the apprenticeship of Thomas Hanigan of Hatfield, Massachusetts to John D. Brown, a farmer.

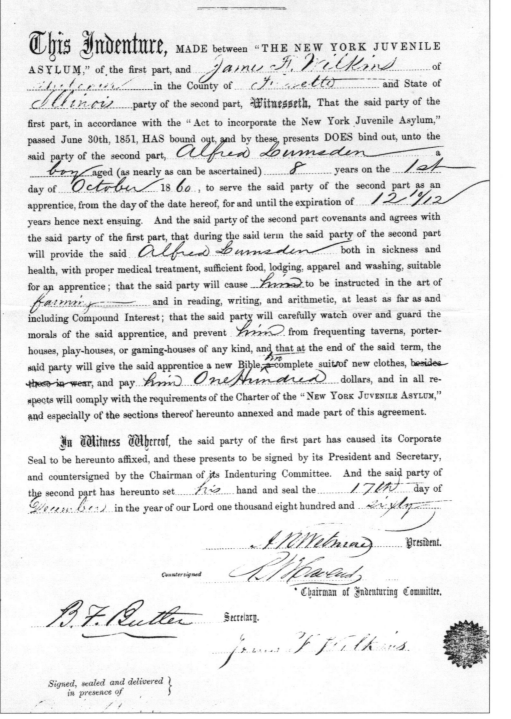

Figure 22

A nineteenth century apprentice indenture agreement. In addition to providing biographical information, the language in legal documents can also provide insight to the values and mores of the time period.

Archival Collections at the Local, State, and Federal Level

LOCAL ARCHIVAL COLLECTIONS

There are a large number of local, municipal, and county archives throughout the United States that hold original records generated by county and city agencies and private entities. Records that might be found in an archival collection include: vital records, naturalization records, divorce records, coroners' case files, voter lists, private papers, probate estate files, registrations and charters of religious and other societies, almshouse records, county surveyor's records, voter registrations, real estate valuation records, and city directories. While not every city in the country has its own archives, some cities such as Baltimore, Philadelphia, and New York City have collections that are worth exploring.

STATE ARCHIVAL COLLECTIONS

Almost every state stores in manuscript (unpublished) form public records of historical value created by state agencies and local units of government. Collections may hold state-created censuses, tax assessment rolls, and state military rosters. Also available in most state archives are microfilm copies of various federal records such as federal population schedules, as they relate to the state served. A few states have created unique card catalogs and databases to facilitate finding specific individuals. Some state archives have extensive collections of old newspapers.

Almost all state archives have a presence on the Internet with Web sites describing their holdings and access policies. Searchable databases are being added regularly. Most institutions will provide a descriptive brochure upon request. As a courtesy, some may also suggest genealogical sources in other facilities that serve their state.

FEDERAL ARCHIVAL COLLECTIONS

Records created by the U.S. Government comprise a valuable source of information. While federal records were not created with family historians in mind, many are rich in historical and biographical information. Original archival records that pertain to the nation as a whole (such as census, military, immigration, and land records) are held by the National Archives and Records Administration (NARA) in Washington, D.C., and in Archives II in College Park, Maryland. Some of the records that are used regularly by family historians have been microfilmed by NARA and are available in the regional archives system and in many libraries across the country. Beyond the heavily used microfilmed records, however, the National Archives has custody of a permanently valuable treasure trove of original documents that unlocks national and personal history. Hundreds of record groups representing the activities of diverse federal agencies are preserved and made available in the nation's capital and in other regions. The holdings of NARA include almost 2 million cubic feet of textual records; over 300,000 rolls of microfilm; more than 2 million maps and charts; more than 2 million architectural and engineering plans; over 9 million aerial photographs; over 7 million still pictures; and thousands of motion picture reels, video recordings, sound recordings, and computer data sets.

Unique sources can be found in the regions of the National Archives (see address list in appendix A). *The*

Archives: A Guide to the National Archives Field Branches (Salt Lake City: Ancestry, 1988) points out a great number of obscure collections that can be rewarding for the family historian. The National Archives – New England Region in suburban Boston, for example, has court records for the area that relate to such diverse matters as admiralty disputes, infringement of patent and copyrights, mutiny and murder, illegal manufacturing or sale of alcoholic beverages, and many others. The New England Region also has the original naturalization records of the federal courts for the six New England states dating back to 1790. Federal court records at the National Archives – Central Plains Region in Kansas City provide firsthand accounts of life in urban centers in the "Wild West." Available only at the National Archives – Mid-Atlantic Region in Philadelphia is a list of individuals who came before the U.S. District Court, for the Eastern District of Pennsylvania, during the Quasi War with France. Significant information regarding individuals involved in the San Francisco Earthquake of 1906 can be extracted from material in a number of record groups at the National Archives – Pacific Sierra Region in San Bruno, California. Some of the least known, genealogically rich records are described in *The Archives*.

In addition to court records, the National Archives has records such as those of the Adjutant General's Office;

Figure 23
Archives are among the best places to find photographic collections.

agricultural bureaus; Alaska Territorial Government; Office of Alien Property; Army Commands; Attorneys and Marshals; Boundary and Claims Commissions; Bureau of the Census; Civil Service Commission; Coast Guard; Department of Commerce; Bureau of Customs; Office of the Chief of Engineers; Farm Credit Administration; Farmers Home Administration; Federal Extension Service; Food Administration; Immigration and Naturalization Service; Bureau of Indian Affairs; Office of the Secretary of the Interior; Internal Revenue Service; Justice Department; Bureau of Land Management; Bureau of Marine Inspection and Navigation; Maritime Administration; Bureau of Mines; National Park Service; Naval Districts and Shore Establishments; Bureau of Ordnance; Patent Office; Postal Service; Bureau of Prisons; Bureau of Public Debt; Public Health Service; Public Housing Administration; Bureau of Public Roads; Railroad Retirement Board; Bureau of Reclamation; Bureau of Refugees, Freedmen, and Abandoned Lands; Selective Service System; Small Business Administration; State Department; Office of the Surgeon General (Army); Tennessee Valley Authority; Veterans Administration; and the Work Projects Administration.

Selected Readings:

A Summary Guide to Local Governmental Records in the Illinois Regional Archives. Springfield, Ill.: Illinois State Archives, 1992.

Barker, Bette Marie, Daniel P. Jones, and Karl J. Niederer, comps. *Guide to Family History Sources in the New Jersey State Archives.* 2d ed. Trenton, N.J.: Division of Archives and Records Management, 1990.

Daly, John. *Descriptive Inventory of the Archives of the City of Philadelphia.* Philadelphia: Department of Records, 1970.

Guide to Genealogical Research in the National Archives. Washington, D.C.: National Archives Trust Fund Board, 1985.

Guide to Records in the New York State Archives. Albany, N.Y.: State Archives and Records Administration, 1993.

Szucs, Loretto Dennis, and Sandra Hargreaves Luebking. *The Archives: A Guide to the National Archives Field Branches.* Salt Lake City: Ancestry, 1988.

Internet Sites of Interest:

National Archives and Records Administration
http://www.nara.gov/

Genealogical Searchable Database - NAIL
http://www.nara.gov/genealogy/genindex. html

Figure 24
An overview of the holdings that can be found in a local archival collection.

The Cuyahoga County Archives, a department of the Board of County Commissio... ...as organized in the summer of 1975. The ... reas, and a research library are loc... ... Rhodes House, a Victori... ... 4.

...ository for the ...urrent records ...s encourages ...ecords and ...he depart... ...s for all

A ... ...ce of persons ... ...per- sonnel are ...ific research p... ...at care and c... ... especially req... ...ers are not allowe... ...embers of the archival ... ...u records to the library area. Pho... ...ue on a cost basis. For the general health a ... ., all persons using the Archives, smoking is not per ...ned in any section of the building.

The Cuyahoga County Archives is open to the public, without charge, Monday through Friday from 8:30 a.m. until 4:30 p.m. The reference library is open for the use of records Monday through Friday from 8:30 a.m. to 4:00 p.m. The address of the Archives is the Rhodes House, 2905 Franklin Boulevard, N.W., Cleveland, Ohio 44113; the telephone number is (216) 443-7250.

The Cuyahoga County Archives holds these records of interest:

- Board of County Commissioners Journals, 1810 - 1984
- Tax Duplicates, 1819-1986 (not inclusive)
- Common Pleas Journals, 1810-1914
- Marriage records, 1810-1941, originals; and an index, 1810 to the present, available on microfiche.
- Divorce case files, 1876-1882, Court of Common Pleas; also Ohio Supreme Court records, 1811-1858, and Court of Common Pleas Special Docket files, 1876-1922.
- Naturalization records, 1818-1971, Court of Common Pleas; also Probate Court naturalization records, 1852-1901
- Birth records, 1849-1908
- Death records, 1840-1908
- Abstract of Votes, 1893-1974, Board of Elections
- List of Electors, 1893-1945, Board of Elections
- Coroner's case files, 1833-1900 (not inclusive)
- Township and ward maps, 1860, 1870, 1880, and 1890
- Atlases: Cuyahoga County, 1852, 1874 and 1892; also City of Cleveland, 1881 and 1898
- County Building Commission Journals, including County Court House, Soldiers' and Sailors' Monument, and certain other County buildings and bridges
- Probate Court estate case files, 1813-1913; index, 1811-1896
- Registration and Charters of Religious and Other Societies, 1845-1924

THE CUYAHOGA COUNTY ARCHIVES

Army Corps of Engineers

The Army Corps of Engineers, established in 1775 as the Office of the Chief of Engineers (OCE), has played a vital role in making the infrastructure of the United States what it is today. Its primary responsibilities included planning, constructing, and repairing military fortifications and encampments; map making; and building roads. Over the years, the corps expanded to include civil projects such as developing and maintaining inland waterways and harbors; surveying for canals, roads, and railroads; designing and constructing flood-control dams and levees; reviewing and approving plans for structures built on and over navigable waters; and disaster relief and recovery work. The Corps is also charged with the purchase and disposal of military land holdings.

With the expansion of responsibilities after the Civil War, the OCE found it necessary to branch out from its Washington, D.C. headquarters and establish district offices throughout the United States. In traditional military fashion, engineers were required to submit reports to superiors in the field offices, and district reports were compiled and submitted to the OCE by the engineer officer in charge.

Field reports sometimes provide amazing detail of conditions endured by the engineers at project sites. Handwritten journals from individuals posted at military fortifications offer firsthand accounts of their experiences. One example is the narrative of Colonel J.J.

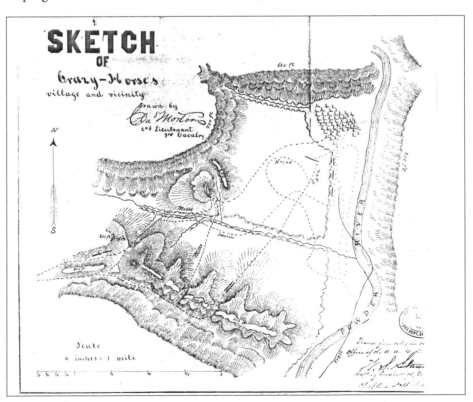

Figure 25
A handwritten page from the journal of Col. J.J. Reynolds included this sketch of Crazy Horse's village and vicinity, drawn by Lt. Charles Morton. Both men were in the 3rd Cavalry, Big Horn Expedition.

31

Reynolds, 3rd Cavalry, shown in Figure 26, in which he reports of the operations of the "Big Horn Expedition," which "left Fort Fetterman on the 1st of March and returned to the same point on the 26th of March 1876." For March 11, 1876, Reynolds recorded the following: "Thermometer at 8 A.M. 23 degrees below zero. Marched at 10 A.M., to Tongue River, moved down that river and after crossing it five times on the ice camped on left bank. (8 miles) Cut through ice two feet thick to reach water which was very fine. Course N."

Also of great interest to both historical and genealogical researchers are the maps created by the corps. Dating as far back as the eighteenth century, these maps—which pertain to both civil and military projects and exploration—frequently include roads, canals, and waterways that could have been migration routes; land ownership or the names of residents; the boundaries of civil divisions and their names or numbers; and additional place name information including inns, mills, churches, mountains, and other cultural and physical features.

The more recent records, dating back fifty years, are usually held by the district offices of the U.S. Army Corps of Engineers. The USACE Web site (www.usace.army.mil/whatwedo) describes current work of the Corps, including a digital visual library containing thousands of images of USACE projects, and people and programs. The digital library is searchable by mission, location, or organization. Most of the older records of the USACE are housed in the National Archives and its regional branches. The collection at the National Archives also includes photographs from many of the Corps's projects, some of which have been digitized.

Selected Readings:

National Archives and Records Administration. *Guide to Genealogical Research in the National Archives.* revised edition. Washington, D.C.: National Archives Trust Fund Board, 1985.

Szucs, Loretto Dennis, and Sandra Hargreaves Luebking. *The Archives: A Guide to the National Archives Field Branches.* Salt Lake City: Ancestry, 1988.

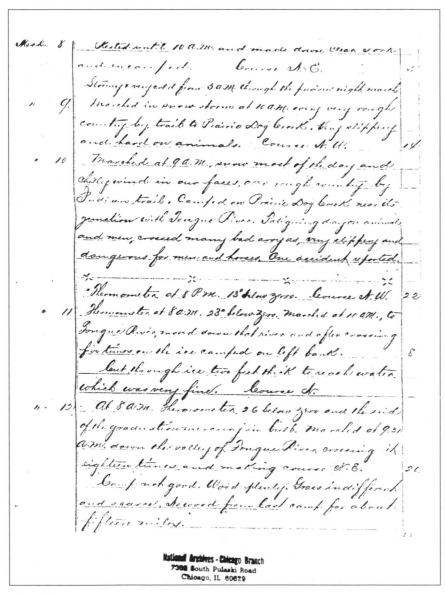

Figure 26
A handwritten page from the journal of Col. J.J. Reynolds, April 15, 1876 [Letters, Reports and Graphic Materials Received, 1868-1903; Department of the Platte, Omaha, Nebraska; Records of Topographical Engineer Departments; Chicago District; U.S. Army Corps of Engineers, Record Group 77; National Archives and Records Administration - Great Lakes Region (Chicago)].

Artifacts

Memorabilia passed down through generations may provide clues as to what direction to take in a search. While the value of some may be obvious, such as a family record sampler listing names and birth dates of family members, even the smallest of trinkets can help open doors to the past.

Wedding bands, pocket watches, school rings, mourning jewelry, cuff links, lockets, and other pieces of jewelry were often inscribed with initials and significant dates. These and other items, like monogrammed handkerchiefs and funeral memorial cards found tucked inside a family Bible, can lead a family historian to previously unexplored avenues of research. Other artifacts that may be useful include fraternal lodge buttons, military buttons and ribbons, uniforms, awards and trophies, and books containing inscriptions and addresses. Heirlooms that do not bear an inscription or seem to have a connection to an ancestor should not be overlooked. A knowledgeable antique dealer may be able to identify the manufacturer or region and approximate year of production for a piece of furniture, a set of dishes, a steamer trunk, or a piece of artwork.

Selected Readings:

Henry, Barbara R. "Family Record Samplers for Genealogists." *Ancestry* 13 (5) (September/October 1995): 25–26.

Melchiori, Marie Varrelman. "Ancestral Artifacts." *APG Quarterly* Vol. XIII, No. 3 (September 1998): 80–81.

Morgan, George G. "Engraved Heirlooms Can Provide Clues." *Along Those Lines...* 13 November 1998. Online column at www.ancestry.com.

Yeargin, Frances Grimes. "Who Was Eliza Walter?" *Ancestry* 14 (2) (March/April 1996): 30–31.

Figure 27
A police badge (shown with a night stick) provided the necessary information—an occupation—to distinguish an ancestor (inset) from the many other individuals with the same name listed in a city directory. The precinct number on the badge also helped to narrow the search to a particular locality.

Association Records

Associations, professional and social, often maintain records containing information of value to family historians. Details that may be found in such records are a member's name, address, and in some cases, educational background and details about the member's business. A search of these records sometimes surfaces published biographies as well.

Associations often print directories of members. Even the smallest public libraries usually have a good collection of directories in their reference sections. To determine if a particular association published a directory, researchers may consult one of the many printed sources available, such as *Directories in Print*, 13th ed. (Detroit: Gale Research Co., 1996) or Dorothea N. Spear's *Bibliography of American Directories Through 1860* (Worcester, Mass.: American Antiquarian Society, 1961). The *Encyclopedia of Associations* (Detroit: Gale Research Co., annual) can be helpful in locating an association with which an ancestor was affiliated.

See also *American Medical Association Records, Fraternal Organization Records, Licenses,* and *Occupational Records.*

Selected Readings:

Directories in Print, 13th ed. Detroit: Gale Research Co., 1996.

Encyclopedia of Associations. Detroit: Gale Research Co., annual.

Spear, Dorothea N. *Bibliography of American Directories Through 1860.* Worcester, Mass.: American Antiquarian Society, 1961.

Figure 28

Organizations such as the Czechoslovak Society published biographical sketches and photographs like the one above in *One Hundred Years of the CSA* (Cicero, Illinois, 1955).

Autobiographies

An autobiography, the story of an individual's life told in his or her own words, provides a look at an ancestor's life that can't be seen from a birth certificate or death certificate.

Authors of autobiographies often include their own family history—sometimes in great detail. However, because an autobiography is written with the expectation that others will read it, a reader should be cautioned to view the contents with at least some degree of objectivity.

Autobiographies can be difficult to locate, since most libraries carry only those on individuals of notable fame. Bibliographical references, such as Louis Kaplan's *A Bibliography of American Autobiographies* (Madison: University of Wisconsin Press, 1961), and Mary Louise Briscoe's *American Autobiography 1945–1980: A Bibliography* (Madison: University of Wisconsin Press, 1982) can be of help in locating autobiographical publications, if they exist.

Selected Readings:

Briscoe, Mary Louise. *American Autobiography 1945–1980: A Bibliography.* Madison: University of Wisconsin Press, 1982.

Kaplan, Louis. *A Bibliography of American Autobiographies.* Madison: University of Wisconsin Press, 1961.

Meyerink, Kory L. ed. *Printed Sources: A Guide to Published Genealogical Records.* Ch. 18: 670–706. Salt Lake City: Ancestry, 1998.

Figure 29
Your ancestor's autobiography will likely include important, as well as interesting, insights into his or her life.

Bankruptcy Records

Laws were enacted as early as 1800 to help individuals and businesses recover from extreme financial hardship. Those overwhelmed with debt, whether brought on by a depressed economy or by financial mismanagement, were able to seek protection in federal courts under bankruptcy laws.

While most bankruptcy cases do not provide the vital statistics genealogists seek, they can provide valuable insight into the lifestyle of an ancestor prior to a bankruptcy. Filings include schedules of assets and liabilities and may have extensive accounts of real and personal property, and occasionally, for corporations, a surprising number of artifacts, photographs, or maps.

To locate a bankruptcy case, the researcher must know the name of the petitioner and the county of residence during the pertinent period, as well as an approximate date of filing. (Public notices printed in local newspapers may be a way to locate the date and place of a bankruptcy.) A small percentage of cases can be accessed through major indexes. Most files, though, can be located only by visiting a region of the National Archives and going through individual indexes of districts, ledger by ledger. Of special interest to those with roots in the South are the records of the Southern Claims Commission, which was organized to settle with Union sympathizers who had supplied northern forces without compensation. Due to the tremendous numbers of filings, only fifteen to twenty percent of files created after 1920 can be saved by the National Archives, and the case files now go through a three-step process to determine which files will be kept.

Selected Readings:

Blake, Kellee Green. *Prosperity Did Forsake Me: Family History in 19th Century Federal Bankruptcy Cases at the National Archives – Mid Atlantic Region.* Audiotape of lecture presented at the National Genealogical Society 1997 Conference in the States, Valley Forge, Pennsylvania. Hobart, Ind.: Repeat Performance, 1997.

BRB Publications Research and Editorial Staff. *The Sourcebook of Federal Courts, U.S. District and Bankruptcy: The Definitive Guide to Searching for Case Information at the Local Level Within the Federal Court System.* Tempe, Ariz.: BRB Publications, 1993.

Owens, James K. "Documenting Regional Business History: The Bankruptcy Acts for 1800 and 1841." *Business History* 179 (1989).

Szucs, Loretto Dennis, and Sandra Hargreaves Luebking. *The Archives: A Guide to the National Archives Field Branches.* Salt Lake City: Ancestry, 1988.

Szucs, Loretto Dennis. "To Whom I Am Indebted: Bankruptcy Records." *Ancestry* 12 (5) (September-October 1994): 26–27.

Watkins, Beverly. "To Surrender All His Estate: The 1867 Bankruptcy Act." *Prologue* 21 (Fall 1989): 206–13.

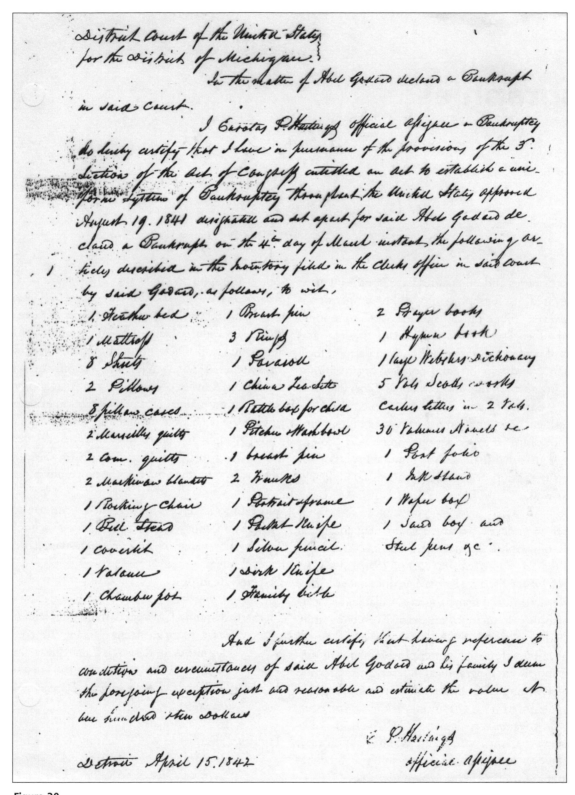

Figure 30

A bankruptcy filing from the U.S. District Court of Michigan found at the National Archives - Great Lakes Region. From a glance at the list of assets, one might assume that this individual was well-read and had led a fairly comfortable existence to this point.

Biographies

Most libraries and bookstores have significant areas devoted to biographies of well-known personalities. However, biographical sketches are commonly published of company officers, industry leaders, and members of professional associations, foundations, local governments, and religious and political organizations. Included in most are the subject's name, birth date and birthplace, parents' names, spouse's name, children's names, residence, occupation, education, achievements, and memberships in organizations. Some may provide accounts of an individual's defining moments, his or her impact on the group or organization, and family background as well.

A number of indexes are available to help locate an ancestor's biography, if one exists. *Printed Sources: A Guide to Published Genealogical Records* (Salt Lake City: Ancestry, 1998), edited by Kory Meyerink, has an entire chapter devoted to the many sources available for locating biographies. It includes an extensive bibliography section listing national biographical indexes, national biographical encyclopedias, American biographical dictionaries, multistate biographical indexes, and statewide biographies arranged alphabetically by state. One of exceptional interest is Fremont Rider's *American Genealogical-Biographical Index (AGBI)*, vols. 1–188+ (Middletown, Conn.: Godfrey Memorial Library, 1952–), an every-name index that includes such collective biographies as Brockett's *Men of Our Day*, Harper's *Colonial Men and Times*, Hinman's *Puritan Settlers of the Colony of Connecticut*, and Holme's *Directory of Ancestral Heads of New England Families*. It is now available on the Internet at <www.ancestry.com> and is also available on CD-ROM.

Another helpful index is the *Biography and Genealogy Master Index (BGMI)*, 2d ed., 8 vols. (Detroit: Gale Research Co.) which contains the names of more than five million individuals, focusing on Americans in the late eighteenth and early nineteenth centuries who have biographical sketches in "Who's Who" publications and other similar sources. A major portion of this index is also available at <www.ancestry.com>. With the exception of persons born after 1920 (who were excluded to protect their privacy), each biography referenced in *BGMI* includes the individual's name, years of birth and death (if known), and an abbreviation for the source of the biography.

Biographical sketches of ancestors can sometimes be located in county atlases and histories, school alumni files, local newspapers, and occupational records.

Selected Readings:

Herbert, Miranda C., and Barbara McNeil. *Biography and Genealogy Master Index*. 2d ed., 8 vols. Detroit: Gale Research Co., 1980; supplement 1982; 1981–85; 1986–90; 1991. First edition published as *Biographical Dictionaries Master Index 1975–76*.

Hinckley, Kathleen W. "Tracking Twentieth-Century Ancestors." *The Source: A Guidebook of American Genealogy*. Rev. ed. Ch. 18: 628–653. Salt Lake City: Ancestry, 1997.

Meyerink, Kory L. ed. *Printed Sources: A Guide to Published Genealogical Records*. Ch.18: 670–706. Salt Lake City: Ancestry, 1998.

_____. "Genealogy's Best-Kept Secret: American Genealogical-Biographical Index." *Ancestry* 17 (2) (March/April 1999): 36-40.

Meyerink, Kory L., and Johni Cerny. "Research in Business, Employment, and Institutional Records." *The Source: A Guidebook of American Genealogy.* Rev. ed. Ch. 10: 336–383. Salt Lake City: Ancestry, 1997. (Provides a bibliography of selected vocational collective biographies.)

Slocum, Robert B. *Biographical Dictionaries and Related Works.* 2 vols. Detroit: Gail Research Co., 1986.

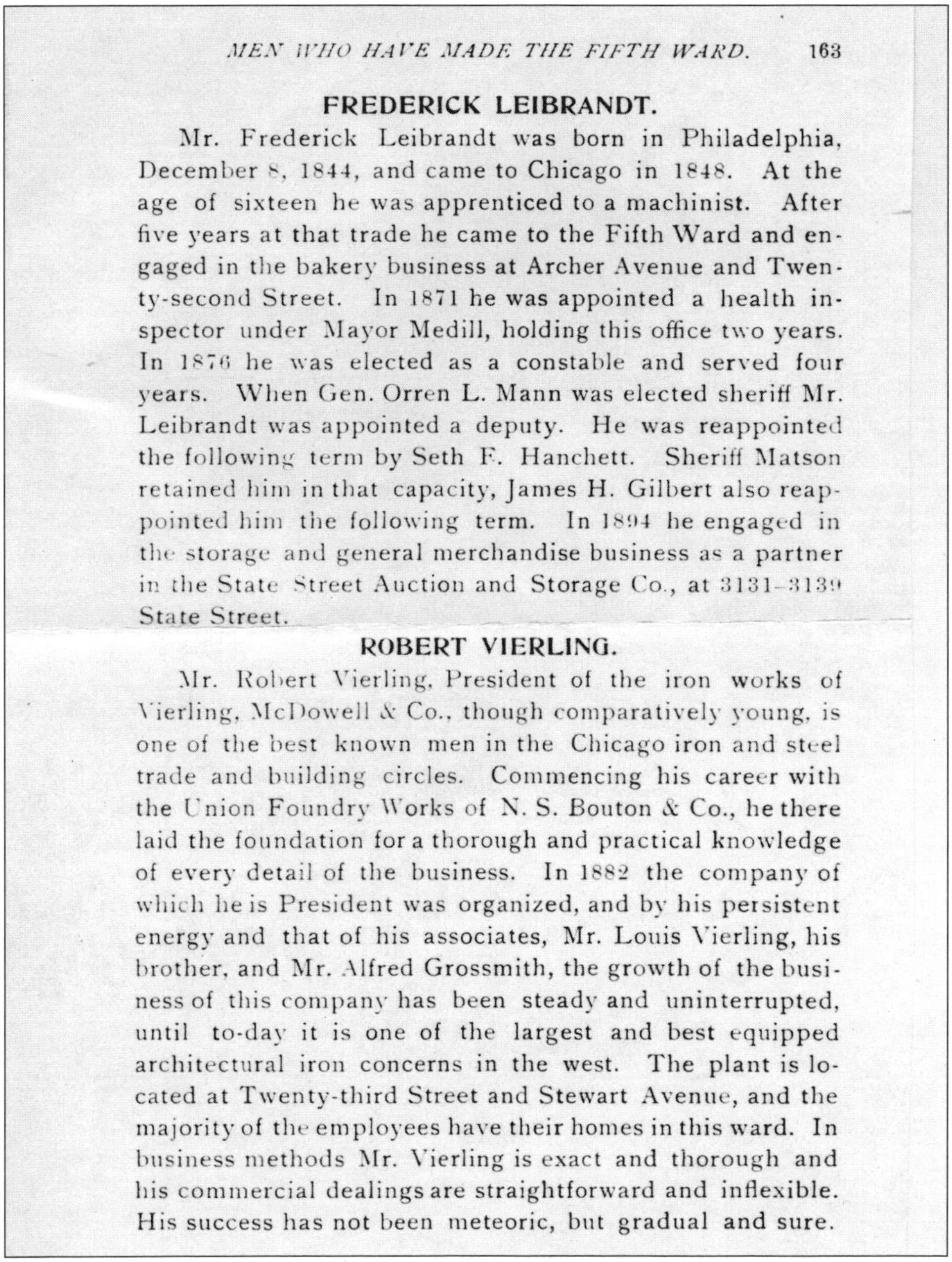

MEN WHO HAVE MADE THE FIFTH WARD.   163

FREDERICK LEIBRANDT.

Mr. Frederick Leibrandt was born in Philadelphia, December 8, 1844, and came to Chicago in 1848. At the age of sixteen he was apprenticed to a machinist. After five years at that trade he came to the Fifth Ward and engaged in the bakery business at Archer Avenue and Twenty-second Street. In 1871 he was appointed a health inspector under Mayor Medill, holding this office two years. In 1876 he was elected as a constable and served four years. When Gen. Orren L. Mann was elected sheriff Mr. Leibrandt was appointed a deputy. He was reappointed the following term by Seth F. Hanchett. Sheriff Matson retained him in that capacity, James H. Gilbert also reappointed him the following term. In 1894 he engaged in the storage and general merchandise business as a partner in the State Street Auction and Storage Co., at 3131–3139 State Street.

ROBERT VIERLING.

Mr. Robert Vierling, President of the iron works of Vierling, McDowell & Co., though comparatively young, is one of the best known men in the Chicago iron and steel trade and building circles. Commencing his career with the Union Foundry Works of N. S. Bouton & Co., he there laid the foundation for a thorough and practical knowledge of every detail of the business. In 1882 the company of which he is President was organized, and by his persistent energy and that of his associates, Mr. Louis Vierling, his brother, and Mr. Alfred Grossmith, the growth of the business of this company has been steady and uninterrupted, until to-day it is one of the largest and best equipped architectural iron concerns in the west. The plant is located at Twenty-third Street and Stewart Avenue, and the majority of the employees have their homes in this ward. In business methods Mr. Vierling is exact and thorough and his commercial dealings are straightforward and inflexible. His success has not been meteoric, but gradual and sure.

Figure 31

While biographies usually center on individuals who were prominent for one reason or another, they should not be overlooked for their value in shining a light on the life, times, and people known to that person. Shorter biographical sketches are often found in county, local, and organizational histories, in newspapers, and in obscure sources such as the above for Frederick Leibrandt which appeared in *Men Who Made the Fifth Ward* (Chicago: Schroeder, Forbrich & Co., 1895).

Bird's-eye View Maps

Panoramic, or "bird's-eye view," maps of an ancestor's hometown, which provide an aerial perspective of streets and buildings, can add a new dimension to a family history. These drawings, which were especially popular during the Civil War era, were usually commissioned by chambers of commerce, real estate companies, and businessmen whose establishments were frequently advertised on its borders.

Historical societies and libraries often hold map collections and may have them cataloged by date or subject. Two collections of note are those of the Library of Congress and the New York Public Library, which currently has one of the largest city map collections in the United States.

Selected Readings:

Library of Congress. *Panoramic Maps of Cities in the United States and Canada: A Checklist of Maps in the Collections of the Library of Congress, Geography, and Map Division*. 2d ed. Washington, D.C.: Library of Congress, 1984.

Figure 32
An 1859 "bird's-eye" map of New York City.

Body Transit Records

In an effort to stem the spread of communicable diseases, local governments in many states required that bodies arriving in their jurisdiction be registered. The resulting records cover a large number of individuals.

As B-Ann Moorhouse, C.G., F.G.B.S., suggested in an article in *The NYG& B Newsletter* (Moorhouse, 1992), "The Board of Health of the City of New York required that any body arriving in Manhattan via ship, train, or even local ferry be registered. Thus the vacationer who died out West and whose body was being shipped back for burial in Green-Wood Cemetery in Brooklyn, the New Jersey resident or Staten Island housewife whose body was being shipped across the river for burial in Upstate New York, the Civil War soldier and sailor whose bodies were being shipped back to New England for burial, all were registered with the City." Moorhouse also notes that the registrations also applied to bodies being shipped in the opposite direction. An example given in this article is that of the transit of Abraham Lincoln, whose body passed through New York City on April 24, 1865. Biographical information included in the Lincoln record includes his age (52 y 2 m), nativity (Kentucky), place of death (Washington, D.C.), date of death (April 15, 1865), disease (pistol shot), place of interment (Springfield, Ill.), and name and address of person having charge of the body (P. Relyea).

"Bodies in Transit," the records for New York City covering the years 1859 to 1894, have been microfilmed and are available at the Municipal Archives of the City of New York, and through the Family History Library. Body transit records are also available for a number of other locations, including Camden, New Jersey, as shown in figure 33. Transit permits may also be interfiled with death records in the place where the burial took place.

Selected Reading:

Moorehouse, B-Ann. "Little-Publicized New York City Sources." *The NYG& B Newsletter*. New York: New York Genealogical and Biographical Society (summer 1992, p. 11).

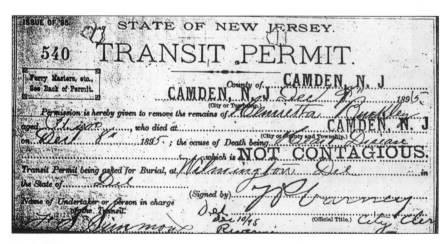

Figure 33

A body transit permit issued in Camden, New Jersey for Henrietta Buckley. The deceased—"aged 31 years"—died at Camden, N.J., Dec. 8, 1895 of heart disease, "which is not contagious." The transit permit is for burial in Wilmington, Delaware.

Cemetery Records

A person's final resting place is often a significant source of information. Burial records maintained by cemeteries often include the date a plot was purchased; who purchased it; the names of individuals buried in the plot, along with death and burial dates (and in some cases, the relationship of those individuals); notations of grave openings for exhumation or for transfer to another burial site; and the name of the person being billed for perpetual care, if applicable.

Locating old records can be the most challenging aspect of this kind of research, as cemeteries were often forced to move as the landscape around it changed. Fortunately, a great effort has been made to document the movement of cemeteries and to preserve older cemeteries, including family burial plots that may have been forgotten as property changed hands. State and local historical and genealogical societies are continually working to conserve valuable cemetery information.

Once genealogical societies in the area have been searched for cemetery locations and transcriptions, libraries and state and county archives are often among the next best places to look. Some states have cemetery associations that can provide locations of cemeteries. Old local and county histories are sometimes useful in identifying former names and localities of cemeteries that have been moved and there are a few contemporary printed guides that will be useful for tracking down even the most hidden burial grounds. An example is *The Graveyard Shift: A Family Historian's Guide to New York City Cemeteries*, (Inskeep, 2000), a guide to the more than 300 former and still-existing cemeteries in New York City.

Burial locations are often noted on the death certificate, in obituaries, or in the family Bible. Researchers unable to locate a reference to a cemetery should consult a map of the area the family resided in. A local historical society will likely have information on older cemeteries. Religious and military cemeteries should not be overlooked in the search. In both cases, records may be preserved in a central location.

See also *Body Transit Records, Tombstone and Monument Inscriptions.*

Selected Readings:

Burek, Deborah, ed. *Cemeteries of the United States.* Detroit: Gale Research Co., 1994.

Cerny, Johni. "Research in Birth, Death, and Cemetery Records." *The Source: A Guidebook of American Genealogy.* Rev. ed. Salt Lake City: Ancestry, 1997.

Inskeep, Carolee. *The Graveyard Shift: A Family Historian's Guide to New York City Cemeteries.* Orem: Ancestry, 2000.

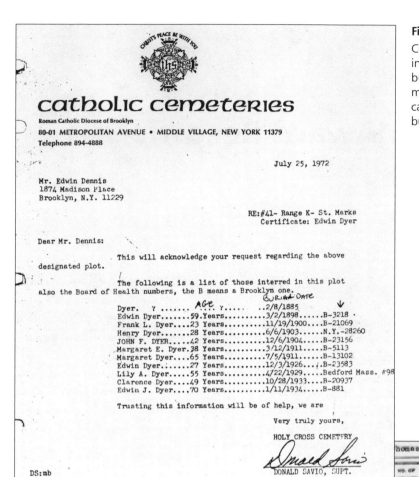

catholic cemeteries

Roman Catholic Diocese of Brooklyn

80-01 METROPOLITAN AVENUE • MIDDLE VILLAGE, NEW YORK 11379

Telephone 894-4888

July 25, 1972

Mr. Edwin Dennis
1874 Madison Place
Brooklyn, N.Y. 11229

RE:#41- Range K- St. Marks
Certificate: Edwin Dyer

Dear Mr. Dennis:

This will acknowledge your request regarding the above designated plot.

The following is a list of those interred in this plot also the Board of Health numbers, the B means a Brooklyn one.

```
                          AGE          BURIAL DATE
Dyer.   γ ....... γ ..... ..2/8/1885         ↓
Edwin Dyer.......59.Years..........3/2/1898......B-3218 ·
Frank L. Dyer....23 Years..........11/19/1900....B-21069
Henry Dyer.......28 Years..........6/6/1903......N.Y.-28260
JOHN F. DYER.....42 Years..........12/6/1904.....B-23156
Margaret E. Dyer.38 Years..........3/12/1911.....B-5113
Margaret Dyer....65 Years..........7/5/1911......B-13102
Edwin Dyer.......27 Years..........12/3/1926.....B-23583
Lily A. Dyer.....55 Years..........4/22/1929.....Bedford Mass. #98
Clarence Dyer....49 Years..........10/28/1933....B-20937
Edwin J. Dyer....70 Years..........1/11/1934.....B-881
```

Trusting this information will be of help, we are

Very truly yours,

HOLY CROSS CEMETERY

DONALD SAVIO, SUPT.

DS:mb

Figure 34

Correspondence from a cemetery can be useful in providing the specific location of a grave or burial plot, in identifying and linking family members, in providing death dates, and in some cases, in determining the place of death and the burial permit or death certificate numbers.

Figure 35

A cemetery plot record from Calvary Cemetery, Evanston, Illinois, showing the names of individuals buried in a certain plot, the dates of internment, burial location in the plot, and in some cases, a notation has been made indicating relationship, age of death, residence at the time of death, and previous burial information.

DATE OF INTERMENT	NAME OF DECEASED	TYPE AND SIZE OF BOX	LOCATION
6/13/14	Johanna Harrington		Birr Place
1/27/36	James Harrington	Pine	North of Center East Row
12/6/47	Nellie T. McCaffery	6-6XX Wood	S.E. Corner
9/11/61	James C. Harrington	29 Mon	S.W.C
9/26/89	Thomas Hart		Street
11/25/1963	Jessie Harrington	29sp Mon	N.W.C-9/7
7/17/1873	Thomas Hart & others	—	Removed from Old Cemetery
12/20/1963	Frank Harrington	29sp Mon	2nd S.E.C
12/28/1887	Fanny A. Wilson (6-0-0)	104- 13th St.	
3/8/1886	Andrew C. Hart (0-1-4)		
1/26/1881	Ellen McDonnell (3-4-10)		
11/10/1878	Catherine Hart		

				Card No. 2		
HART	Thomas			6	9	K
OWNER			PART OF LOT	LOT	BLOCK	
DATE OF PURCHASE:	NO. OF GRAVES:	INCOME CARE			SEE FILE	
SIZE OF LOT:	X	NO. OF SQ. FT.				

DATE OF INTERMENT	NAME OF DECEASED	TYPE AND SIZE OF BOX	LOCATION
4/21/1875	Margaret Murphy (0-10-0)		
9/31/1973	George Murphy (0-7-0)		
11/4/1975	Rose Ann Harrington	#9 C.V.	N.E.Corner

Centennial Farm Award Records

The records of centennial farm award programs that have been active in many states can be useful sources of family information. The main criteria for a farm or ranch to receive this type of award is that the farm or ranch must be in continuous ownership and operation by a family for at least one hundred years. Lineal descent must typically be traced through either a son, daughter, grandson, or granddaughter (including in-laws) of the previous owner. While the quality and quantity of documentation submitted varies, it often includes property deeds, pedigree charts, names of all owners and their relationships to one another, dates of each individual's ownership, a description of the farm's current operation, and a short written history of the farm operation.

The name of the award program varies from state to state. In some areas it is called the Centennial Farm Award Program, in others it is called the Century Farm Distinction Award, or the Historical Farm Award Program.

Although most states have or are participating in some type of centennial award program, it is administered by different agencies in different states. The county-level cooperative extension service may administer the program in some states, the land-grant college in others, and in still others the program is administered by the state's department of agriculture. Sometimes the Farm Bureau, a private, nongovernment agency serving farm families, is involved in some capacity. In some states, such as Iowa, the program was administered by an American Revolution Bicentennial Commission. Often it is a partnership of several such agencies.

Each centennial award given represents one hundred years worth of genealogy, for at least one line of descendancy. The records provided by the farm family to confirm lineal descent are usually available to the general public, depending on the policies of the agency administering the program. The records for some states, such as Iowa, have been microfilmed and are available at and through the Family History Library.

Selected Readings:

Angelastro, Lynda. "Centennial Farm Award Program." *Ancestry* 14, (5) (September/October 1996): 20-21.

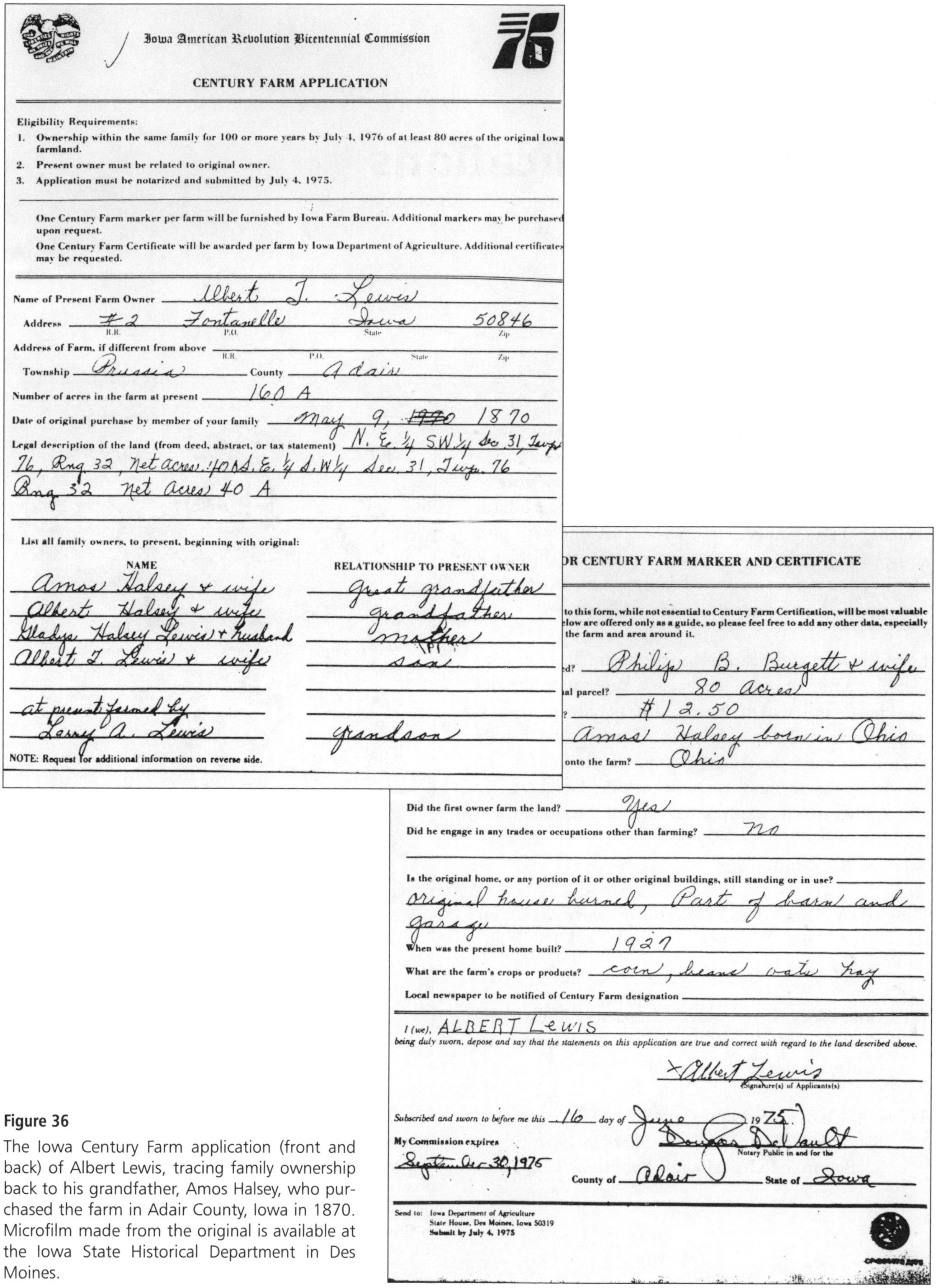

Iowa American Revolution Bicentennial Commission

76

CENTURY FARM APPLICATION

Eligibility Requirements:

1. Ownership within the same family for 100 or more years by July 4, 1976 of at least 80 acres of the original Iowa farmland.
2. Present owner must be related to original owner.
3. Application must be notarized and submitted by July 4, 1975.

One Century Farm marker per farm will be furnished by Iowa Farm Bureau. Additional markers may be purchased upon request.

One Century Farm Certificate will be awarded per farm by Iowa Department of Agriculture. Additional certificates may be requested.

Name of Present Farm Owner: Albert T. Lewis

Address: #2 (R.R.) Fontanelle (P.O.) Iowa (State) 50846 (Zip)

Address of Farm, if different from above: R.R. P.O. State Zip

Township: Prussia County: Adair

Number of acres in the farm at present: 160 A

Date of original purchase by member of your family: May 9, ~~1970~~ 1870

Legal description of the land (from deed, abstract, or tax statement): N. E. 1/4 SW 1/4 Sec. 31, Twp. 76, Rng. 32, Net Acres: 40 A S. E. 1/4 S. W 1/4 Sec. 31, Twp. 76 Rng. 32 Net Acres 40 A

List all family owners, to present, beginning with original:

NAME	RELATIONSHIP TO PRESENT OWNER
Amos Halsey + wife	Great grandfather
Albert Halsey + wife	grandfather
Gladys Halsey Lewis + husband	mother
Albert T. Lewis + wife	son
at present farmed by Larry A. Lewis	grandson

NOTE: Request for additional information on reverse side.

...OR CENTURY FARM MARKER AND CERTIFICATE

...to this form, while not essential to Century Farm Certification, will be most valuable ...low are offered only as a guide, so please feel free to add any other data, especially ...the farm and area around it.

...d? Philip B. Burgett + wife

...al parcel? 80 acres

...? $12.50

...? Amos Halsey born in Ohio

...onto the farm? Ohio

Did the first owner farm the land? Yes

Did he engage in any trades or occupations other than farming? no

Is the original home, or any portion of it or other original buildings, still standing or in use? original house burned, Part of barn and garage

When was the present home built? 1927

What are the farm's crops or products? corn, beans oats hay

Local newspaper to be notified of Century Farm designation

I (we), ALBERT Lewis

being duly sworn, depose and say that the statements on this application are true and correct with regard to the land described above.

Albert Lewis (Signature(s) of Applicants(s))

Subscribed and sworn to before me this 16 *day of* June 19 75

My Commission expires September 30, 1975 Douglas DeVault Notary Public in and for the County of Adair State of Iowa

Send to: Iowa Department of Agriculture State House, Des Moines, Iowa 50319 Submit by July 4, 1975

Figure 36

The Iowa Century Farm application (front and back) of Albert Lewis, tracing family ownership back to his grandfather, Amos Halsey, who purchased the farm in Adair County, Iowa in 1870. Microfilm made from the original is available at the Iowa State Historical Department in Des Moines.

Centennial Publications

National centennial celebrations provided the impetus for many counties to record their local histories. Centennial publications usually include a history of the county and its townships and have biographical sketches of many of the county residents who were alive at the time of publication. Those compiled in the North often had complete rosters of Union soldiers from the county who had fought in the Civil War as well.

Local libraries and historical societies are likely to have histories published for the area, and larger state libraries may have copies of materials that pertain to regions within their state. The Library of Congress, the Family History Library, the Allen County Public Library, the Newberry Library, and the New York Public Library are also known to have exceptional historical collections.

Selected Readings:

Filby, P. William. *A Bibliography of American County Histories.* Baltimore: Genealogical Publishing Co., 1985.

Meyerink, Kory L. ed. *Printed Sources: A Guide to Published Genealogical Records.* Salt Lake City: Ancestry, 1998.

Peterson, Clarence Stewart. *Consolidated Bibliography of County Histories in Fifty States in 1961.* 2d ed. Baltimore: Genealogical Publishing Co., 1963.

Figure 37

Typical centennial publications include photographs, maps, and biographical sketches of important individuals. Centennials were published for schools, religious institutions, businesses, associations, towns, cities, and other entities.

City Directories

The first listing of residents for an American city is believed to have been compiled in 1752 for Baltimore, Maryland, followed by Charleston, South Carolina in 1782. Many other cities throughout the country followed suit in the succeeding years.

While the obvious use of a city directory is to confirm an address of an ancestor, directories can provide much more. Many of them list an individual's occupation and have an abbreviation indicating whether the occupant is a homeowner, a relative of the homeowner, or an unrelated boarder. Some directories also include an alphabetical listing of streets with the names of the people residing at each address. This can be especially helpful in locating an immigrant who settled with family members or friends from the old country who had different last names. Directories can also link ancestors to churches, fraternal organizations, businesses, and other groups in the area.

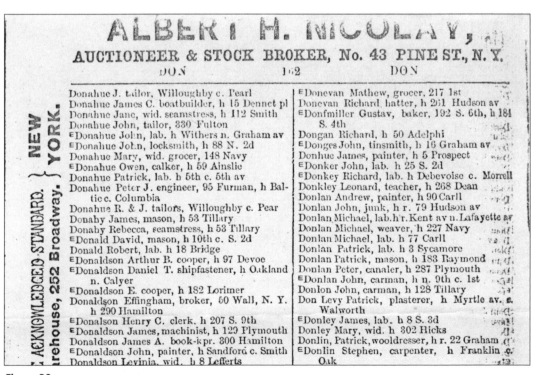

Figure 38

A page from an 1867-68 Brooklyn, New York City directory, showing name, occupation, and street address. Many directories are available on microfilm and microfiche at various libraries.

47

Most larger public libraries and state archives hold collections of in-state directories. The Library of Congress and the American Antiquarian Society in Worcester, Massachusetts hold major city directory collections on the national level.

Selected Readings:

Burton, Robert E. "City Directories in the United States, 1784–1820: A Bibliography with Historical Notes." M.S. thesis, University of Michigan, 1956. (Gives locations of directories)

Catalog of City, County, and State Directories Published in North America. New York: North American Directory Publishers, 1967. (May help to identify and locate directories no longer in print)

City and State Directories in Print, 1990–1991. 1st ed. Detroit: Gale Research Co., 1989.

City Directories of the United States Pre 1860 Through 1901: Guide to the Microfilm Collection. Woodbridge, Conn.: Research Publications, 1983.

"Directories in the Library of Congress." *The American Genealogist* 13 (1937): 46–53; 27 (1951): 142.

Kirkham, E. Kay. *A Handy Guide to Record Searching in the Larger Cities of the United States.* Logan, Utah: The Everton Publishers, 1974.

Moriarty, John H. "Directory Information Materials for New York City Residents, 1626–1786: A Bibliographic Study." *Bulletin New York Public Library* (October 1942).

Parker, Nathan C. *Personal Name Index to the 1856 City Directories of California.* Genealogy and Local History Series, vol. 10. Detroit: Gale Research Co., 1980.

Remington, Gordon Lewis. "Research In Directories." *The Source: A Guidebook of American Genealogy.* Rev. ed. Salt Lake City: Ancestry, 1997.

Sopp, Elsie L. *Personal Name Index to the 1856 City Directories of Iowa.* Genealogy and Local History Series, vol. 13. Detroit: Gale Research Co., 1980.

Figure 39

If an individual's name is not found in the regular listing, it may be listed in a special section, such as the one shown, found in either the front or the back of the directory.

The Street Directory of the Principal Cities of the United States . . . to April 1908. 5th ed. 1908. Reprint. Detroit: Gale Research Co., 1973.

Figure 40

Advertisements found throughout old city directories can provide clues to occupations and family-owned businesses.

College and University Records

Many colleges and universities maintain historical archives that contain faculty and student records such as admissions applications. Student records can provide information on the course of study and the date of graduation. A number of schools also maintain alumni files containing the year of graduation along with address and employment information. More detailed directories may also include previous residences, subsequent education, maiden name (if applicable), and children's names.

vide information on the types of records available and the location of those records. The college or university library may have copies of old yearbooks, campus newspapers, and alumni directories. Local libraries, historical societies, and archives sometimes hold collections from institutions of higher learning.

See also *School Records.*

Fraternities and sororities are another potential source of information resulting from an ancestor's college career. Publications of fraternities and sororities often contain information like that found in alumni directories. An example is *The Sigma Chi Fraternity Manual and Directory* (Nate, 1922), which includes both a geographical and an alphabetical index of members dating back as far as 1775.

The college or university in question, if still in existence, can pro-

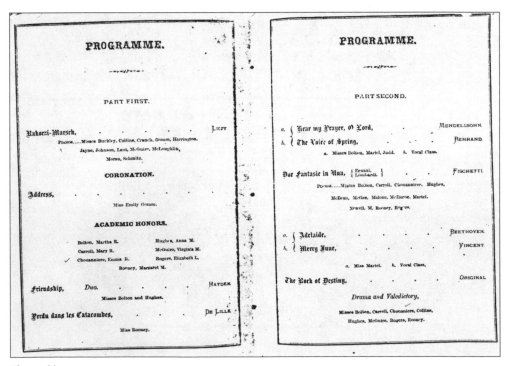

Figure 41
A college graduation program reveals that Emma R. Chouanniere participated in drama, played the piano, and excelled in academics, insights into personality and facts that may otherwise have been lost over time.

JOSEPH R. DENNIS, A.B.

"JOEY"

Brooklyn Prep

Class Football (2, 4).

"JOEY" has eluded the nickname hounds for his three years at Fordham. Since the advent of the gipsy scholar caravan from Brooklyn, in the memorable days of Sophomore, the youth from the unfenced ranges of Flatbush has moved quietly in and around the classroom for all the world like one of Conan Doyle's insubstantial tourists; yet opposing ends have found him all too substantial in his materializations on the Interclass Football field.

Versatility is his maiden name; like Joe Cook, about the only thing he can do is to imitate four Hawaiians. It is related that his first articulate speech on this sphere was an offer to the kid next door to meet him at catchweights in any line of infant sport, from crying for the moon to making faces at his maiden aunt. If the thesis on objective evidence is more than so many words, it must be so; for "Joe" can manage with remarkable facility the pigskin, the palaver, and the pasteboards.

He is by no means a politician, as the word is used among the boys. He has no need to be, for fortune has blessed him with the finest trait that anyone could wish for—an unusual aptitude for contracting sincere and lasting friendships. Wish him "best of luck?" But there, you see, he has it.

Figure 42

A page from *The Maroon*, Fordham University's yearbook, 1924.

Computerized Genealogies

An ever-growing number of researchers are turning to the Internet, seeking information from other family historians who are tracking the same surnames. With the help of computer programs like Wholly Genes' *The Master Genealogist*, Sierra's *Generations*, and Brøderbund's *Family Tree Maker*, individuals have made their family trees available online in various formats through their personal Web pages. Thousands of individuals have submitted their pedigree charts to collections such as Ancestry.com's World Tree and Brøderbund's World Family Tree (Web addresses follow) as well. Such collections are usually in GEDCOM format, a common computer language that communicates with most popular genealogy programs, thereby allowing a researcher to download the information found into their own program. Another collection, in fact one of the largest collections of lineage-linked databases, is the Ancestral File™, maintained by The Church of Jesus Christ of Latter-day Saints. This database is not available on the Internet, but can be accessed through the Family History Library and its Family History Centers.

A surname search using an Internet search engine is the best way to locate a page containing genealogical information for a particular surname. In using a search engine, it is recommended that the surname be followed by the word "family" or "genealogy" to narrow the search and the return of possible sites. There are also Web sites available, such as Juliana's Links at <www.ancestry.com>, which provide direct links to personal Web pages containing genealogical information.

A researcher utilizing computerized genealogies should keep in mind that the information in these databases is a secondary source that is often undocumented and subject to errors in transcription. If a discrepancy is found, the name and address of the submitter is included in the database so sources can be compared and any necessary corrections can be made. It is also important to compare the collections available online in terms of the number of names and fees. For example, Brøderbund charges a fee to access World Family Tree, while access to Ancestry.com's World Tree is free.

See also *FamilySearch*® and *Internet Sources*.

Selected Readings:

Bonner, Laurie, and Steve Bonner. *Searching for Cyber-Roots: A Step-By-Step Guide to Genealogy on the World Wide Web*. Salt Lake City: Ancestry, 1997.

Gehring, Jake. "Lineage-Linked Databases." *Ancestry* 15 (1) (January/February 1997): 27–28.

Helm, Matthew, and April Leigh Helm. *Genealogy Online for Dummies*. Foster City, CA: IDG Books Worldwide, Inc., 1998.

Meyerink, Kory L. "Databases, Indexes, and Other Finding Aids." *The Source: A Guidebook of American Genealogy*. Rev. ed. Salt Lake City: Ancestry, 1997.

Morgan, George G. *The Genealogy Forum on America Online*. Salt Lake City: Ancestry, 1998.

Descendants of William Dennis

Generation No. 1

1. WILLIAM[1] DENNIS was born in Ireland. He married MARY POLAND.

   Child of WILLIAM DENNIS and MARY POLAND is:
2.   i.   WILLIAM HENRY[2] DENNIS, b. 10 July 1834, Brooklyn, New York, d. 07 January 1906, 115 2nd Place, Brooklyn, New York.

Generation No. 2

2. WILLIAM HENRY[2] DENNIS (WILLIAM[1]) was born 10 July 1834 in Brooklyn, New York, and died 07 January 1906 in 115 2nd Place, Brooklyn, New York. He married CATHERINE HUGGINS 11 April 1865 in St. Paul's R.C. Church, Brooklyn, NY, daughter of WILLIAM HUGGINS and BRIDGET DWYER.

More About WILLIAM HENRY DENNIS:
Fact 1: 02 August 1870, Clerk in Store Age 35
Fact 2: 20 July 1834, Christened, St. James Cathedral, Brooklyn
Fact 3: 10 January 1906, Buried, St. John Cemetery, NY

More About CATHERINE HUGGINS:
Fact 1: 1848, Came to U.S.

Marriage Notes for WILLIAM DENNIS and CATHERINE HUGGINS:
St. Paul's R.C. Church
234 Congress Street
Brooklyn. Ny 11201

Witnesses: James Kean
    Julia Huggins
Rev. E.J. O'Reilly officiating

   Children of WILLIAM DENNIS and CATHERINE HUGGINS are:
        i.   WILLIAM J.[3] DENNIS, b. October 1859; m. KATHLEEN O'MERRA.
       ii.   HENRY J. DENNIS. b. 1860.
      iii.   MARIA DENNIS, b. 1865.
       iv.   CHARLES E. DENNIS, b. March 1868.
3.   v.   GEORGE WILLIAM DENNIS, b. 05 December 1870, Brooklyn, New York; d. 07 April 1935, Brooklyn, or Bronx, New York.
       vi.   ANN E. DENNIS, b. 1874.
      vii.   ROBERT M. DENNIS, b. May 1876.
     viii.   MARGARET J. DENNIS, b. 21 February 1878.

              Notes for MARGARET J. DENNIS:
              Sister M. Pacifica, Franciscan

4.   ix.   BENJAMIN J. DENNIS, b. January 1881.
        x.   FRANCIS B. DENNIS, b. March 1887.

Generation No. 3

Figure 43

Genealogy software programs have facilitated record keeping and the exchange of information among family historians.

Coroner's Inquests

Although coroners are often associated with murder, their records should not be overlooked. A coroner may have been called in to investigate deaths occurring under the following circumstances as well: accident, suicide, sudden death when in apparent good health, unattended by a licensed physician at time of death, suspicious or unusual causes, poisoning or adverse reaction to drugs or alcohol, disease constituting a threat to public health, employment related illness or injury, during medical diagnostic or therapeutic procedures, in any prison or penal institution or while in police custody, dead on arrival at hospital, unclaimed bodies, any body brought into a new medico-legal jurisdiction without proper medical certification, or any body to be cremated, dissected, or buried at sea.

As with most records, the contents and condition of an individual's inquest file may vary greatly from county to county, and even from year to year. Many inquest files contain sworn statements made by family and friends of the deceased and any other witnesses present at the time of death or when a body was discovered. A 1935 Chicago inquest, for example, included a form requesting the full name of the deceased

```
THE DEPUTY:   Q  When did you last see your hus-
band alive?

   THE WITNESS:  A  Sunday.

   Q  Sunday?   A  Sunday, I seen him.

   Q  And were you and your husband living together?

   A  No.

   Q  Or apart?  A  No,  we are apart seven years.

   Q  How did he act Sunday when you last saw him?

   A  Well, he acted very good.  He always was
down by me, and he promised me this Sunday he
would take me to the cemetery, and he didn't get
there any more.

   Q  He never said anything about taking his
life or anything, did he?

   A  No.

   Q  That proved that way that he would do that
or anything?  A  No, sir.

   Q  Did he act melancholy in any way?  A  No, he
didn't.  He always acted fine, and he talked nice
and everything.

   Q  Was he in good health?  A  He was in good
```

Figure 44

A page of testimony concerning the 1933 death of Joseph Kustak.

54

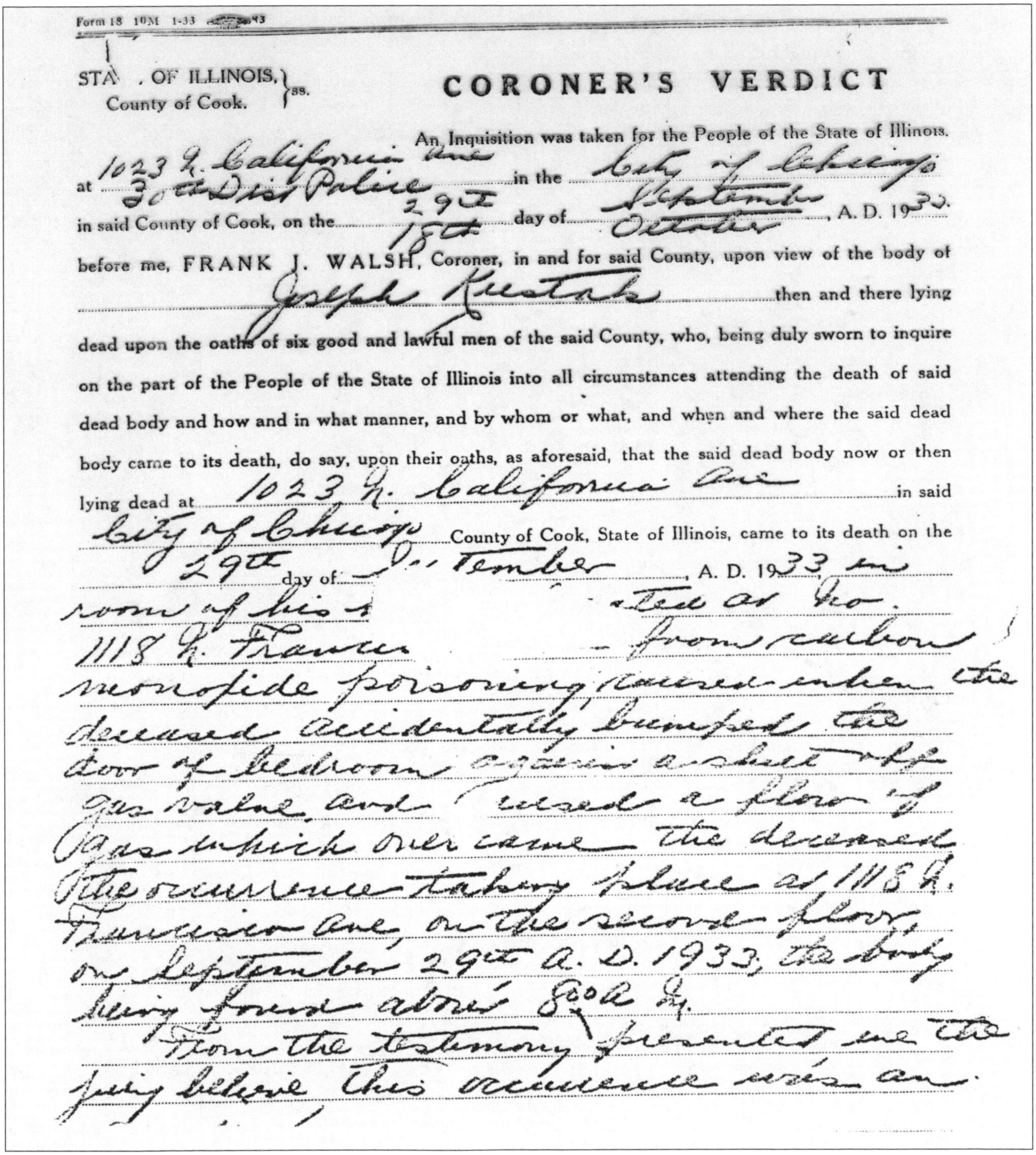
Form 18 10M 1-33

STA . OF ILLINOIS, } ss.
County of Cook.

CORONER'S VERDICT

An Inquisition was taken for the People of the State of Illinois, at 1023 N. California Ave / 30th Dist Police in the City of Chicago in said County of Cook, on the 29th / 18th day of September / October, A. D. 1933, before me, FRANK J. WALSH, Coroner, in and for said County, upon view of the body of Joseph Kustak then and there lying dead upon the oaths of six good and lawful men of the said County, who, being duly sworn to inquire on the part of the People of the State of Illinois into all circumstances attending the death of said dead body and how and in what manner, and by whom or what, and when and where the said dead body came to its death, do say, upon their oaths, as aforesaid, that the said dead body now or then lying dead at 1023 N. California Ave in said City of Chicago County of Cook, State of Illinois, came to its death on the 29th day of September, A. D. 1933 in room of his ... ated at No. 1118 N. Francisco — from carbon monoxide poisoning caused when the deceased accidentally bumped the door of bedroom against a shut off gas valve, and caused a flow of gas which overcame the deceased. The occurrence taking place at 1118 N. Francisco Ave, on the second floor, on September 29th A. D. 1933; the body being found about 8:00 A M.

From the testimony presented me the jury believe this occurrence was an

Figure 45
The coroner's verdict on the cause of death of Joseph Kustak in 1933.

along with the person's address, age, sex, marital status, color, birthplace, length of residence in the United States, length of residence in the city, occupation, employer, past occupation, wages or salary due, amount of life insurance and to whom it was payable, value of personal and real estate property, level of education, number of dependents, and ten questions regarding the decedent's physical and mental health at the time of death.

Personnel in the county coroner's office should be able to provide information on the location of files.

Selected Readings:

Naanes, Ted, and Loretto Dennis Szucs. "Dead Men Do Tell Tales." *Ancestry* 12 (2) (Mar-Apr 1994): 6.

Roebuck, Haywood. "North Carolina Colonial Coroners' Inquests, 1738–75." *North Carolina Genealogical Society Journal* 1 (1975): 11–37.

Scott, Kenneth. *Coroners' Reports, New York City, 1843-1849*. New York: New York Genealogical and Biographical Society, 1991.

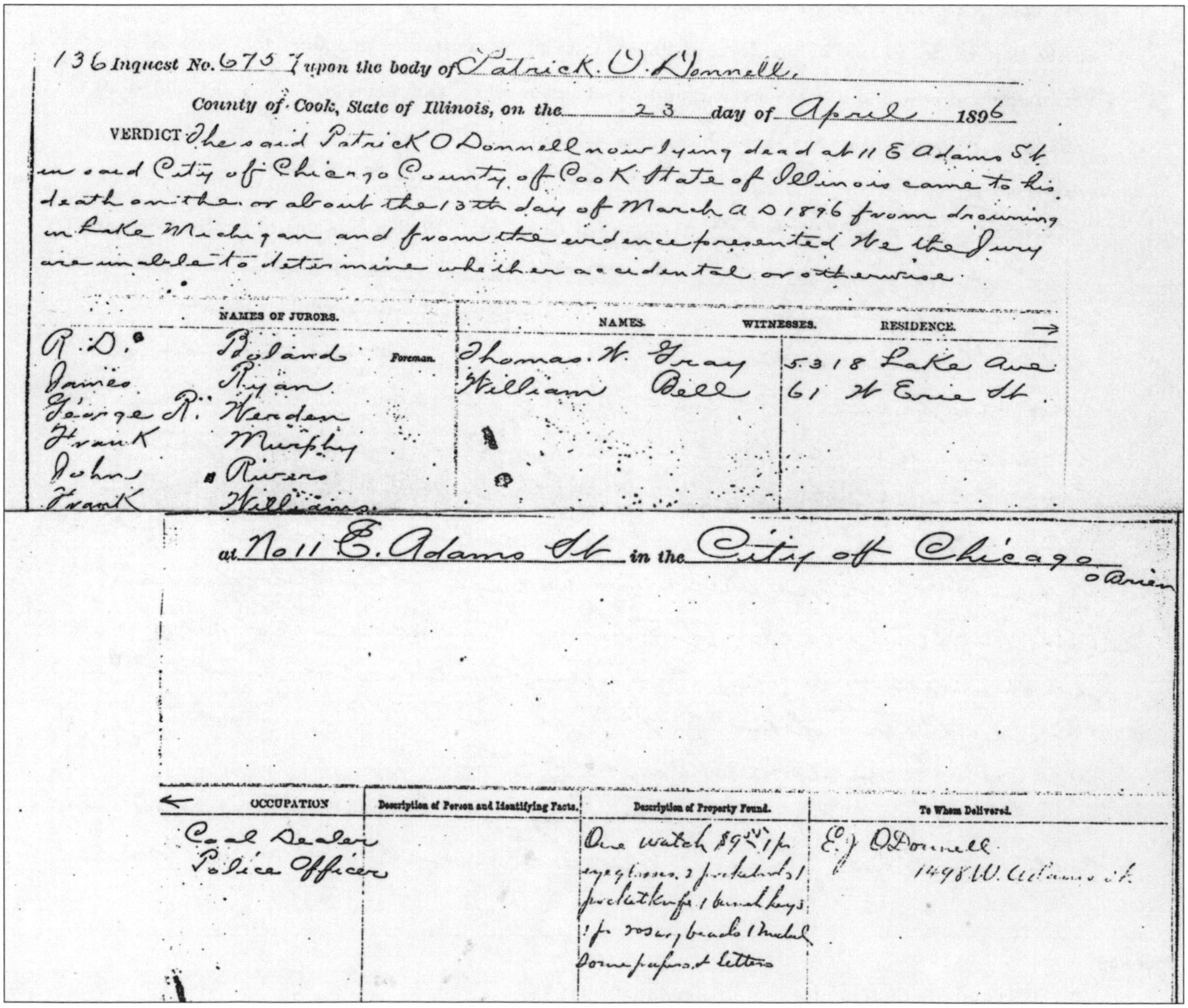

136 Inquest No. 675 upon the body of Patrick O. Donnell,

County of Cook, State of Illinois, on the 23 day of April 1896

VERDICT The said Patrick O Donnell now lying dead at 11 E Adams St in said City of Chicago County of Cook State of Illinois came to his death on the or about the 13th day of March A D 1896 from drowning in Lake Michigan and from the evidence presented We the Jury are unable to determine whether accidental or otherwise.

NAMES OF JURORS.		WITNESSES. NAMES.	RESIDENCE.
R. D. Boland	Foreman.	Thomas W. Gray	5318 Lake Ave
James Ryan		William Bell	61 W Erie St.
George R. Herden			
Frank Murphy			
John Rivers			
Frank Williams			

at No 11 E. Adams St in the City of Chicago

O'Brien

OCCUPATION	Description of Person and Identifying Facts.	Description of Property Found.	To Whom Delivered.
Coal Dealer Police Officer		One watch $9.50 1 pr eyeglasses, 2 pocketbooks 1 pocketknife 1 bunch keys 1 pr rosary beads 1 medal some papers & letters	E. J. O'Donnell 1498 W. Adams St.

Figure 46

The 1896 inquest on the body of Patrick O'Donnell resulted in the record shown. Two short pages provide the approximate date and probable cause of death, names of jurors and witnesses, description of property found on the body, and to whom it was delivered.

County, Farmers', or Rural Directories

As with the city directory, county or rural directories can be helpful in placing an ancestor in a certain place at a certain time. These directories, sometimes called farmers' directories, cover a much larger area (an entire county or, in the regional directories, several counties) and were used to advertise goods and services in rural areas.

Because of the larger geographic area of coverage, these directories can be especially helpful to a researcher who knows the region an ancestor was from, but doesn't know the exact town. County directories may contain biographical information on residents and advertisers, such as age and place of birth, length of residence in the area, and names of spouse and any children; however, the greater the area covered, the fewer biographical details are likely to be included.

Selected Readings:

Catalog of City, County, and State Directories Published in North America. New York: North American Directory Publishers, 1967.

Remington, Gordon Lewis. "Research in Directories." *The Source: A Guidebook of American Genealogy.* Rev. ed. Ch. 11: 384–410. Salt Lake City: Ancestry, 1997.

1918

Southern Cook County
Farmers' Directory

Abbreviations Used in This Directory

a—Acres; Ch—Children; O—Owner; T—Tenant or Renter; R—Rural Route; S—Section; Maiden name of wife follows directory name in parentheses ( ); figures at end of information—year became resident of county. Name of farm follows names of children in quotation marks. In case of a tenant, the farm owner's name follows the figures giving size of farm. Names of children not at home are preceded by a star (*).

EXAMPLE

Adair, H. W. (Delia Moren) Ch Marion, George, Floyd, Walter, Margorie; Chicago Heights R1 Bloom S23 O11a T345a Chicago Heights Land Assn (1891) Tel. Chicago Heights

Means

Adair, H. W.—Name.
(Delia Moren)—Wife's maiden name.
Ch Marion, George, Floyd, Walter, Margorie—Children's names.
Chicago Heights R1—Postoffice Chicago Heights R. F. D. 1
Bloom S23—Bloom Township, Section 23.
O11a—Owner 11 acres.
T345a—Tenant on 345 acres.
Chicago Heights Land Assn.—Owner's name.
(1891)—Lived in county since 1891.
Chicago Tel., Chicago Heights—Chicago Telephone, Chicago Heights Exchange.

A

Abbe, George M. (Bertha Rauch); Tinley Park R2 Bremen S15 O140a T40a William Abbe and Burr Sub. Div. (1895)

Abbe, Henry (Marie Kuech) **Ch** Norman; Tinley Park R2 Bremen S16 T120a Christ Abbe (1891)

Adair, H. W. (Delia Moren) Ch Marion, George, Floyd, Walter, Margorie; Chicago Heights R1 Bloom S23 O11a T345a Chicago Heights Land Assn. (1891) Tel. Chicago Heights

Agate, David (Alta Kettering) Ch Ralph, George; Orland R2 Orland S5 O100a S6 T80a Mrs. Susan Agate (1865) Bell Tel. Orland

Agate, Mrs. George Ch George, David, Mary, Henry, Minnie "Oak Farm" Orland R2 Orland S6 O80a (1860) Bell Tel. Orland

Aggen, John J. (Ellen Yager) Ch Harry, Nettie, Alfred, Stephen, John, George, Jacob; Worth R1 Worth S28 T40a Fred Hohn (1875)

Ahrens, August (Rike Eicker) Ch George, *Albert, Clara; Lemont R2 Lemont S31 O80a (1863)

Ahrens, George F. W. (Caroline Hischer) Ch Esther; Lemont R2 Lemont S31 T80a August Ahrens (1892)

Andersen, Lauritz (Elna Johanne) Ch Grace, Margaret; Lemont R2 Lemont S33 O38½a (1906)

Anderson, Bartel (Emma Shultz) Ch Bartel, Emma, Johnnie, Dora, Alice, Mary, Minnie, Hellen, Hazel, Amanda, George, Henry, Edward, Laura, Alma; "High View Farm" Orland R1 Orland S30 O243¾a (1866) Bell Tel. Orland

Figure 47
A page from the 1918 *Southern Cook County Farmers' Directory* provides a legend of abbreviations and a glimpse of the valuable biographical information contained in these publications.

Court Records

Court records are a valuable yet underutilized source of family and local history. Many of the matters brought into court in colonial times would be considered trivial by today's standards. Until the Civil War era, criminal prosecution in many towns included gossip, witchcraft, scolding a husband, being disrespectful to a clergy member, and refusing to attend church services. In addition to being the judicial centers, local courts were also units of government with power to issue licenses to attorneys, physicians, merchants, peddlers, innkeepers, midwives, farriers, and the clergy. Courts also regulated apprenticeships, established weights and measures, provided for inspection of goods and services, paid bounties for heads and animal skins, oversaw education of orphans, looked after the poor, called local militia units, and assessed and collected taxes. Since the colonial period, the responsibilities of the courts have expanded with the population. Court records, which are open to the public, now take up miles of space in courthouses and archives. With so many functions being performed by the courts, the chances of finding at least one ancestor among the many records are good.

The most useful types of court records for family historians include adoption, bankruptcy, civil, claims, criminal, deposition, divorce, guardianship, land dispute, naturalization, orphan, and probate.

Probate proceedings, perhaps the most-used court files, contain personality-revealing messages from the past. County courts commonly handle these cases, which relate to a decedent's estate and its distribution to named heirs, and at times, the appointment of a guardian for a minor or a disabled person. Some coun-

Court docket books, which are open to the public, can be a quick and fascinating overview of a town or city's activities, or of a specific case file for an individual or group.

ties have master indexes for court proceedings, but more often than not, registers must be examined by year. When names are distinguished only by a case number, a search of docket books, providing a synopsis of the case, may be helpful.

Locating court records can be an intimidating process, but the results are often well worth the effort. Fortunately, there are a number of sources available to help researchers find what they seek. An entire chapter has been devoted to court records research in both *The Source: A Guidebook of American Genealogy*. Rev. ed. (Salt Lake City: Ancestry, 1997) and *Printed Sources: A Guide to Published Genealogical Records* (Salt Lake City: Ancestry, 1998). Also useful is *The Guide to Genealogical Research in the National Archives*. Rev. ed. (Washington, D.C.: National Archives Trust Fund Board, 1991), which provides detailed listings of holdings at the National Archives and its regional offices.

Before visiting any court, it is advisable to call in advance to check on research policies and hours of operation.

See also *Admiralty, Adoption, Almshouse, Apprentice, Archives, Bankruptcy, Deeds, Divorce, Guardianship, Indentures, Licenses, Naturalization,* and *Probate.*

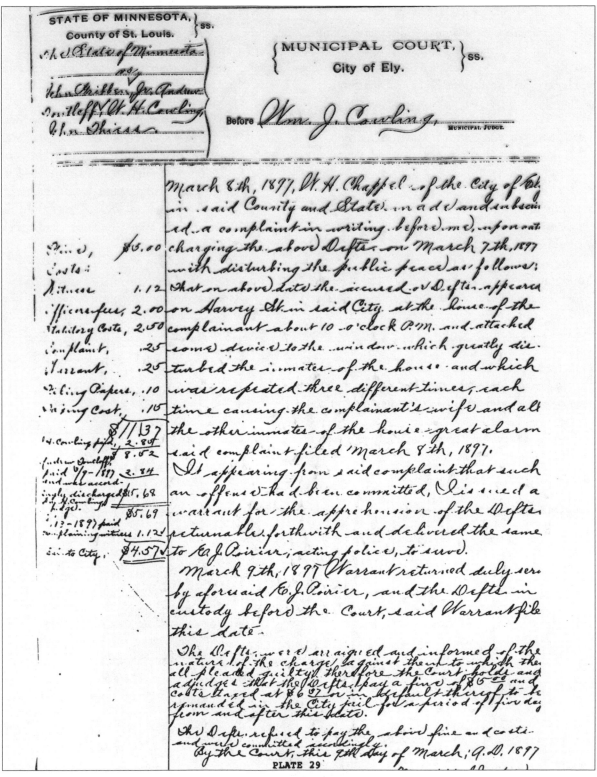

Figure 48

Court docket books often provide a synopsis of a court case from beginning to end and are often a shortcut to finding needed court records. Shown is a page form the 1897 Criminal Docket book from the Municipal Court of St. Louis County, Minnesota. The complaint charges four men with disturbing the public peace. The defendants were served with a warrant for their apprehension, and they were arraigned and informed of the nature of the charge against them, to which they all pleaded guilty. The court adjudged that the defendants pay a fine of $5 and costs. The defendants refused to pay the fine and "were committed accordingly."

Selected Readings:

Bentley, Elizabeth P. *County Courthouse Book.* Baltimore: Genealogical Publishing Co., 1992.

Black, Henry Campbell. *Black's Law Dictionary.* St. Paul, Minn.: West Publishing Co., rpt. 1979.

Eichholz, Alice, ed. *Ancestry's Red Book: American State, County and Town Sources.* Rev. ed. Salt Lake City: Ancestry, 1992.

Greenwood, Val. D. *The Researcher's Guide to American Genealogy.* 2d ed. Baltimore: Genealogical Publishing Co., 1990.

New York State Archives. *List of Pre-1874 Court Records in the State Archives.* Albany: Office of Cultural Education, New York State Education Dept., 1984.

Ryskamp, George R. *What is Fee Simply Absolute? How Understanding American Legal Concepts Helps Research.* Audiotape of lecture presented at the National Genealogical Society 1995 Conference in the States, San Diego, California. Hobart, Ind.: Repeat Performance, 1995. Order from Repeat Performance, 2911 Crabapple Lane, Hobart, IN 46342.

Szucs, Loretto Dennis. "American Courts: Mirror of a Nation." *Ancestry* 17 (2) (March/April 1999): 14-21.

Warren, James W. *Ancestors Hanging on Your Family Tree: Using Court and Institutional Records.* Audiotape of a lecture presented at the National Genealogical Society 1997 Conference in the States, Valley Forge, Pennsylvania. Hobart, Ind.: Repeat Performance, 1997. Order from Repeat Performance, 2911 Crabapple Lane, Hobart, IN 46342.

Wilson, Don W. "Federal Court Records in the Regional Archives System." *Prologue: Quarterly of the National Archives* 21 (3) (Fall 1989): 176–77.

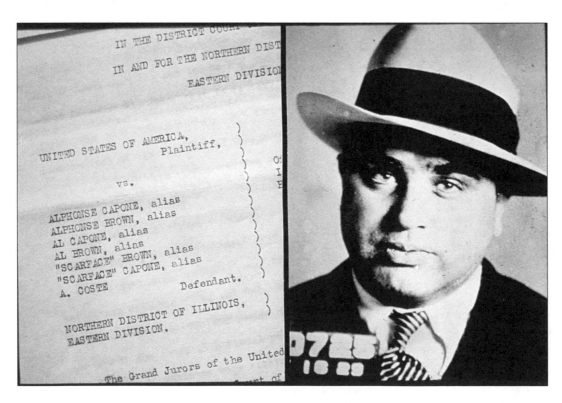

Figure 49

Prohibition-era gangster Al Capone was indicted for income tax evasion in the U.S. District Court of the Northern District of Illinois. Capone's court records are filed with thousands of other less notorious individuals at the National Archives - Great Lakes Region, Chicago.

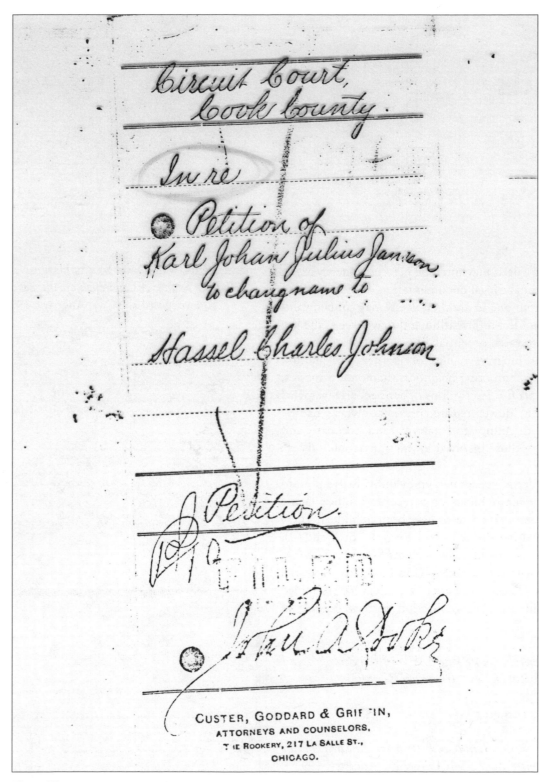

Figure 50

In some court indexes, cases will not be listed alphabetically under the surnames of the plaintiff or defendant, but rather with the "Inre" cases, under the letter "I" ("in regards to," or "in the matter of.") Shown is the "Inre" petition of Karl Johan Julius Johnson, who changed his name to Hassel Charles Johnson because he grew tired of receiving bills of a neighbor of the same name.

Deeds

While a deed may often be perceived merely as the mundane legal documentation of the transfer of property from one to another, deeds may contain valuable biographical information and may serve as the key to further research potential. Typically uniform in content, deeds include: names of grantee and grantor, watercourses, bordering neighbors, names of witnesses, arrangements for descriptions of acreage, arrangements for payment, dower release, previous owner's names, type of deed, county and state of residence, date, and signatures of those involved in the transaction.

Generally, deeds were drawn up by individuals and transcribed into deed books at a recorder's office. Some deeds and abstracts of deeds have been published. These are discussed in "Printed Land Records" by Wendy B. Elliott and Karen Clifford in *Printed Sources: A Guide to Published Genealogical Records* (Salt Lake City: Ancestry, 1997). The Genealogical Society of Utah has assembled a significant microfilm collection of these records as well.

See also *American State Papers, Homestead Records, Land Grants* and *Patents,* and *Territorial Records.*

Selected Readings:

Hone, E. Wade. *Land and Property Research in the United States.* Salt Lake City: Ancestry, 1997.

Meyerink, Kory L., ed. *Printed Sources: A Guide to Published Genealogical Records.* Salt Lake City: Ancestry, 1997.

Szucs, Loretto Dennis, and Sandra Hargreaves Luebking. *The Source: A Guidebook of American Genealogy.* Rev. ed. Salt Lake City: Ancestry, 1997.

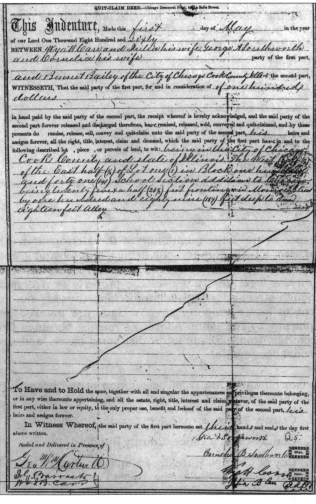

Figure 51
A deed dated 1 May 1860 from Cook County, Illinois.

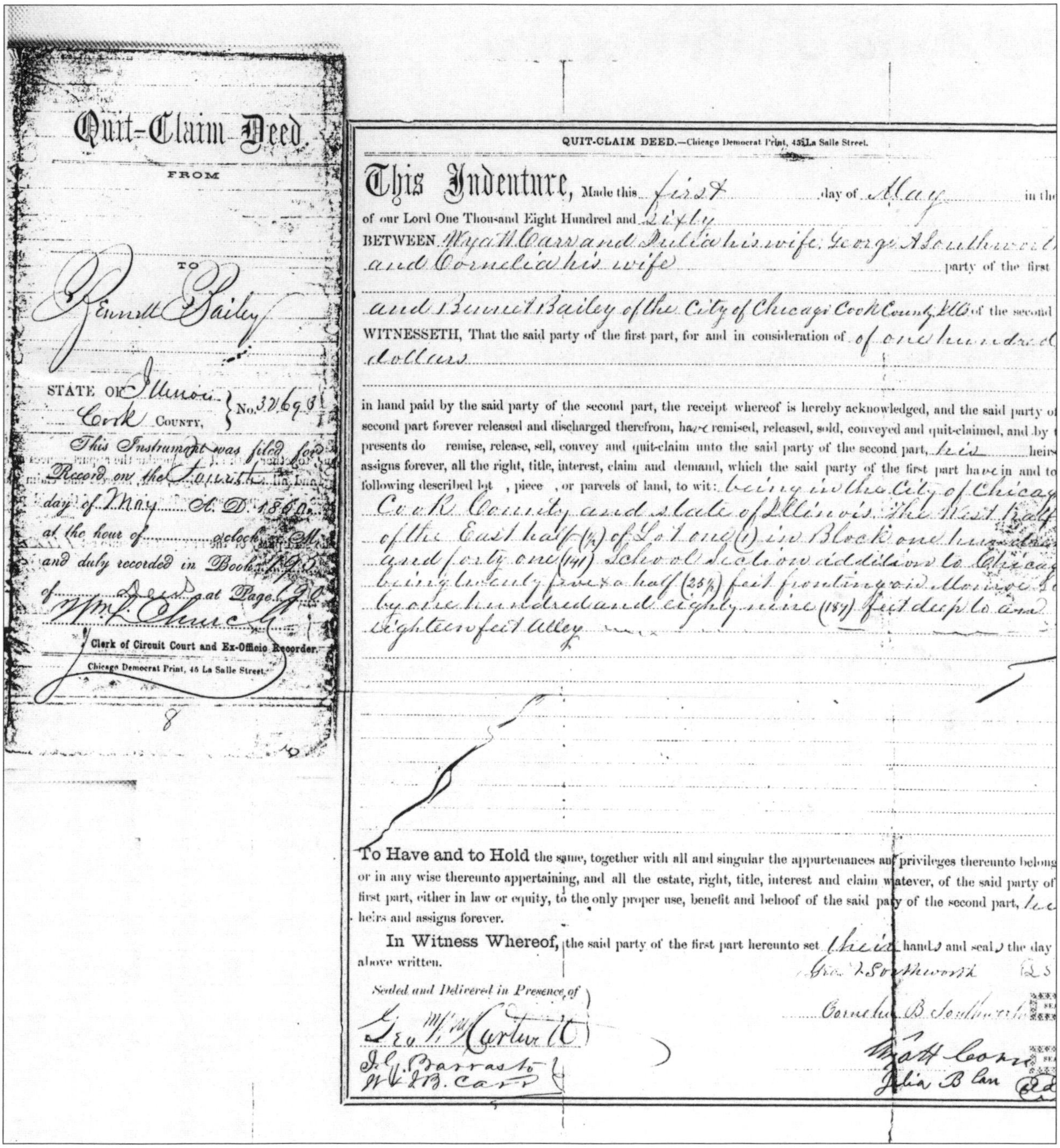

Quit-Claim Deed.

FROM

TO

Bennett Bailey

STATE OF Illinois, } No. 32698
Cook COUNTY,

This Instrument was filed for Record on the fourth day of May A. D. 1860 at the hour of ...... o'clock ... M., and duly recorded in Book 195 of Deeds at Page 190

Wm. Church

Clerk of Circuit Court and Ex-Officio Recorder.

Chicago Democrat Print, 45 La Salle Street.

QUIT-CLAIM DEED.—Chicago Democrat Print, 45 La Salle Street.

This Indenture, Made this first day of May in the year of our Lord One Thousand Eight Hundred and Sixty BETWEEN Wyatt Carr and Julia his wife, George A Southworth and Cornelia his wife party of the first part and Bennet Bailey of the City of Chicago Cook County Ills of the second part WITNESSETH, That the said party of the first part, for and in consideration of of one hundred dollars in hand paid by the said party of the second part, the receipt whereof is hereby acknowledged, and the said party of the first part forever released and discharged therefrom, have remised, released, sold, conveyed and quit-claimed, and by these presents do remise, release, sell, convey and quit-claim unto the said party of the second part, his heirs and assigns forever, all the right, title, interest, claim and demand, which the said party of the first part have in and to the following described lot, piece, or parcels of land, to wit: being in the City of Chicago Cook County and State of Illinois. The West half of the East half (½) of Lot one (1) in Block one hundred and forty one (141) School Section addition to Chicago being twenty five & a half (25½) feet fronting on Monroe St by one hundred and eighty nine (189) feet deep to an eighteen feet alley

To Have and to Hold the same, together with all and singular the appurtenances and privileges thereunto belonging or in any wise thereunto appertaining, and all the estate, right, title, interest and claim whatever, of the said party of the first part, either in law or equity, to the only proper use, benefit and behoof of the said party of the second part, his heirs and assigns forever.

In Witness Whereof, the said party of the first part hereunto set their hands and seals the day above written.

Sealed and Delivered in Presence of

Geo. W. McCarter
J. G. Barrasto
W. & B. Carr

Geo. A Southworth
Cornelia B Southworth
Wyatt Carr
Julia B Carr

Figure 52

This copy of a quit-claim deed provides names of spouses of grantor and grantees, important dates, and the legal description of the property.

Delayed Birth Records

Many states were not required to record vital statistics until 1910 or well after. For documentation of births prior to that year, researchers have looked to church records, family Bibles, notices in newspapers, or other secondary sources. Often overlooked are delayed birth records that are available for many births during the mid- to late 1800s and the early 1900s.

Individuals born before the issuance of birth certificates may have applied for a delayed birth certificate to document their age for Social Security or passport applications, insurance, or other benefits. Those applying for a delayed birth certificate had to provide some evidence of their age. In some cases, the 1880 and 1900 census enumerations were used to document the applicant's age. Others submitted baptismal certificates, pages from the family Bible, school records, or affidavits from the attending physician, midwife, or relatives. Information recorded on the delayed birth certificate includes the applicants' name, date of birth, and the name, place of birth, and race of the mother and father. Also noted on the certificate is the evidence that was presented with the application.

These records can usually be located in the county in which the individual filed the application. The Family History Library has indexes of birth records that include some delayed birth records on microfilm.

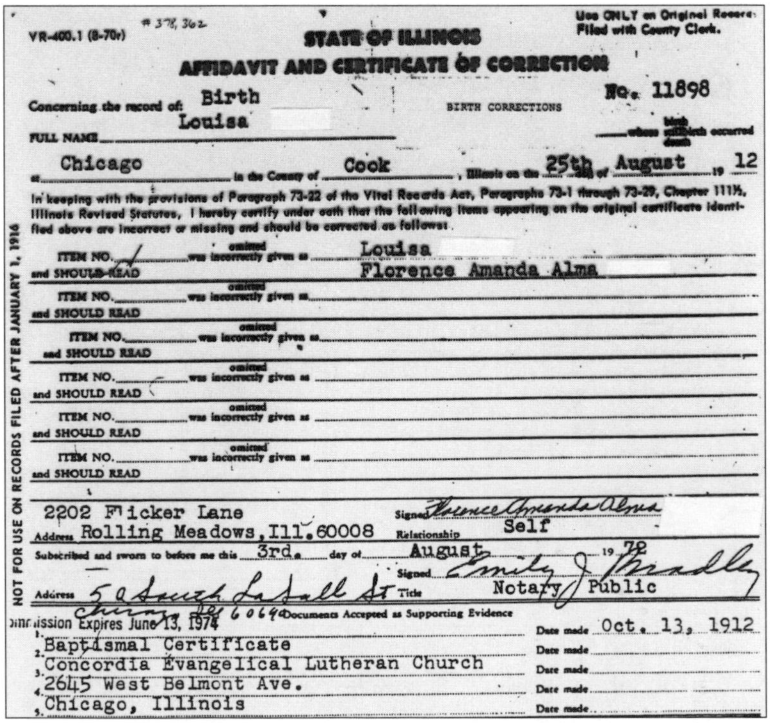

Selected Readings:

Kemp, Thomas J. *International Vital Records Handbook*. 3d ed. Baltimore: Genealogical Publishing Co., 1994.

Szucs, Loretto Dennis, and Sandra H. Luebking, eds. *The Source: A Guidebook of American Genealogy*. Rev. ed. Salt Lake City: Ancestry, 1997.

Figure 53

An Affidavit and Certificate of Correction (in this case, a delayed birth registration) from Chicago, Illinois. The mention of a baptismal certificate from Concordia Evangelical Lutheran Church provides additional clues and places to look for further information.

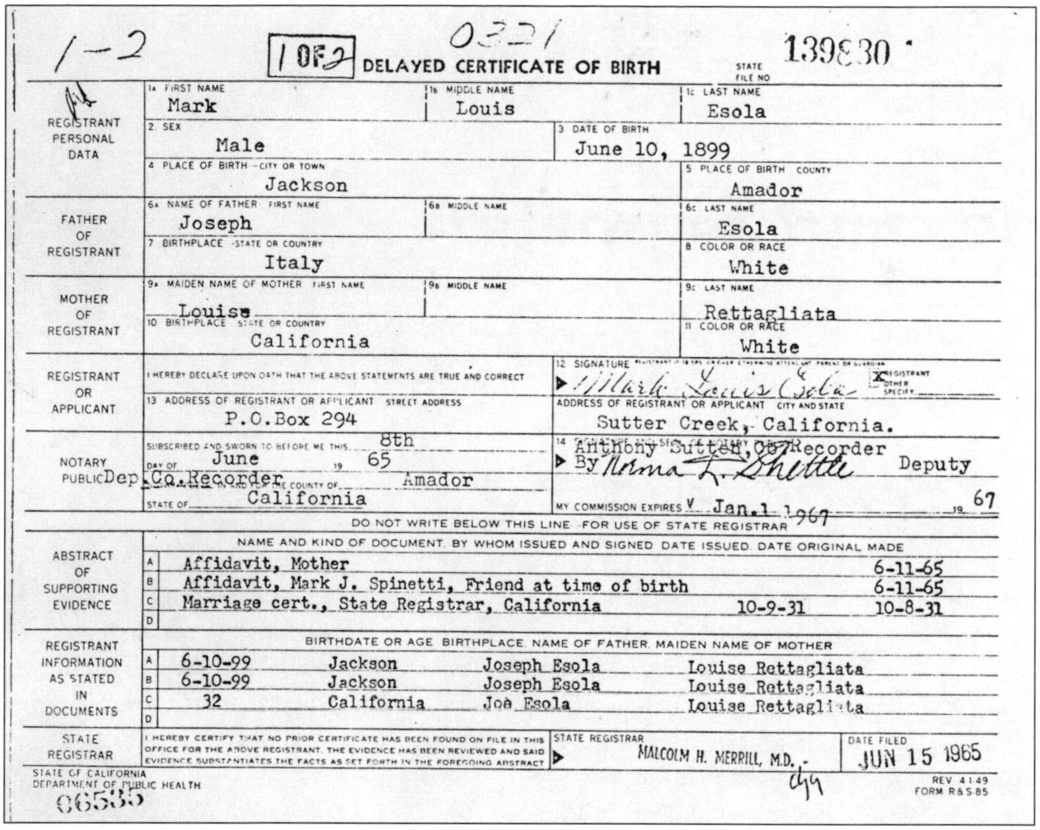

1-2 0321

1 OF 2 DELAYED CERTIFICATE OF BIRTH

STATE FILE NO 139830

REGISTRANT PERSONAL DATA
1a FIRST NAME: Mark | 1b MIDDLE NAME: Louis | 1c LAST NAME: Esola
2 SEX: Male | 3 DATE OF BIRTH: June 10, 1899
4 PLACE OF BIRTH—CITY OR TOWN: Jackson | 5 PLACE OF BIRTH COUNTY: Amador

FATHER OF REGISTRANT
6a NAME OF FATHER FIRST NAME: Joseph | 6b MIDDLE NAME | 6c LAST NAME: Esola
7 BIRTHPLACE—STATE OR COUNTRY: Italy | 8 COLOR OR RACE: White

MOTHER OF REGISTRANT
9a MAIDEN NAME OF MOTHER FIRST NAME: Louise | 9b MIDDLE NAME | 9c LAST NAME: Rettagliata
10 BIRTHPLACE STATE OR COUNTRY: California | 11 COLOR OR RACE: White

REGISTRANT OR APPLICANT
I HEREBY DECLARE UPON OATH THAT THE ABOVE STATEMENTS ARE TRUE AND CORRECT
12 SIGNATURE: Mark Louis Esola — X REGISTRANT
13 ADDRESS OF REGISTRANT OR APPLICANT STREET ADDRESS: P.O.Box 294 | ADDRESS OF REGISTRANT OR APPLICANT CITY AND STATE: Sutter Creek, California.

NOTARY PUBLIC Dep Co.Recorder
SUBSCRIBED AND SWORN TO BEFORE ME THIS 8th DAY OF June 19 65 | 14 Anthony Sutter, Co. Recorder By Norma L. Shettle Deputy
COUNTY OF Amador
STATE OF California | MY COMMISSION EXPIRES Jan. 1 1967 19 67

DO NOT WRITE BELOW THIS LINE—FOR USE OF STATE REGISTRAR

ABSTRACT OF SUPPORTING EVIDENCE
NAME AND KIND OF DOCUMENT. BY WHOM ISSUED AND SIGNED. DATE ISSUED. DATE ORIGINAL MADE

	Document	Date issued	Date original made
A	Affidavit, Mother		6-11-65
B	Affidavit, Mark J. Spinetti, Friend at time of birth		6-11-65
C	Marriage cert., State Registrar, California	10-9-31	10-8-31
D			

REGISTRANT INFORMATION AS STATED IN DOCUMENTS
BIRTHDATE OR AGE. BIRTHPLACE. NAME OF FATHER. MAIDEN NAME OF MOTHER

	Birthdate or age	Birthplace	Name of father	Maiden name of mother
A	6-10-99	Jackson	Joseph Esola	Louise Rettagliata
B	6-10-99	Jackson	Joseph Esola	Louise Rettagliata
C	32	California	Joe Esola	Louise Rettagliata
D				

STATE REGISTRAR
I HEREBY CERTIFY THAT NO PRIOR CERTIFICATE HAS BEEN FOUND ON FILE IN THIS OFFICE FOR THE ABOVE REGISTRANT. THE EVIDENCE HAS BEEN REVIEWED AND SAID EVIDENCE SUBSTANTIATES THE FACTS AS SET FORTH IN THE FOREGOING ABSTRACT
STATE REGISTRAR: MALCOLM H. MERRILL, M.D. | DATE FILED: JUN 15 1965

STATE OF CALIFORNIA DEPARTMENT OF PUBLIC HEALTH
06535
REV 4-1-49 FORM R&S-85

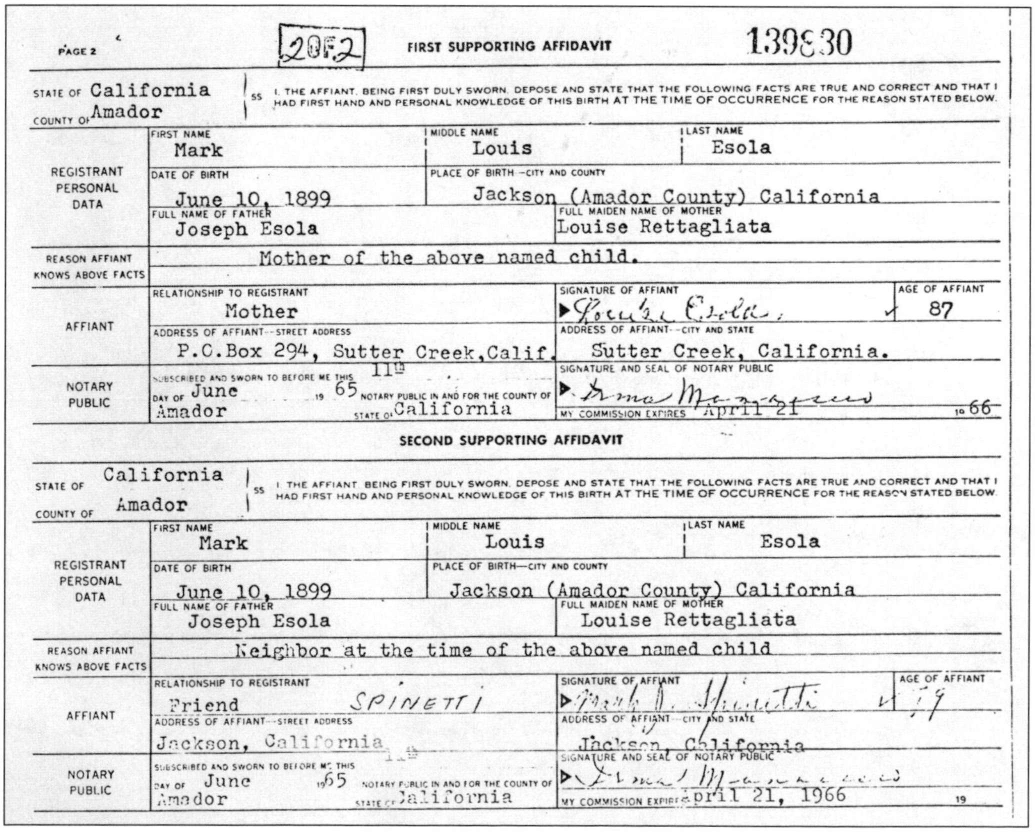

PAGE 2 — 2 OF 2 — FIRST SUPPORTING AFFIDAVIT — 139830

STATE OF California
COUNTY OF Amador } SS
I, THE AFFIANT, BEING FIRST DULY SWORN, DEPOSE AND STATE THAT THE FOLLOWING FACTS ARE TRUE AND CORRECT AND THAT I HAD FIRST HAND AND PERSONAL KNOWLEDGE OF THIS BIRTH AT THE TIME OF OCCURRENCE FOR THE REASON STATED BELOW.

REGISTRANT PERSONAL DATA
FIRST NAME: Mark | MIDDLE NAME: Louis | LAST NAME: Esola
DATE OF BIRTH: June 10, 1899 | PLACE OF BIRTH—CITY AND COUNTY: Jackson (Amador County) California
FULL NAME OF FATHER: Joseph Esola | FULL MAIDEN NAME OF MOTHER: Louise Rettagliata

REASON AFFIANT KNOWS ABOVE FACTS: Mother of the above named child.

AFFIANT
RELATIONSHIP TO REGISTRANT: Mother | SIGNATURE OF AFFIANT: Louise Esola | AGE OF AFFIANT: 87
ADDRESS OF AFFIANT—STREET ADDRESS: P.O.Box 294, Sutter Creek, Calif. | ADDRESS OF AFFIANT—CITY AND STATE: Sutter Creek, California.

NOTARY PUBLIC
SUBSCRIBED AND SWORN TO BEFORE ME THIS 11th DAY OF June 19 65 NOTARY PUBLIC IN AND FOR THE COUNTY OF Amador STATE OF California
SIGNATURE AND SEAL OF NOTARY PUBLIC: Irma Manzzanares
MY COMMISSION EXPIRES April 21 19 66

SECOND SUPPORTING AFFIDAVIT

STATE OF California
COUNTY OF Amador } SS
I, THE AFFIANT, BEING FIRST DULY SWORN, DEPOSE AND STATE THAT THE FOLLOWING FACTS ARE TRUE AND CORRECT AND THAT I HAD FIRST HAND AND PERSONAL KNOWLEDGE OF THIS BIRTH AT THE TIME OF OCCURRENCE FOR THE REASON STATED BELOW.

REGISTRANT PERSONAL DATA
FIRST NAME: Mark | MIDDLE NAME: Louis | LAST NAME: Esola
DATE OF BIRTH: June 10, 1899 | PLACE OF BIRTH—CITY AND COUNTY: Jackson (Amador County) California
FULL NAME OF FATHER: Joseph Esola | FULL MAIDEN NAME OF MOTHER: Louise Rettagliata

REASON AFFIANT KNOWS ABOVE FACTS: Neighbor at the time of the above named child

AFFIANT
RELATIONSHIP TO REGISTRANT: Friend SPINETTI | SIGNATURE OF AFFIANT: Mark J. Spinetti | AGE OF AFFIANT: 79
ADDRESS OF AFFIANT—STREET ADDRESS: Jackson, California | ADDRESS OF AFFIANT—CITY AND STATE: Jackson, California

NOTARY PUBLIC
SUBSCRIBED AND SWORN TO BEFORE ME THIS 11th DAY OF June 19 65 NOTARY PUBLIC IN AND FOR THE COUNTY OF Amador STATE OF California
SIGNATURE AND SEAL OF NOTARY PUBLIC: Irma Manzzanares
MY COMMISSION EXPIRES April 21, 1966

Figure 54

An example of a California delayed certificate of birth and its supporting affidavits.

Diaries and Journals

A diary or journal is a wonderful find for a family historian. Either one can provide insight into an ancestor's personality; offer details of family events such as births, marriages, and deaths; and may make mention of a previously unknown relation. Even the published diaries and journals of others living during the same time period can be useful. The personal accounts that depict events with details not found in history books can afford a researcher a perspective of what an ancestor's life may have been like.

An ancestor's diary or journal is likely to be found among other personal effects that have been passed

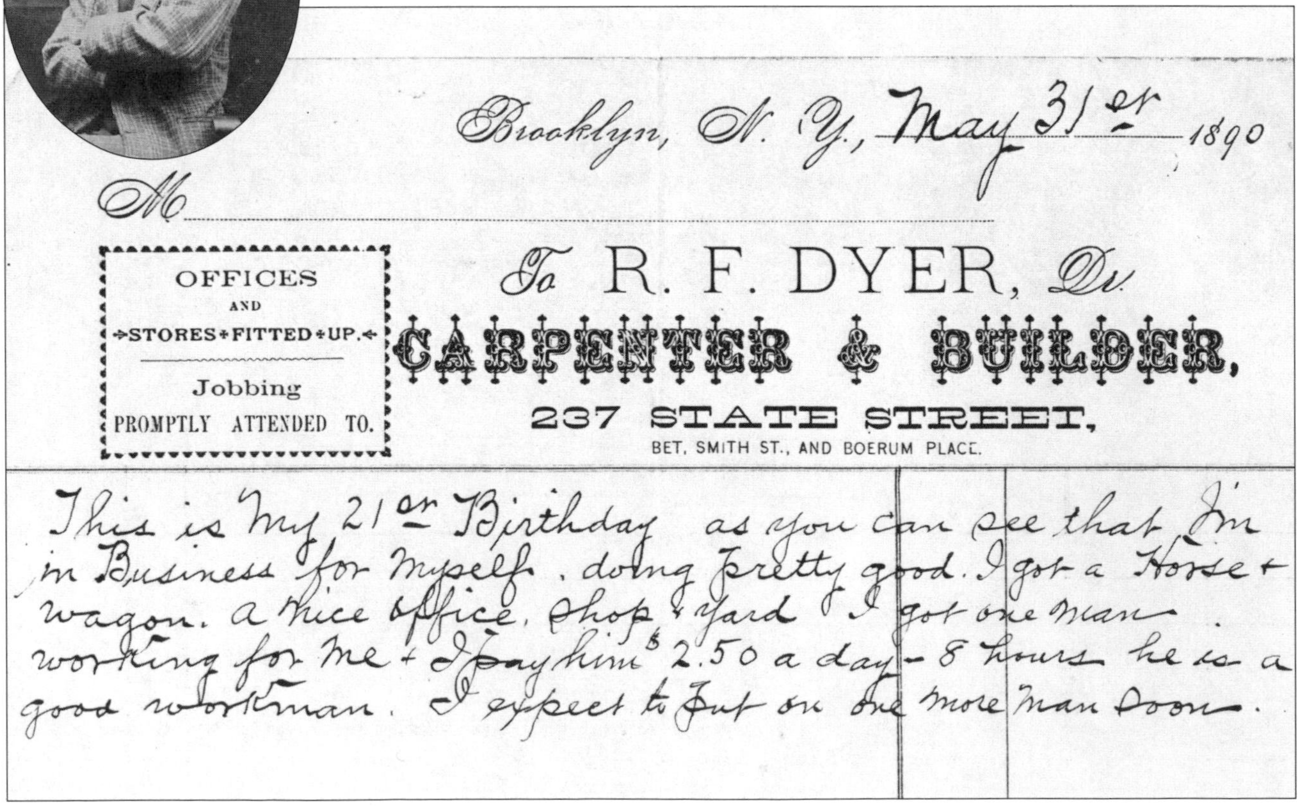

Brooklyn, N. Y., May 31st 1890

M_____

To R. F. DYER, Dr.

CARPENTER & BUILDER,

237 STATE STREET,

BET. SMITH ST., AND BOERUM PLACE.

OFFICES AND
STORES FITTED UP.
Jobbing
PROMPTLY ATTENDED TO.

This is My 21st Birthday as you can see that I'm in Business for myself, doing pretty good. I got a Horse + wagon. a nice office, shop + yard + I got one man working for me + I pay him $2.50 a day – 8 hours he is a good workman. I expect to put on one more man soon.

Figure 55
Figures 55-57 show excerpts from the personal journals of Raymond F. Dyer. The photographs are of Dyer as well.

66

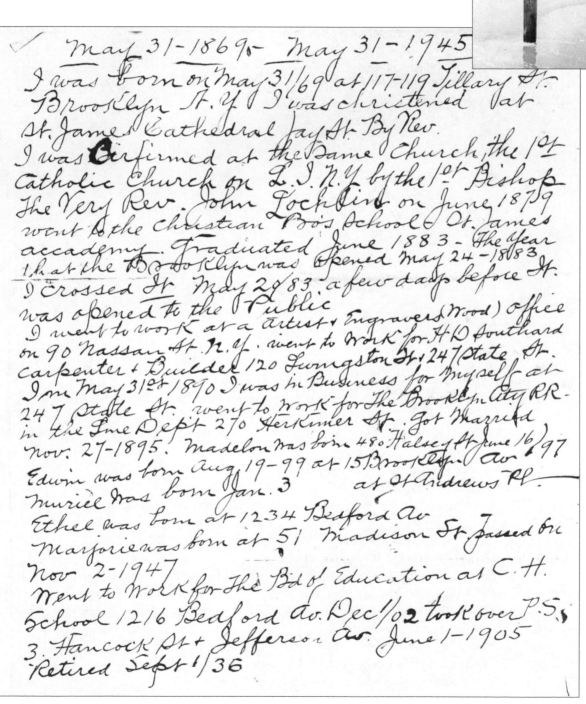

May 31-1869 - May 31-1945

I was born on May 31/69 at 117-119 Tillary St.
Brooklyn N.Y. I was christened at
St. James Cathedral Jay St. By Rev.
I was Confirmed at the Same Church, the 1st
Catholic Church on L.I. N.Y. by the 1st Bishop
The Very Rev. John Lochlin on June 1879
went to the Christian Bro's School St. James
accademy. Graduated June 1883 - The Year
that the Brooklyn was opened May 24 - 1883
I Crossed It May 29/83 a few days before It
was opened to the Public
    I went to work at a Artist + Engravers (Wood) office
on 90 Nassau St. N.Y. went to work for H.D. Southard
carpenter + Builder 120 Livingston St, 247 State St.
    I in May 31st 1890 I was in Business for myself at
247 State St. went to work for The Brooklyn City RR
in the Line Dept 270 Herkimer St. Got Married
Nov. 27-1895. Madelon was born 480 Halsey St June 16/97
Edwin was born Aug. 19-99 at 15 Brooklyn Av
Muriel was born Jan. 3   at St Andrews Pl.
Ethel was born at 1234 Bedford Av
Marjorie was born at 51 Madison St Passed On
Nov 2-1947
Went to work for The Bd of Education as C.H.
School 1216 Bedford Av. Dec 1/02 took over P.S.
3. Hancock St + Jefferson Av. June 1-1905
Retired Sept 1/36

Figure 56

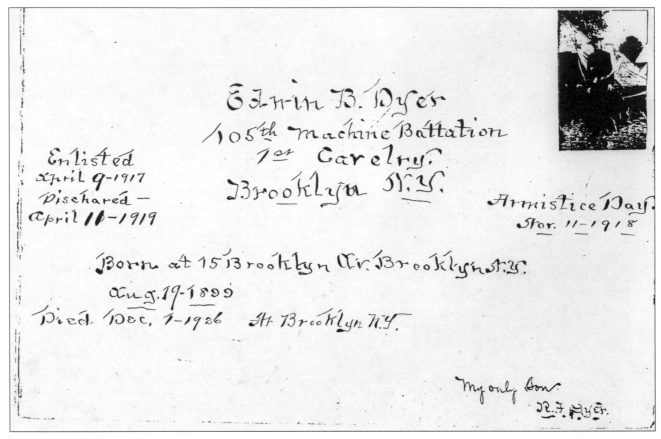

Figure 57

down through the generations. An elderly relative may have such a treasure packed away in an attic. If nothing turns up in the family collections, a search of manuscripts held by public libraries and historical societies may turn up a relative's papers or those of an individual who shared a similar lifestyle or experience. The *National Union Catalog of Manuscript Collections* (Washington, D.C.: Library of Congress, 1962–present), or *NUCMC*, and the *Index to Personal Names in the National Union Catalog of Manuscript Collections, 1959–1984* (Alexandria, Va.: Chadwyck-Healey, 1988), which can be found in large reference libraries, are good places to start. *NUCMC* is an index containing descriptions of manuscript collections held by public, private, and academic libraries. As its name implies, the *Index to Personal Names in the National Union Catalog of Manuscript Collections, 1959–1984* is an alphabetical listing of the surnames mentioned in the descriptions of the manuscript collections during that time period.

Selected Readings:

Arksey, Laura, Nancy Pries, and Marcia Reed. *American Diaries: An Annotated Bibliography of Published American Diaries and Journals*, vol. 1, 1492–1844; vol. 2, 1845–1980. Detroit: Gale Research, 1983, 1987.

Carmack, Sharon DeBartolo. *A Genealogist's Guide to Discovering Your Female Ancestors*. Cincinnati: Betterway Books, 1998.

Holmes, Kenneth. *Covered Wagon Women: Diaries and Letters from the Western Trails, 1840–1890*. Glendale, Calif.: and Spokane, Wash.: Arthur H. Clark Co., 1981–91.

Internet Site of Interest:

National Union Catalog of Manuscript Collections http://lcweb.loc.gov/coll/nucmc/nucmc.html

Divorce Records

If a divorce in the family is suspected, a search of court records is a worthwhile endeavor. Information usually found in divorce case files are the names of the couple dissolving the marriage, their ages or dates of birth, their places of birth, and the names and ages of children involved. One may also find names of other family members entered for custody purposes.

Divorce records are usually found in county or circuit courts; however, this may vary as some states have different procedures for handling divorces. Local newspapers may include divorce notices or, in some cases, detailed articles about the circumstances surrounding the divorce. Some divorces are recorded in state legislation proceedings, most notably those cases filed in the years just following a territory becoming a state. For cases prior to that, territorial or colonial legislative records should be searched. Another possible source for these earlier divorce records are Colonial Office volumes, since colonies were required to submit copies of all laws passed to the British government for approval. These volumes can be found in large research libraries.

Selected Readings:

Cerny, Johni, and Sandra H. Luebking. "Research in Marriage and Divorce Records." *The Source: A Guidebook of American Genealogy.* Rev. ed. Ch. 4: 86–100. Salt Lake City: Ancestry, 1997.

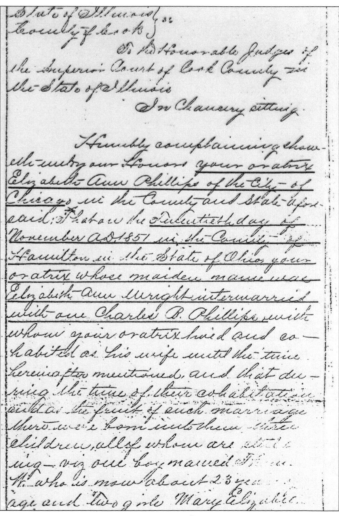

Figure 58

An 1876 Cook County, Illinois divorce record involving Elizabeth Ann and Charles B. Phillips of Chicago. Included in the court transcript is Elizabeth's maiden name, the date and county in which the marriage took place, the names and ages of the children born into the marriage, and other biographical information.

Draft Records

As discussed in greater detail under the heading "Military Records," records pertaining to service in the United States Military are among the most useful in terms of genealogical information. Among these records are draft records from the Civil War, World War I, and World War II.

Civil War

From 1863 to 1865, white males between the ages of twenty and forty-five (including aliens who had declared their intention to naturalize) were registered for draft by the United States government. The resulting records provide each individual's name, place of residence, age, occupation, marital status, and the state, territory, or country of birth. Some of the records may also contain a physical description as as well as notation as to whether he was accepted or rejected for service. Indexes and some records for the Civil War draft are available on microfilm through the National Archives and at the Family History Library and its Family History Centers. Many of these records are arranged by congressional district, and if the soldier was from a large city, it is necessary to know in which ward he resided. Researchers with ancestors who served in the Confederate army may be able to locate records through a microfilmed index of Confederate soldiers at the National Archives.

World War I

In 1917, the Selective Service System began the first of three draft registrations, which, combined, resulted in the registration of more than 24 million men between the ages of eighteen and forty-five. Eligible males (citizens and aliens) filled out cards that requested name, address, date of birth, place of birth, age, race, citizenship, occupation and employer,

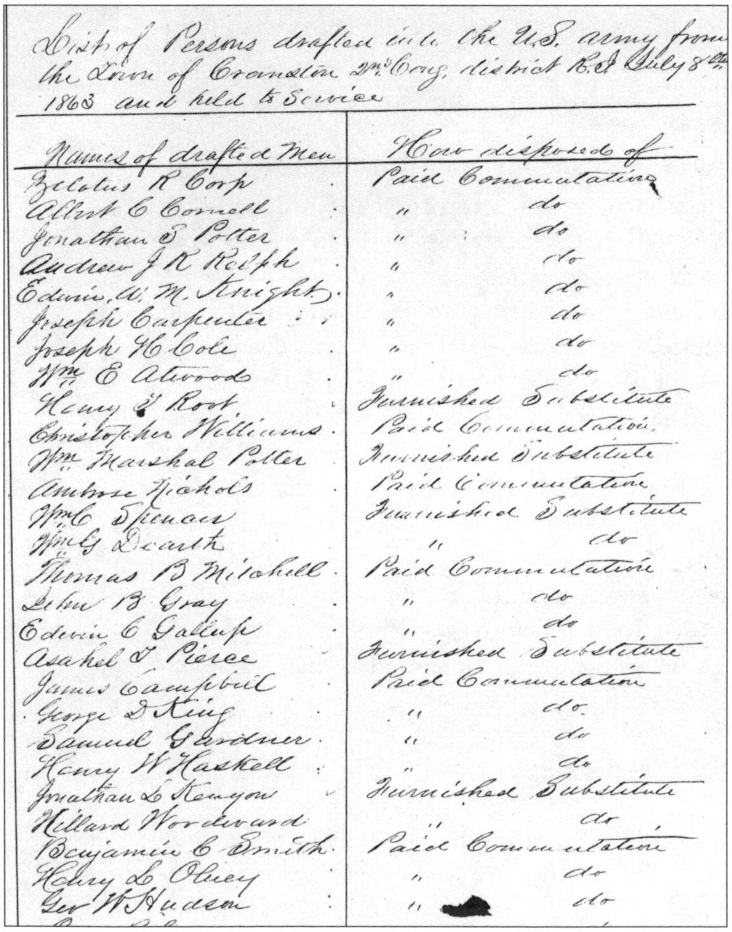

List of Persons drafted into the U.S. army from the Town of Cranston 2nd Cong. district R.I. July 8th 1863 and held to Service

Names of drafted Men	How disposed of
Zelotus R Corp	Paid Commutation
Albert C Cornell	" do
Jonathan S Potter	" do
Andrew J R Rolph	" do
Edwin W. M. Knight	" do
Joseph Carpenter	" do
Joseph H Cole	" do
Wm E Atwood	" do
Henry T Root	Furnished Substitute
Christopher Williams	Paid Commutation
Wm Marshal Potter	Furnished Substitute
Ambrose Nichols	Paid Commutation
Wm C Spencer	Furnished Substitute
Wm G Death	" do
Thomas B Mitchell	Paid Commutation
John B Gray	" do
Edwin C Gallup	" do
Asahel T Pierce	Furnished Substitute
James Campbell	Paid Commutation
George D King	" do
Samuel Gardner	" do
Henry W Haskell	" do
Jonathan L Kenyon	Furnished Substitute
Willard Woodward	" do
Benjamin C Smith	Paid Commutation
Henry L Olney	" do
Geo W Hudson	" do

Figure 59

List of Persons Drafted into the U.S. Army from the town of Cranston, Rhode Island, 1863. (Courtesy of Rhode Island State Archives).

dependent relatives, marital status, father's place of birth, name and address of next of kin, and a brief physical description.

The National Archives – Southeast Region in Georgia has the original registration cards. Microfilm copies are available through the regional branches of the National Archives for the states they serve and through the Family History Library and its centers.

WORLD WAR II

Registration cards from World War II contain much of the same information as the World War I cards, with the exception of marital status, dependent relatives, and father's birthplace. Selected regional branches of the National Archives have recently acquired some of the registration cards from this draft. The remaining cards are in the custody of the Selective Service System and are subject to privacy laws.

Selected Readings:

Knapp, Michael. "World War I Service Records." *Prologue: Quarterly of the National Archives* 22:3 (Fall 1990): 300–303.

Morebeck, Nancy Justus. *Civil War Draft Records, An Index to the 38th Congressional Districts of 1863.* Published by author.

_____. "Civil War Union Draft Records." *Forum.* 9 (4) (Winter 1991): 14–15.

Neagles, James C. *U.S. Military Records: A Guide to Federal & State Sources, Colonial America to the Present.* Salt Lake City: Ancestry, 1994.

Szucs, Loretto Dennis, and Sandra Hargreaves Luebking, eds. *The Source: A Guidebook of American Genealogy.* Rev. ed. Salt Lake City: Ancestry, 1997.

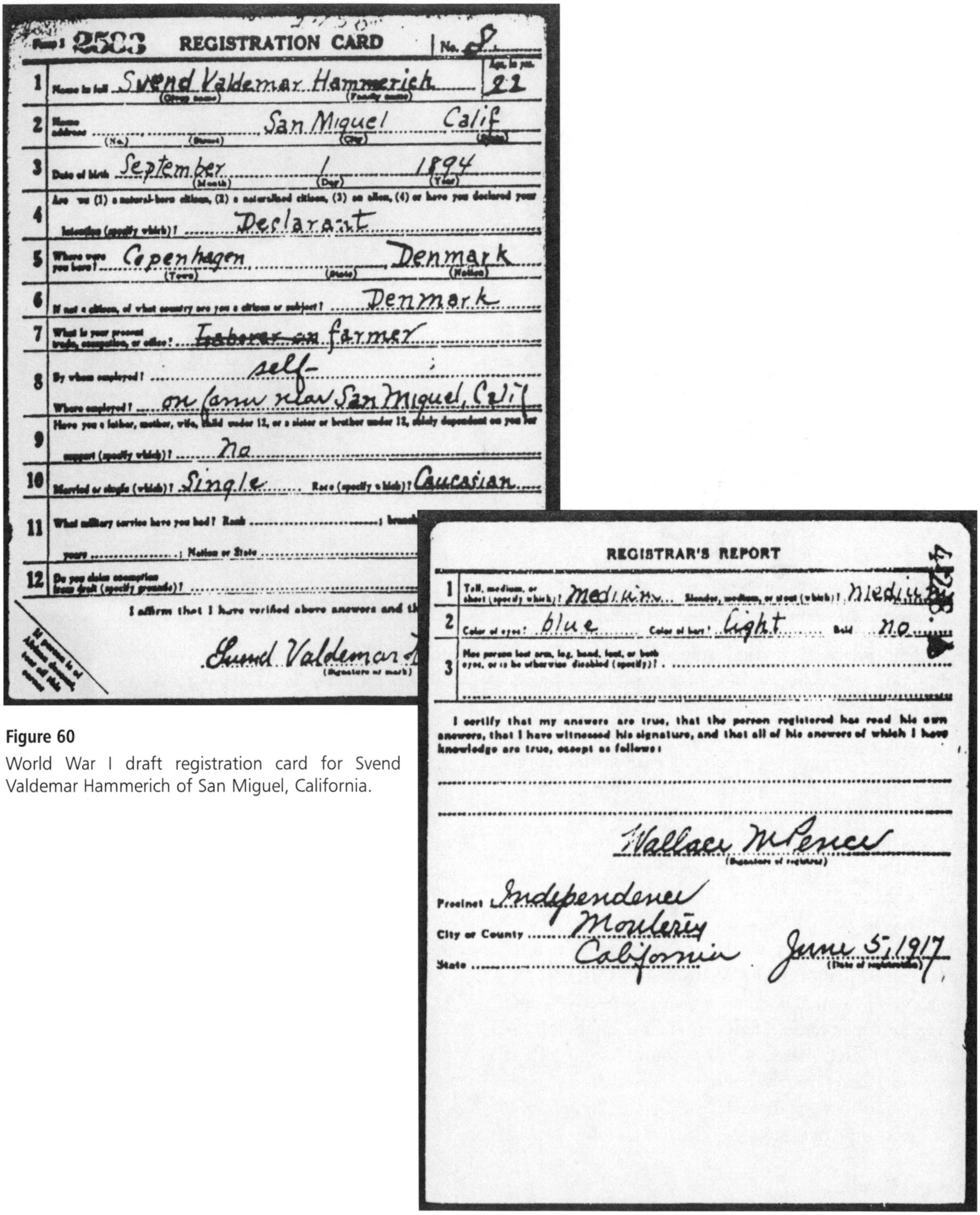

Figure 60

World War I draft registration card for Svend Valdemar Hammerich of San Miguel, California.

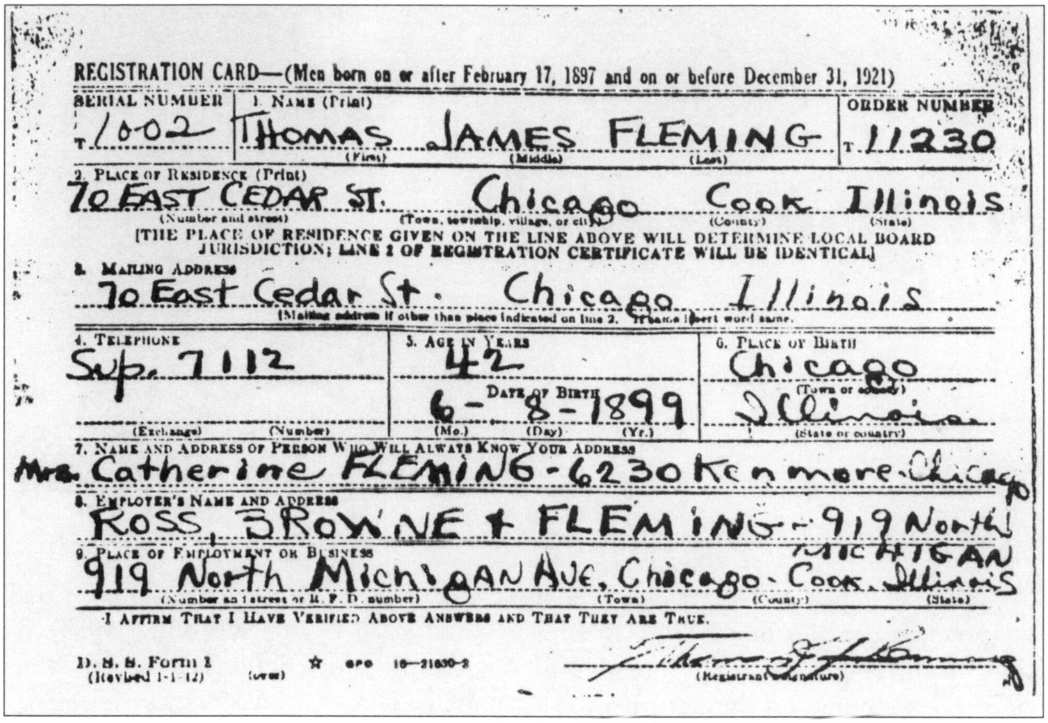

Figure 61

World War II draft card for Thomas James Fleming of Chicago, Illinois.

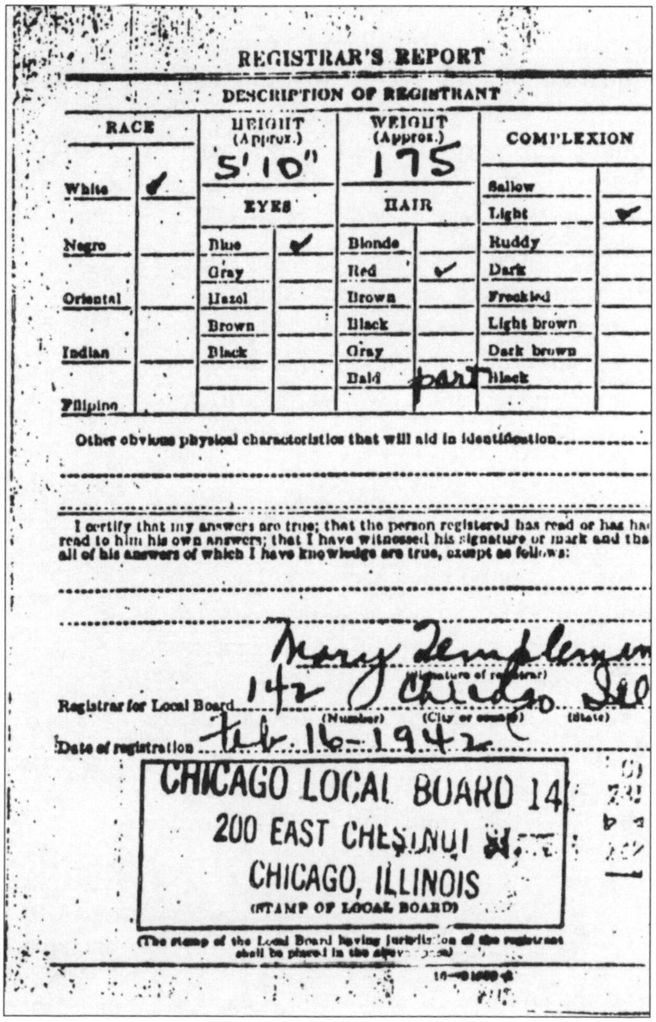

Draper Manuscripts

Lyman Copeland Draper (1815-91) dedicated himself to preserving the history of the "heroes of the Revolution" in the South. With the intention of publishing a series of volumes on the settlement and history of the Trans-Allegheny West, Draper recorded individual recollections and collected papers and unique information for a time period that is often difficult to document. While most of the collection consists of his notes and correspondence, also included are maps, land records, muster rolls, transcripts of official documents, extracts from newspapers, and other published sources. The names of countless pioneers, some with references to their lineage, are among the treasures to be found in this unusual source. Even if one's ancestors are not included here, the researcher will at least come away with a true sense of what life was like during this time period.

At his death, Draper's manuscripts were bequeathed to the State Historical Society of Wisconsin, where he had been employed as corresponding secretary. The collection, consisting of 491 volumes, is arranged by geographic area, subject, and individual and covers the period from the mid-1700s through the War of 1812. Most of the material relates to the area known as "Trans-Allegheny West," which included the western Carolinas and Virginia, some portions of Georgia and Alabama, the entire Ohio River Valley, and parts of the Mississippi River Valley.

The entire Draper manuscript collection has been microfilmed, and copies are available in at least eighty libraries across the country. An important tool to help navigate this extensive collection is Josephine Harper's *Guide to the Draper Manuscripts* (Madison: State Historical Society of Wisconsin, 1983). This publication provides descriptions of the fifty series that comprise the Draper manuscripts, as well as an index of the individuals and places named within the manuscripts.

Selected Readings:

Danky, James P. *Genealogical Research: An Introduction to the Resources of the State Historical Society of Wisconsin*. Madison, WI: State Historical Society of Wisconsin, 1986.

Harper, Josephine. *Guide to the Draper Manuscripts*. Madison: State Historical Society of Wisconsin, 1983.

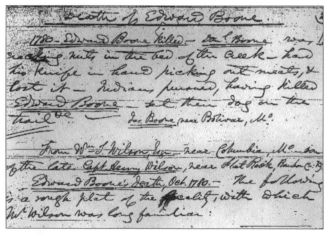

Figure 62

An portion of an interview conducted by Draper with William T. Wilson near Columbia, Missouri in 1851 [page 296 of volume 6 of series S (Draper's Notes)]. Compliments of James L. Hansen, FASG, State Historical Society of Wisconsin.

Ethnic Sources

An examination of home sources, obituaries, military records, census records, and naturalization records typically furnish clues of a forebear's ethnic origin. Once an origin is found, knowledge of an ancestor's ethnic group, its history, and its laws and customs can lead a family historian to specific and often unique record sources. There are a number of cultural publications available to those seeking a better understanding of personality traits and traditions that have been passed on from generation to generation. Large ethnic collections can be found in public and private libraries in the United States. These collections contain a wide variety of original and published material, including ethnic newspapers and records of churches, cultural societies, and fraternal organizations that deal with ethnic groups and their experiences in America. The most significant of these collections can be found at the Balch Institute for Ethnic Studies in Philadelphia, the Immigration History Research Center at the University of Minnesota in St. Paul, the Family History Library in Salt Lake City,

Figure 63
Franco-American Club, Fort Wayne, Indiana. (Courtesy of Rev. Charles Banet)

and the Center for Migration Studies in New York, Staten Island. A number of "single-ethnic" societies have been organized to promote the study and preservation of specific cultures. *The Ancestry Family Historian's Address Book: A Comprehensive List of Local, State, and Federal Agencies and Institutions and Ethnic and Genealogical Organizations* (Salt Lake City: Ancestry, 1997) lists addresses, telephone numbers, and Internet addresses for hundreds of ethnic genealogical societies.

Sources are available for most ethnic groups at ethnic and local historical societies, public libraries, and the LDS Family History Library.

The newsletters and quarterlies put out by local genealogical and historical societies can also be especially rich sources of information, as they often focus on the ethnic groups in their respective areas.

Several publications are available to help researchers locate the many sources that exist. Among them is *Ethnic Information Sources of the United States*, 2d ed., 2 vols. (Detroit: Gale Research Co., 1983), edited by Paul Wasserman and Alice E. Kennington, which identifies standard sources and research institutions as well as the less familiar ethnic fraternal organizations, ethnic newspaper collections, and ethnic museums. Lubomyr Wynar's *Encyclopedic Directory of Ethnic Organizations in the United States* (Littleton, Colo.: Libraries Unlimited, 1975), while dated, is another guide that lists 1,475 major ethnic organizations, representing seventy-three ethnic groups, and briefly describes the nature of the organizations' holdings. A valuable source of information on printed ethnic materials is Lubomyr and Anna T. Wynar's *Encyclopedic Directory of Ethnic Newspapers and Periodicals in the United States* (Littleton, Colo.: Libraries Unlimited, 1976). An extensive bibliography at the end of the "Ethnic Sources" chapter in *Printed Sources: A Guide to Published Genealogical Records* (Salt Lake City: Ancestry, 1998) cites a number of excellent sources for specific ethnic groups.

See also *Immigrants' Letters.*

Selected Readings:

Buenker, John D., Nicholas C. Burckel, and Rudolph J. Vecoli. *Immigration and Ethnicity: A Guide to Information Sources*. Detroit: Gale Research Co., 1977. (Contains more than 1,500 annotated bibliographic entries)

Miller, Wayne Charles. *Comprehensive Bibliography for the Study of American Minorities*. 2 vols. New York: New York University Press, 1976.

Szucs, Loretto Dennis. "Ethnic Sources." *Printed Sources: A Guide to Published Genealogical Records*. Salt Lake City: Ancestry, 1998.

Thernstrom, Stephan. *Harvard Encyclopedia of American Ethnic Groups*. Cambridge, Mass.: Belknap Press of Harvard University Press, 1980.

Wasserman, Paul, and Alice E. Kennington, eds. *Ethnic Information Sources of the United States*. 2d ed. 2 vols. Detroit: Gale Research Co., 1983.

Wynar, Lubomyr. *Encyclopedic Directory of Ethnic Organizations in the United States*. Littleton, Colo.: Libraries Unlimited, 1975.

_____, and Anna T. Wynar. *Encyclopedic Directory of Ethnic Newspapers and Periodicals in the United States*. Littleton, Colo.: Libraries Unlimited, 1976.

Figure 64

A page from *Poles in Chicago 1837-1937: A History of One Century of Polish Contribution to the City of Chicago, Illinois*. (Chicago: Polish Pageant, 1937)

Figure 65

A sample biographical sketch from the *World's Fair Memorial of the Czechoslovak Group* (Chicago: International Exposition, 1933). Information published in the work about John Toman included his parents' names (including the mother's maiden name); his birth date and place; when he came to Chicago; name of his wife (and year of marriage); names of his children; where he was educated; and an outline of his career as an alderman.

FamilySearch®

FamilySearch® is a collection of databases that was developed by the Family History Department of The Church of Jesus Christ of Latter-day Saints and is an excellent starting point for any family history researcher. The collection consists of Ancestral File®, the International Genealogical Index (IGI)®, the Social Security Death Index, the U.S. Military Index, Scottish Church Records, and the Family History Library Catalog®. A description of Ancestral File can be found in this book under the heading "Computerized Genealogies," and the Social Security Death Index is discussed in a section of the same name. IGI is an alphabetically arranged, international index of more than 240 million names of deceased people.

The database is divided into regional sections (e.g. United States and Canada), therefore it may be necessary to conduct more than one search for a particular surname. All names included have been obtained from birth, baptismal/christening, and marriage records and include the names of parents or spouse and the date of the genealogical event from which the documents originated. Since contributions to the database are accepted without question, researchers should document any potential links to their family line. The U.S. Military Index includes the names, dates of birth and death, race, and marital status of more than 100,000 individuals who died while in service during the Korean and Vietnam Wars between 1950 and 1975. The Scottish Church Records database consists of the names of 10 million deceased persons derived from Scottish church records. Finally, the Family History Library Catalog contains bibliographic information on the collection of records located at the Family History Library in Salt Lake City. FamilySearch® is available online, or on CD-ROM at the Family History Library and its Family History Centers, and in some public and private libraries. Information can be printed out or downloaded onto diskette via GEDCOM. IGI is available on microfiche at Family History Centers. The Social Security Death Index is also accessible via the Internet at <www.ancestry.com>.

Selected Readings:

Meyerink, Kory L. "Databases, Indexes, and Other Finding Aids." *The Source: A Guidebook of American Genealogy*. Rev. ed. Salt Lake City: Ancestry, 1997.

Nichols, Elizabeth L. *Genealogy in the Computer Age: Understanding FamilySearch*. Rev. ed. Salt Lake City: Family History Educators, 1994.

_____. "The International Genealogical Index, 1993 Edition," FGS *Forum* 5 (4) 6 (3) (1993–94).

Sperry, Kip. "Published Indexes." *Printed Sources: A Guide to Published Genealogical Records*. Ch. 6: 192–214.

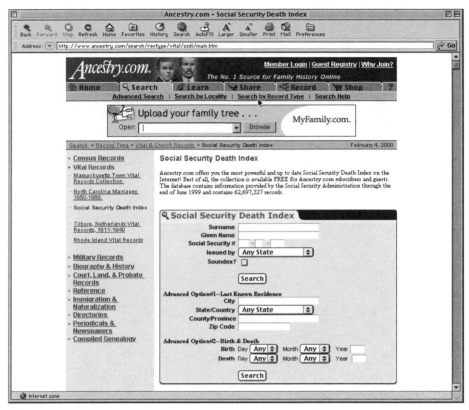

Figure 66
The Social Security Death Index search page at Ancestry.com.

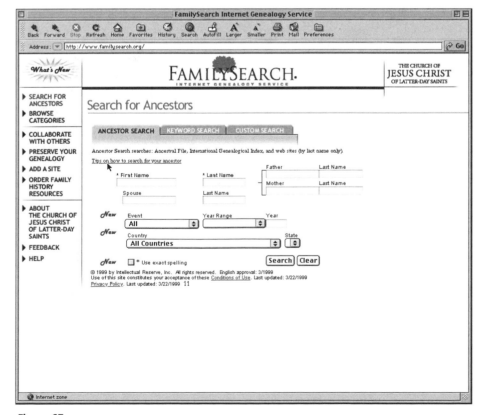

Figure 67
Search page at FamilySearch.org.

Fire Insurance Maps

If an ancestor's home or business address is known, fire insurance maps can provide interesting information about the building in which they lived or worked. Used by insurance companies to determine the risk factors in underwriting a building, the maps are color coded to indicate the construction material as well as its size and shape, and the location of doors, windows, firewalls, ditches, water mains, and sprinkling systems, if any.

The Library of Congress has a list of the maps available for each town and city. Photocopies can be requested from the Library of Congress, Photoduplication Services, Washington, DC 20540. Copies of the maps can also be found at some libraries and state historical societies.

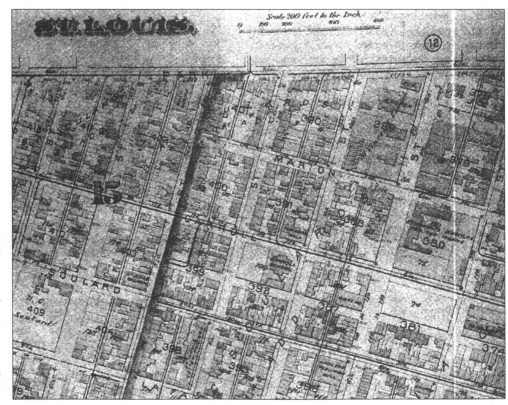

Figure 68

St. Louis Fire Insurance Map from G.M. Hopkins, Atlas of the City of St. Louis, Missouri (1883).

Selected Readings:

Oswald, Diane L. *Fire Insurance Maps: Their History and Applications*. College Station, Texas: Lacewing Press, 1997.

Neagles, James C. *The Library of Congress: A Guide to Genealogical and Historical Research*. Salt Lake City: Ancestry, 1990.

Foreign Birth, Marriage, and Death Records

American consular offices abroad record the births, deaths, and marriages of civilian U.S. citizens in foreign countries, with death records dating back as far as 1792. Included among these are records of births and deaths occurring en route to a foreign destination. The U.S. consular office, upon notification of the event, prepares a Consular Report of Birth (form DS-1350) or the Report of the Death of an American Citizen Abroad (form OF-180), which is filed with the U.S. Department of State. Notices of birth include the name and sex of the child, date and place of birth, and the names and residence of the parents. Death notices typically show the name, place of former residence in the United States, date and place of death, and name and post of the reporting official. The notices, in some cases, provided information about the estate of the deceased as well.

With written authorization from the individual born abroad, or proof of death and relation, copies of the Consular Report of Birth can be requested from Passport Services, Correspondence Branch, U.S. Department of State, 1425 K St. N. W., Room 386, Washington, DC 20522-1705. Notices of death created prior to 1960, including copies of

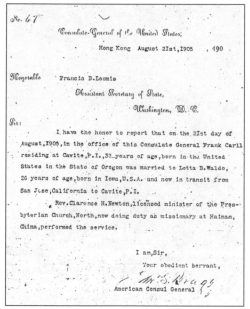

Figure 69

A U.S. Consulate record of the marriage of Frank Carll, who was born in Oregon and married 21 August 1905 to Lotta B. Waldo, born in Iowa.

those sent to newspapers by the Department of State, may be located among other consular dispatches in Record Group 59 and in the Records of Foreign Service Posts of the Department of State, Record Group 84, at the National Archives. Records created in 1960 and beyond can be requested by writing to Passport Services at the address previously listed. Records pertaining to foreign deaths of military personnel or persons employed by the Department of Defense are in the custody of the National Personnel Records Center (Military Personnel Records), 9700 Page Blvd., St. Louis, MO 63132-5100.

Selected Readings:

Hinckley, Kathleen W. "Tracking Twentieth-Century Ancestors." *The Source: A Guidebook of American Genealogy.* Rev. ed. Ch. 18: 628–53.

Kemp, Thomas J. *International Vital Records Handbook.* 3d ed. Baltimore: Genealogical Publishing Co., 1994.

Foreign Records of Emigration

If a search of American records fails to yield the name of the town from which an ancestor emigrated, records from the country of origin may provide the missing information. Many countries in Europe have fully indexed, compiled records that may list the emigrant. Records of departure (or emigration records) giving name, age, close relatives or traveling companions, and usually the last place of residence, may exist if the ancestor had permission to leave the country.

The archives in some countries have prepared indexes of emigrants from particular regions, and private authors have made significant contributions to the effort as well. Two such examples are *The Wuerttemberg Emigration Index* (Salt Lake City: Ancestry, 1986), 7 volumes, in which Trudy Schenk and Ruth Froelke have transcribed handwritten lists and indexed the names of 100,000 individuals who emigrated from Wuerttemberg, Germany from 1750 to 1900, and Peter Wilson Coldham's *The Complete Book of Emigrants*, 4 volumes (Baltimore: Genealogical Publishing Co., 1987–93), listing those emigrating from the British Isles to the United States during the period 1607–1776.

Many other emigration records, indexed and abstracted by government order or by genealogists, are available on microfilm at some libraries and through the Family History Library and its Centers. Among the most important of those on microfilm with the Family History Library are the Hamburg passenger lists (Hamburg was one of two chief ports of embarkation for Central and Eastern European emigrants in the nineteenth century), which contain the names of virtually all the persons who sailed from that port between 1850 and 1934.

Selected Readings:

Szucs, Loretto Dennis, and Kory L. Meyerink. "Immigration: Finding Immigrant Origins." *The Source: A Guidebook of American Genealogy*. Salt Lake City: Ancestry, 1997. Chapter 13, 441–519.

Wright, Raymond S., III. "Immigrant and Emigrant Indexes." *Ancestry* 14 (2) (March/April 1996): 26–7.

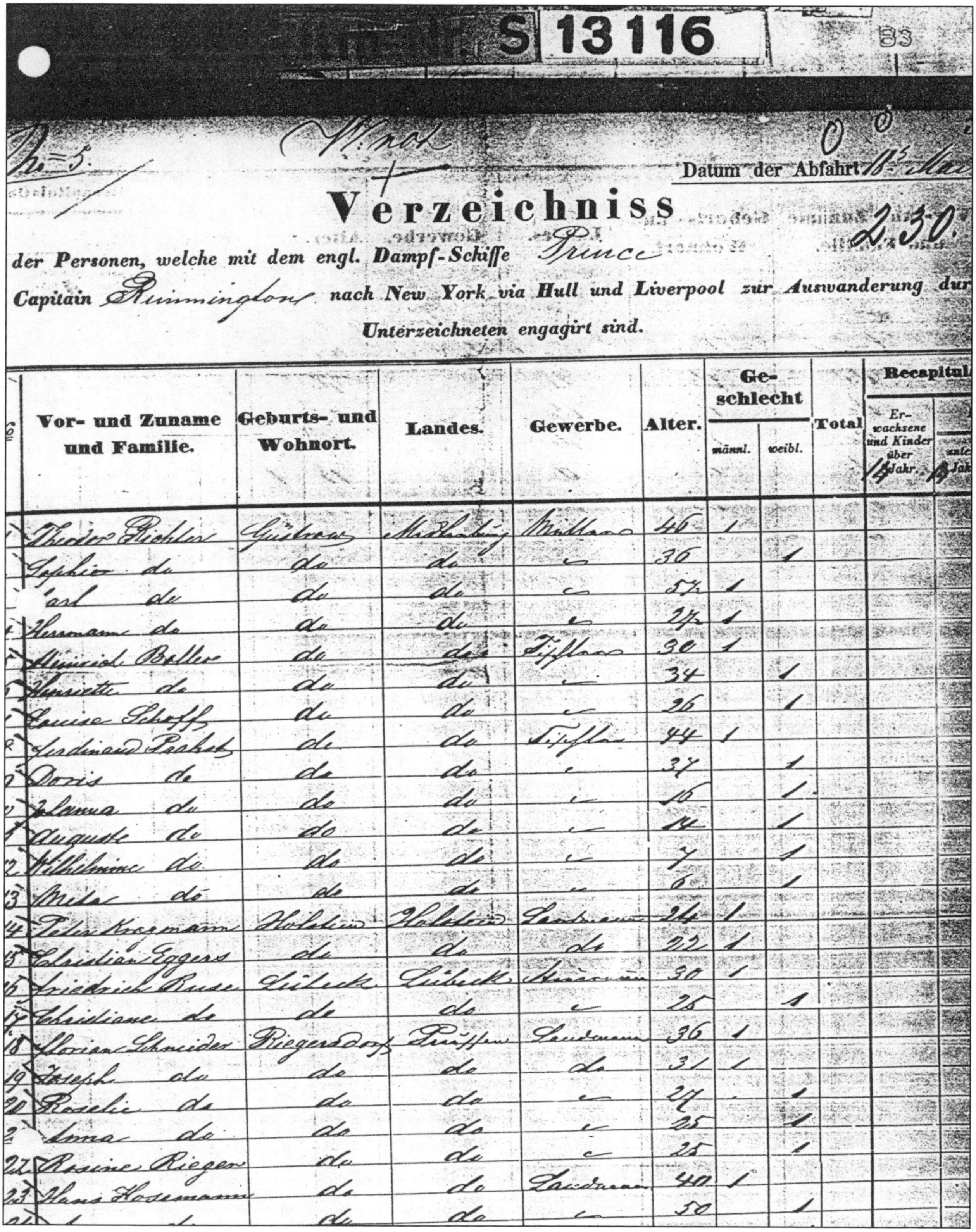
S 13116

No. 5

Datum der Abfahrt 15 März

Verzeichniss

der Personen, welche mit dem engl. Dampf-Schiffe Prince Capitain Rimmington nach New York via Hull und Liverpool zur Auswanderung dur[ch] Unterzeichneten engagirt sind.

	Vor- und Zuname und Familie.	Geburts- und Wohnort.	Landes.	Gewerbe.	Alter.	Geschlecht männl.	Geschlecht weibl.	Total	Recapitul[ation] Erwachsene und Kinder über 14 Jahr.	unter 14 Jahr.
1	Theodor Richter	Güstrow	Mecklenburg	[illegible]	46	1				
2	Sophie do	do	do	"	36		1			
3	Carl do	do	do	"	5½	1				
4	Hermann do	do	do	"	2½	1				
5	Heinrich Boller	do	do	Tischler	30	1				
6	Henriette do	do	do	"	34		1			
7	Louise Scheff	do	do	"	26		1			
8	Ferdinand [illegible]	do	do	Tischler	44	1				
9	Doris do	do	do	"	37		1			
10	Johanna do	do	do	"	16		1			
11	Auguste do	do	do	"	14		1			
12	Wilhelmine do	do	do	"	7		1			
13	Meta do	do	do	"	6		1			
14	Peter Kregmann	Holstein	Holstein	Landmann	24	1				
15	Christian Eggers	do	do	do	22	1				
16	Friedrich Buse	Lübeck	Lübeck	[illegible]	30	1				
17	Christiane do	do	do	"	25		1			
18	Florian Schneider	Riegersdorf	Preussen	Landmann	36	1				
19	Joseph do	do	do	do	31	1				
20	Rosalie do	do	do	"	27		1			
21	Anna do	do	do	"	25		1			
22	Rosine Riegen	do	do	"	25		1			
23	Hans Hosemann	do	do	Landmann	40	1				
24	[illegible]	do	do	"	50		1			

Figure 70

A Hamburg passenger emigration list dated March 1852 for the steamship *Prince* lists passenger names, place of birth and residence, country, trades, age, and sex.

Fraternal Organization Records

From the colonial period to the present, the United States has been home to thousands of fraternal organizations and chapters. It is human nature to seek the company of those who have common interests or similar backgrounds. The emergence of fraternal societies, such as the Masons organization that dates back several centuries, is evidence of this. Whether the society met for business, social, or philanthropic purposes, or to maintain ethnic identity, most kept records of activities and members. The archives of fraternal organizations such as the Masons, Odd Fellows, Knights of Columbus, Elks, Moose, and Czechoslovak Society of America often preserve membership records that include some or all of the following items: name of member, date and place of birth, names of parents, places of residence, names of spouse and children, religious and other affiliations, education, occupation, personal description, and date and place of joining the organization. More recent records may also include a photograph of the individual. It is

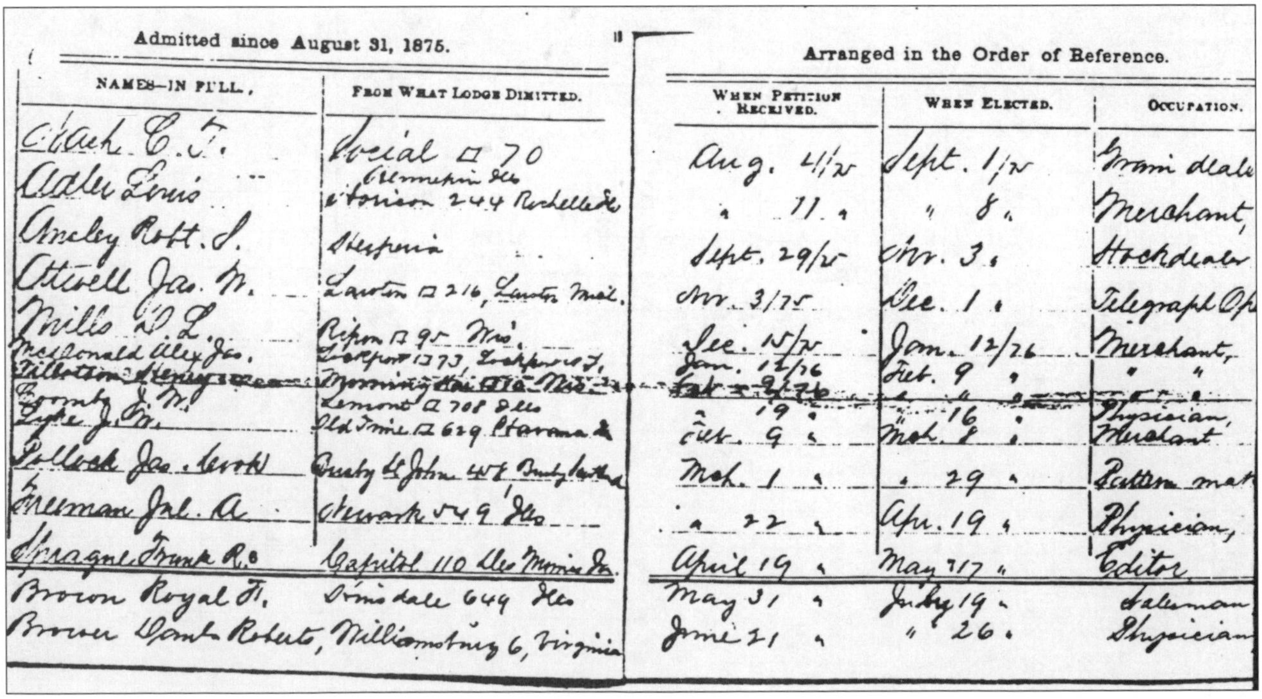

Figure 71
A page from the Annual Report of Hesperia Lodge No. 411 (1876), which shows Brother Tillotson becoming affiliated with the lodge on February 9, 1876, coming from Morning Star Lodge No. 10 (Wisconsin), and being received from the Grand Secretary of Illinois A. T. & A. M. (Masons). (Courtesy of Linda Lamberty)

important to mention that a successful search may require research of the history and functions of more complex organizations, such as the aforementioned Masonic group.

The initial step is to determine an individual's membership in a specific organization. While the contents and existence of the records are varied among the different organizations, a diligent search may turn up clues where conventional sources have failed. In some cases, biographical information of members can be located in published works. Newsletters and centennial papers may include notices of birthdays, anniversaries, obituaries, and mentions of significant events in the lives of its members. Cemeteries may also provide clues in the form of headstones with fraternal emblems and specific areas of cemeteries reserved for those belonging to specific organizations. Probate files and personal possessions, such as jewelry with insignias and photographs, may open the way to further investigation.

Many libraries and historical societies list a variety of printed sources that will lead to needed information regarding a specific organization and its subgroups. An understanding of the workings and history of an organization will greatly improve the chances of success in finding records. If the organization still exists, the *Encyclopedia of Associations: Regional, State, and Local Organizations,* 4th ed., 5 vols. (Detroit: Gale Research Co., 1961–) is a likely source for addresses to write for information. Section 10 of that work lists "Fraternal, Nationality, and Ethnic." The Rotary Club is one of a growing number of organizations that has a Web page listing local chapters with addresses. Local libraries and historical societies may hold records of those that are no longer in existence.

Selected Readings:

Chicago Directory of Lodges for the Year 1883. Chicago: C. F. Lichtner & Bro., 1883.

Eldridge, Grant J., ed. *Encyclopedia of Associations: Regional State, and Local Organizations.* 4th ed. 5 vols. Detroit: Gale Research Co., 1994.

Fraternal Directory. San Francisco: The Bancroft Co., 1889.

Wynar, Lubomyr R. *Encyclopedia Directory of Ethnic Organizations in the United States.* Littleton, Colo.: Libraries Unlimited, 1975.

Internet Sites of Interest:

B.P.O. Elks Online
http://www.elks.org/default.cfm

Fraternal Organizations
http://www.wvu.edu/~socialwk/faculty/RAL/E/fraternities.html

Friendly Societies
http://www.wvu.edu/~socialwk/faculty/RAL/E/friendly.societies.html

Freemasons
http://www.freemasonry.org/

IOF Foresters
www.iof.org/

IOOF Lodge Phone Directory
http://www.ioof.org/IOOF/IOOFPhoneDirectory.html

Knights of Columbus
http://www.kofc.org/

Lions International
http://www.lions.org/

Masonic Library and Museum Association
http://www.erols.com/bessel/mlma.htm

National Grange
http://www.nationalgrange.org/

Rotary International
http://www.rotary.org/

Freedmen's Bureau

Established by the federal government in 1865, the Bureau of Refugees, Freedmen, and Abandoned Lands, more commonly known as the Freedmen's Bureau, assisted ex-slaves in a number of ways, including drawing up labor contracts, conducting marriages, leasing abandoned land, and providing transportation to those seeking to relocate after the war. The contents of the records vary greatly among the district field offices; however, some contain important genealogical information. For example, records from Mississippi contain local marriage registers from 1865 and 1866, validating marriages that took place before and after emancipation, and labor contracts drawn up between 1866 and 1868 that, in many cases, name both the laborer and family members. It was not uncommon for the contracts to be executed between an ex-slave and a former owner, providing names that can lead to additional sources of information.

Also of interest are the signature records from the Freedmen's Savings and Trust Company. Completed by the depositor when the account was opened, information recorded often included the account holder's name, age, birthplace, residence, names of family members, and former owner.

The records of the Freedmen's Bureau and the Freedmen's Savings and Trust Company are available on microfilm at the National Archives. To use the records of the Freedmen's Savings and Trust Company, a researcher must know the city in which the account was held.

See also *Slavery Records.*

Selected Readings:

Black Studies: A Select Catalog of National Archives Microfilm Publications. Washington, D.C.: National Archives, 1984.

Everly, Elaine C. "Freedmen's Bureau Records: An Overview." *Prologue: Quarterly of the National Archives* 29 (2) (Summer 1997): 95–99.

Guide to Genealogical Research in the National Archives. Washington, D.C.: National Archives Trust Fund Board, 1982.

Hester, Gwendolyn Lynette. *Freedmen and Colored Marriage Records, 1865–1890, Sumter County, Alabama.* Heritage Books, 1996.

Kavasch, E. Barrie, ed. *An Index of African Americans Identified in Select Records of the Bureau of Refugees, Freedmen, & Abandoned Lands.* Heritage Books, 1995.

Thackery, David T. "African American Family History." *The Source: A Guidebook of American Genealogy.* Rev. ed. Salt Lake City: Ancestry, 1997.

Washington, Reginald. "The Freedmen's Savings and Trust Company and African-American Genealogical Research." *Prologue: Quarterly of the National Archives* 29 (2) (Summer 1997): 170–181.

Internet Sites of Interest:

Christine's Genealogy Web site Freedmen's Bureau Records
http://www.ccharity.com/contents/freedmens.htm

Freedmen's Marriages, State of Virginia
http://www.msstate.edu/listarchives/afrigeneas/199703/msg00109.html

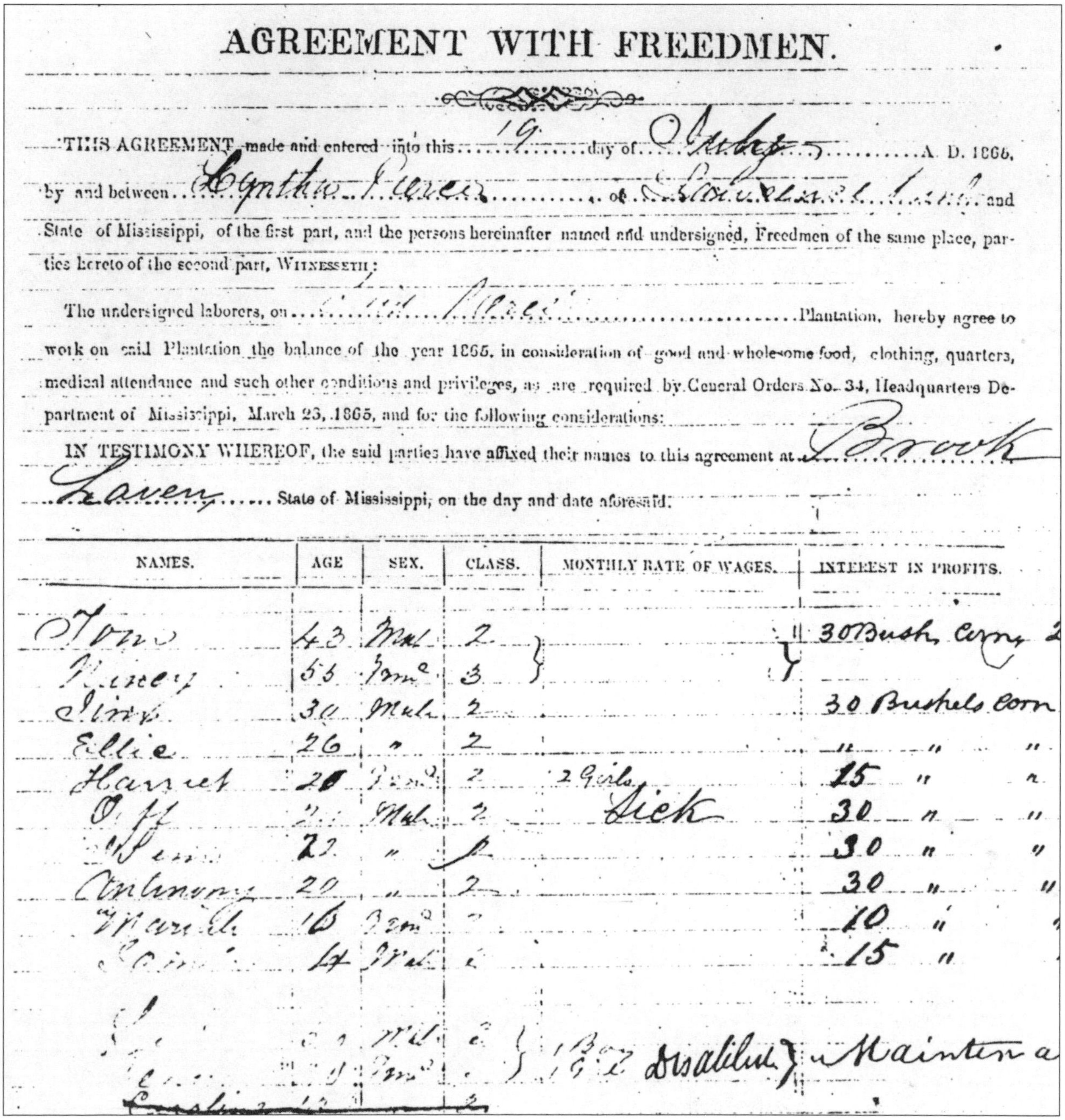

Figure 72
An 1865 Freedmen's Agreement from Brookhaven, Mississippi.

Genealogical Society Records

Genealogical societies provide a number of important services to their members. Possibly the most valuable of those services are the publishing and indexing of information valuable to family historians. Among the resources one might find are indexes of newspaper birth, death, and marriage notices, local cemetery records, compilations of tombstone inscriptions, mortuary records, court records, and lists of members interested in a particular surname. In addition to articles of interest, regular publications for members may include voter registration lists, immigration lists, and censuses for the region.

Selected Readings:

Devine, Donn. "Societies Contribute Indispensable Sources." *Ancestry* 13 (5) (September-October 1995): 16–17.

Smith, Juliana Szucs. *The Ancestry Family Historian's Address Book: A Comprehensive List of Local, State, and Federal Agencies and Institutions and Ethnic and Genealogical Organizations.* Salt Lake City: Ancestry, 1997. (An extensive list of societies indexed by state, including street address, mailing address, telephone number, fax number, and e-mail and Internet addresses, where applicable).

Internet Sites of Interest:

Federation of Genealogical Societies Society Hall
www.familyhistory.com/societyhall/

Centennial Family Certificate Questionnaire 25-5

Name of applicant
as it is to appear on the Certificate

Address Zip

Name of ancestor Hiram Adams

Date born 1805 Where New York Died 1887 Where Flint, Mich.

Where buried Flint, Mich. Date married 1826 Where N.Y state?

Name of spouse Elizabeth Staats Date born 1803 Where N.Y. state ?

Died 1859 Where Flint, Mich. Where buried Flint, Mich.

Where in Michigan did ancestor settle?
Township Atlas County Genesee

Date ancestor settled in Michigan 1855-60 Did spouse accompany? yes

Place from which ancestor came, if known Erie County, New York

Proof of arrival date see obituaries of TEW Adams & Wm.H.Adams.
Ellis. History of Genesee Co, Mich. 1879 lists
Hiram as 1859 supervisor of Atlas twp.-p.256
* * * * * * * * * * Also: Hiram's obituary
(Not listed in 1860 census, have not checked 1870)

LINEAGE CHART

Generation 1. My Michigan Pioneer ancestor was Hiram Adams
He/She was born March 27, 1805 at central New York
Died November 12, 1887 at Flint, Michigan
Married to: Elizabeth Staats on January 5, 1826

Generation 2. Their child Theron Edwin Winfield was my great- grandfather
He/She was born July 16, 1835 at Davenport, New York
Died August 10, 1910 at Pontiac, Michigan
Married Melissa Hayes Rice on March 3, 1866

Generation 3. Their child Edwin Hayes "Hayes" was my grandfather
He/She was born March 19, 1885 at Chesaning, Michigan
Died July 21, 1975 at Chesaning, Michigan
Married Lelia Maude Hall on June 26, 1908

Figure 73

A certificate questionnaire generated by the Michigan Genealogical Council. This and other Michigan Council records have been microfilmed and are available through the Family History Library.

ILLINOIS STATE GENEALOGICAL SOCIETY
PRAIRIE PIONEER CERTIFICATE APPLICATION

NAME OF APPLICANT (as it is
to appear on certificate) Rita J HOTCHKISS

ADDRESS 210 E. 56th Street A Long Beach, Calif 90805

NAME OF PIONEER ANCESTOR Sarah Jane PAULIN (HOTCHKISS)

DATE OF BIRTH 30 March 1847 PLACE OF BIRTH Fulton Co., Ill
          Day Month Year City County State

DATE OF DEATH 6 July 1936 PLACE OF DEATH Marshalltown, Marshall Co., Iowa
          Day Month Year City County State

PLACE BURIED Riverside Cemt. Marshalltown Marshall Co., Iowa
          Name of Cemetery City County State

PIONEER'S FATHER'S NAME Jack W. PAULIN

PIONEER'S MOTHER'S NAME Hanna DEFORDE

PIONEER'S SPOUSE'S NAME Lyman Luther HOTCHKISS
          (maiden name if woman)

SPOUSE'S DATE & PLACE OF BIRTH (9 Dec 1846 Cattersugus Co., New York
          Day Month Year City County State

SPOUSE'S DATE & PLACE OF DEATH 18 Jan 1912 Marshalltown, Marshall Co., Iowa
          Day Month Year City County State

PLACE BURIED Riverside Cemt Marshalltown, Marshall Co., Iowa
          Name of Cemetery City County State

DATE OF MARRIAGE 4 July 1864 PLACE Marshalltown Marshall Co. Iowa
          Day Month Year City County State

DATE & LOCATION PIONEER SETTLED IN ILLINOIS 1847 Fulton Co.
          Year City County

CHILDREN OF ANCESTOR

Name	Born	Where	Died	Where	Spouse	Date Married
Cora	?	?	?	?	?	?
Julie	?	?	?	?	?	?
C.M. Perry	1872	Iowa	?	?	?	?
Bird Lucius	1872	Iowa	1957	Iowa	Maybell ADAMS	?
Mary J	?	?	?	?	?	?

Please list other children on a separate sheet

Harry W.	1877	Iowa	1943	Iowa	Blanche YOKOM	?

PERMISSION RELEASE
I hereby give permission to the Illinois State Genealogical Society
to use my material submitted for the Prairie Pioneer Certificate for
their publications in the future.

Signed this ___ day of ___ Aug ___ 1983.
Signature Rita J. Hotchkiss
Address 210 E. 56th St "A" Long Beach, Ca. 90805

Figure 74

Many genealogical societies have ongoing projects to document and publish information about the pioneers who settled in the locale. This sample from the Illinois Genealogical Society is typical of most in supplying rich biographical details about the pioneer and other family members.

Genetics Studies

With almost daily advances occurring in the field of genetic studies, a family historian's research has taken on new significance. Armed with knowledge of ancestors' causes of death, an individual may be able to detect a particular illness or disease to which the family line seems to be predisposed and take measures to reduce the risk of reoccurrence in present and future generations. Genetic testing is now available for over one hundred inherited diseases, such as familial breast cancer and colon cancer, and professional genetic counselors are available to help individuals and families determine if the tests are appropriate for them.

Due to possible ramifications on insurance coverage and employment, most individuals undergoing genetic testing or participating in genetics studies seek total confidentiality. This hasn't always been the case, however, and earlier studies like those conducted by the Eugenics Record Office during the first half of the twentieth century are available to the public. The information in this particular study, which solicited family medical histories throughout the country from volunteers, including college students, individuals with particular hereditary defects, and patients in mental institutions, is available on microfilm through the LDS Family History Library.

Selected Readings:

Anderson, Robert Charles. "Records of the Eugenic's Records Office." *Forum* 4:2:6 (Summer 1992).

Carmack, Sharon DeBartolo. *A Genealogist's Guide to Discovering Your Female Ancestors.* Cincinnati, Ohio: Betterway Books, 1998.

Gormley, Myra Vanderpool. *Family Diseases. Are You At Risk?* Baltimore, Md.: Genealogical Publishing Co., 1989.

Krause, Carol. *How Healthy Is Your Family Tree?* New York: Fireside (Simon & Schuster), 1995.

Nelson-Anderson, Danette L., and Cynthia V. Waters. *Genetic Connections: A Guide to Documenting Your Individual and Family Health History.* Washington, Missouri: Sonters Publishing, 1995. (This book discusses genetic inheritance, explains a number of inherited illnesses, and provides forms for documenting your family health history)

Olson, Pamella S. "Genealogical Records: Invaluable Aid to Marrow Donor Search." *Heritage Quest* 43: 16–18.

Roderick, Thomas H. "Umbilical Lines and the mtDNA Project." *National Genealogical Society Quarterly* 82 (2) (June 1994): 144–45.

_____. "Files of the Eugenics Record Office: A Resource for Genealogists." *National Genealogical Society Quarterly* 82 (2) (June 1994): 97–113.

FATHER'S FATHER.

1. Full name _August Graff_   2. Date of birth
3. Birthplace: Town _Lithuania_   State or Country _Europe_
4. Education   Favorite studies
5. Residences, principal _Lithuania_
6. Age at marriage _30_ Total No. of sons _4_ of daughters _3_ Ages of those that died early, sons _52_ daughters _52_   55   53
7. Occupations at successive ages _Agricultural_
8. Lesser diseases to which there was special liability: In youth   In middle age
9. Grave illnesses in youth
10. Surgical operations unde
11. If dead, cause of death a
11a. State whether blood rela
12. Special tastes, gifts or pe

Please do not write here.

Gra-53

Articulated family records.

Gra-54

Carnegie Institution of Washington,

EUGENICS RECORD OFFICE

FOUNDED BY MRS. E. H. HARRIMAN

COLD SPRING HARBOR,
LONG ISLAND, N. Y.

Please do not write here.

No. _45891_
Sent _MAR 3   1925_
Returned
Ack'd
Collab. _Geo. E. Fisher_

Record of
Family Traits

Name of person responsible for filling out this schedule _Julia Florence Graff_
Important.—Please do not neglect.
Date _May 6, 1928_ Permanent Address _229 Pine Street_
Town and State _Kulpmont, Pennsylvania_

INSTRUCTIONS.

1. This schedule is given out in duplicate in order that, after filling out both copies, one may be added to the family archives of the person filling them out and the second may be returned to the Eugenics Record Office, which is by this method building up a good index of the natural traits of the better American families. Preserve carefully your copy of the schedule and enter new data on it from time to time.

2. In filling out this schedule decide first on your own place in the pedigree—father, mother, child, or the like, depending upon which place will give you the greatest number of connections. Make entry for yourself and then assign the other members of the family to their appropriate places.

3. It is important to bear in mind that this record will be much more accurate and complete if consultation be had with the oldest living members of the family.

4. It is especially suggested that, after filling out this schedule, the person making the study interest other branches of his family in making similar records, in order that they may be articulated into a scientific genealogy—a record of natural inheritance within the pedigree.

5. On request to the Eugenics Record Of   ll be sent free to other branches of the family, or to friends and associates simi-larly interested in adding such records to thei

6. The data contained in these schedules   as confidential, and no names will be publishe

7. All schedules received will be given a

8. In case this blank schedule is lost, acc   as many fresh copies as the particular collabo

9. It is expected that 10 years later you

WHEN FILLED OUT PLEASE RET

Tenth Edition.
6M, 1-'25.
Lancaster Press, Lancaster, Pa.

FATHER'S MOTHER.

1. Full maiden name _Francis Dugan_   2. Date of birth
3. Birthplace: Town _Lithuania_   State or Country _Europe_
4. Education   Favorite studies
5. Residences, principal _Lithuania_
6. Date of marriage   Place of Marriage _Lithuania_ Total No. of sons _4_ of daughters _3_
7. Occupations at successive ages _Housewife_
8. Lesser diseases to which there was special liability: In youth   In middle age
9. Grave illnesses in youth   in middle age
10. Surgical operations undergone
11. If dead, cause of death and age at death _Fever – age of 40._
12. Special tastes, gifts or peculiarities of mind or body. Character, favorite pursuits, amusements, etc _Singing_

Figure 75

Pages from a schedule filed with the Eugenics Records Office, copied from microfilm at the Family History Library.

Grand Army of the Republic

Records created by the many posts of the Grand Army of the Republic, a fraternal organization of Union veterans of the Civil War, may be useful to those tracking ancestors who were honorably discharged veterans of the Union army, navy, marine corps, or the Revenue Cutter Service. Of particular interest would be the membership applications and descriptive books listing the members of each post, which at its strongest point numbered more than 490,000 in total, and in most cases include their age, birthplace, residence, occupation, and war records.

The last Grand Army of the Republic post was disbanded in 1949. In many cases, post records have been

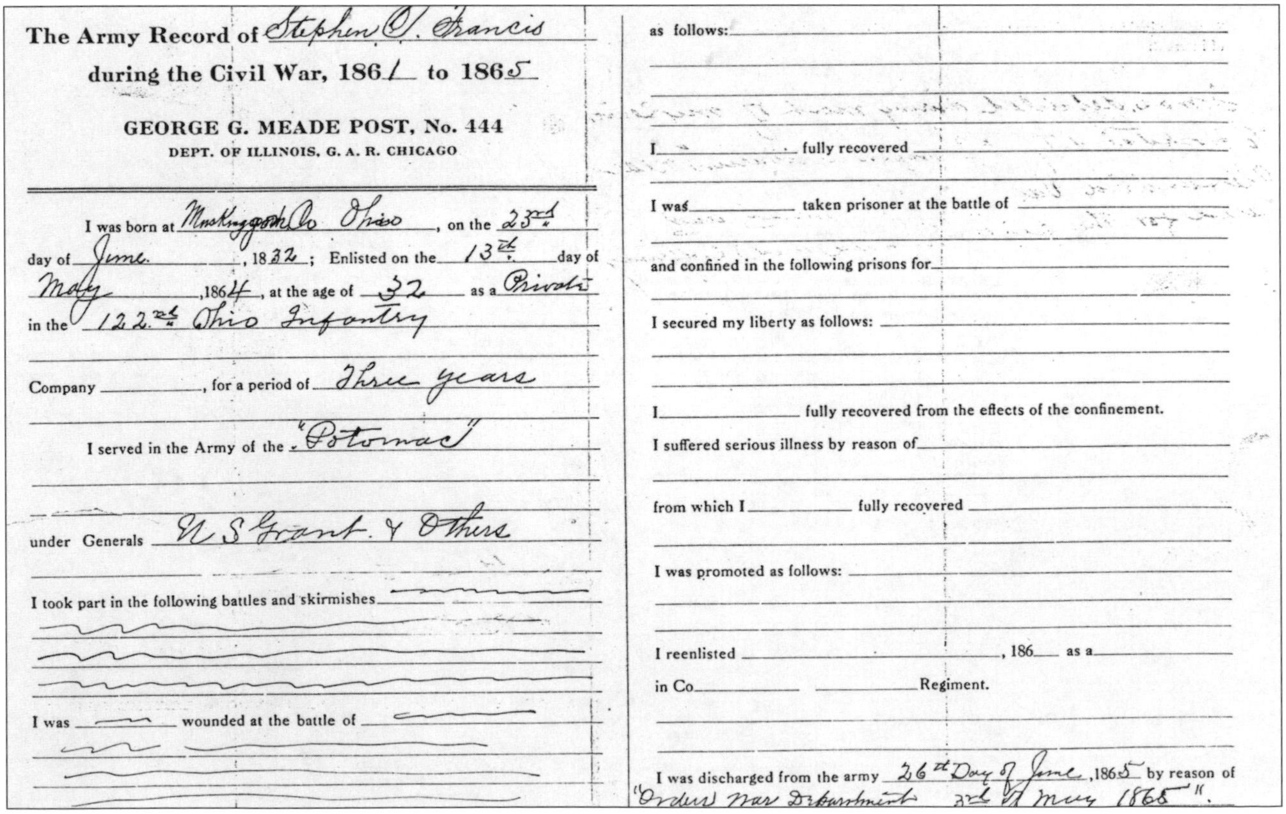

The Army Record of Stephen C. Francis
during the Civil War, 1861 to 1865

GEORGE G. MEADE POST, No. 444
DEPT. OF ILLINOIS, G. A. R. CHICAGO

I was born at Muskingum Co Ohio, on the 23rd day of June, 1832; Enlisted on the 13th day of May, 1864, at the age of 32 as a Private in the 122nd Ohio Infantry

Company ____, for a period of Three years

I served in the Army of the "Potomac"

under Generals U S Grant & Others

I took part in the following battles and skirmishes ____

I was ____ wounded at the battle of ____

as follows: ____

I ____ fully recovered ____

I was ____ taken prisoner at the battle of ____

and confined in the following prisons for ____

I secured my liberty as follows: ____

I ____ fully recovered from the effects of the confinement.

I suffered serious illness by reason of ____

from which I ____ fully recovered ____

I was promoted as follows: ____

I reenlisted ____, 186__ as a ____

in Co. ____ ____ Regiment.

I was discharged from the army 26th Day of June, 1865 by reason of "Orders War Department 3rd of May 1865".

Figure 76

A copy of the Army Record of Stephen C. Francis during the Civil War, filed with a Grand Army of the Republic post in Chicago, Illinois. (Courtesy of Linda Lamberty)

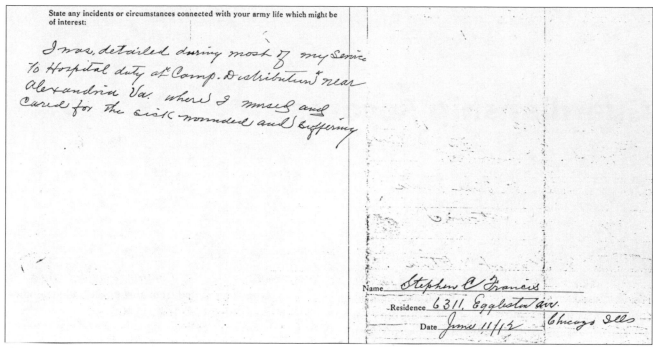

State any incidents or circumstances connected with your army life which might be of interest:

I was detailed during most of my Service to Hospital duty at Camp Distribution near Alexandria Va. where I nursed and cared for the sick wounded and Suffering

Name *Stephen C Francis*

Residence *6311, Eggleston av.*

Date *June 11/92   Chicago Ills*

Figure 77
The reverse side of the Army Record of Stephen C. Francis. (Courtesy of Linda Lamberty)

Figure 78
A record of Post 210, Albion, Michigan Grand Army of the Republic, showing names, ages, birthplaces, residence, and information regarding military service of members.

donated to the state historical societies, libraries, and archives the post operated in. The U.S. Army Military History Institute, 22 Ashburn Drive, Carlisle Barracks, Carlisle, PA 17013, also has records pertaining to various posts located in Maine, Maryland, Massachusetts, New York, and Pennsylvania.

Selected Readings:

Neagles, James C. *U.S. Military Records: A Guide to Federal & State Sources, Colonial America to the Present.* Salt Lake City: Ancestry, 1994.

Internet Sites of Interest:

Grand Army of the Republic Civil War Mus. and Lib.
http://suvcw.org/garmus.htm

Grand Army of the Republic Memorial Museum
http://suvcw.org/gar.htm

Ladies of the Grand Army of the Republic
http://suvcw.org/lgar.htm

U.S. Army Military History Institute
http://carlisle-www.army.mil/usamhi/

Guardianship Records

The appointment of a guardian may be legally required in a number of situations, most commonly to manage an inheritance left to a minor or to care for the minor in the event of the parents' deaths. (Guardians were also appointed for adult individuals considered incapable of handling their own concerns.) Depending on the case, resulting records can include the appointment, the bond the guardian may be required to post, periodic reports filed with the court, and a final account required when the minor is allowed to take charge of his or her own affairs.

Information that may be included among the records are the names of the minor, the guardian, and the natural parents. Details of inherited property and the minor's relationship to the benefactor are sometimes revealed, and the dates of the documents can provide clues to the age of the minor.

Guardianship records are typically held by the same court that handles probate proceedings and may, in fact, be a part of a probate file. In some cases, they may have been turned over to a state depository. The Genealogical Society of Utah has microfilmed records from various locations and has made them available through the Family History Library.

See also *Probate Records*.

Selected Readings:

Eakle, Arlene H. "Research in Court Records." *The Source: A Guidebook of American Genealogy*. Rev. ed. Chapter 7: 173–238. Salt Lake City: Ancestry, 1997.

Greenwood, Val D. *The Researcher's Guide to American Genealogy*. 2d ed. Baltimore, Md.: Genealogical Publishing Co., Inc., 1990.

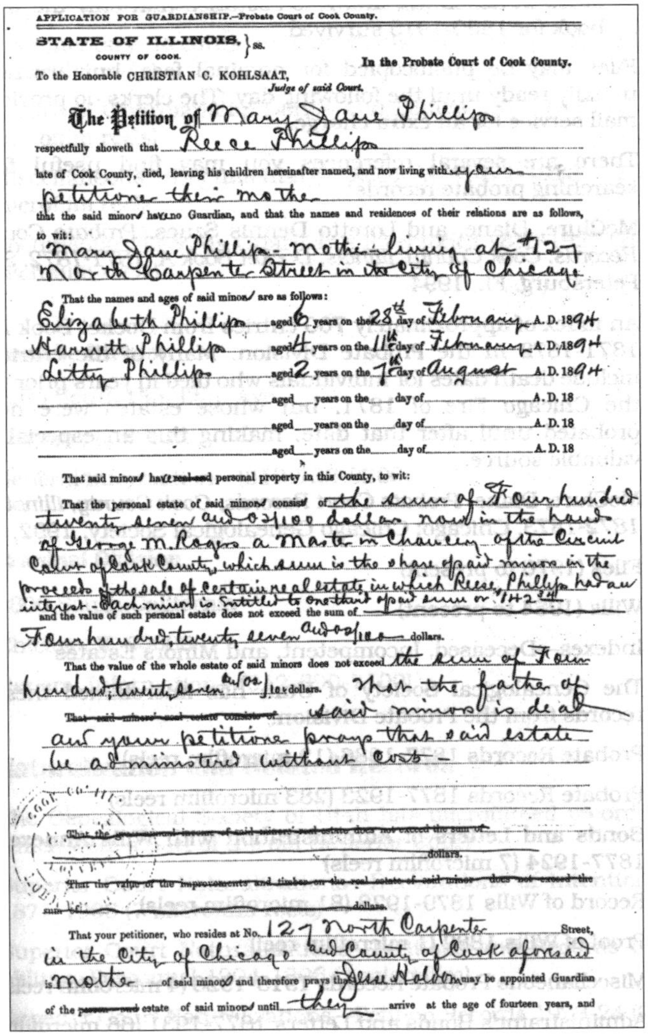
APPLICATION FOR GUARDIANSHIP.—Probate Court of Cook County.

STATE OF ILLINOIS, COUNTY OF COOK. } ss.

In the Probate Court of Cook County.

To the Honorable CHRISTIAN C. KOHLSAAT, Judge of said Court.

The Petition of Mary Jane Phillips respectfully showeth that Reece Phillips late of Cook County, died, leaving his children hereinafter named, and now living with your petitioner their mother

that the said minors have no Guardian, and that the names and residences of their relations are as follows, to wit:

Mary Jane Phillips - mother - living at 127 North Carpenter Street in the City of Chicago

That the names and ages of said minors are as follows:

Elizabeth Phillips aged 6 years on the 28th day of February A.D. 1894

Harriett Phillips aged 4 years on the 11th day of February A.D. 1894

Letty Phillips aged 2 years on the 7th day of August A.D. 1894

aged ___ years on the ___ day of ___ A.D. 18

aged ___ years on the ___ day of ___ A.D. 18

aged ___ years on the ___ day of ___ A.D. 18

That said minors have ~~real and~~ personal property in this County, to wit:

That the personal estate of said minors consist of the sum of Four hundred twenty seven and 02/100 dollars now in the hands of George M. Rogers a Master in Chancery of the Circuit Court of Cook County, which sum is the share of said minors in the proceeds of the sale of certain real estate in which Reese Phillips had an interest - Each minor is entitled to one third of said sum or 142.34 and the value of such personal estate does not exceed the sum of Four hundred, twenty seven and 02/100 dollars.

That the value of the whole estate of said minors does not exceed the sum of Four hundred, twenty seven and 02/100 dollars. That the father of said minors is dead and your petitioner prays that said estate be administered without cost -

~~That said minors' real estate consists of~~

~~That the annual income of said minors' real estate does not exceed the sum of~~ dollars.

~~That the value of the improvements and timber on the real estate of said minor does not exceed the sum of~~ dollars.

That your petitioner, who resides at No. 127 North Carpenter Street, in the City of Chicago and County of Cook aforesaid is mother of said minors and therefore prays that Jesse Holden may be appointed Guardian of the ~~person and~~ estate of said minors until they arrive at the age of fourteen years, and

Figure 79

Guardianship Application, Cook County Probate Court.

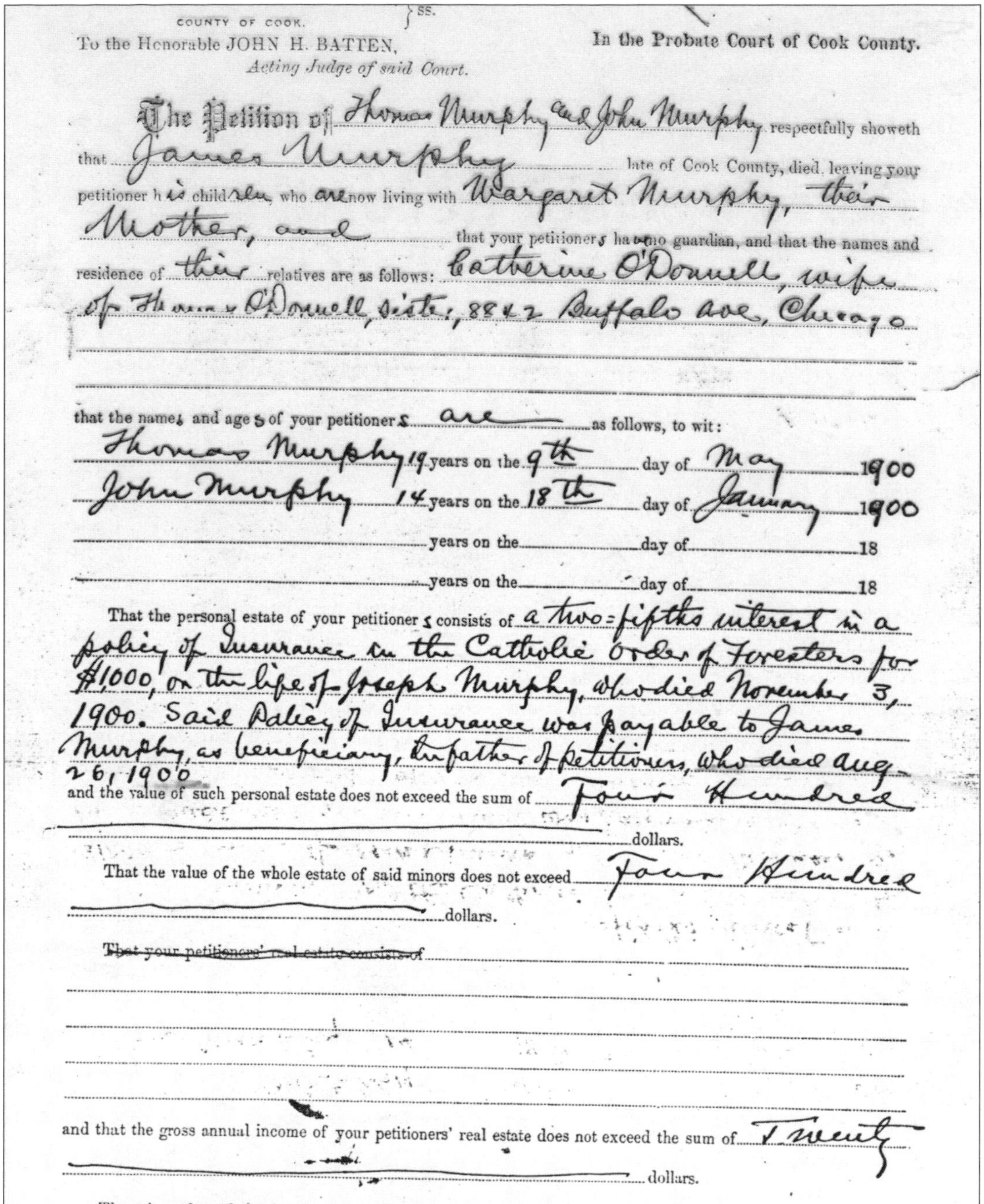
COUNTY OF COOK. } SS.

To the Honorable JOHN H. BATTEN, *Acting Judge of said Court.*

In the Probate Court of Cook County.

The Petition of Thomas Murphy and John Murphy respectfully showeth that James Murphy late of Cook County, died, leaving your petitioner his children who are now living with Margaret Murphy, their Mother, and that your petitioners have no guardian, and that the names and residence of their relatives are as follows: Catherine O'Donnell, wife of Thomas O'Donnell, sister, 8842 Buffalo ave, Chicago

that the names and ages of your petitioners are as follows, to wit:

Thomas Murphy 19 years on the 9th day of May 1900

John Murphy 14 years on the 18th day of January 1900

years on the day of 18

years on the day of 18

That the personal estate of your petitioners consists of a two-fifths interest in a policy of Insurance in the Catholic Order of Foresters for $1000, on the life of Joseph Murphy, who died November 3, 1900. Said Policy of Insurance was payable to James Murphy, as beneficiary, the father of petitioners, who died Aug. 26, 1900 and the value of such personal estate does not exceed the sum of Four Hundred dollars.

That the value of the whole estate of said minors does not exceed Four Hundred dollars.

~~That your petitioners' real estate consists of~~

and that the gross annual income of your petitioners' real estate does not exceed the sum of Twenty dollars.

~~That the value of the improvements and timber on the real estate of your petitioner does not exceed the sum of~~ ~~dollars;~~

and that your petitioners are over the age of fourteen years, and hereby select Margaret Murphy as their guardian; and that said Margaret Murphy

Figure 80

The court guardianship petition of Thomas and John Murphy, showing that their father James Murphy of Cook County Illinois died August 26, 1900, leaving the petitioners—his children—living with their mother, Margaret Murphy. The record states that the petitioners have no guardian, and it provides the name and address of an aunt as a relative. The ages of and birth dates of the boys are provided in the document, as well as the fact that their personal estate is two-fifths interest in a $1,000 life insurance policy from the Catholic Order of Foresters. This guardianship record, like most, provides a number of clues leading to other sources.

Hereditary Society Records

A number of hereditary or lineage societies are in existence throughout the United States for descendants whose ancestors shared a common past. Many societies are based on the military service of ancestors, such as the National Society of the Daughters of the American Revolution, while other societies base membership on the ship an ancestor arrived on, the colony settled in, religion, nationality, or royal lineage. Family societies have experienced significant growth in recent years as well.

Hereditary societies have published volumes of membership rosters and ancestor indexes, some containing the complete lineage of all members, in addition to biographical sketches of ancestors. A comprehensive guide to the most active hereditary societies in the United States and their printed sources is Grahame Thomas Smallwood, Jr.'s chapter "Tracking Through Hereditary and Lineage Organizations" in *The Source: A Guidebook to American Genealogy* (Salt Lake City: Ancestry, 1997). Libraries with large genealogical collections may have copies of various publications.

Ancestry.com has an online database of lineage books of the Daughters of the American Revolution, National Society. These volumes contain information submitted by tens of thousands of individuals with ancestral connections to Revolutionary War patriots (http://www.ancestry.com/search/rectype/inddbs/3174.htm).

Selected Readings:

Smallwood, Grahame Thomas, Jr. "Tracking Through Hereditary and Lineage Organizations." *The Source: A Guidebook of American Genealogy.* Salt Lake City: Ancestry, 1997. (Chapter includes the names, addresses, membership requirements, and printed works of the most active hereditary societies in the United States)

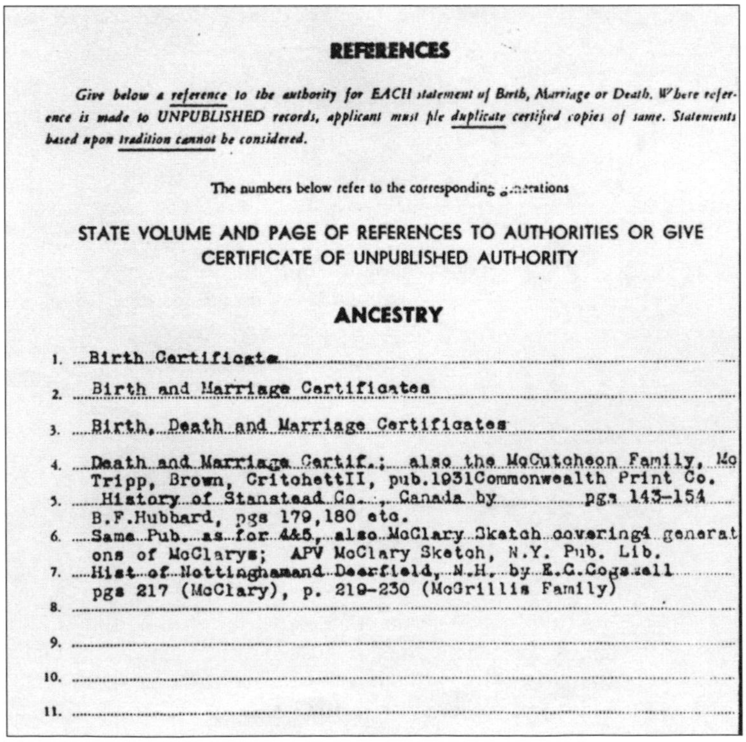

REFERENCES

Give below a reference to the authority for EACH statement of Birth, Marriage or Death. Where reference is made to UNPUBLISHED records, applicant must file duplicate certified copies of same. Statements based upon tradition cannot be considered.

The numbers below refer to the corresponding generations

STATE VOLUME AND PAGE OF REFERENCES TO AUTHORITIES OR GIVE CERTIFICATE OF UNPUBLISHED AUTHORITY

ANCESTRY

1. Birth Certificate
2. Birth and Marriage Certificates
3. Birth, Death and Marriage Certificates
4. Death and Marriage Certif.; also the McCutcheon Family, Mc Tripp, Brown, CritchettII, pub.1931Commonwealth Print Co.
5. History of Stanstead Co., Canada by pgs 143-154 B.F.Hubbard, pgs 179,180 etc.
6. Same Pub. as for 4&5, also McClary Sketch covering4 generat ons of McClarys; APV McClary Sketch, N.Y. Pub. Lib.
7. Hist of Nottinghamand Deerfield, N.H. by E.C.Cogswell pgs 217 (McClary), p. 219-230 (McGrillis Family)
8.
9.
10.
11.

Figure 81

A list of references provided on a membership application for the National Society of New England Women.

Internet Sites of Interest:

Daughters of the American Revolution, National Society (DAR)
http://www.chesapeake.net/DAR/

Daughters of Union Veterans of the Civil War (DUV)
http://suvcw.org/duv.htm

Genealogy Society of Mayflower Descendants
http://members.aol.com/calebj/mayflower.html

Order of Descendants of Ancient Planters
http://tyner.simplenet.com/PLANTERS.HTM

Sons and Daughters of the Pilgrims, National Society
http://www.nssdp.org

Sons of the American Revolution, National Society
http://www.sar.org/

Sons of Confederate Veterans
http://scv.org

Sons of Union Veterans of the Civil War
http://suvcw.org/

United Daughters of the Confederacy (UDC)
http://www.hqudc.org/

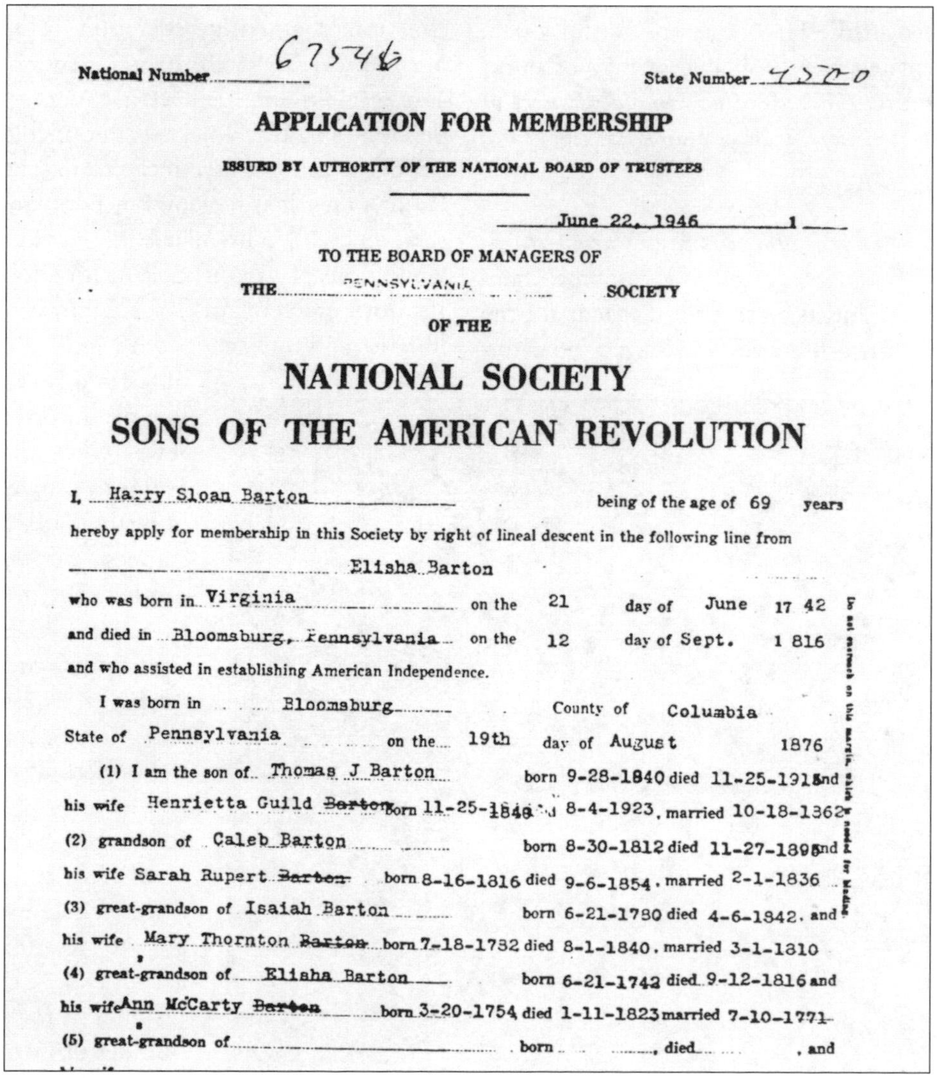

National Number 67546 State Number 4520

APPLICATION FOR MEMBERSHIP

ISSUED BY AUTHORITY OF THE NATIONAL BOARD OF TRUSTEES

June 22, 1946

TO THE BOARD OF MANAGERS OF

THE PENNSYLVANIA SOCIETY

OF THE

NATIONAL SOCIETY

SONS OF THE AMERICAN REVOLUTION

I, Harry Sloan Barton being of the age of 69 years hereby apply for membership in this Society by right of lineal descent in the following line from Elisha Barton

who was born in Virginia on the 21 day of June 1742

and died in Bloomsburg, Pennsylvania on the 12 day of Sept. 1816

and who assisted in establishing American Independence.

I was born in Bloomsburg County of Columbia

State of Pennsylvania on the 19th day of August 1876

(1) I am the son of Thomas J Barton born 9-28-1840 died 11-25-1918 and

his wife Henrietta Guild ~~Barton~~ born 11-25-1848 died 8-4-1923, married 10-18-1862

(2) grandson of Caleb Barton born 8-30-1812 died 11-27-1898 and

his wife Sarah Rupert ~~Barton~~ born 8-16-1816 died 9-6-1854, married 2-1-1836

(3) great-grandson of Isaiah Barton born 6-21-1780 died 4-6-1842, and

his wife Mary Thornton ~~Barton~~ born 7-18-1782 died 8-1-1840, married 3-1-1810

(4) great-grandson of Elisha Barton born 6-21-1742 died 9-12-1816 and

his wife Ann McCarty ~~Barton~~ born 3-20-1754 died 1-11-1823 married 7-10-1771

(5) great-grandson of ... born ..., died ..., and

Do not write on this margin, which is needed for binding

Figure 82

An application for membership submitted to the Pennsylvania Society of the National Society Sons of the American Revolution.

Holocaust Records

As a result of the efforts to ensure that the millions of Jews killed in the Holocaust are not forgotten, survivors have created some valuable sources of information. These sources include the *National Registry of Jewish Holocaust Survivors*, yizkor books, and pages of testimony.

The *National Registry of Jewish Holocaust Survivors* lists approximately 80,000 names of survivors and their families residing in the United States and Canada and can be found in many major libraries. (To have a letter for-warded to a survivor listed in the register, write to: American Gathering/Federation of Jewish Holocaust Survivors, 122 W. 30th St., New York, NY 10001.) Yizkor books offer detailed accounts of towns that were devastated by the Holocaust and include detailed histories of the community, stories from survivors about their families as well as remembrances of families that had no survivors, and a list of all the victims from the town. Collections of yizkor books can be found at the YIVO Institute of New York, the Library of Congress, and libraries and universities with Judaica collections. Pages of testimony can provide the following information on many Jews who died during the Holocaust: name; place and year of birth; place, date, and circumstances of death; name of mother, father, and spouse; and in some cases, information about children. For information on pages of testimony, write to: Yad Vashem, P.O. Box 3477, 91034 Jerusalem, Israel.

Recent efforts by Holocaust survivors to track down family assets seized by the Nazi party and to reclaim dormant bank accounts have created additional resources for researchers. A number of institutions have created lists of such accounts that have remained unclaimed since the end of World War II, some

Figure 83
A memorial garden to the victims of the holocaust on the grounds of Dachau prizon camp near Munich, Germany. (Courtesy of Matthew Wright)

including the foreign addresses of account holders. The Web site for the Simon Weisenthal Center (see Internet Sites of Interest below) contains a searchable database of lists created by several Swiss, Swedish, French, and British banks, as well as some insurance companies.

Selected Readings:

Guzik, Estelle M., ed. *Genealogical Resources in the New York Metropolitan Area*. New York: Jewish Genealogical Society, 1989. (This guide to agencies in New York and New Jersey provides information on specific records, hours of operations, finding aids, fees, and restrictions. Appendixes include bibliography and location of yizkor books, vital record application forms, Soundex codes, U.S. city directories, available foreign telephone directories, and Jewish cemeteries).

Klarefeld, Serge. *Memorial to Jews Deported From France*. New York: Klarefeld Foundation, 1983. (Contains information about some 70,000 Jews deported from France to concentration camps, primarily Auschwitz. Gives name, birth date, and place of birth.)

Mokotoff, Gary, and Sallyann Amdur Sack. *Where Once We Walked: A Guide to the Jewish Communities Destroyed in the Holocaust*. Teaneck, N.J.: Avotaynu, 1991.

Mokotoff, Gary. *How to Document Victims and Locate Survivors of the Holocaust*. Bergenfield, N.J.: Avotaynu, 1995.

_____. "Jewish-American Family History." *The Source: A Guidebook of American Genealogy*. Salt Lake City: Ancestry, 1997.

Sack, Sallyann Amdur. *A Guide to Jewish Genealogical Research in Israel*. Bergenfield, N.J.: Avotaynu, 1995. (A detailed guide to the accessibility and holdings of each agency. Appendixes include yizkor books and landsmanshaftn listed at Yad Vashem Library and a list of towns represented at the 1981 World Gathering of Holocaust Survivors)

Internet Sites of Interest:

AMCHA
Israeli Centers for Holocaust Survivors and the Second Generation
http://www.amcha.org/

Avotaynu, Inc.
http://www.avotaynu.com

Beit Theresienstadt
http://www.cet.ac.il/terezin/ndx_e.htm

Center for Jewish History
http://www.cjh.org/

International Association of Jewish Genealogical Societies
http://www1.jewishgen.org/ajgs/

JewishGen
http://www.jewishgen.org

Office of Survivor Affairs
United States Holocaust Memorial Museum
http://www.ushmm.org/%7Eosa/index.htm

Simon Wiesenthal Center
http://www.wiesenthal.com/index.html

Holocaust Assets
Swiss, Swedish, French and British bank and insurance accounts
http://www.wiesenthal.com/swiss/index.html

United States Holocaust Memorial Museum
http://www.ushmm.org/

YIVO Institute for Jewish Research
http://www.baruch.cuny.edu/yivo/

Home Sources

Typically, the best place to begin family history research is in the home. Home sources often provide a link to past generations that cannot be found elsewhere. Most families keep copies of important documents such as birth, marriage and death certificates, wills, military papers, and tax returns. Oftentimes these documents are boxed up and passed along with other belongings when a family member dies. These records and other mementos, when given careful consideration, can lead a researcher to numerous other sources.

Family Bibles, photographs, personal papers, diaries, scrapbooks, newspaper clippings, or engraved pieces of jewelry can all hold clues such as names, significant dates and events, or where the family resided during a particular period of time.

Whenever possible, relatives should be contacted and asked if they might have genealogical records. An aunt may be able to put a story with a picture, or a distant cousin may be reminded of a box of neglected papers sitting in an attic.

See also *Artifacts* and *Diaries and Journals*.

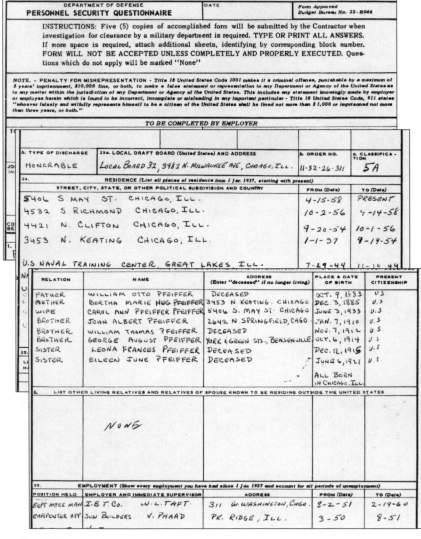

Figure 84

Documents found in the home can contain many important clues. This personnel security form leads a researcher to several other record sources in addition to providing the names, addresses, and birth information for numerous relatives.

Selected Readings:

Frisch-Ripley, Karen. *Unlocking the Secrets in Old Photographs*. Salt Lake City: Ancestry, 1992.

Szucs, Loretto Dennis and Sandra Hargreaves Luebking, eds. *The Source: A Guidebook of American Genealogy*. Rev. ed. Salt Lake City: Ancestry, 1997.

Kyvig, David E., and Myron A. Marty. *Nearby History: Exploring the Past Around You*. Nashville: American Association for State and Local History, 1982.

Figure 85

A student ID card provides a date of birth and a home address, and leads to another potential source of information at the University of Notre Dame.

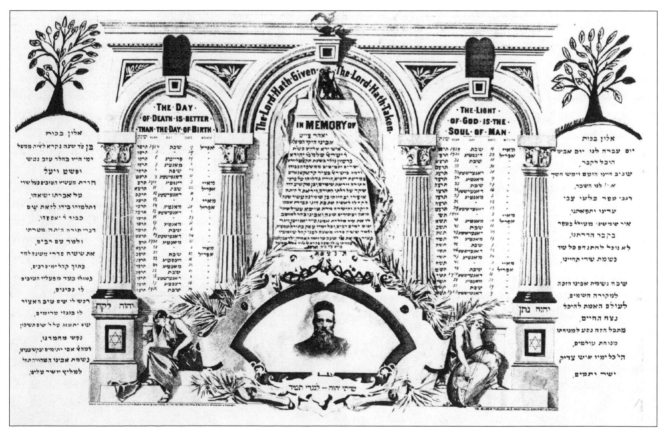

Figure 86

This unusually ornate, fifty-year yahrzeit calendar from the turn of the century contains information of genealogical significance. The middle section, which is a eulogy to the deceased, shows his name was Israil Solomon, son of Yehudah Gershon. He was born in 1838 (no specific date given) in Krakanava, Russia, which today is Krekenava, Lithuania. It ends with his death date reckoned on the Hebrew calendar as the 24th day of Nisan, 5663, equivalent to April 21, 1903. The columns on each side give the month, day, and year, reckoned by the secular calendar, for the yahrzeit dates; the left side for the years 1904-28, the right side, the years 1929-50. The calendar was found in an attic of a home in upper New York State, which had been abandoned by the previous owner. (Courtesy of Gary Mokotoff)

Homestead Records

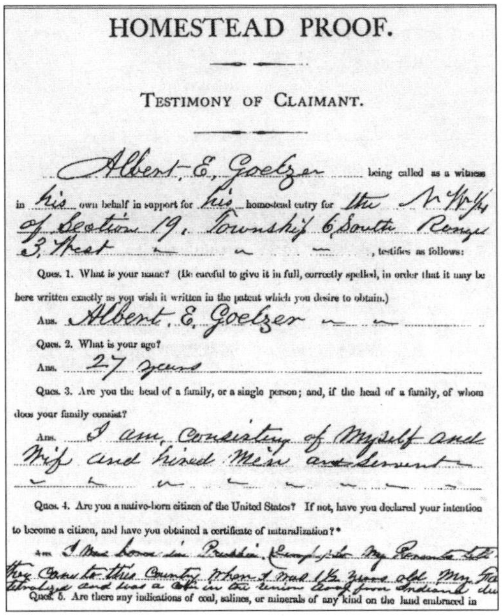

HOMESTEAD PROOF.

TESTIMONY OF CLAIMANT.

Figure 87

This homestead proof contains valuable biographical information, as well as clues to other potential record sources with the references to the claimant's father's naturalization and his own service in the Union Army during the Civil War.

Following the Homestead Act of 1862, approximately 285 million acres of public land was granted to individuals through various subsequent acts. As is the case with most bureaucratic processes, the transfer of land required a small mountain of paperwork. The resulting data, which is contained in homestead files, includes the homestead application and final proof of homesteading, and it is rich in genealogical information.

Nearly 2 million claims were filed (most between 1863 and 1917), and although more than 1,185,000 of the entries were never patented, files were created for each one. After selecting a piece of land, individuals would file a claim through the local land office or directly at the General Land Office (GLO) in Washington, D.C. and take an oath that they were at least twenty-one years old or married and the head of a family. The claimant was also required to provide information about citizenship, including the date and place of naturalization, if applicable.

For the remaining claims—an estimated 783,000—that were patented, a homestead final certificate file was created. Usually included in that file are the homestead application and final proof documents, which provide the claimant's name, age, post office address, description of the tract and the house, date of the establishment of residence, number and relationship of family members, status of citizenship (a copy of naturalization papers may be included), crops, acres under cultivation, and testimony of witnesses.

Homestead records, including claims that were not completed, are available through the National Archives and Records Administration. In some cases, clues as to why the claim was not completed can be found.

Selected Readings:

Hone, E. Wade. *Land and Property Research in the United States*. Salt Lake City: Ancestry, 1997.

Luebking, Sandra Hargreaves. "Research in Land and Tax Records." *The Source: A Guidebook of American Genealogy*. Rev. ed. Salt Lake City: Ancestry, 1997.

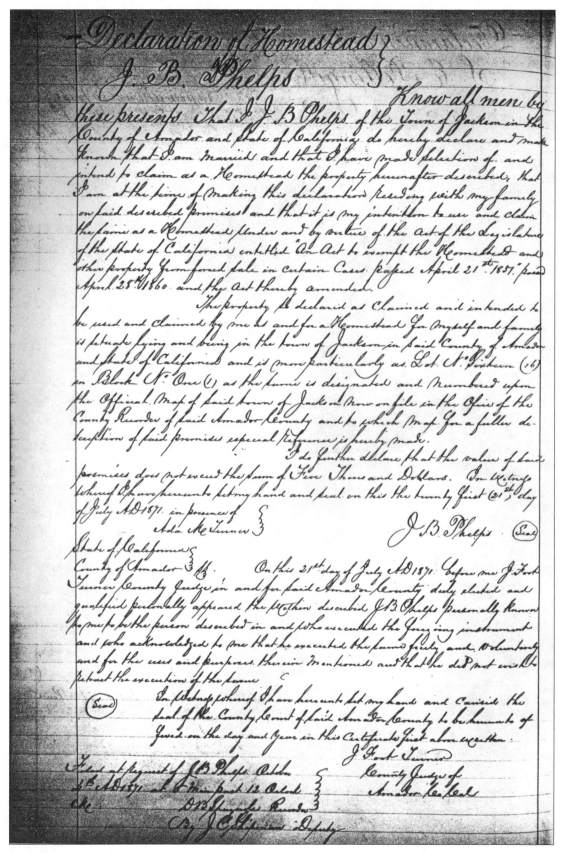

Figure 88

A declaration of homestead, filed in Amador County, California on 21 July 1871 by J. B. Phelps, provides a legal description of the property.

Hospital Records

Hospital registers and early death records are valuable sources of information. Most will include the patient's name, age, birthplace, date of entry or admission, reason for hospitalization, and the date of discharge or death.

While they may be difficult to obtain due to confidentiality requirements, some hospitals will release records with proper identification and proof of relationship. The Genealogical Society of Utah has microfilmed some nineteenth century records.

Selected Readings:

Clay, Robert Y. "Patients in the Hospital at Williamsburg, 1800–37." *Virginia Genealogist* 24 (1980): 23–28, 90–94.

Figure 89
A horse-drawn ambulance in Brooklyn, New York, ca. 1900.

Gilliam, Charles Edgar. "Mount Malado." *Tyler's Quarterly* 20 (1938–39): 138–42, 250. (Virginia's earliest hospital)

New York Down-State Medical Center. *History of Long Island College Hospital: Alumni Association Highlights, 1880–1955 and Biographies of Graduates, 1900–1955.* New York: New York Alumni Association, 1961.

Johns, Frank S., and Anne Page. "Chimborazo Hospital and J. B. McCaw, Surgeon in Chief." *Virginia Magazine of History and Biography* 62 (1954): 190–200. (Provides information on Revolutionary War hospitals)

Kelner, Joseph. "Examination of Hospital Records." *Case and Comment* 84 (1979): 51–54. (Describes access to modern records)

Larrabee, Eric. *The Benevolent and Necessary Institution: New York Hospital, 1771–1971.* Garden City, N.Y.: Doubleday, 1971.

Uppedegraff, Marie. *The Story of Stamford Hospital, 1896–1971.* Stamford, Conn.: Stamford Hospital, 1971.

Williams, William H. "The Industrious Poor and the Founding of the Pennsylvania Hospital." *Pennsylvania Magazine of History and Biography* 97 (1973): 431–43.

RETURN OF THE HOSPITAL CORPS

at Field Hospital No.3, Walter Reed General Hospital, Takoma Park, D.C.

(Here insert name of post or station, and department; or, in the field, name of camp and nearest town, also the field army, division, and regiment or command to which attached)

for the period from November 30th., 1911 , to January 31st., 1912.

Enlisted strength of command on last day of period: 137.

LINEAL NO. BY GRADES (Designate colored men by a "C")	NAMES (SURNAMES FIRST) (See Instruction 2)	RANK (Use ditto marks when applicable)	NO. OF HOURS OF INSTRUCTION DURING PERIOD	REMARKS
1	Wood, Richard A.	Sgt.1.Cl.		In general charge. Single.
2	Anderson, Cecil H.	"		Asst.Instructor in Materia Medica and Pharmacy. In charge of instruction records. Married.
3	Donovan, Thomas F.	"		In charge of property. Asst.Instructor in clerical work. Single.
1	Hester, Thomas G.	Sergeant		Asst.Instructor in Anatomy and Physiology and company drills.
2	Burke, Edmund	"		Asst.Instructor in First Aid and Diet Cooking and Company Drills. Relieved from duty as Mess Sergeant Jan.9th.1912 per Ord.#10, Field Hosp.No.3.Jan.8,1912
3	Chamberlin, Frank W.	"		Asst.Instructor in Equitation,Packing and Driving and Identification Work, and company drills.
4	Mitchell, Edward H.	"		Asst.Instructor in Nursing and Ward Management and company drills. Absent sick at Ft.Myer,Va.,from Dec.19th.,1911 to Jan.8th.,1912, In line of duty.
5	Abernethy, Welborn B.	"		Appointed Mess Sergeant Jan.10th. 1912 per Ord.#10.Field Hosp.No.3.

Figure 90
U.S. Army Hospital Corps Return, 1911-12. (Courtesy of National Archives)

Immigrant Letters

Letters from people who had emigrated to America were often treasured by those who remained in their homelands. In days before any means of rapid communication, those left behind were particularly eager to read firsthand accounts of life in the New World. Often, letters were the last remaining link with family and friends who would never be seen again.

Some letters have been saved and printed in magazines, newspapers, and books. Many letters that were saved by families are finding their way into print on a regular basis. The possibility that some letters may be in the care of distant cousins should not be overlooked. While a researcher may have no luck finding a letter written by family members, a letter written by someone of the same ethnic group or the same locality, religion, or time period can often tell more about what an ancestor saw and felt than any other source. Not all printed immigrant letters are easily found, for a great number are hidden among the titles of thousands of books and periodicals on ethnic origins and immigration. The *Periodical Source Index* (*PERSI*) and the *National Union Catalog of Manuscript Collections* (NUCMC) may be helpful in narrowing the search.

See also *National Union Catalog of Manuscript Collections (NUCMC)* and *PERSI*.

Selected Readings:

Barkai, Avraham. Branching Out: German Jewish Immigration to the United States, 1820–1914. New York: Holmes and Meier, 1984.

Barton, H. Arnold. *Letters from the Promised Land: Swedes in America, 1840–1914*. Minneapolis: University of Minnesota Press, 1975.

Blegen, Theodore C. *Land of Their Choice: The Immigrants Write Home*. St. Paul, Minn., 1955.

Conway, Alan, ed. *The Welsh in America: Letters from the Immigrants*. St. Paul, Minn., 1961.

Emerson, Everett, ed. *Letters from New England: The Massachusetts Bay Colony, 1629–1638*. Amherst, Mass., 1976.

Erickson, Charlotte. *Invisible Immigrants: The Adaptation of English and Scottish Immigrants in Nineteenth-Century America*. Coral Gables: University of Miami Press, 1972.

Hale, Frederick, ed. *Danes in North America*. Seattle, 1984.

Kamphoefner, Walter D., et al. *News from the Land of Freedom: German Immigrants Write Home*. Ithaca, N.Y.: Cornell University Press, 1991.

Newman, George Frederick. *Letters from Our Palatine Ancestors, 1644–1689*. Hershey, Pa.: Gary T. Hawbaker, 1984.

Peyser, Joseph L. *Letters from New France: The Upper Country*. Urbana: University of Ill. Press, 1992.

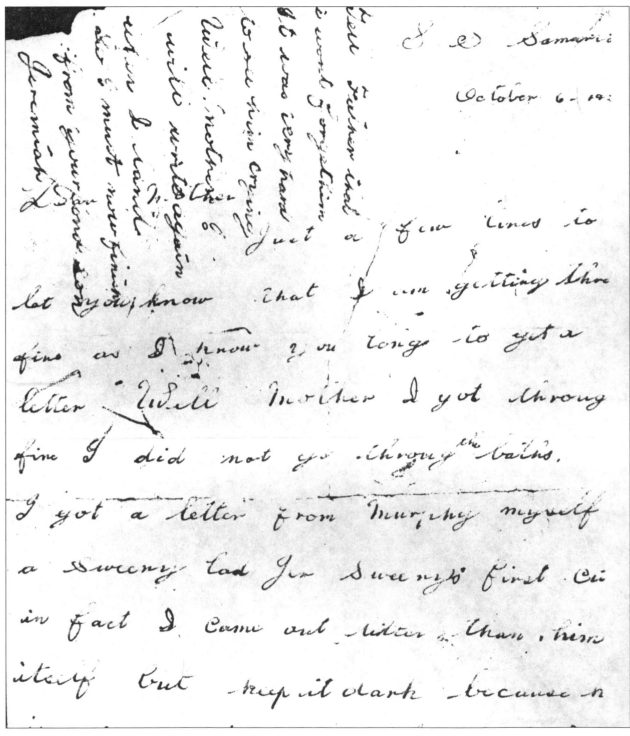

Figure 91
A portion of a letter from Jeremiah Curtin. (Courtesy of Gerry Curtin Ganley)

Smith, Clifford Neal. *Letters Home: Genealogical and Family Historical Data on Nineteenth-Century German Settlers in Australia, Bermuda, Brazil, Canada, and the United States.* McNeal, Ariz.: Westland Publishing, 1988.

Zempel, S. *In Their Own Words: Letters from Norwegian Immigrants.* St. Paul: University of Minnesota Press, 1991.

Indentured Servants

Original seaport cities of the American colonies thrived on a merchant-dominated, laborer-scarce economy of trade relations. In ports such as Boston, New York, Philadelphia, Baltimore, Charleston, Savannah, and New Orleans, merchants and sea captains became wealthy trading sugar, cotton, tobacco, lumber, and slaves. The English system of indentured servitude was adopted to populate the colonies and to provide labor. Emigrants who could not afford to pay for their journey to the New World would sell themselves into service for a specific period of time in return for the cost of passage and provisions. They would sometimes negotiate a contract with an emigrant agent that would be carried with them to be sold to employers when they arrived. Others would auction themselves off to the highest bidder upon arrival. (The latter group is also referred to as "redemptioners.") Disadvantaged children were also candidates for indenture. Children as young as eighteen months were bound out for periods that would often last until they reached adulthood.

The indenture business was extensive and included a high number of English, German, and Irish people who came to America. States such as Pennsylvania and Maryland used indentured servants as a primary means of development.

A few of these records have been published, such as those noted in Coldham's lists (see the selected readings that follow in this section); others are still hidden in their original form, mostly in archives and historical collections.

Selected Readings:

Coldham, Peter Wilson. *The Complete Book of Emigrants 1607–1660: A Comprehensive Listing Compiled from English Public Records of Those Who Took Ship to the Americas for Political, Religious, and Economic Reasons; of Those Who Were Deported for Vagrancy, Roguery, or Non-Conformity; and Those Who Were Sold to Labour in the New Colonies.* Baltimore: Genealogical Publishing Co., 1987. [1219.4] {30,000}

_____. *The Complete Book of Emigrants, 1661–1699.* Baltimore: Genealogical Publishing Co., 1990. [——] {30,000}

_____. *The Complete Book of Emigrants, 1700–1750.* Baltimore: Genealogical Publishing Co., 1992. [——] {25,000}

_____. *The Complete Book of Emigrants, 1751–1776.* Baltimore: Genealogical Publishing Co., 1993. [——] {15,000}

_____. *The Complete Book of Emigrants in Bondage, 1614–1755.* Baltimore: Genealogical Publishing Co., 1988. Supplement, 1993. [——]{53,000} (Most of these names were published earlier in the nine volumes of *Bonded Passengers to America* and two volumes of *English Convicts in Colonial America*, but this does include some new records)

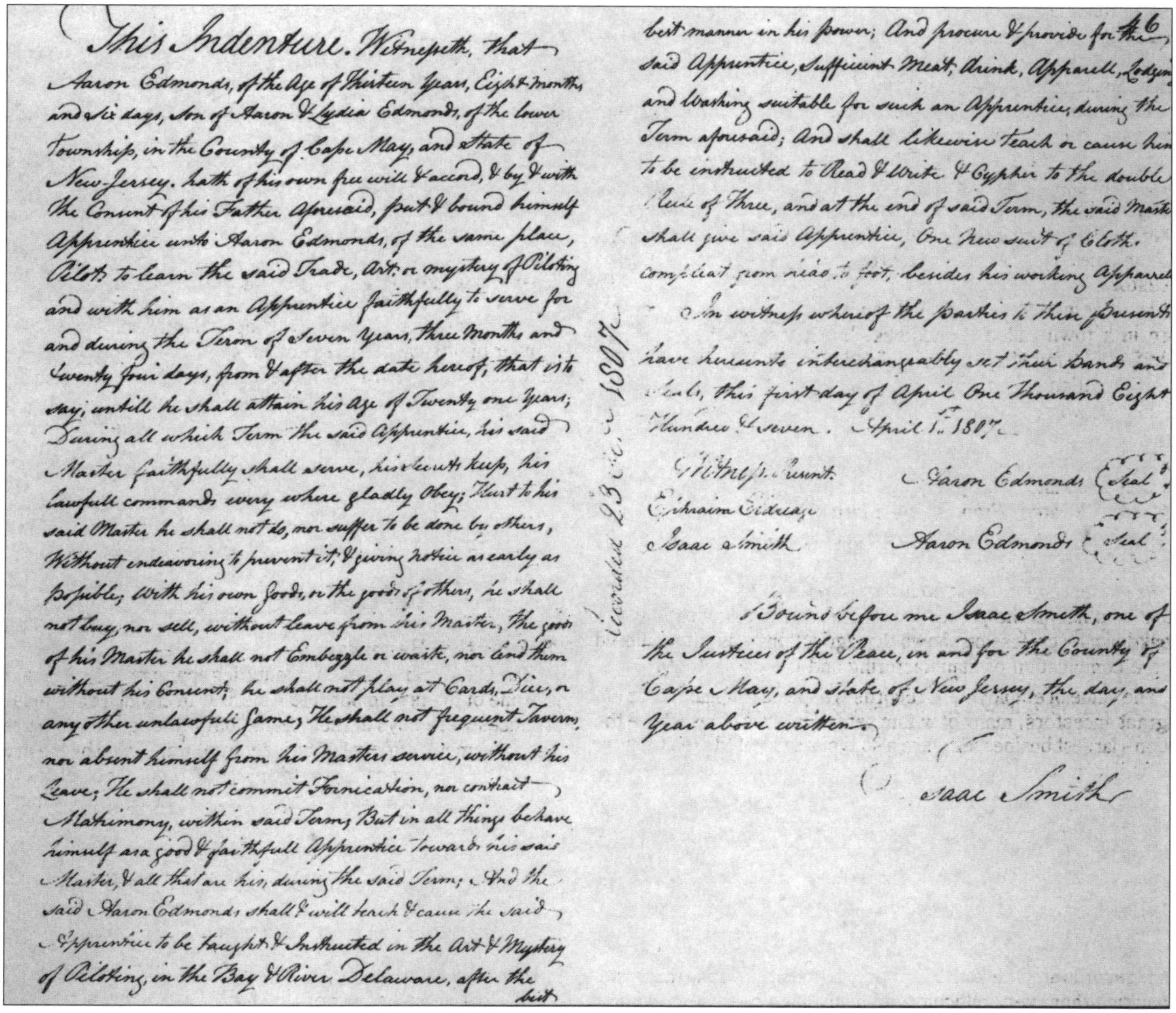

This Indenture. Witnesseth, that
Aaron Edmonds, of the Age of Thirteen Years, Eight months
and six days, Son of Aaron & Lydia Edmonds, of the lower
Townships, in the County of Cape May, and State of
New-Jersey. hath of his own free will & accord, & by & with
the Consent of his Father aforesaid, put & bound himself
Apprentice unto Aaron Edmonds, of the same place,
Pilot, to learn the said Trade, Art or mystery of Piloting
and with him as an Apprentice faithfully to serve for
and during the Term of Seven Years, three Months and
twenty four days, from & after the date hereof, that is to
say; untill he shall attain his Age of Twenty one Years;
During all which Term the said Apprentice, his said
Master faithfully shall serve, his secrets keep, his
lawfull commands every where gladly Obey; Hurt to his
said Master he shall not do, nor suffer to be done by others,
Without endeavoring to prevent it, & giving notice as early as
possible; With his own goods, or the goods of others, he shall
not buy, nor sell, without leave from his Master, the goods
of his Master he shall not Embezzle or waste, nor lend them
without his Consent; he shall not play at Cards, Dice, or
any other unlawfull Game, He shall not frequent Taverns,
nor absent himself from his Masters service, without his
Leave; He shall not commit Fornication, nor contract
Matrimony, within said Term; But in all things behave
himself as a good & faithfull Apprentice towards his said
Master, & all that are his, during the said Term; And the
said Aaron Edmonds shall & will teach & cause the said
Apprentice to be taught & Instructed in the Art & Mystery
of Piloting, in the Bay & River Delaware, after the
best

Recorded 23 Oct 1807

best manner in his power; And procure & provide for the 46
said Apprentice, Sufficient Meat, drink, Apparell, Lodging
and Washing suitable for such an Apprentice, during the
Term aforesaid; And shall likewise teach or cause him
to be instructed to Read & Write & Cypher to the double
Rule of Three, and at the end of said Term, the said Master
shall give said Apprentice, One new suit of Cloth,
compleat from head to foot, besides his working Apparrell

In witness whereof the parties to these Presents
have hereunto interchangeably set their hands and
Seals, this first day of April One Thousand Eight
Hundred & seven. April 1st 1807.

Witness Present — Aaron Edmonds {Seal}
Ephraim Eldredge
Isaac Smith — Aaron Edmonds {Seal}

Bound before me Isaac Smith, one of
the Justices of the Peace, in and for the County of
Cape May, and State of New Jersey, the day and
Year above written

Isaac Smith

Figure 92

Indenture of Aaron Edmonds to Aaron Edmonds, 23 October 1807, Port of Philadelphia, Pensssylvania. (Courtesy of Genealogical Society of Utah)

Daniels, Roger. *Coming to America: A History of Immigration and Ethnicity in American Life.* New York: Harper Collins, 1990.

Diffenderffer, Frank R. *The German Immigration Into Pennsylvania Through the Port of Philadelphia form 1700 to 1775, and the Redemptioners. 1900.* Reprint. Baltimore: Genealogical Publishing Co., 1988. (Mostly background history; five pages have lists)

Drudy, P. J. *Irish Studies. Vol. 4. The Irish in America: Emigration, Assimilation and Impact.* London: Cambridge University Press, 1985.

Smith, Abbot Emerson. *Colonists in Bondage: White Servitude and Convict Labor in America, 1607–1776.* New York: 1947.

Wehmann, Howard H. comp. *A Guide to Pre-Federal Records in the National Archives.* Revised by Benjamin L. DeWhitt. Washington, D.C.: National Archives Trust Fund Board, 1989.

Internet Site of Interest:

Genealogy Club of Albuquerque, "Indentured Servants." Karen Millian
http://www.abqgen.swnet.com/article8.htm

Indian (Native American) Records

The frequent interaction of the United States government with American Indian tribes has created a significant amount of material for individuals researching Native American heritage. Records relating to the removal of tribes to the West vary according to the tribe, with some including census rolls and emigration lists dating from the early to mid–1800s and others containing miscellaneous muster rolls from the 1830s. Enrollment records created by the Dawes Commission in allotting land to the Cherokee, Choctaw, Chickasaw, Creek, and Seminole tribes consist of the application filed, the tribal rolls from various nations that were used for identification, birth and death affidavits, the approved roll that included the name, age, sex, degree of blood, and the number of the enrollment card for those whom the commission decided were entitled to enrollment. Annual census rolls, required by an act passed in 1884, typically include an individual's Indian and/or English name, roll number, age or date of birth, sex, and relationship to the head of family, with the addition of degree of blood, marital status, ward status, and place of residence for rolls taken after 1929. A thorough description of these and many other records available can be found in the chapter "Tracking Native American Family History," by Curt B. Witcher and George J. Nixon, in *The Source: A Guidebook of American Genealogy*. Rev. ed. (Salt Lake City: Ancestry, 1997).

As most records are grouped according to tribe, it is extremely important to identify the tribe to which an ancestor belonged. Many of the records created by the Bureau of Indian Affairs are available on microfilm through the National Archives. Microfilm copies of the records of the Dawes Commission are also available at

Figure 93

The programs of the Bureau of Indian Affairs (BIA) have had an impact on virtually every phase of tribal development. The sampling shown are from the BIA records at the National Archives - Southwest Region, Fort Worth.

the Oklahoma Historical Society, the University of Oklahoma in Norman, Oklahoma, and the Family History Library and its centers. These same records are available online at <www.ancestry.com>. Records from Indian schools, whether run by a mission or the Bureau of Indian Affairs, can also provide important details.

Selected Readings:

Bantin, Philip C. *Guide to Catholic Indian Mission and School Records in Midwest Repositories*. Milwaukee: Marquette University Libraries, Department of Special Collections and University Archives, 1984.

Carter, Kent. *The Dawes Commission and the Allotment of the Five Civilized Tribes, 1893–1914*. Salt Lake City: Ancestry, 1999.

DEPARTMENT OF THE INTERIOR.
COMMISSION TO THE FIVE CIVILIZED TRIBES.
MUSKOGEE, I.T., FEBUARY 12th, 1901.

IN THE MATTER OF THE APPLICATION OF   Ephraim Thorne for the enrollment of himself and children as citizens of the Cherokee Nation,
and he being sworn and examined by Commissioner, C. R. Breckinridge,
testified as follows;

Q Give me your full name?   A Ephraim Thorne.
Q How old are you Mr. Thorne?   A About forty nine.
Q What is your Postoffice? A Wagoner.
Q In what district do you live?   A Tahlequah.
Q Who is it you want to enroll; yourself and family? A
A Just myself and three children.
Q You do not apply for a wife? A No sir, she's dead.
Q Do you claim to be a Cherokee by blood? A Yes sir.
Q How long have you lived in the Cherokee Nation?
A You might say all my life.
Q All your life? A Very near all my life.
Q Where were you living when not living in the Cherokee Nation?
A I was railroading from 1880 to 1890 from here to Denison and from
Denison to Muskogee, and part of the time I was stationed at Deni-
son; I was working in the shops.
Q Were you born in the Cherokee Nation? A Yes sir.
Q Give me the name of your father?   A Jacob Thorne.
Q Is he dead?   A Yes sir.
Q, Give me the name of your mother?   A Nancy Thorne.
Q Is she dead?   A Yes sir.
Q Give me the names of these children? A   The oldest one is Wil-
liam R Thorne.
Q How old is that child?   A He was born in 1888.
Q Twelve years old? A Yes sir.
Q The next child? A Louella.
Q How old is that child?   A Born in '91.
Q About nine years old? A Yes sir.
Q Next child?   A James Willard.
Q How old is that child?   A Born on the 10th of this last January.
Q Are these children all living now? A Yes sir.
Q Give me the name of the mother of these children?
A The mother of the two first ones was Carrie.
Q What was her name when you married her? A Manley.
Q When did you marry her? A I married her in '84.
Q Was she a white woman or a Cherokee? A Yes sir, she was a
white woman.
Q Were you ever married before you married that woman? A No sir.
Q Was she ever married before she married you? A No sir.
Q Is she dead? A yes sir.
Q When did she die? A She died in September of the Fall of 1895 I
believe.
Q Did you and she live together until she died?   A Yes sir.
   Q Have you a certificate of your marriage to her? A No sir, I
was married in Texas.
Q Married to her in 1884 in Texas? A Yes sir.
Q What were you doing in Texas?   A I was railroading.
Q You said you began railroading in 1880? A I began here in '80.
Q Where did she die?   A She died in the Cherokee Nation, Tahle-
quah District, five miles east of Tahlequah.
Q You had a license when you married her? A Yes sir.
Q Married by a preacher? A yes sir.
Q Give me the name of the mother of your youngest child, James
W.   A Why, Sallie.
Q What was her name when you married her? A McPhearson.
Q Is she living or dead? A She's dead.
Q When did she die? A She died the 11th of January; this last
January.
Q Was she a Cherokee or white woman? A She was a white woman.
Q Have you a certificate of your marriage to her? A Yes sir.

Figure 94

The first page of a three-page application of Ephraim Thorne for the enrollment of himself and his children as citizens of the Cherokee Nation. The record is among thousands like it at the National Archives
- Southwest Region. The database index of the applications is available at Ancestry.com.

Chepesiuk, Ron, and Arnold Shankman. *American Indian Archival Material: Guide to the Holdings in the Southeast*. Westport, Conn.: Greenwood Press, 1982.

Dewitt, Donald L. *American Indian Material in the Western History Collections, University of Oklahoma*. Norman: University of Oklahoma Press, 1990.

Hill, Edward, comp. *Guide to Records in the National Archives of the United States Relating to American Indians*. Washington, D.C.: National Archives and Records Administration, 1981.

Hogue, Arthur R. "The Record of an Indian School District, 1837–1844." *Indian Magazine of History* 48 (1952): 185–92.

Johnson, Steven L. *Guide to American Indian Documents in the Congressional Serial Set, 1817–1899*. A project of the Institute for the Development of Indian Law. New York: Clearwater Publishing Co., 1977.

Kirkham, E. Kay. *Our Native Americans and Their Records of Genealogical Value*. Logan, Utah: The Everton Publishers, 1980.

Swanton, John R. *The Indian Tribes of North America*. Smithsonian Institution, Bureau of American Ethnology, Bulletin 145. Washington, D.C.: Smithsonian Institution Press, 1984.

U.S. Department of the Interior Library. *Bibliographic and Historical Index of American Indians and Persons Involved in Indian Affairs*. 8 vols. Boston: G. K. Hall, 1966.

Witcher, Curt Bryan. *A Bibliography of Sources for Native American Family History*. Fort Wayne, Ind.: Allen County Public Library, 1988.

______, and George J. Nixon. "Tracking Native American Family History." *The Source: A Guidebook of American Genealogy*. Rev. ed. Ch. 14: 520–72. Salt Lake City: Ancestry, 1997.

Internet Sites of Interest:

Bureau of Indian Affairs—Genealogy Resources
http://www.doi.gov/bureau-indian-affairs.html

Native American Heritage Museum at Highland Mission
http://www.kshs.org/places/highland.htm

Index of Native American Resources on the Internet
http://www.hanksville.org/NAresources/

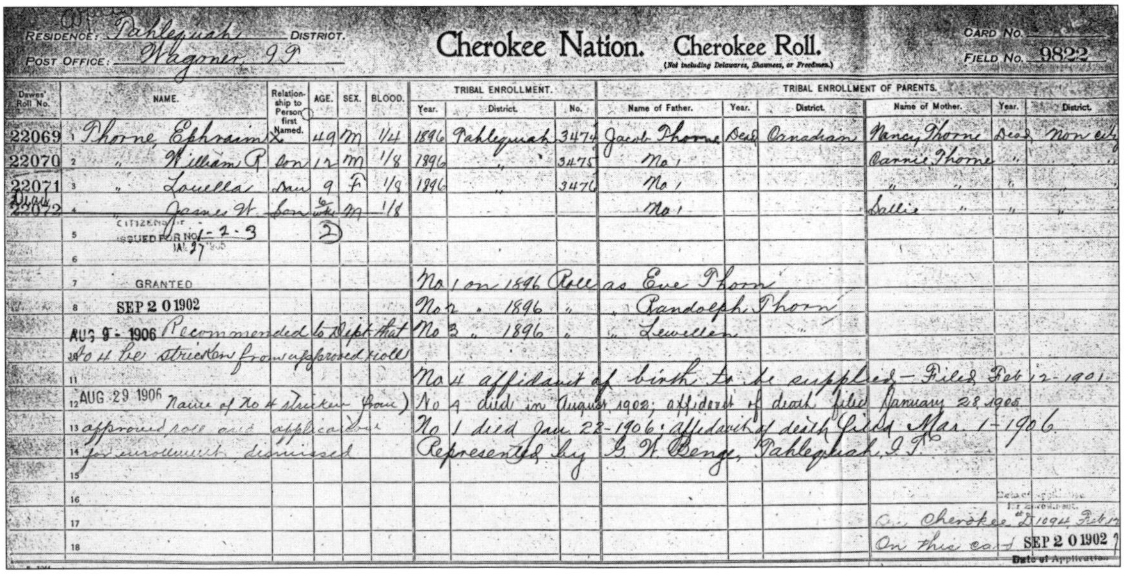

RESIDENCE: Tahlequah DISTRICT.
POST OFFICE: Wagoner, I.T.

Cherokee Nation. Cherokee Roll.
(Not including Delawares, Shawnees, or Freedmen.)

CARD NO.
FIELD NO. 9822

Dawes' Roll No.		NAME.	Relationship to Person first Named.	AGE.	SEX.	BLOOD.	Tribal Enrollment Year.	District.	No.	Name of Father.	Year.	District.	Name of Mother.	Year.	District.
22069	1	Thorne, Ephraim	X	49	M	1/4	1896	Tahlequah	3474	Jacob Thorne	Dead	Canadian	Nancy Thorne	Dead	Non citz
22070	2	" William R	Son	12	M	1/8	1896	"	3475	No 1			Carrie Thorne	"	"
22071	3	" Louella	Dau	9	F	1/8	1896	"	3476	No 1			" "	"	"
Died 22072	4	" James W.	Son	6 wks	M	1/8				No 1			Sallie "	"	"

CITIZENSHIP CERTIFICATE ISSUED FOR No 1-2-3 JAN 27 1903

GRANTED SEP 2 0 1902

AUG 9 - 1906 Recommended to Dept that No 4 be stricken from approved roll

AUG 29 1906 Name of No 4 stricken from approved roll and application for enrollment dismissed

No 1 on 1896 Roll as Eve Thorn
No 2 " 1896 " " Randolph Thorn
No 3 " 1896 " " Lewellen
No 4 affidavit of birth to be supplied—Filed Feb 12-1901
No 4 died in August 1902; affidavit of death filed January 28 1905
No 1 died Jan 22-1906: Affidavit of death filed Mar 1-1906
Represented by G. W. Benge, Tahlequah, I.T.

SEP 2 0 1902
Date of Application

Figure 95
A Dawes Census Card and Application for the family of Ephraim Thorne. The original record is at the National Archives - Southwest Region (Ft. Worth), and the database index to the collection is available through Ancestry.com on its Web site:<www.ancestry.com>.

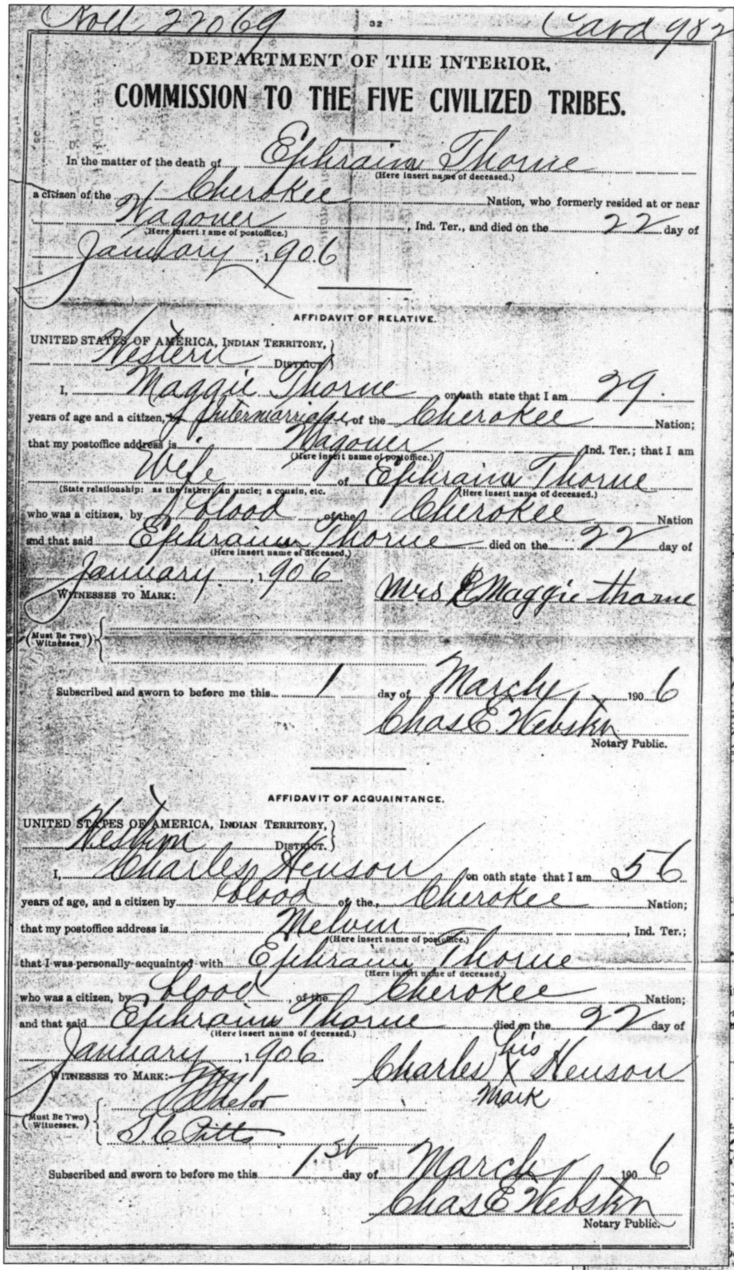

Roll 22069 Card 982

DEPARTMENT OF THE INTERIOR,

COMMISSION TO THE FIVE CIVILIZED TRIBES.

In the matter of the death of Ephraim Thorne (Here insert name of deceased.)
a citizen of the Cherokee Nation, who formerly resided at or near Wagoner (Here insert name of postoffice.), Ind. Ter., and died on the 22 day of January 1906

AFFIDAVIT OF RELATIVE.

UNITED STATES OF AMERICA, INDIAN TERRITORY, Western District.

I, Maggie Thorne on oath state that I am 29 years of age and a citizen, by intermarriage of the Cherokee Nation; that my postoffice address is Wagoner (Here insert name of postoffice.) Ind. Ter.; that I am Wife (State relationship: as the father, an uncle, a cousin, etc.) of Ephraim Thorne (Here insert name of deceased.) who was a citizen, by blood of the Cherokee Nation and that said Ephraim Thorne (Here insert name of deceased.) died on the 22 day of January 1906

WITNESSES TO MARK: (Must Be Two Witnesses.)

Mrs Maggie Thorne

Subscribed and sworn to before me this 1 day of March 1906

Chas E Webster
Notary Public.

AFFIDAVIT OF ACQUAINTANCE.

UNITED STATES OF AMERICA, INDIAN TERRITORY, Western District.

I, Charles Henson on oath state that I am 56 years of age, and a citizen by blood of the Cherokee Nation; that my postoffice address is Melvin (Here insert name of postoffice.), Ind. Ter.; that I was personally acquainted with Ephraim Thorne (Here insert name of deceased.) who was a citizen, by blood of the Cherokee Nation; and that said Ephraim Thorne (Here insert name of deceased.) died on the 22 day of January 1906

WITNESSES TO MARK: (Must Be Two Witnesses.)
[illegible]
S. C. Pitts

Charles his X mark Henson

Subscribed and sworn to before me this 1st day of March 1906

Chas E Webster
Notary Public.

Figure 96

This affidavit of Maggie Thorne, concerning the death of her husband, Ephraim Thorne, is among the records of the Five Civilized Tribes at the National Archives - Southwest Region.

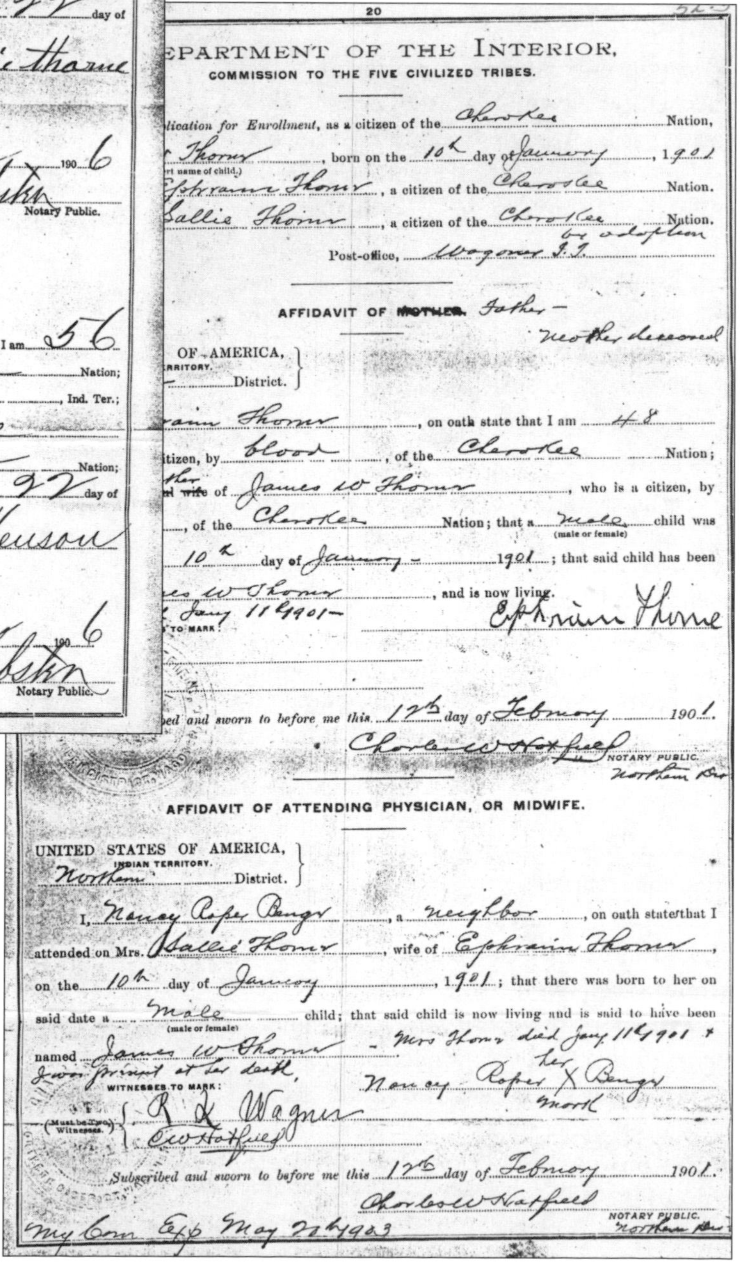

20

DEPARTMENT OF THE INTERIOR,

COMMISSION TO THE FIVE CIVILIZED TRIBES.

...lication for Enrollment, as a citizen of the Cherokee Nation, ... Thorne ..., born on the 10th day of January, 1901 ... Ephraim Thorne, a citizen of the Cherokee Nation. ... Sallie Thorne, a citizen of the Cherokee by adoption Nation.

Post-office, Wagoner I.T.

AFFIDAVIT OF ~~MOTHER~~ Father — mother deceased

... OF AMERICA, ... ERRITORY. ... District.

...raim Thorne, on oath state that I am 48 ... citizen, by blood, of the Cherokee Nation; ... father ... of James W Thorne, who is a citizen, by ..., of the Cherokee Nation; that a male (male or female) child was ... 10th day of January 1901; that said child has been ... James W Thorne, and is now living. ... Jany 11th 1901 —

Ephraim Thorne

...bed and sworn to before me this 12th day of February 1901.

Charles W Hatfield
NOTARY PUBLIC. Northern Dist

AFFIDAVIT OF ATTENDING PHYSICIAN, OR MIDWIFE.

UNITED STATES OF AMERICA, INDIAN TERRITORY. Northern District.

I, Nancy Roper Benge, a neighbor, on oath state that I attended on Mrs. Sallie Thorne, wife of Ephraim Thorne, on the 10th day of January, 1901; that there was born to her on said date a male (male or female) child; that said child is now living and is said to have been named James W Thorne — Mrs Thorne died Jany 11th 1901 + I was present at her death.

WITNESSES TO MARK: (Must be Two Witnesses.)
R L Wagner
C W Hatfield

Nancy Roper her X mark Benge

Subscribed and sworn to before me this 12th day of February 1901.

Charles W Hatfield
NOTARY PUBLIC. Northern Dist

My Com Exp May 22nd 1903

Figure 97

Application submitted to the Commission to the Five Civilized Tribes by James W. Thorne for enrollment as a citizen of the Cherokee Nation.

Insurance Records

Insurance companies traditionally keep extensive records of the people they insure. The most commonly issued policies include life, health, dental, automobile, property, unemployment, and disability.

Life insurance records, including applications, history cards, and renewal cards, are often kept by the issuing company for many years. To protect themselves legally, some companies even keep original applications permanently or microfilm them. Due to the nature of the insurance, such records may provide information regarding the policyholder's lifestyle, health, age, residence, and beneficiaries. By 1865, medical information on diseases or health conditions was included, and in 1889, Mutual Life began attaching a medical examination to the policy.

Insurance certificates, policies, or payment books held by a relative, or found in family files, may help determine the company that insured an ancestor. Fraternal organizations should not be overlooked in the search of family documents, since many, such as Woodmen of the World, offered insurance benefits to members. While most companies will not search their files for a genealogist, some may allow individuals to see them, provided they can prove a relationship to the policyholder in question.

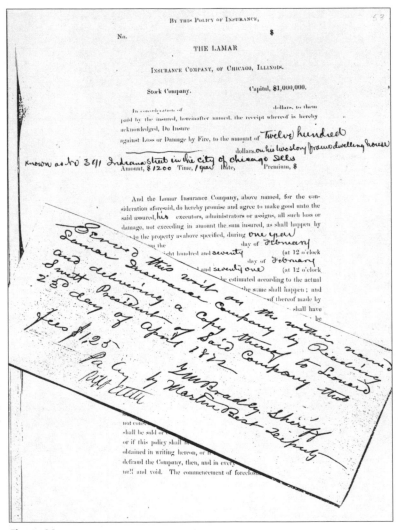

Figure 98

A property insurance policy found in a court file concerning an individual who lost his home in the Great Chicago Fire. It is not uncommon to find insurance records among court files. In fact, after the fire thousands of these were filed in Cook County court.

114

Insurance companies regularly rely on computer databases for obtaining past health and insurance histories on nearly everyone who has been insured. While every contemporary insurance company has safeguards in place to protect privacy rights, some will release information on older policies, especially those of the deceased. The addresses for two insurance reporting agencies follow.

Medical Information Bureau
Box 105 Essex Station
Boston, MA 02112

American Warranty Life Insurance Co.
1433 SW 6th Avenue
Portland, OR 97201

Selected Readings:

Clough, Shepard B. *A Century of American Life Insurance: A History of the Mutual Life Insurance Company of New York 1843–1943.* New York: Columbia University Press, 1946.

Directory of Health/Life Insurance Companies. Modesto, Calif.: HRS Geriatric Publishing, 1989.

Galles, Duane. "Using Life Insurance Records in Genealogical Research." *Genealogical Journal* 20 (1992): 156–71.

Larkin, Harold F. "Retention of Life Insurance Records." *American Archivist* 5 (April 1942): 93–99.

Copy of Application

"Application to The Travelers Insurance Company, Hartford, Connecticut.

What is your full name? Joseph R. Dennis
A. What is your age? 39 Date of birth? 8-10-01 Place of birth? U. S. A. (State or Country)
B. Color? W C. Height? 5 ft. 3½ in. D. Weight? 165 lbs.
E. Where do you reside? 1744 Ryder St. (Street and No.) Brooklyn (City or Town)
County of? Kings State of? N.Y.
F. Are you member of firm or employee? ~~(Member of firm?)~~ (Employee?) The Travelers Ins. Co.-
(Name of firm and business engaged in?)
Located at? 130 Clinton Street, Town of? Brooklyn State of? New York
G. State fully your occupation—position, nature of business engaged in and the duties performed? Attorney - Usual Duties For Travelers Insurance Co.
*H. To whom shall Policy be payable in case of death? {Name? Muriel D. Dennis Address? as above
{Age? Height? ft. in. Weight? lbs.
What is relationship of the beneficiary to you? Wife
I. Do your average weekly earnings exceed the aggregate single weekly indemnity payable under this Policy and all other similar policies now carried by you? Yes
J. What life, accident or health insurance have you in this Company? None except group Life Insurance.
What accident or health insurance have you in other companies or associations? None
Have you ever received indemnity for any injury or illness? No
K. Have you ever been declined or postponed for life, accident or health insurance? No
Have you ever made application for life, accident or health insurance upon which you have not been notified of the action thereon? No
Has any life, accident or health policy issued to you been canceled or has any renewal thereof been refused, by this or any other company or association? No
L. Have you in contemplation any special journey or hazardous undertaking? No
Do you ever engage in motorcycling or aeronautics? No
Do you own or operate an automobile? Operate.
M. Have any of your relatives ever been insane or had tuberculosis? No
N. Are your habits temperate? Yes
O. Are you maimed or deformed? No
Is your sight or hearing impaired? No
Have you ever had a hernia or worn a truss? No
Have you ever had any of the following: Epilepsy? No Syphilis? No
Vertigo or Dizziness? No Diabetes? No Tuberculosis? No
Mental disorder? No Disease of Brain or Nervous System? No
Disease of Tonsils, Nose or Throat? Tonsils removed abt. 1915 - complete recovery.
P. Have you within the past five years had medical or surgical advice or treatment or any departures from good health? If so, state when and what, and duration. No
(Month—Year) (Nature of Ailment) (Duration of Ailment)
Q. Have you ever had, or ever been advised to have, an operation? Tonsils removed about 1915 - Complete recovery.

Figure 99
An application for life insurance filed with the Travelers Insurance Company.

Internal Revenue Service Records, 1862-66

The Office of the Commissioner of Internal Revenue was established in the Department of the Treasury by an act of 1 July 1862 to help finance the Civil War. The agency, under the Commissioner, was known as the Bureau of Internal Revenue until 1953, and thereafter as the Internal Revenue Service (IRS). Wartime taxes were gradually abolished until 1883, when only taxes on liquor and tobacco existed. In addition to taxes on these commodities, the bureau began collecting a corporation income tax after 1909. With the adoption of the sixteenth amendment in 1913, the collection of income taxes became one of the bureau's principal functions.

The Internal Revenue Act of July 1862 was supposed "to provide Internal Revenue to support the Government and to pay Interest on the Public Debt." Monthly, annual, and special taxes were levied on personal property such as carriages and yachts, and on the receipts of certain businesses. These assessment lists date primarily from 1862 to 1873 and are arranged by collection districts, and therein, chronologically by tax period. The Civil War period tax lists are on microfilm and are the same lists held textually in some branches. They include two general lists, each in alphabetical order: (1) a list of names of all persons residing in the division who were liable for taxation, and (2) a list of names of all persons residing outside the division who were owners of property in the division. Under each person's name, the value, assessment, or enumeration of taxable income or items and the amount of duty or tax due is shown.

All regions of the National Archives hold IRS records, and while the date spans vary, some have been microfilmed. Microfilm copies of these Civil War period Internal Revenue Service tax records are available for the states of Alabama, Arkansas, California, Colorado, Delaware, Florida, Georgia, Idaho, Illinois, Kentucky, Louisiana, Maryland, Mississippi, Montana, North Carolina, Pennsylvania, South Carolina, Texas, Virginia, and West Virginia.

Selected Readings:

Fox, Cynthia G. "Income Tax Records of the Civil War Years." *Prologue.* (1986): 250.

Genealogical & Biographical Research: A Select Catalog of National Archives Microfilm Publications. Washington: National Archives Trust Fund Board, 1983. (A complete breakdown, by state and country, of each collection district, the type and dates of lists, and the microfilm roll number appears on pages 24–41)

Holdcamper, Forrest R., comp. *Records of the Internal Revenue Service.* Washington, D.C.: National Archives and Records Service, 1967.

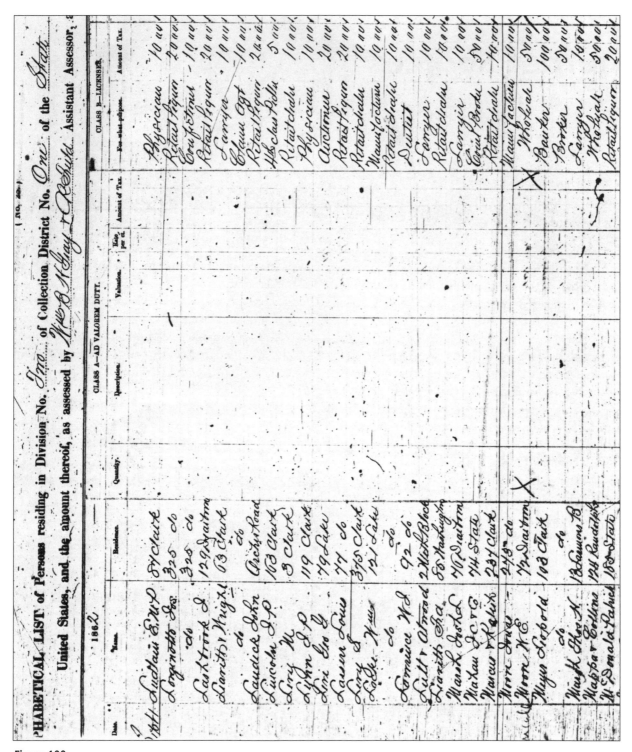

Figure 100

Internal Revenue Service records for Chicago, Illinois dated 1 September 1962, showing residents, their addresses, occupations, and the amount of tax assessed.

Internet Sources

The Internet is bringing a vast number of resources to the fingertips of the researcher who knows where to look. Resources available include thousands of searchable databases of names, such as the Social Security Death Index, the *Periodical Source Index* (*PERSI*), the *American Genealogical-Biographical Index* (*AGBI*), and the Bureau of Land Management's database of land patents. There are hundreds of thousands of Web sites devoted entirely to genealogical research. The Family History Department of The Church of Jesus Christ of Latter-day Saints has launched a site making available selected records from its holdings. With over 500 million names and new databases added everyday, Ancestry.com has one of the largest collection of material of use to family historians, with some not available elsewhere. Its AIS Census Index, for example, has made available a 35 million-name index to state and federal census records dating from 1790 through 1870. RootsWeb, located at <www.rootsweb.com>, is host to a list of over 500,000 surnames, Cyndi Howell's famous list of genealogical links, thousands of Web pages, and mailing lists. The Web site is also home to the USGenWeb Archives and a large portion of the USGenWeb pages.

The USGenWeb Project, a volunteer undertaking, is well on its way to meeting its goal to provide Internet Web sites for genealogical research in every county and every state of the United States. A typical county Web page contains useful tips, lists of online databases particular to the area, surname inquiries, descriptions of local libraries and their genealogical holdings, local genealogical and historical society addresses and links to its Web sites (if applicable), and a historical perspective of the county. The county pages are then grouped together at the state and national level. The success of the USGenWeb Project has now sparked the creation of the World GenWeb. While the content varies from region to region, the project is progressing steadily.

Figure 101

A search page from the Civil War Database on Ancestry.com.

118

Figure 102

The Land Patent page of the Bureau of Land Management opens the door to over five million title documents issued between 1820 and 1908 <http:www.glorecords.blm.gov>.

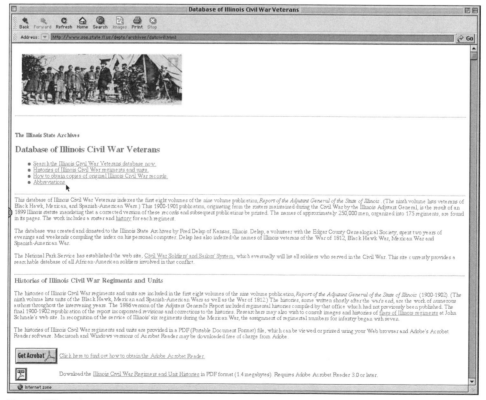

Figure 103

The names of approximately 250,000 Illinois Civil War Veterans appear on the pages of the Illinois State Archives Internet site at <http://www.sos.state.il.us/depts/archives/datcivil.html>.

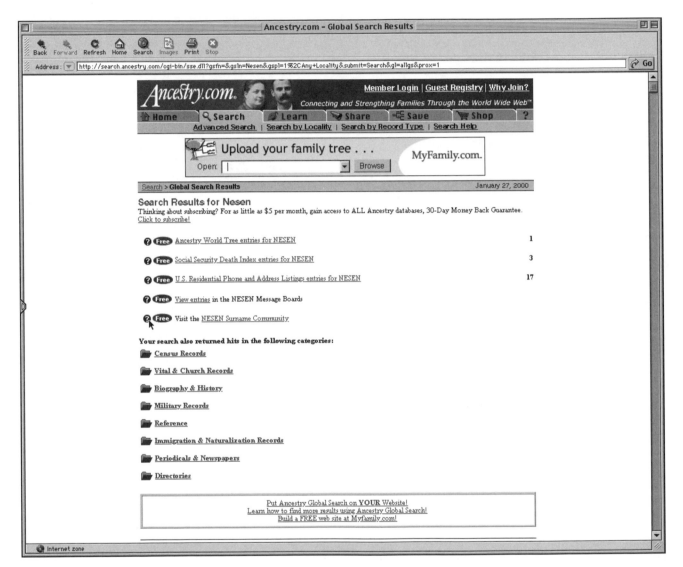

Figure 104

The once time-consuming labor of searching for an individual in separate state indexes for every year has been eliminated with the global search capabilities of the Internet. Shown above is a page showing search results for the name Nesen on Ancestry.com. A single search points to the presence of the name in seven states.

Those with Eastern European ancestry may be interested in visiting the Federation of Eastern European Family History Societies Web site, which features homepages for regional societies, databases, mailing lists, and an incredible collection of historical maps for this area of rapidly changing borders. The site is cross-indexed and also keyword/surname searchable to make it easy to navigate the vast resources available.

A number of genealogical societies and historical societies also have Web sites that provide information on their collections. Mailing lists available through various listserve groups can put a researcher in contact with others tracking a common surname, geographic area, or ethnic group.

Publications on how to use the Internet as a research tool are cropping up almost as quickly as the Web sites. Juliana Szucs Smith's *The Family Historian's Address Book: A Comprehensive List of Local, State, and Federal Agencies and Institutions and Ethnic and Genealogical Organizations* (Salt Lake City: Ancestry, 1998) contains over 540 pages of addresses that include URLs and e-mail addresses for genealogical societies, libraries, archives, and other repositories of interest to the family historian. There is also a special section with a list of Web sites to help researchers get started online.

See also *American Genealogical Biographical Index, PERSI,* and *Social Security Index.*

Selected Readings:

Bonner, Laurie, and Steve Bonner. *Searching for Cyber-Roots: A Step-By-Step Guide to Genealogy on the World Wide Web.* Salt Lake City: Ancestry, 1997.

Gehring, Jake. "Accessing the World's Card Catalogs." *Ancestry* 15 (3) (May/June 1997): 22–23.

_____. "Internet Search Engines." *Ancestry* 15 (2) (March/April 1997): 20–21.

_____. "The USGenWeb Project." *Ancestry* 15 (4) (July/August 1997): 46–47.

Helm, Matthew, and April Leigh Helm. *Genealogy Online for Dummies.* Foster City, Calif.: IDG Books Worldwide, Inc., 1998.

Kemp, Thomas Jay. *Virtual Roots: A Guide to Genealogy and Local History on the World Wide Web.* Wilmington, Delaware: Scholarly Resources Inc., 1997.

Meyerink, Kory L. "Databases, Indexes, and Other Finding Aids." *The Source: A Guidebook of American Genealogy.* Rev. ed. Salt Lake City: Ancestry, 1997.

Internet Sites of Interest:

Ancestry.com
http://www.ancestry.com

Bureau of Land Management
http://www.blm.gov/

Cyndi's List of Genealogy Sites on the Internet
http://www.cyndislist.com

Family History Department of The Church of Jesus Christ of Latter-day Saints
FamilySearch Internet Genealogy Service
http://www.familysearch.org

Federation of Eastern European Family History Societies
http://feefhs.org/

Helm's Genealogy Toolbox
http://www.genealogytoolbox.com/

Juliana's Links
http://www.ancestry.com/ancestry/testurllinks/search.asp

National Archives and Records Administration
http://www.nara.gov/

RootsWeb
http://www.rootsweb.com

U.S. GenWeb Project
http://www.usgenweb.com/index.html

World GenWeb Project
http://www.worldgenweb.org/

Land Grants and Patents

While land records are not filled with biographical data, they are one of the few kinds of records that can be used to identify individuals in the early settlement periods of America. Since statistics indicate that approximately ninety percent of adult white males owned land in the United States in the mid-1800s, there is a reasonably good chance of locating people in times and places where other documentation may be scarce. For the pre-Revolutionary War era, land records administered by the British, French, Mexican, and Spanish governments can be lucrative sources for research. British Crown charters and grants, for example, were an integral part of each colony. France followed the example of the British, granting charters to companies, and Spanish land transactions can be searched from approximately 1763. In 1821, Mexico officially gained its independence from Spain and began its own administration of what is now the southwestern portion of the United States (Foreign land grants and charters are described in detail in *Land & Property Research in the*

United States by E. Wade Hone). The importance of land records has not diminished over time; contemporary records continue to play an important role in identifying individuals.

Land distributed by governments on any level is defined as a land grant. Lands were provided for an agreed set of

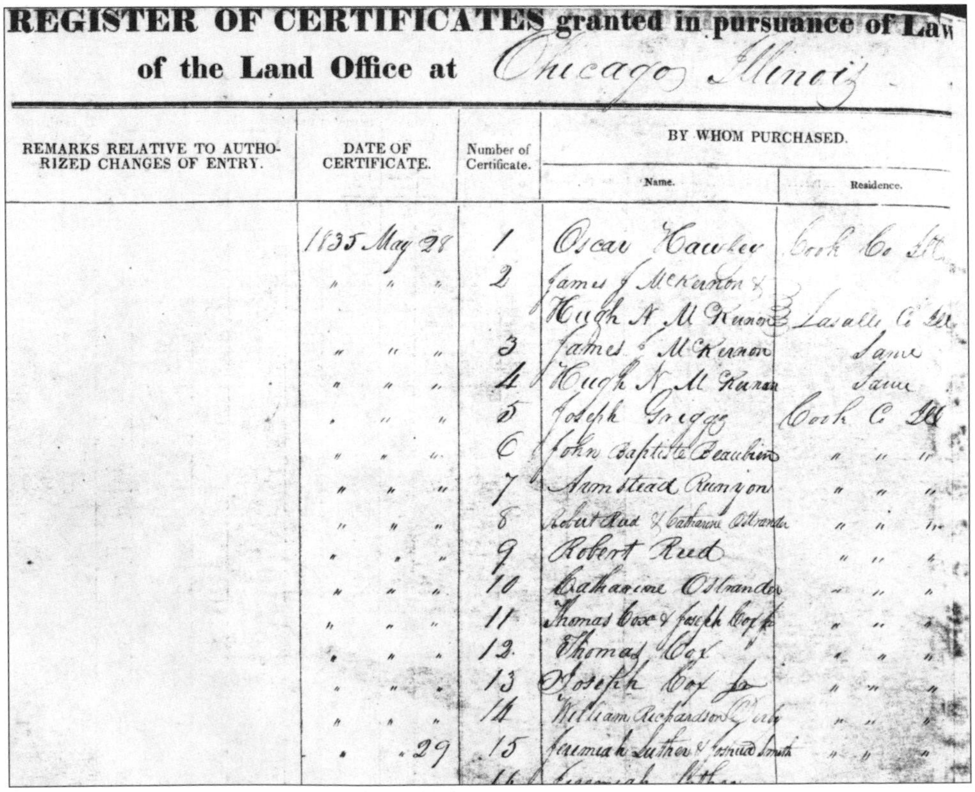

Figure 105

A copy of a page from a ledger of original land transactions recorded at the Land Office at Chicago, Illinois in 1835. (Courtesy of the National Archives - Great Lakes Region, Chicago, Illinois).

terms and/or sum of money by the first titleholder. Title to government land was in the form of a patent, the first sale of a piece of property. After a patent was issued, the property became part of the private or individual sector of land ownership and was thereafter sold in the form of a deed. Twenty states, including the thirteen original colonies, are known as state-land states. Individual states granted lands for a variety of reasons, generally to generate revenue and to encourage settlement. These records will be found at the state level. Many states have indexed and published early land grants.

The U.S. Government has sold or given away more than 1 billion acres of land, creating 5 million patents that are kept by the Bureau of Land Management. The National Archives has records granting the patents. Federal patents dated from the late 1780s to 1 July 1908 are indexed for a number of Public Domain States in a database that can be accessed by computer terminals at the Bureau of Land Management office in northern Virginia and on the Internet at <www.blm.gov>.

See also *American State Papers, Deeds, Homestead Records,* and *Territorial Records.*

Selected Readings:

E. Wade Hone. *Land & Property Research in the United States*. Salt Lake City: Ancestry, 1997.

Guide to Genealogical Research in the National Archives. Washington, D.C.: National Archives Trust Fund Board, 1985.

Meyerink, Kory L., ed. *Printed Sources: A Guide to Published Genealogical Records*. Salt Lake City: Ancestry, 1998.

Szucs, Loretto Dennis, and Sandra Hargreaves Luebking. *The Archives: A Guide to the National Archives Field Branches*. Salt Lake City: Ancestry, 1988.

_______, eds. *The Source: A Guidebook of American Genealogy*. Rev. ed. Salt Lake City: Ancestry, 1997.

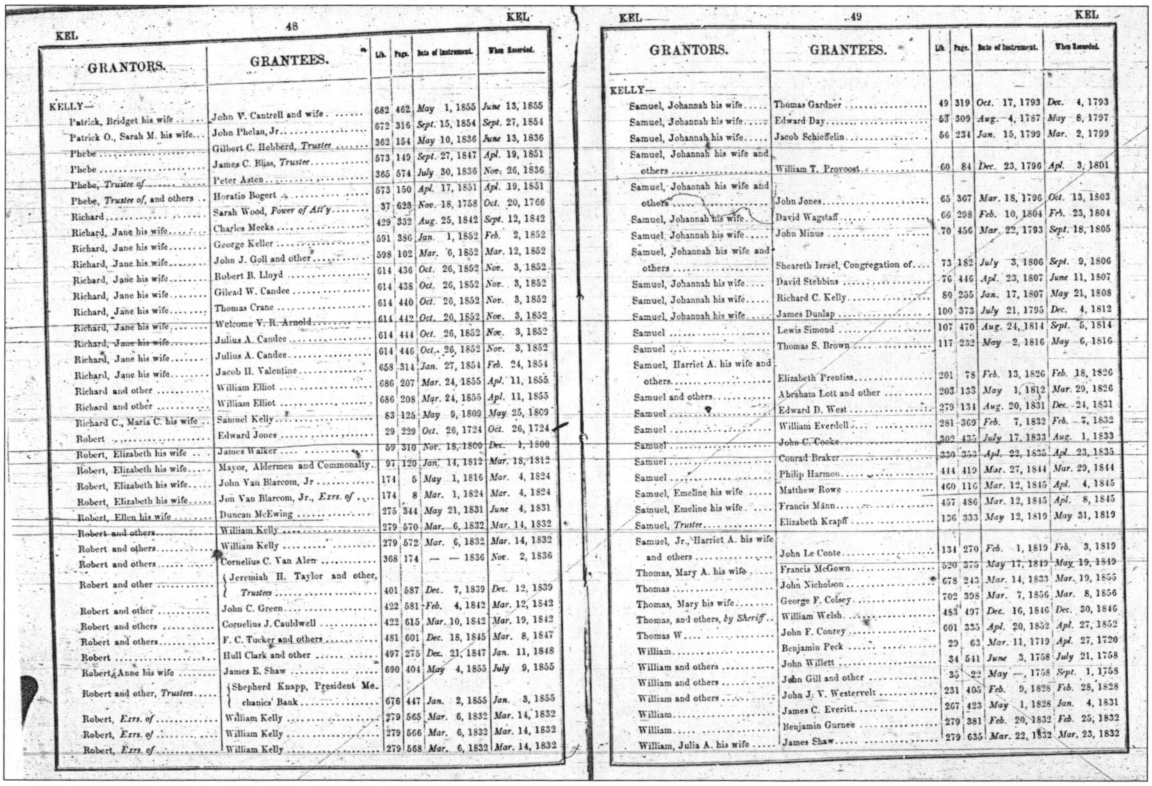

KEL 48 KEL

GRANTORS.	GRANTEES.	Lib.	Page.	Date of Instrument.	When Recorded.
KELLY—					
Patrick, Bridget his wife	John V. Cantrell and wife	682	462	May 1, 1855	June 13, 1855
Patrick O., Sarah M. his wife	John Phelan, Jr.	672	316	Sept. 15, 1854	Sept. 27, 1854
Phebe	Gilbert C. Hebberd, *Trustee*	362	154	May 10, 1836	June 13, 1836
Phebe	James C. Bliss, *Trustee*	573	149	Sept. 27, 1847	Apl. 19, 1851
Phebe, *Trustee of*	Peter Asten	365	574	July 30, 1836	Nov. 26, 1836
Phebe, *Trustee of*, and others	Horatio Bogert	573	150	Apl. 17, 1851	Apl. 19, 1851
Richard	Sarah Wood, *Power of Att'y*	37	628	Nov. 18, 1758	Oct. 20, 1766
Richard, Jane his wife	Charles Meeks	429	332	Aug. 25, 1842	Sept. 12, 1842
Richard, Jane his wife	George Keller	591	386	Jan. 1, 1852	Feb. 2, 1852
Richard, Jane his wife	John J. Goll and other	598	102	Mar. 6, 1852	Mar. 12, 1852
Richard, Jane his wife	Robert B. Lloyd	614	436	Oct. 26, 1852	Nov. 3, 1852
Richard, Jane his wife	Gilead W. Candee	614	438	Oct. 26, 1852	Nov. 3, 1852
Richard, Jane his wife	Thomas Crane	614	440	Oct. 26, 1852	Nov. 3, 1852
Richard, Jane his wife	Welcome V. R. Arnold	614	442	Oct. 26, 1852	Nov. 3, 1852
Richard, Jane his wife	Julius A. Candee	614	444	Oct. 26, 1852	Nov. 3, 1852
Richard, Jane his wife	Julius A. Candee	614	446	Oct. 26, 1852	Nov. 3, 1852
Richard, Jane his wife	Jacob H. Valentine	658	314	Jan. 27, 1854	Feb. 24, 1854
Richard and other	William Elliot	686	207	Mar. 24, 1855	Apl. 11, 1855
Richard and other	William Elliot	686	208	Mar. 24, 1855	Apl. 11, 1855
Richard C., Maria C. his wife	Samuel Kelly	83	125	May 9, 1809	May 25, 1809
Robert	Edward Jones	29	229	Oct. 26, 1724	Oct. 26, 1724
Robert, Elizabeth his wife	James Walker	59	310	Nov. 18, 1800	Dec. 1, 1800
Robert, Elizabeth his wife	Mayor, Aldermen and Commonalty	97	120	Jan. 14, 1812	Mar. 18, 1812
Robert, Elizabeth his wife	John Van Blarcom, Jr	174	5	May 1, 1816	Mar. 4, 1824
Robert, Elizabeth his wife	Jon Van Blarcom, Jr., *Exrs. of*	174	8	Mar. 1, 1824	Mar. 4, 1824
Robert, Ellen his wife	Duncan McEwing	275	344	May 21, 1831	June 4, 1831
Robert and others	William Kelly	279	570	Mar. 6, 1832	Mar. 14, 1832
Robert and others	William Kelly	279	572	Mar. 6, 1832	Mar. 14, 1832
Robert and others	Cornelius C. Van Alen	368	174	— — 1836	Nov. 2, 1836
Robert and other	Jeremiah H. Taylor and other, *Trustees*	401	587	Dec. 7, 1839	Dec. 12, 1839
Robert and other	John C. Green	422	581	Feb. 4, 1842	Mar. 12, 1842
Robert and others	Cornelius J. Cauldwell	422	615	Mar. 10, 1842	Mar. 19, 1842
Robert and others	F. C. Tucker and others	481	601	Dec. 18, 1845	Mar. 8, 1847
Robert	Hull Clark and other	497	275	Dec. 21, 1847	Jan. 11, 1848
Robert, Anne his wife	James E. Shaw	690	404	May 4, 1855	July 9, 1855
Robert and other, *Trustees*	Shepherd Knapp, President Mechanics' Bank	676	447	Jan. 2, 1855	Jan. 3, 1855
Robert, *Exrs. of*	William Kelly	279	565	Mar. 6, 1832	Mar. 14, 1832
Robert, *Exrs. of*	William Kelly	279	566	Mar. 6, 1832	Mar. 14, 1832
Robert, *Exrs. of*	William Kelly	279	568	Mar. 6, 1832	Mar. 14, 1832

KEL 49 KEL

GRANTORS.	GRANTEES.	Lib.	Page.	Date of Instrument.	When Recorded.
KELLY—					
Samuel, Johannah his wife	Thomas Gardner	49	319	Oct. 17, 1793	Dec. 4, 1793
Samuel, Johannah his wife	Edward Day	53	309	Aug. 4, 1787	May 8, 1797
Samuel, Johannah his wife	Jacob Schieffelin	56	234	Jan. 15, 1799	Mar. 2, 1799
Samuel, Johannah his wife and others	William T. Provoost	60	84	Dec. 23, 1796	Apl. 3, 1801
Samuel, Johannah his wife and others	John Jones	65	367	Mar. 18, 1796	Oct. 13, 1803
Samuel, Johannah his wife	David Wagstaff	66	298	Feb. 10, 1804	Feb. 23, 1804
Samuel, Johannah his wife	John Minus	70	456	Mar. 22, 1793	Sept. 18, 1805
Samuel, Johannah his wife and others	Shearith Israel, Congregation of	73	182	July 3, 1806	Sept. 9, 1806
Samuel, Johannah his wife	David Stebbins	76	446	Apl. 23, 1807	June 11, 1807
Samuel, Johannah his wife	Richard C. Kelly	80	255	Jan. 17, 1807	May 21, 1808
Samuel, Johannah his wife	James Dunlap	100	373	July 21, 1795	Dec. 4, 1812
Samuel	Lewis Simond	107	470	Aug. 24, 1814	Sept. 5, 1814
Samuel	Thomas S. Brown	117	232	May 2, 1816	May 6, 1816
Samuel, Harriet A. his wife and others	Elizabeth Prentiss	201	78	Feb. 13, 1826	Feb. 18, 1826
Samuel and others	Abraham Lott and other	203	133	May 1, 1812	Mar. 29, 1826
Samuel	Edward D. West	279	134	Aug. 20, 1831	Dec. 24, 1831
Samuel	William Everdell	281	369	Feb. 7, 1832	Feb. 7, 1832
Samuel	John C. Cooke	302	435	July 17, 1833	Aug. 1, 1833
Samuel	Conrad Braker	330	353	Apl. 22, 1835	Apl. 23, 1835
Samuel	Philip Harmon	444	419	Mar. 27, 1844	Mar. 29, 1844
Samuel, Emeline his wife	Matthew Rowe	460	116	Mar. 12, 1845	Apl. 4, 1845
Samuel, Emeline his wife	Francis Mann	457	486	Mar. 12, 1845	Apl. 8, 1845
Samuel, *Trustee*	Elizabeth Krapff	136	333	May 12, 1819	May 31, 1819
Samuel, Jr., Harriet A. his wife and others	John Le Conte	134	270	Feb. 1, 1819	Feb. 3, 1819
Thomas, Mary A. his wife	Francis McGown	520	375	May 17, 1849	May 19, 1849
Thomas	John Nicholson	678	243	Mar. 14, 1833	Mar. 19, 1855
Thomas, Mary his wife	George F. Colsey	702	398	Mar. 7, 1856	Mar. 8, 1856
Thomas, and others, *by Sheriff*	William Welsh	483	497	Dec. 16, 1846	Dec. 30, 1846
Thomas W.	John F. Conrey	601	335	Apl. 20, 1852	Apl. 27, 1852
William	Benjamin Peck	29	63	Mar. 11, 1719	Apl. 27, 1720
William and others	John Willett	34	541	June 3, 1758	July 21, 1758
William and others	John Gill and other	35	22	May —, 1758	Sept. 1, 1758
William and others	John J. V. Westervelt	231	405	Feb. 9, 1828	Feb. 28, 1828
William	James C. Everitt	267	423	May 1, 1828	Jan. 4, 1831
William	Benjamin Gurnee	279	381	Feb. 20, 1832	Feb. 25, 1832
William, Julia A. his wife	James Shaw	279	635	Mar. 22, 1832	Mar. 23, 1832

Figure 106

Two pages showing a few of the Kellys listed in the Grantor/Grantee Index for New York City. The conveyances for 1654 to 1866 were microfilmed from original records at the New York County Courthouse and are available at and through the National Archives.

Library Guides

Guides to libraries with genealogy collections can be direct routes to information on cities. For example, Joseph Oldenburg's *A Genealogical Guide to the Burton Historical Collection: Detroit Public Library* (Salt Lake City: Ancestry, 1988) provides information on city directories, local history sources, newspapers, atlases and maps, and picture collections for the Detroit area, as well as some other Michigan counties and other states. Sources that would be difficult for the average researcher to discover, such as a description of vital records transcribed by a local chapter of the National Society of the Daughters of the American Revolution, are brought to light in this guide.

Peggy Tuck Sinko's *Guide to Local and Family History at The Newberry Library* (Salt Lake City: Ancestry, 1987) prepares the researcher for the fact that, like most other libraries, the Newberry does not have official Chicago or Cook County birth, death, marriage, probate, or land records, but it does have some important yet obscure sources for the city. In addition to all of the available Chicago city directories (1838 to 1928–29), the guide calls attention to "Sam Fink's Marriages and Deaths From Chicago Newspapers, 1834–1889," and the Newberry's unique Chicago and Cook County Biographical File, an ever-growing source.

The New England Historic Genealogical Society has published the *Circulating Library Catalog* in two volumes; the first volume is a list of genealogies, while the second includes research aids.

Selected Readings:

Cerny, Johni, and Wendy Elliott. *The Library: A Guide to the LDS Family History Library*. Salt Lake City: Ancestry, 1988.

New England Historic Genealogical Society. *Circulating Library Catalog*. 2 vols. Boston: New England Historic Genealogical Society, 1998.

Oldenburg, Joseph. *A Genealogical Guide to the Burton Historical Collection: Detroit Public Library*. Salt Lake City: Ancestry, 1988.

Sinko, Peggy Tuck. *Guide to Local and Family History at The Newberry Library*. Salt Lake City: Ancestry, 1987.

Internet Sites of Interest:

Allen County Public Library
http://www.acpl.lib.in.us/

Family History Library, The
http://www.familysearch.org

Library of Congress - Local History & Genealogy Division
http://lcweb.loc.gov/

New England Historic Genealogical Society
http://www.nehgs.org

Newberry Library, Chicago
http://www.newberry.org/

Licenses

The requirement to hold a license to operate a business or to practice in certain professions has resulted in an additional source of information for researchers. Municipal records contain licensing applications filed by shopkeepers, saloon keepers, peddlers, and other local business owners requesting permission to operate a business in a particular city or state. Applications often include the applicant's age, birthplace, marital status, and residence. Professional organizations often keep records on licensed professionals. Such organizations include the American Medical Association for medical practitioners, the National Education Association for teachers, and the American Bar Association for lawyers. The St. Louis Board of Pharmacy has records of druggists' licenses for the period 1893 to 1909. State and county archives sometimes have licensing records as well. For example, the Pennsylvania State Archives has medical and dental licenses dating back to the late 1800s. Owners and masters of ships, yachts, and other marine vessels were licensed by the Bureau of Marine Inspection and Navigation. Some licenses include birth dates and places, as well as citizenship status. Marine licenses can be found in the regions of the National Archives.

Marriage licenses, containing significant amounts of genealogical materials, date back to the latter half of the nineteenth century. Copies can usually be obtained from the county in which the marriage took place.

See also *Medical Records, Motor Vehicle Registration Records, Maritime Records,* and *Occupational Records.*

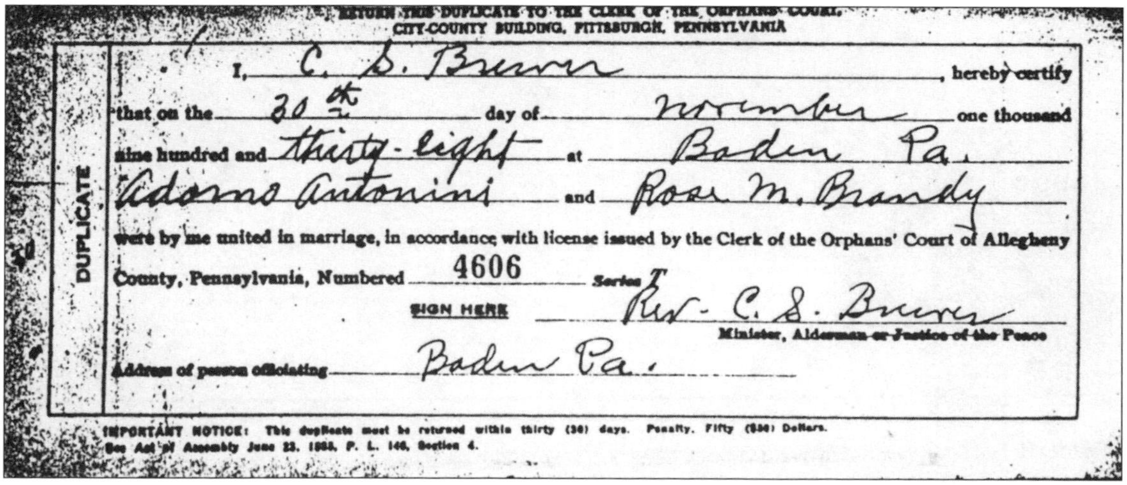

RETURN THIS DUPLICATE TO THE CLERK OF THE ORPHANS' COURT,
CITY-COUNTY BUILDING, PITTSBURGH, PENNSYLVANIA

DUPLICATE

I, ________________, hereby certify that on the 30th day of November one thousand nine hundred and thirty-eight at Baden Pa. Adorno Antonini and Rose M. Brandy were by me united in marriage, in accordance with license issued by the Clerk of the Orphans' Court of Allegheny County, Pennsylvania, Numbered 4606 Series T

SIGN HERE ________________
Minister, ~~Alderman or Justice of the Peace~~

Address of person officiating Baden Pa.

IMPORTANT NOTICE: This duplicate must be returned within thirty (30) days. Penalty, Fifty ($50) Dollars.
See Act of Assembly June 23, 1885, P. L. 146, Section 4.

Figure 107
Document from the Clerk of the Orphan's Court, Allegheny County, Pennsylvania, pertaining to a 1938 marriage license for Adorno Antonini and Rose M. Bradley.

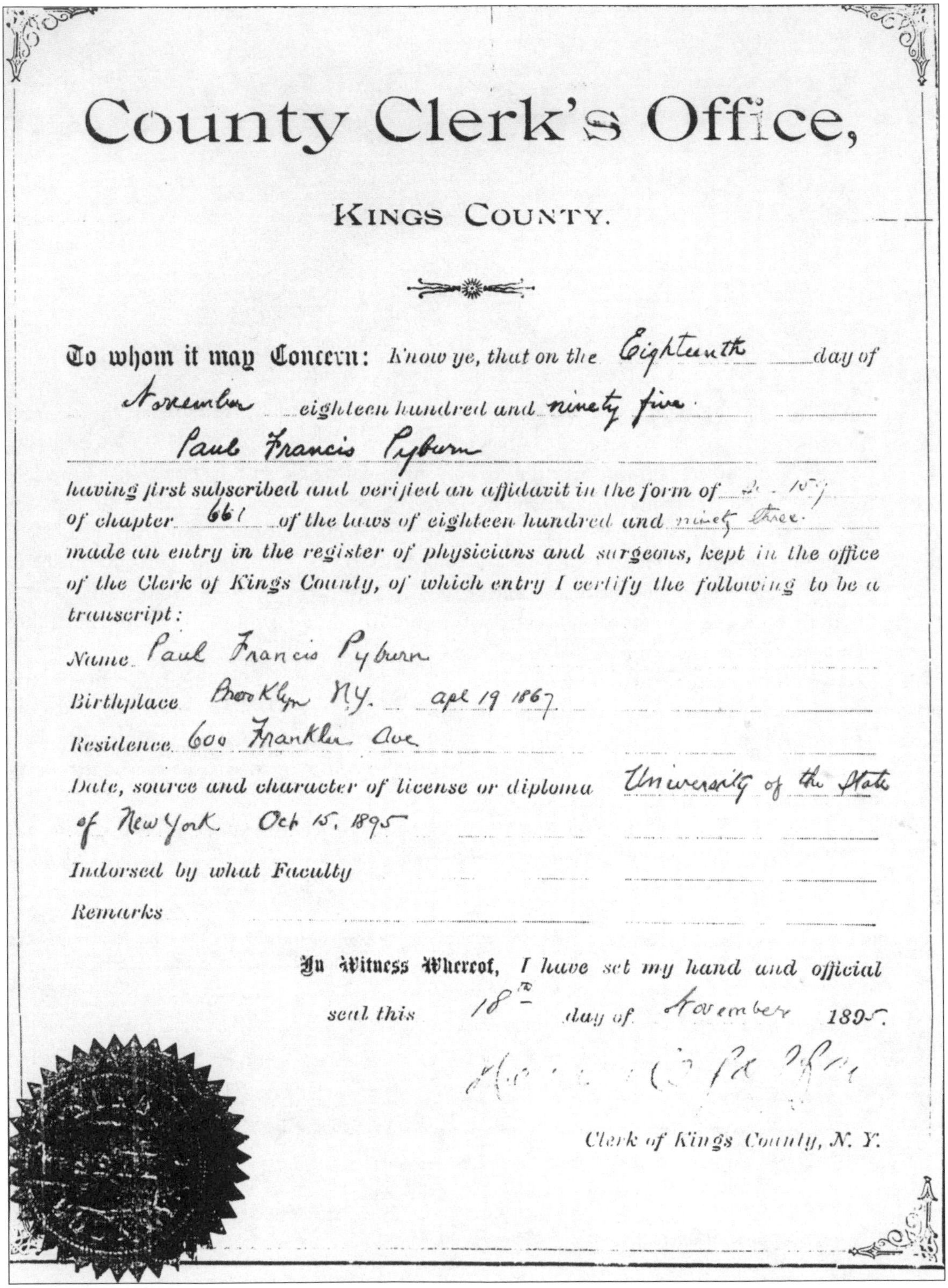

Figure 108
A medical license issued in 1895 by the Clerk of Kings County, New York.

Selected Readings:

Brownstone, David M., and Gordon Carruth. *Where to Find Business Information*. New York: John Wiley and Sons, 1979.

Daniels, Lorna M. *Business Information Sources*. 3d ed. Berkeley: University of California Press, 1993.

Meyerink, Kory L., and Johni Cerny. "Research in Business, Employment, and Institutional Records." *The Source: A Guidebook of American Genealogy*. Rev. ed. Salt Lake City: Ancestry, 1997.

Szucs, Loretto Dennis, and Sandra Hargreaves Luebking. *The Archives: A Guide to the National Archives Field Branches*. Salt Lake City: Ancestry, 1988.

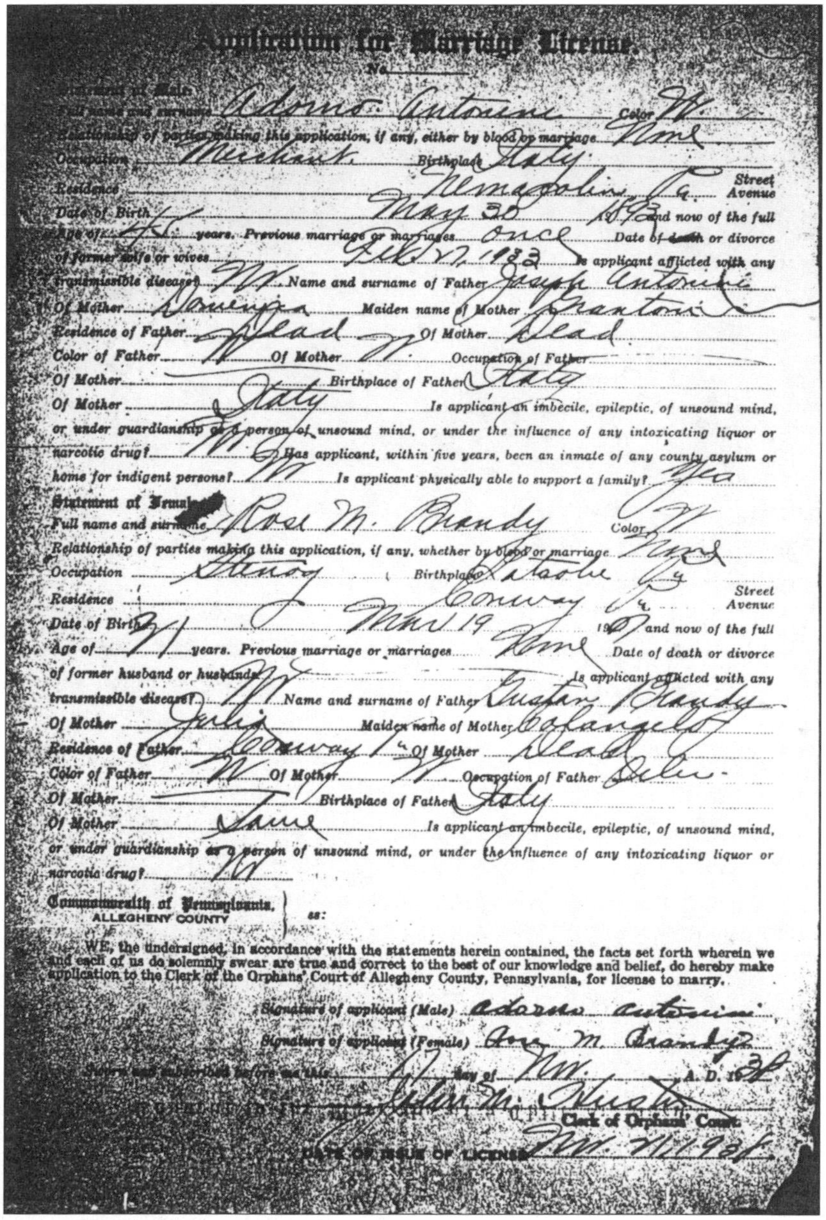

Application for Marriage License.

No. ______

Statement of Male:

Full name and surname Adorno Antonini Color W.

Relationship of parties making this application, if any, either by blood or marriage None

Occupation Merchant Birthplace Italy

Residence Nemacolin Pa. Street Avenue

Date of Birth May 30 189_ and now of the full

Age of 45 years. Previous marriage or marriages once Date of death or divorce

of former wife or wives Feb 27 1932 Is applicant afflicted with any

transmissible disease? No Name and surname of Father Joseph Antonini

Of Mother Domenica Maiden name of Mother Grantoni

Residence of Father Dead Of Mother Dead

Color of Father W Of Mother W Occupation of Father ——

Of Mother —— Birthplace of Father Italy

Of Mother Italy Is applicant an imbecile, epileptic, of unsound mind,

or under guardianship as a person of unsound mind, or under the influence of any intoxicating liquor or

narcotic drug? No Has applicant, within five years, been an inmate of any county asylum or

home for indigent persons? No Is applicant physically able to support a family? Yes

Statement of Female:

Full name and surname Rose M. Brandy Color W

Relationship of parties making this application, if any, whether by blood or marriage None

Occupation Steno. Birthplace Latrobe Pa

Residence Conway Pa. Street Avenue

Date of Birth Mar 19 19__ and now of the full

Age of __ years. Previous marriage or marriages None Date of death or divorce

of former husband or husbands —— Is applicant afflicted with any

transmissible disease? No Name and surname of Father Gustav Brandy

Of Mother Julia Maiden name of Mother Colangelo

Residence of Father Conway Pa Of Mother Dead

Color of Father W Of Mother W Occupation of Father Deler

Of Mother —— Birthplace of Father Italy

Of Mother Same Is applicant an imbecile, epileptic, of unsound mind,

or under guardianship as a person of unsound mind, or under the influence of any intoxicating liquor or

narcotic drug? No

Commonwealth of Pennsylvania,
ALLEGHENY COUNTY } ss:

WE, the undersigned, in accordance with the statements herein contained, the facts set forth wherein we and each of us do solemnly swear are true and correct to the best of our knowledge and belief, do hereby make application to the Clerk of the Orphans' Court of Allegheny County, Pennsylvania, for license to marry.

Signature of applicant (Male) adorno antonini

Signature of applicant (Female) Rose M. Brandy

Sworn and subscribed before me this __ day of Nov. A.D. 1938

Clerk of Orphans' Court.

DATE OF ISSUE OF LICENSE Nov. __ 1938

Figure 109

Another document from the Clerk of the Orphan's Court pertaining to a 1938 marriage license for Adorno Antonini and Rose M. Bradley. This document shows birth and occupational information for the couple, a notation of a previous marriage for Adorno, names of parents, including mother's maiden name, and the parents' birthplaces.

Manufacturers' Schedules of the Census (Industry Schedules), 1810-80

The information available in manufacturers' schedules varies, depending on which year it was taken. The first census of manufacturers was taken in 1810; however the returns were incomplete. Most of these schedules have been lost, except for the few bound with the population schedules. The 1820 census provided much more information, including the owner's name, location of the establishment, the number of employees, kind and quantity of machinery invested, articles manufactured, annual production, and general remarks on the business and demand for its products. No schedules were compiled for 1830, and the 1840 schedules included only statistical information. From 1850 to 1870, the schedule was called the "industry schedule" and recorded the name of the company or the owner, the kind of business, the amount of capital invested, and both the quantity and value of the materials, labor, machinery, and products. In 1880, the census was again called "manufacturers' schedule," and agents recorded industrial information for certain large industries and in cities of more than 8,000 inhabitants.

Some of the regional branches of the National Archives have the 1820, 1850, 1860, and 1870 schedules on microfilm. Surviving manufacturers' schedules from the 1810 census are listed in appendix IX of Katherine H. Davidson and Charlotte M. Ashby, comps., *Preliminary Inventory of the Records of the Bureau of the Census,* Preliminary Inventory 161 (Washington, D.C.: National Archives and Records Service, 1964).

Selected Readings:

Davidson, Katherine H., and Charlotte M. Ashby, comps., *Preliminary Inventory of the Records of the Bureau of the Census,* Preliminary Inventory 161. Washington, D.C.: National Archives and Records Service, 1964.

Fishbein, Meyer H. *The Censuses of Manufacturers, 1810-1890.* Reference Information Paper 50 (1973).

Indexes to Manufacturers' Census of 1820: An Edited Printing of the Original Indexes and Information Reprint. Knightstown, Ind.: Bookmark, 1977.

Meyerink, Kory L, ed. *Printed Sources: A Guide to Published Genealogical Records.* Salt Lake City: Ancestry, 1998.

Szucs, Loretto Dennis, and Sandra Hargreaves Luebking, eds. *The Source: A Guidebook of American Genealogy.* Rev. ed. Salt Lake City: Ancestry, 1997.

Internet Sites of Interest:

Ancestry.com
http://www.ancestry.com

National Archives and Records Administration
http://www.nara.gov/publications/microfilm/census/census.html

SCHEDULE 5.—Products of Industry in _____ _____ in the County of _Carbon_ State of _Penna_ during the Year ending June 1, 1850, as enumerated by me, _R Butter_ Ass't Marshal

Name of Corporation, Company, or Individual, producing Articles to the Annual Value of $500.	Name of Business, Manufacture, or Product.	Capital invested in Real and Personal Estate in the Business.	Raw Material used, including Fuel.			Kind of motive power, machinery, structure, or resource.	Average number of hands employed.		Wages.		Annual Product.		
			Quantities.	Kinds.	Values.		Male.	Female.	Average monthly cost of male labour.	Average monthly cost of female labour.	Quantities.	Kinds.	Values.
1	2	3	4	5	6	7	8	9	10	11	12	13	14
F. H. Hackman	Tailor	300		Dry Goods	950	Hand	2		50			Clothing	1725
Thomas Seyfried	Brewer	1000	20000	Barley	2000	Hand	5		10		300 bbl	Porter	1500
			1500 lb	Hops	240						400 "	Ale & Beer	2000
			3½	Fuller	50								
William Gorman	Shoemaker	1000	2 tons	Sole leather	720	Hand	6		150			Boots & Shoes	3500
			½ "	Upper do	350							Caps &c	500
			500	Calf skins	924								
				Trimmings	150								
John Richards	Iron	12000	4000 t	Ore	4000	Water and	25		500		1700 t	Iron	37.300
			3000 t	Coal	6000	Hand							
			700 t	Limestone	560	1 Stack							
George W. Griffin	Cabinet Maker	400	200 lb	Mahogany	40	Hand	1		30			Cabinet ware	550

SCHEDULE 5.—Products of Industry in _Mauch Chunk Borough_ in the County of _Carbon_ State of _Pennsylvania_ during the Year ending June 1, 1850, as enumerated by me, _R Butter_ Ass't Marshal

Name of Corporation, Company, or Individual, producing Articles to the Annual Value of $500.	Name of Business, Manufacture, or Product.	Capital invested in Real and Personal Estate in the Business.	Raw Material used, including Fuel.			Kind of motive power, machinery, structure, or resource.	Average number of hands employed.		Wages.		Annual Product.		
			Quantities.	Kinds.	Values.		Male.	Female.	Average monthly cost of male labour.	Average monthly cost of female labour.	Quantities.	Kinds.	Values.
1	2	3	4	5	6	7	8	9	10	11	12	13	14
Gleasen & Daniel	Cabinet Maker	1000	12000 ft	Poplar	252	Hand	4		100			Cabinet ware	4000
			3000 ft	Pine	48								
				Cherry stuff	350								
				Butter stuff	150								
				Paints Hardware	200								
				Mahogany	30								
W. H. Foster	Saddle Harness maker	1500	2000 lb	Harness leather	575	Hand	11		100			Harness	3500
				Oil cloth &c	200								
			200 lb	Skirting	50								
				Trimmings	300								
Conrad Miller	Boat Builder	5000	30000 ft	Lumber	4500	Hand	12		429		25	Canal boats	9375
			25 bbl	Pitch & tar	50	Rope						Repairing	2000
			2 ½ t	Oakum	350	Windlas							
			2 T	Castings	120								

Figure 110

A two-page entry from an 1850 manufacturers/industrial census schedule for Carbon County, Pennsylvania.

Maps, Atlases, and Gazetteers

Being familiar with the area in which an ancestor lived is essential to a successful search. The location of the city or town will lead the family researcher to record sources, such as historical societies, churches, and cemeteries in the region. In addition to city and town, it is important to determine the county in which an ancestor resided, since many records, including vital statistics and property taxes, were created and are maintained on the county level. Challenging the researcher is the fact that, over the years, as cities grew, most of them expanded by annexing the small towns at their fringes. Wards assumed different configurations and streets were often renamed. Also complicating matters are towns that have been renamed or those with names like Anderson, which is common to ten states.

Many research problems can be solved with the use of maps, atlases and gazetteers. Maps that show the location and approximate size of a town also reveal neighboring communities and nearby landmarks, such as rivers and mountains, which may be noted in an ancestor's diary or photo album. An atlas is a collection of maps and can be useful in more ways than one. In addition to pinpointing the location of a family homestead, commercial atlases include advertisements of local establishments and biographical sketches of its subscribers, in some cases accompanied by lithographs or photographs as well. A

gazetteer is a geographical tool that lists place-names alphabetically and identifies locations, sometimes including historical information. Older gazetteers, published before the turn of the century, are especially useful for locating towns that are no longer in existence or that have changed names.

The residence and family group of Aaron M. Simpson, as depicted in the COMBINATION ATLAS MAP OF KOSCIUSKO COUNTY, INDIANA *(Chicago: Kingman Brothers, 1879), and a map from the* UNILLUSTRATED HISTORICAL ATLAS OF HARRISON COUNTY, MISSOURI *(Philadelphia: Edwards Brothers, 1876).*

Figure 111
The residence and family group of Aaron M. Simpson, as depicted in the *Combination Atlas Map of Kosciusko County, Indiana* (Chicago: Kingman Brothers, 1879).

Maps dating from various periods can be located in many public libraries and local historical societies. The Library of Congress houses one of the largest map collections in the world, with more than 4 million maps. Copies of various maps in this collection are available for purchase from their Photoduplication Services department. The National Archives maintains a collection with nearly 2 million maps from which copies can be requested by writing to the Cartographic and Architectural Branch (NNSC), National Archives at College Park, 8601 Adelphi Road, College Park, MD 20740-6001.

See also *Birds-eye View Maps, Fire Insurance Maps,* and *Post Office Records.*

Selected Readings:

Abate, Frank R., ed. *Omni Gazetteer of the United States of America: Providing Name, Location, and Identification for Nearly 1,500,000 Populated Places and Geographic Features in the Fifty States, the District of Columbia, Puerto Rico, and U.S. Territories.* 11 vols. Detroit: Omnigraphics, 1991.

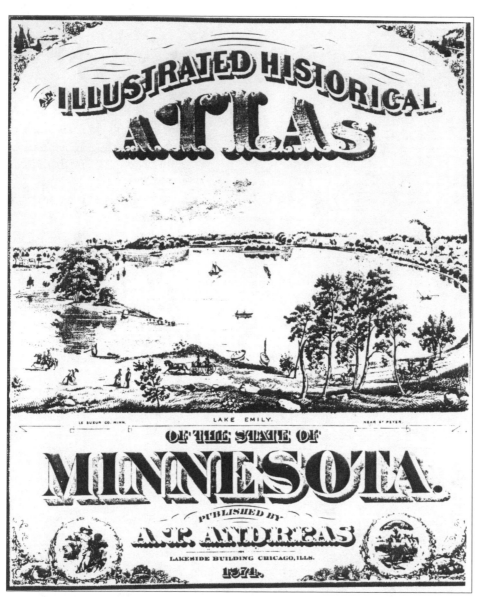

Figure 112

An Illustrated Historical Atlas of the State of Minnesota (Chicago: A.T. Andreas, 1874) is typical of those published in the 1870s. Significant biographical information may be gleaned from county atlases, including statements about birth dates and places, marriage information, previous residences, and names of children and parents for prominent citizens.

American Places Dictionary: A Guide to 45,000 Populated Places, Natural Features, and Other Places in the U.S. 4 vols. Detroit: Omnigraphics, 1994.

Cobb, David A., ed. *Guide to U.S. Map Resources.* Chicago: American Library Association, 1990.

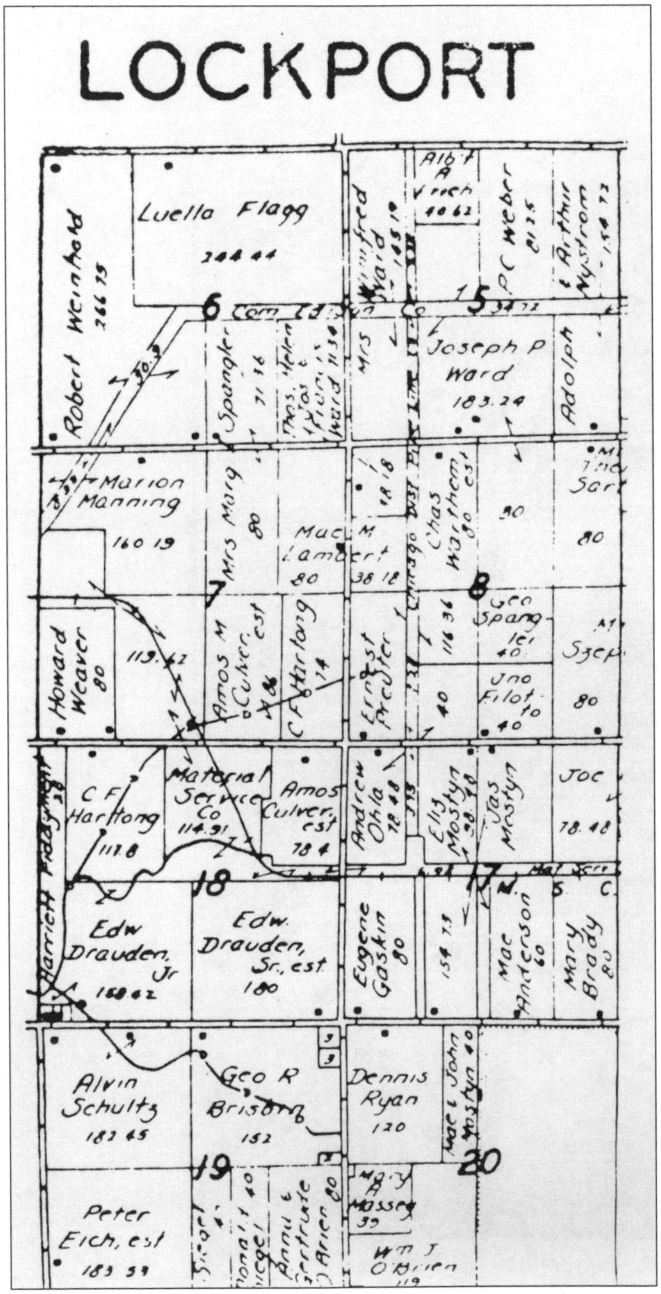

Figure 113

A section of an undated township map of Lockport, Will County, Illinois (T. 36 N-R. 10 E.), showing land ownership and legal descriptions of properties. Township maps are often found in county deed recorder's records and with historical societies and agencies.

Library of Congress. *The Bibliography of Cartography.* 5 vols. Boston: G.K. Hall, 1973, 1st supplement. 2 vols. 1979.

Makower, Joel, ed. *The Map Catalog: Every Kind of Map and Chart on Earth and Even Some Above It.* 2d ed. New York: Vintage Books, 1992.

New York Public Library, Research Libraries. *Dictionary Catalog of the Map Division.* 10 vols. Boston: G.K. Hall, 1971. (The New York Public Library has one of the largest city map collections in the United States)

Schiffman, Carol Mehr. "Geographic Tools: Maps, Atlases, and Gazetteers." *Printed Sources: A Guide to Published Genealogical Records.* Ch. 3: 94–144. Salt Lake City: Ancestry, 1998. Included with this discussion of the uses of geographic tools in genealogical research is an extensive bibliography section, which provides a list of sources alphabetically by state.

Szucs, Loretto Dennis, and Sandra Hargreaves Luebking, eds. *The Source: A Guidebook of American Genealogy.* Rev. ed. Salt Lake City: Ancestry, 1997.

Thackery, David. "County Atlases." *Ancestry* 12 (6) (November/December 1994): 20–21.

_____. "Gazetteers: Identifying Research Localities." *Ancestry* 12 (4) (July/August 1994): 24–5.

Thrower, Norman J. W. "The County Atlases of the United States." *Surveying and Mapping* 21 (1961): 365–73.

Internet Sites of Interest:

Ancestry.com - Maps and Gazetteers
http://www.ancestry.com/ancestry/maps.asp

MapQuest
http://www.mapquest.com/

USGS County/Location Finder
http://www-nmd.usgs.gov/www/gnis/gnisform.html

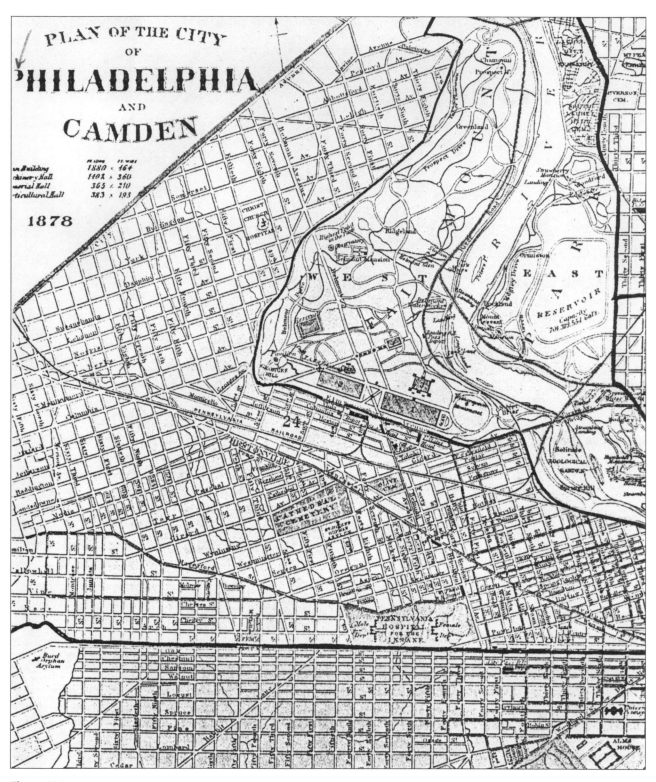

Figure 114

An 1878 street map of Philadelphia, Pennsylvania, showing ward numbers and boundaries that are often critical for locating specific addresses in census records and other sources. Many old maps have been republished and are available from genealogical book and supply vendors.

Maritime Records

Throughout history, the seas, lakes, and rivers have played a dominant role in the movement of commodities and people and have provided a livelihood for millions. A wealth of research material is available for those seeking to learn more about seafaring ancestors. Some provide names and addresses of individuals; some include biographical details and help in placing an ancestor in a given time in history.

Maritime sources, which may focus on specific ports or waterways, or on fishing, whaling, or naval activities, can be difficult to locate. A researcher must know the full name of the person and which records are most likely to hold information on them. Published guides, such as *Great Lakes Maritime History: Bibliography and Sources of Information* (Charles E. Feltner and Jeri Baron Feltner. Dearborn, Mich.: Seajay Publishing, 1982), can be helpful, as can periodical indexes, such as *PERSI* (go to <www.ancestry.com> for information on using this periodical index as a research tool).

Large maritime collections are located in maritime museums, some university libraries, and

Figure 115

Depending on the date and circumstances of the boat or ship wreck, files may contain the testimony of eyewitnesses and photographs, such as this one of wreckage off the coast of Massachusetts.

the National Archives and its field branches. Among the records that can be found in the Archives' collections are licensing documents from maritime and riparian ports, Seamen's Protection Certificate Applications with birth and naturalization information, records of the Coast Guard, records of the Bureau of Customs, Immigration and Naturalization Service, and records of the federal admiralty courts. The National Archives – Northeast Region in New York also holds a collection of records for the period 1835 through 1882 from the Seaman's Retreat, a refuge for sick and impoverished sailors, which in many cases include the sailor's name, country of origin, and the name of the vessel on which he arrived.

See also *Admiralty Records.*

Selected Readings:

Dixon, Ruth Priest. "High Seas Protection." *Forum* Parts I & II. 10 (1), 10 (2) (Spring and Summer 1998).

Dixon, Ruth Priest. Index to Seaman's Protection Certificate Applications and Proofs of Citizenship. Baltimore, Md.: Clearfield Co., Inc., 1998.

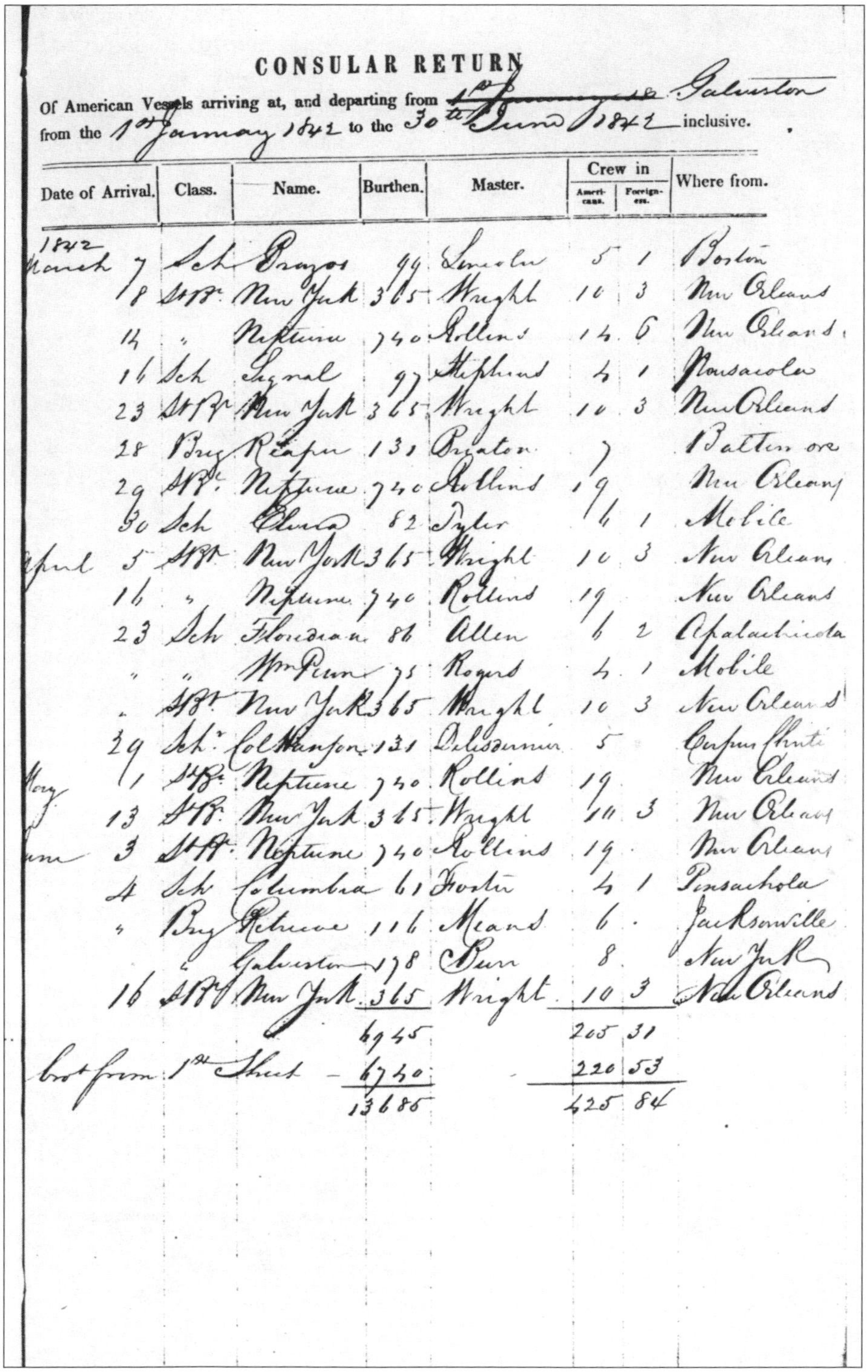

CONSULAR RETURN

Of American Vessels arriving at, and departing from Galveston from the 1st January 1842 to the 30th June 1842 inclusive.

Date of Arrival.		Class.	Name.	Burthen.	Master.	Crew in Americans.	Crew in Foreigners.	Where from.
1842 March	7	Sch	Brazos	99	Lincoln	5	1	Boston
	8	St Bt	New York	365	Wright	10	3	New Orleans
	14	"	Neptune	740	Rollins	14	6	New Orleans
	16	Sch	Signal	97	Stephens	4	1	Pensacola
	23	St Bt	New York	365	Wright	10	3	New Orleans
	28	Brig	Reaper	131	Brigaton	7		Batten ore
	29	St Bt	Neptune	740	Rollins	19		New Orleans
	30	Sch	Elvira	82	Tyler	4	1	Mobile
April	5	St Bt	New York	365	Wright	10	3	New Orleans
	16	"	Neptune	740	Rollins	19		New Orleans
	23	Sch	Floridian	86	Allen	6	2	Apalachicola
	"	"	Wm Penn	75	Rogers	4	1	Mobile
	"	St Bt	New York	365	Wright	10	3	New Orleans
	29	Schr	Col Hanson	131	Delisdernier	5		Corpus Christi
May	1	St Bt	Neptune	740	Rollins	19		New Orleans
	13	St Bt	New York	365	Wright	10	3	New Orleans
June	3	St Bt	Neptune	740	Rollins	19		New Orleans
	4	Sch	Columbia	61	Foster	4	1	Pensachola
	"	Brig	Retrieve	116	Means	6		Jacksonville
		"	Galveston	178	Burr	8		New York
	16	St Bt	New York	365	Wright	10	3	New Orleans
				6945		205	31	
brt from 1st Sheet				6740		220	53	
				13685		425	84	

Figure 116

An 1842 Consular Return showing the names of ship masters, number of crew members, where each ship was from, and other information identifying ships departing from Galveston. These records have been microfilmed and may be found at the National Archives and through the Family History Library.

Feltner, Charles E., and Jeri Baron Feltner. *Great Lakes Maritime History: Bibliography and Sources of Information*. Dearborn, Mich.: Seajay Publishing, 1982.

Guber, Rafael. "When Genealogists Write History - Part II." *Ancestry* 15 (3) (May/June 1997): 36-41.

Guide to Genealogical Research in the National Archives. Rev. ed. Washington, D.C.: National Archives Trust Fund Board, 1991.

Labaree, Benjamin W., William M. Fowler, Jr., John B. Hattendorf, Jeffrey J. Safford, Edward W. Sloan, and Andrew W. German. *America and the Sea: A Maritime History*. Mystic, Connecticut: Mystic Seaport Museum, Inc., 1998.

Szucs, Loretto Dennis. "Watery Treasures: Maritime and Naval Sources." *Ancestry* 12 (3) (May-June 1994): 25–8.

Internet Sites of Interest:

A Guide to Maritime History on the Internet
http://ils.unc.edu/maritime/home.html

Apalachicola Maritime Museum
http://www.homtown.com/apalachicola/maritime.html

Arkansas River Historical Society
http://www.tulsaweb.com/port/

Bernice P. Bishop Museum
http://www.bishop.hawaii.org/

Great Lakes Lore Maritime Museum
http://www.usa.k12.mi.us/~lakes/index.html

Historical Collections of the Great Lakes (HCGL)
http://www.bgsu.edu/colleges/library/hcgl/hcgl.html

Hudson River Maritime Museum
http://www.ulster.net/~hrmm/

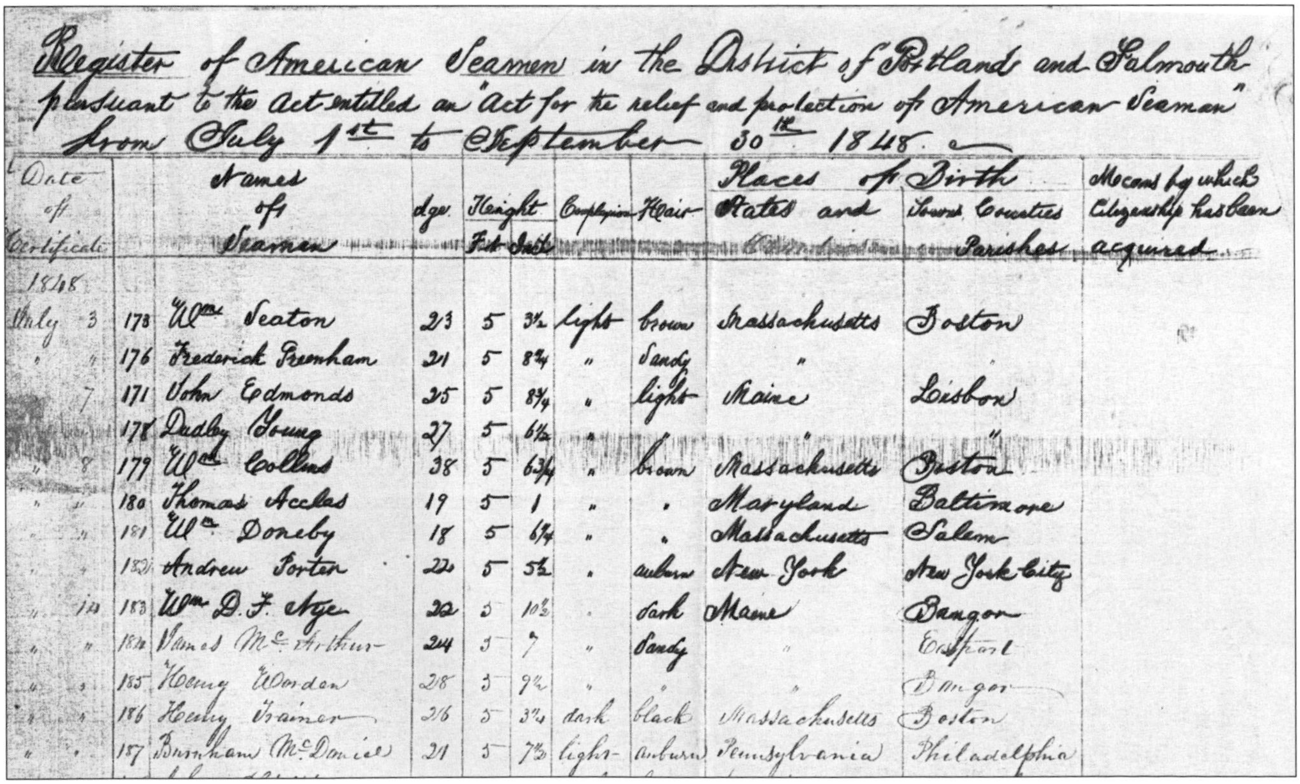

Register of American Seamen in the District of Portland and Falmouth pursuant to the act entitled an "Act for the relief and protection of American Seamen" from July 1st to September 30th 1848.

Date of Certificate		Names of Seamen	Age	Height Feet	Height Inch	Complexion	Hair	Places of Birth: States and	Towns, Counties, Parishes	Means by which Citizenship has been acquired
1848										
July 3	175	Wm Seaton	23	5	3½	light	brown	Massachusetts	Boston	
" "	176	Frederick Greenham	21	5	8¾	"	Sandy	"		
7	177	John Edmonds	25	5	8¼	"	light	Maine	Lisbon	
	178	Dudley Young	27	5	6½				"	
8	179	Wm Collins	38	5	6¾	"	brown	Massachusetts	Boston	
" "	180	Thomas Acclas	19	5	1	"	"	Maryland	Baltimore	
" "	181	Wm Doneby	18	5	6¼	"	"	Massachusetts	Salem	
" "	182	Andrew Porter	22	5	5½	"	auburn	New York	New York City	
" 14	183	Wm D. F. Nye	22	5	10½	"	dark	Maine	Bangor	
" "	184	James McArthur	24	5	7	"	Sandy	"	Eastport	
" "	185	Henry Worden	28	5	9½	"	"		Bangor	
" "	186	Henry Trainor	26	5	3½	dark	black	Massachusetts	Boston	
"	187	Burnham McDonald	21	5	7½	light	auburn	Pennsylvania	Philadelphia	

Figure 117
Register of American seamen in the District of Portland and Falmouth pursuant to the act entitled "Act for the Relief and Protection of American Seamen" from July 1 to September 30 1848. The document includes the date the certificate was issued to the seaman, name of seaman, age, height in feet and inches, complexion, hair color, places of birth (states, towns, counties, or parishes), and means by which citizenship was acquired.

Independence Seaport Museum
http://www.libertynet.org/seaport/

Inland Seas Maritime Museum of the Great Lakes Historical Society
http://www.inlandseas.org/

Maritime History Archive—Memorial University of Newfoundland
http://www.mun.ca/mha/

National Maritime Historical Society
http://seahistory.org/index2.html

Oregon Maritime Center and Museum—Lawrence Barber Library
http://www.teleport.com/~omcm/index.shtml

Robert H. Smith's Master Index to World Wide Maritime Museum Internet Resources
http://www.bobhudson.com/Smiths/index.html

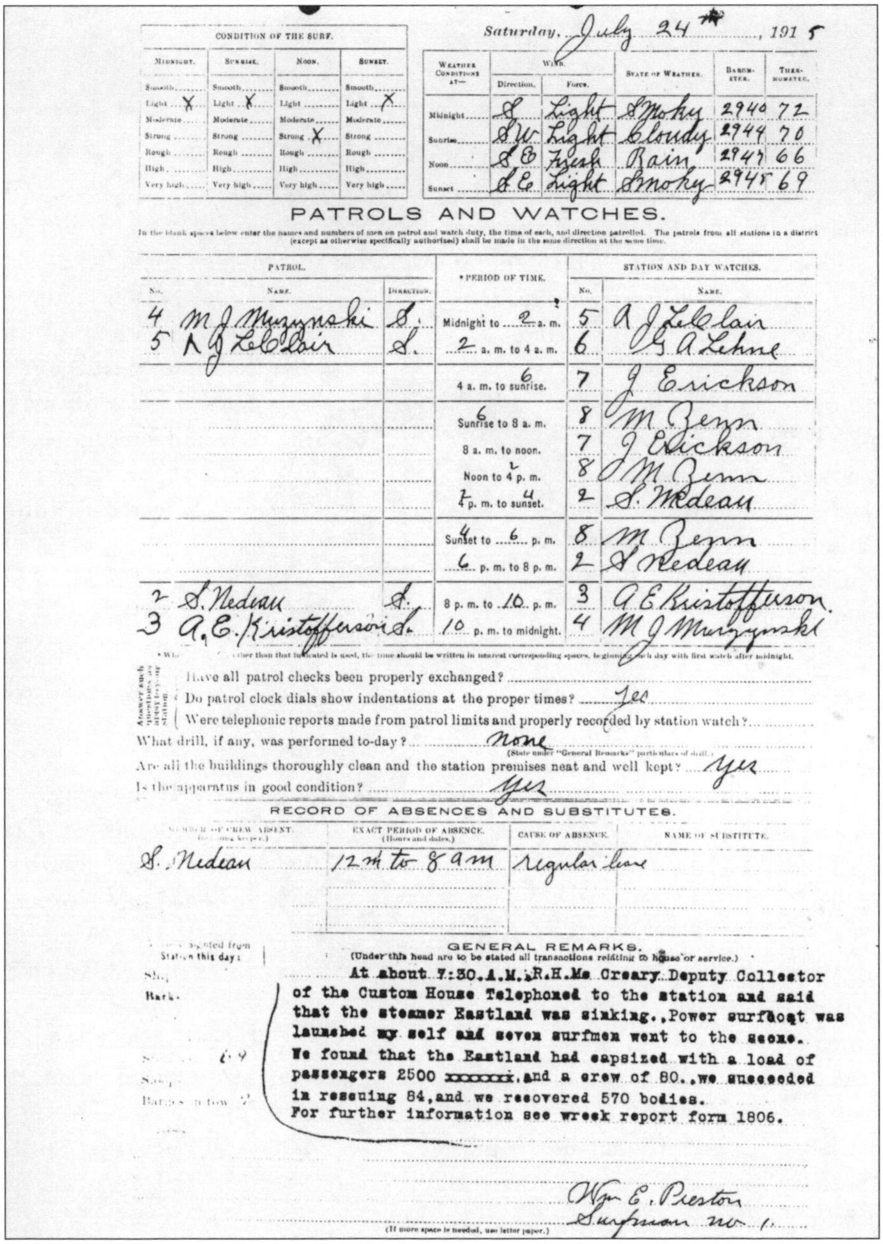

Saturday, July 24th, 1915

CONDITION OF THE SURF.			
Midnight.	Sunrise.	Noon.	Sunset.
Smooth	Smooth	Smooth	Smooth
Light X	Light X	Light	Light X
Moderate	Moderate	Moderate	Moderate
Strong	Strong	Strong X	Strong
Rough	Rough	Rough	Rough
High	High	High	High
Very high	Very high	Very high	Very high

Weather Conditions at—	Wind Direction.	Wind Force.	State of Weather.	Barometer.	Thermometer.
Midnight	S	Light	Smoky	2940	72
Sunrise	SW	Light	Cloudy	2944	70
Noon	SE	Fresh	Rain	2947	66
Sunset	SE	Light	Smoky	2945	69

PATROLS AND WATCHES.

In the blank spaces below enter the names and numbers of men on patrol and watch duty, the time of each, and direction patrolled. The patrols from all stations in a district (except as otherwise specifically authorized) shall be made in the same direction at the same time.

Patrol No.	Patrol Name.	Direction.	* Period of Time.	Station and Day Watches No.	Name.
4	M J Muzynski	S.	Midnight to 2 a. m.	5	A J LeClair
5	A J LeClair	S.	2 a. m. to 4 a. m.	6	G A Lehne
			4 a. m. to sunrise. 6	7	J Erickson
			Sunrise 6 to 8 a. m.	8	M Zenn
			8 a. m. to noon.	7	J Erickson
			Noon to 2 p. m.	8	M Zenn
			2 p. m. to sunset. 4	2	S. Nedeau
			Sunset 4 to 6 p. m.	8	M Zenn
			6 p. m. to 8 p. m.	2	S Nedeau
2	S. Nedeau	S.	8 p. m. to 10 p. m.	3	A E Kristofferson
3	A. E. Kristofferson	S.	10 p. m. to midnight.	4	M J Muzynski

Have all patrol checks been properly exchanged?
Do patrol clock dials show indentations at the proper times? Yes
Were telephonic reports made from patrol limits and properly recorded by station watch?
What drill, if any, was performed to-day? none
Are all the buildings thoroughly clean and the station premises neat and well kept? Yes
Is the apparatus in good condition? Yes

RECORD OF ABSENCES AND SUBSTITUTES.

Number of Crew Absent.	Exact Period of Absence. (Hours and dates.)	Cause of Absence.	Name of Substitute.
S. Nedeau	12 m to 8 am	regular leave	

GENERAL REMARKS.
(Under this head are to be stated all transactions relating to house or service.)

At about 7:30.A.M.,R.H.Mc Creary Deputy Collector of the Custom House Telephoned to the station and said that the steamer Eastland was sinking.,Power surfboat was launched my self and seven surfmen went to the scene. We found that the Eastland had capsized with a load of passengers 2500 xxxxxxx.and a crew of 80.,we succeeded in rescuing 84,and we recovered 570 bodies.
For further information see wreck report form 1806.

Wm E. Preston
Surfman no. 1.

(If more space is needed, use letter paper.)

Figure 118

A page from the *Weekly Journal of the Lifesaving Service*, giving a report on the capsized *Eastland*. The excursion steamer overturned on July 24, 1915 in the Chicago River, killing 812 people. (Courtesy of the National Archives - Great Lakes Region, Chicago)

Marriage Dispensations

In some religions, a dispensation was necessary, under certain circumstances, for a couple to be married in a religious ceremony. Dispensations were requested for various reasons, such as not wanting banns read or posted, a marriage between cousins, or, most commonly, a marriage between a couple of different religious backgrounds. In the Catholic Church, for example, a dispensation is necessary for a Catholic to marry someone of another denomination. In those cases, dispensation records reveal a good deal of biographical information: names of prospective bride and groom, their birthplaces (sometimes including exact towns, which can be especially helpful in learning a foreign origin), residence at the time of filing for the dispensation, and the names of both parents, often including the mother's maiden name.

In order to locate this kind of record, the religious backgrounds of the couple of interest must be determined as well as where and when the marriage took place. If the records have been saved for the time period in question, an inquiry to the religious headquarters, diocese, or archive may be the best starting point. If nothing else, this may narrow the search to a particular congregation or parish.

An example of a published collection of Catholic dispensations is *Bishop Loughlin's Dispensations—Diocese of Brooklyn 1859-1866, Volume 1* by Joseph M. Silinonte.

The value of this particular book of 5,200 dispensations lies not only in its content, but in its coverage—the Diocese of Brooklyn included all of Long Island (then Kings, Queens, and Suffolk counties) and present-day Nassau County, a total of thirty-five churches. Furthermore, this region was the initial stopping-off place for many immigrants, who would later move elsewhere.

Selected Readings:

J. Gordon Melton, III, ed. *The Directory of Religious Organizations in the United States.* Detroit: Gale Research Co., 1993.

Dougherty, Richard W. "Published Church Records" in *Printed Sources: A Guide to Published Genealogical Records* edited by Kory L Meyerink. Salt Lake City: Ancestry, 1988, 269-298.

____. "Research in Church Records" in *The Source: A Guidebook of American Genealogy* edited by Loretto Dennis Szucs and Sandra Hargreaves Luebking. Salt Lake City: Ancestry, 1988, 149-170.

Silinonte, Joseph M. Bishop *Loughlin's Dispensations—Diocese of Brooklyn 1859-1866*, Volume 1. Brooklyn, N.Y: Joseph Silinonte (7901 4th Avenue, #D, Brooklyn, NY 11209), 1996.

Groom's Name Bride's Name	Place of Nativity	Residence	Parents	Date & Church Code	Comments
Dunnigan, Michael	NL	NL	NL	Jan 27, 1863	
Burns, Ellen	NL	NL	NL	12	
Dunnigan, Patrick H	NL	Powers St	NL	Mar 1, 1864	
Holge ?, MaryJane	NL	Stanton St ?	NL	8	
Dunnigan, Thomas	Kings Co	Clinton Av c Lafayette	John, Peggy Kelly ?	Sept 22, 1862	
Quinn, Susan	Armagh	Washington nr Atlantic	NL	15	
Dunning ?, Henry S ?	Brunswick, Maine	4 William St	Elisha, Lidia Lunt	Oct 2, 1866	
Logue, Catherine	Ireland	Graham St&Lafayette Av	John, Ann Callaghan	12	
Dunphy, James	Kilkenny	Bay Ridge	Luke, Honh Grant	Jun 21, 1865	
McCarthy, Margaret	Limerick	11 Elizabeth St NY	NL	18	
Dunphy, John	Kilkenny	Cincinnatti	Jas, Bt O'Neill	Jan 12, 1865	
Walsh, Bridget	Kilkenny	Bay Ridge	Jas, Mrgt McCarthy	18	
Dunworth, Lawrence I	Sheffield	Dobbs Ferry	Andrew, Isabella Bacon	Apr 6, 1863	
Ryan, Margaret	Tipperary	28 W. Warren	Jas, Johanna McEncroe	10	
Dunworth, Patrick	Limerick	15 Graham St	Jere, Jane Kennedy	Jul 22, 1866	
Stone, Mary Ann	Limerick	78 Pacific St	John, — Griffin	10	
Durain, Edwin Doyer	Brooklyn	14 Harper Ct	Jas, Eliza Neson	May 8, 1860	
Doonan, Margaret	Brooklyn	101 Tillary St	John, Eliz Moran	1	
Durkin, Thomas	Roscommon	206 Hamilton Av	Matt, Mrgt Daley	May 3, 1866	
McEntee, Catherine	Monaghan	6 Walworth St	Wm, Cath Carney	12	
Durnery, Thomas	Donegal	NL	Thadeus, Anna Cawley	Dec 1, 1862	
Williamson, Laura	England	NL	NL	31	
Durning, Thomas	NL	NL	NL	Oct 24, 1863	
Williamson, Laura	NL	NL	NL	31	
Durrings ?, James	W. Meath	NY	Ed, Cath	May 16, 1865	
Lally, Ann	Mayo	52 Willow nr Amity	Frs, Mary McGlen ?	10	
Duryee ?, Stephen B	Flatbush	Flatbush	Jacob, Nelly Schumaker	Sept 23, 1862	
Kelly, Mary A	N.Y.	270 2 St	John, Ann Reilly	9	
Duscold, Charles	NY	143 Hudson Av	John, Mary	Sept 24, 1866	
Nolan, Ann E	Morristown NJ	191 Fulton	NL	1	
Dusptery ?, Abraham	?	Greenpoint	John, Rebecca Townsend ?	Apr 11, 1863	
O'Connor, Bridget	Ireland	Greenpoint	Thos, Cath Farrell	1	
Dusser ?, John H	Queens	14 Lincoln Pl	Thos, Cath Carroll	Oct 7, 1861	
Cawden ?, Mary Ellen	Brooklyn	Johnson&Union Av	Thos, NL	9	
Dwyer, Denis	Clare	143 Court	Dl, Bt Murphy	Frb 6, 1863	
Hackett, Mary E	Tipperary	222 Court	Pk, Ellen	2	
Dwyer, Edward	Kilkenny	Love Lane	Tim'y, Julia Hughes	Sept 28, 1860	
Kelly, Bridget	NL	Love Lane	NL	4	
Dwyer, James	Tipperary	28 Butler St	Jere, Honh Meara	Aug 6, 1864	
Shanahan, Mary	Tipperary	148 Butler	Tim'y, Bt Dunn	2	
Dwyer, Jeremiah	Tipperary	Pierpont House	Jere, Ellen Kennedy	Oct 9, 1865	
Dunn, Ann	Kildare	Pierpont House	Denis, NL	4	
Dwyer, John	Limerick	14 Pacific St	Ml, Ellen Ryan	Dec 31, 1865	
Noonan, Mary	Clare	14 Pacific St	Denis, Bt Nelson	10	
Dwyer, Michael	Kildare	545 Columbia	Wm, Ellen Kelly	Jan 24, 1866	
Mackin, Margaret	Ireland	29 Carrol	NL	3	
Dwyer, Patrick	Limerick	Washington Av nr Bergen	Bart, Mary Hannon ?	May 30, 1863	
Feely, Sarah	NL	Washington Av nr Bergen	NL	15	
Dwyer, Patrick	Tipperary	101 Columbia	Ml, Mrgt Hayes	Feb 2, 1864	
Dorsey, Anna	Tipperary	106 Duffield	Thos, Cath	1	
Dwyer, Timothy	NY	22 Amity	Wm, Honh Murray	Jan 6, 1861	
Callanan, Ellen	Cork	22 Amity	John, Mrgt Dwyer	10	
Dynan, Thomas	Clare	Pacific&Willow	Johm, Mrgt Kelly	Jan 28, 1862	
Manix, Bridget	Clare	Congress nr Columbia	NL	10	
Dyott, William	Dublin	New Rochelle	Wm Hy, - Willett	Sept 9, 1861	
O'Leary, Ellen	Kerry	186 2 St ED	John, Gubby ? Horrigan	9	
Eagan, James	NL	Union St	NL	Feb 15, 1863	
Murphy, Catherine	NL	Union St	NL	1	
Eagan, James P	NL	NL	NL	Oct 24, 1863	
Spelman, B ?	NL	NL	NL	21	
Eagan, John	Longford	171 Jay St	Owen, Rose Trainer	Nov 24, 1859	
Smith, Ellen	NL	Myrtle Av & Jay	NL	1	
Eagan, Rody ?	Kings	4 Av & 21 St	Chs, Eliza Fitzpatrick	Oct 3, 1860	
Cuniff, Bridget	Ireland	4 Av & 21 St	NL	6	
Eagan, Thomas	Galway	Utica Av	Peter, Anne Mee	July 24, 1865	
Daley, Mary	Galway	Utica Av	NL	32	
Eagan, William	Cork	29 Sackett St	Wm, Julia Murray	Sept 22, 1865	
Gilbride, Elizabeth	Brooklyn	13 Summit St	John, NL	11	
Early, James	W. Meath	Washington Av&Bergen	John, Mary Walsh	Feb 7, 1866	
Kelly, Ann	Donegal	Washington nr ?	NL	15	67

54

Figure 119

A page taken from Joseph M. Silinonte's Bishop Loughlin's *Dispensations - Diocese of Brooklyn 1859-1866, Volume 1*. (Reproduced with permission)

Medical Records

Medical records often contain valuable genealogical information, including name, date of birth, place of birth, parents' names, and sometimes family medical histories. Confidentiality laws severely limit access to medical records, with access typically restricted to physicians, the individual to whom they pertain, or that person's legal guardian. Medical records pertaining to military personnel may be available through the National Archives. Collections held there include medical records for the periods 1821–84 and 1894–1912, containing information relating to regular army personnel admitted to hospitals for treatment; abstracts of medical records for Civil War soldiers treated at medical facilities in posts and camps, and in the field; records from the Bureau of Medicine and Surgery pertaining to sick or wounded naval personnel; and hospital records for residents of some of the National Homes for Disabled Volunteer Soldiers.

See also *Genetics Studies, Hospital Records,* and *Insurance Records.*

Selected Readings:

Guide to Genealogical Research in the National Archives. Washington, D.C.: National Archives Trust Fund Board, 1982.

Neagles, James C. *U.S. Military Records: A Guide to Federal & State Sources, Colonial America to the Present.* Salt Lake City: Ancestry, 1994.

Figure 120

Register of patients from 1906 when the Office of the Surgeon General in San Francisco set up shelters and cared for thousands of residents after the earthquake and fire. The records are at the National Archives - Pacific Region, San Bruno, California.

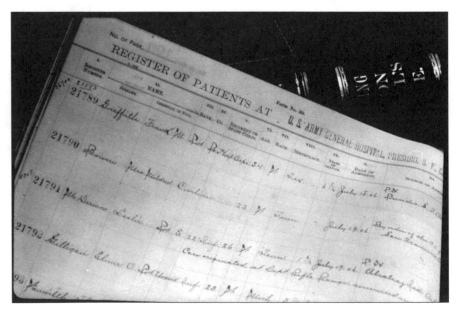

Midwife Records

Throughout American history, midwives were commonly used to assist in childbirth. The journals of some midwives, in which they recorded the births they attended, have been published and microfilmed. Typically included in each entry is the date, time, and place of birth; sex of the baby; the names of the infant and parents; and the name of the attending midwife or physician. In some cases, the family address, the mother's maiden name, and the father's occupation may be listed as well.

An example of one such journal is Laurel Thatcher Ulrich's *A Midwife's Tale: The Life of Martha Ballard, Based on Her Diary, 1785–1812* (New York: Vintage Books, 1991). A collection of midwife records at Northwestern Memorial Hospital Archives in Chicago, which contains over 100,000 entries, was microfilmed by the Genealogical Society of Utah and is available from the LDS Family History Library and its Family History Centers. Similar manuscripts exist for other places, although some degree of searching is required to locate them.

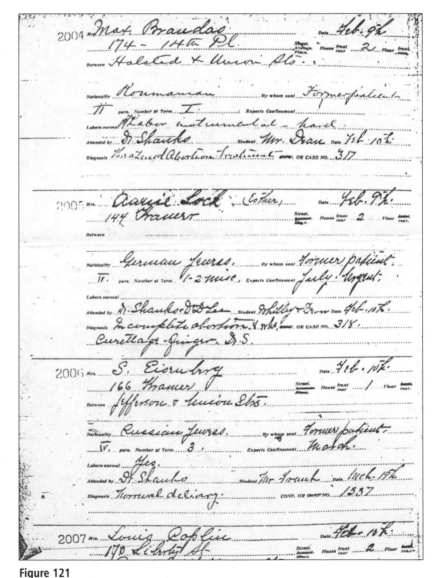

Figure 121

A page from a midwife's journal from the collection at Northwestern Memorial Hospital Archives in Chicago.

Military Records

Military records are among the most important and most extensive U.S. records of genealogical value. The military needs to verify the identities of soldiers who fought and the veterans who receive pensions. Therefore, birth information is common in military records. As is the case with most records used in family history research, more recent records include more information than do earlier records. Revolutionary War service records seldom identify the birthplace of the soldier, let alone his native origins. Civil War enlistment records usually indicate the country where an immigrant was born, and sometimes the town. However, military enlistment records from the end of the nineteenth century almost always indicate the town of birth. In addition to service and enlistment records, valuable information can be found in draft records, medical records, pension records, and burial records.

To locate military records for an ancestor, it is essential to know when and where in the armed forces he or she served, and whether that person served in the enlisted ranks or was an officer. Family sources such as letters, photographs, military but-

tons and ribbons, service medals, and discharge papers may provide the necessary information. The National Archives has military records relating to service and pensions prior to World War I. Records relating to military service from World War I and thereafter are housed in the National Personnel Records Center, 9700 Page Boulevard, St. Louis, MO 63132. The Family History Library has a large collection of military records with over 25,000 microfilms of the major indexes to the military records at the National Archives and many of the service and pension records. A Cemetery Service, operated by the Department of Veterans Affairs, maintains an alphabetical card index of almost all soldiers who have been buried in national cemeteries and other cemeteries under federal jurisdiction since 1861.

Ancestry.com has made a number of military databases available, such as the Civil War Research Database, a work in progress, with well over 2 million names in it as this volume goes to print.

See also *Draft Records, FamilySearch® (Military Index), Medical Records,* and *Pension Records.*

Selected Readings:

Cerny, Johni. "Research in Military Records." *The Source: A Guidebook of American Genealogy.* Rev. ed. Ch. 9: 288–334 (revised by Lloyd DeWitt Bockstruck and David Thackery). Salt Lake City: Ancestry, 1997.

Deputy, Marilyn, and Pat Barben. *Register of Federal United States Military Records, a Guide to Manuscript Sources at the Genealogical Library Salt Lake City and the National Archives in Washington, D.C.* 3 vols. Bowie, Md.: Heritage Books, 1986.

Guide to Genealogical Research in the National Archives. Washington, D.C.: National Archives Trust Fund Board, 1982.

Neagles, James C. *U.S. Military Records: A Guide to Federal & State Sources, Colonial America to the Present.* Salt Lake City: Ancestry, 1994.

Internet Sites of Interest:

Ancestry.com Military Resource Page
http://www.ancestry.com/dailynews/military.htm

Commonwealth War Graves Commission
http://www.cwgc.org/

Department of Veterans Affairs
http://www.va.gov/foia/index.htm

Guide to Requesting Military Records (World War I and later)
http://www.ancestry.com/research/military80.htm

National Personnel Records Center Military Personnel Records - National Archives and Records Administration
http://www.nara.gov/regional/stlouis.html

Marine Corps Historical Center
http://www.usmc.mil/history.nsf/table+of+contents

Naval Historical Center
http://www.history.navy.mil/

U.S. Army Center of Military History
http://www.army.mil/cmh-pg/default.htm

Full-text Listings of Medal of Honor Citations
http://www.army.mil/cmh-pg/moh1.htm

U.S. Army Military History Institute
http://carlisle-www.army.mil/usamhi/

Military Records continued on page 146

I certify, on honor, that Thomas Howley a Private of Captain J. E. Flynn's Company (K) of the 9th Regiment of H. Artillery VOLUNTEERS, of the State of New York, born in Ireland, State of ——, aged 35 years; 5 feet 7 inches high; Sandy complexion, Blue eyes, light hair, and by occupation a Laborer, having joined the company on its original organization at Auburn N.Y. and enrolled in it at the muster into the service of the United States at Auburn N.Y., on the 8th day of September, 1862, (or was mustered in service as a recruit, by ..., at ..., on the ... day of ..., 186 , or was drafted and mustered into the service of the United States from the ... Enrollment District of the State of ..., at ..., on the ... day of ..., 186 ,) to serve in the Regiment, for the term of Three Years: and having served HONESTLY and FAITHFULLY with his Company in 9th N.Y. Arty to the present date, is now entitled to a DISCHARGE by reason of Death. Was Killed in action at Monocacy Md. July 9th 1864.

The said Thomas Howley was last paid by Paymaster [illegible] to include the 29th day of February, 1864, and has pay due him from that time to the present date; he is entitled to pay and subsistence for TRAVELING to place of enrollment, and whatever other allowances are authorized to volunteer soldiers, drafted men, or militia, so discharged. He has received from the United States CLOTHING amounting to 31 96/100 dollars, since the 8th day of September 1863, when his clothing account was last settled. He has received from the United States 35 100 dollars advanced BOUNTY.

There is to be stopped from him, on account of the State of ..., or other authorities, for CLOTHING, &c., received on entering service, ... 100 dollars; and for other stoppages, viz: One (1) [illegible] 30 ... 100 dollars.

He has been furnished with TRANSPORTATION in kind from the place of his discharge to ...; and he has been SUBSISTED for TRAVELING to his place of enrollment, up to the ..., 186–.

He is indebted to ..., SUTLER, Nothing 100 dollars.
He is indebted to ..., LAUNDRESS, " 100 dollars.

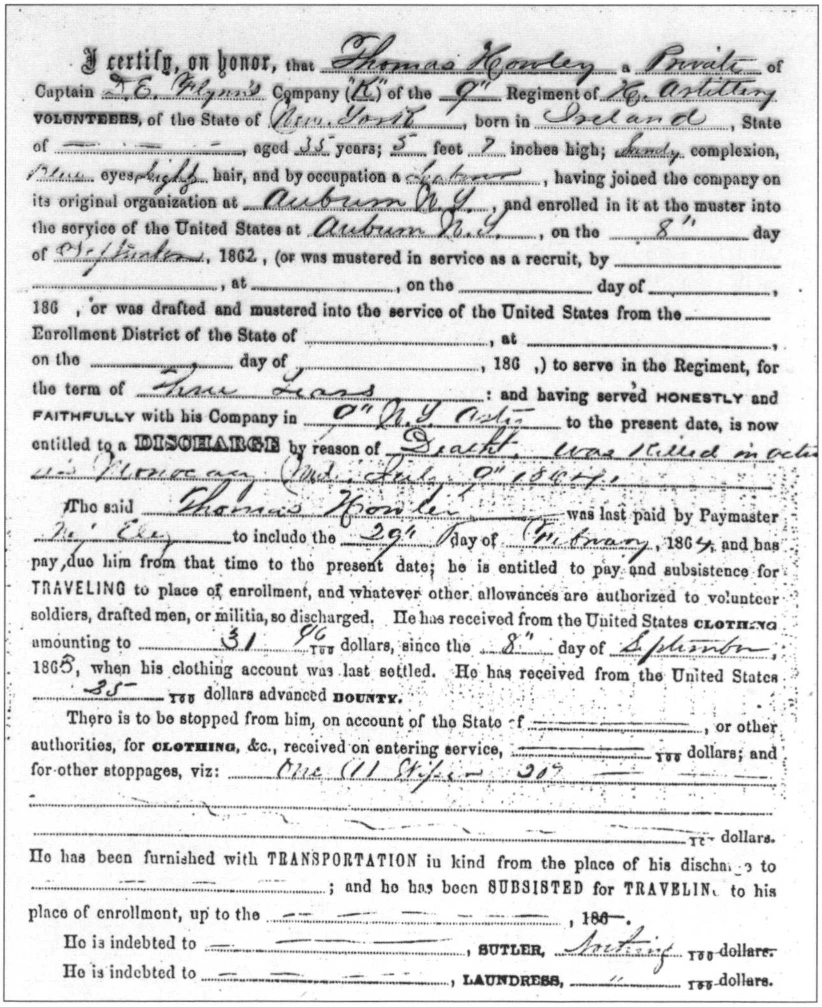

Figure 122

These Civil War discharge papers from 1864 for Thomas Howley includes his regiment, his native country, age, a physical description, and the fact that he was killed in action on 9 July 1864 in the "Battle that Saved Washington" in Monocacy, Maryland.

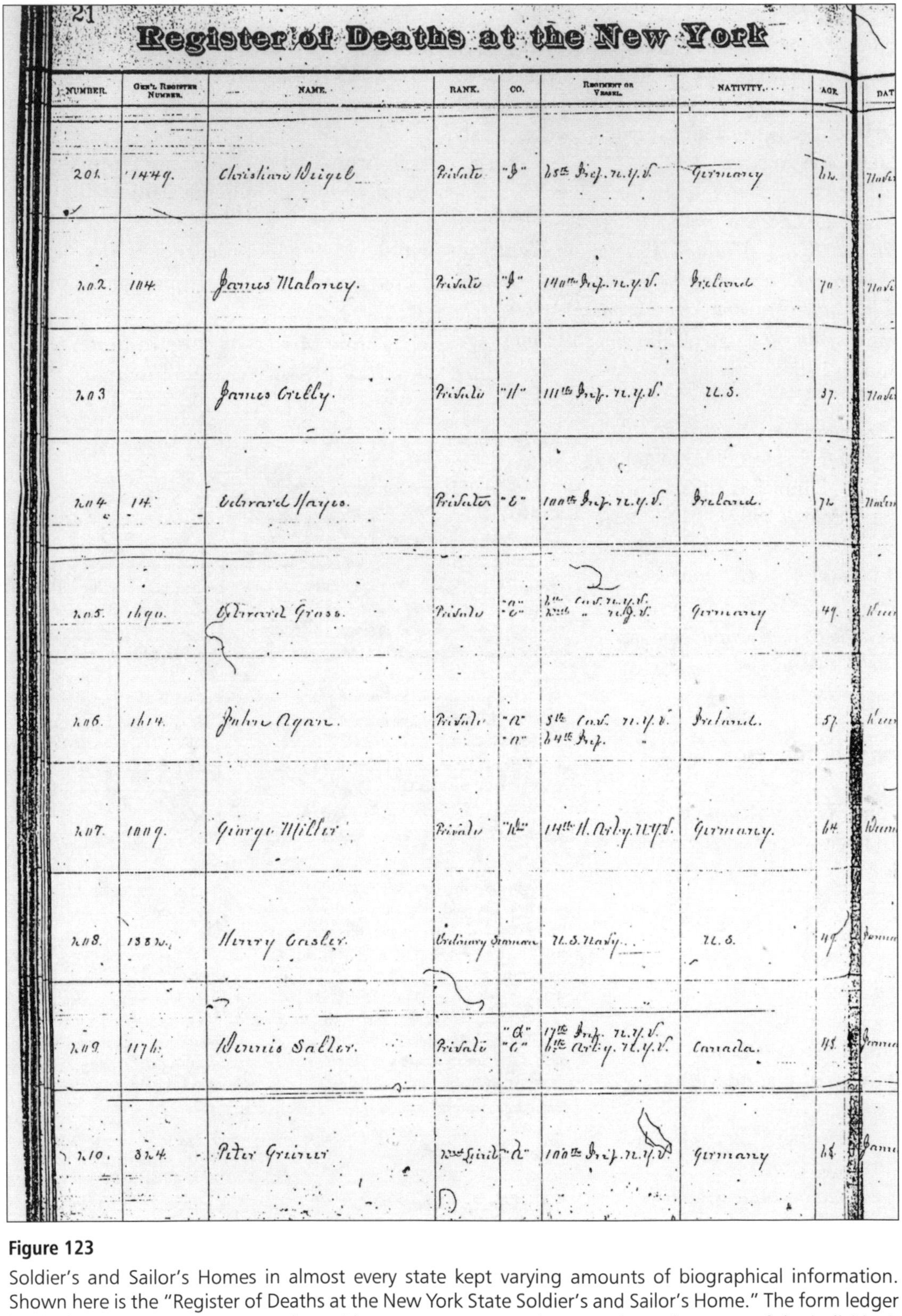

Register of Deaths at the New York

NUMBER.	Gen'l Register Number.	NAME.	RANK.	CO.	Regiment or Vessel.	NATIVITY.	AGE.	DAT
201.	1449.	Christian Weigel	Private	"I"	65th Inf. N.Y.V.	Germany	62.	Nove
202.	104	James Maloney.	Private	"I"	140th Inf. N.Y.V.	Ireland	70	Nove
203		James Crilly.	Private	"H"	111th Inf. N.Y.V.	U.S.	37.	Nove
204	14.	Edward Hayes.	Private	"C"	100th Inf. N.Y.V.	Ireland.	72	Nove
205.	1490.	Edward Gross.	Private	"C" "C"	6th Cav. N.Y.V. 2nd " N.Y.V.	Germany	49.	Nove
206.	1614.	John Agan.	Private	"A" "A"	8th Cav. N.Y.V. 64th Inf.	Ireland.	57	Nove
207.	1009.	George Miller.	Private	"K"	14th H. Arty. N.Y.V.	Germany.	64	Nove
208.	1382.	Henry Gasler.	Ordinary Seaman		U.S. Navy.	U.S.	47	Nove
209.	1176.	Dennis Saller.	Private	"A" "C"	17th Inf. N.Y.V. 6th Arty. N.Y.V.	Canada.	48	Nove
210.	324.	Peter Gruner	1st Lieut.	"A"	100th Inf. N.Y.V.	Germany	68	Nove

Figure 123

Soldier's and Sailor's Homes in almost every state kept varying amounts of biographical information. Shown here is the "Register of Deaths at the New York State Soldier's and Sailor's Home." The form ledger books (running across two pages) provide spaces to enter register numbers, the name of the individual, rank, company, regiment or vessel, nativity, age, date of death, cause of death, place of death, where buried, number of grave, and remarks. The records of some states have been indexed, and some have been microfilmed. State archives are among the best places to start a search for these records. The New York Soldier's and Sailor's Home records have been microfilmed and are available at and through the Family History Library.

State Soldier's & Sailor's Home.

AGE	DATE OF DEATH.	CAUSE OF DEATH.	PLACE OF DEATH.	WHERE BURIED.	NUMBER OF GRAVE.	REMARKS.
62.	November 6. 1883	Apoplexy & Paralysis.	Hospital.	Home Cemetery	173.	No friends in this country.
70	November 19. 1883		Hospital. Rochester. N.Y.	Rochester. N.Y.	—	Died while on furlough
37.	November 24 1883	General Dropsy.	Hospital.	Seneca Falls. N.Y.	—	Peter & Barney (brothers) notified. Order recd thro telephone to send remains to Seneca Falls. N.Y.
72.	November 25. 1883	Apoplexy.	Hospital.	Home Cemetery	174.	Mary Hayes (sister) notified. Palace Grange. Co. Limerick Ireland.
49.	December 10. 1883	Congestion of the Brain and Epilepsy.	Hospital	Home Cemetery.	175.	No relatives in this country.
57.	December 16. 1883	General Dropsy. due to Disease of the Heart	Hospital	Home Cemetery.	176.	Notified. Terrence Duffy. friends N.Y.
64.	December 30. 1883	Paralysis	Hospital.	Home Cemetery.	177.	No friends.
49.	January 4. 1884	Insanity.	Hospital	Home Cemetery.	178.	Thg Eli Casler (Son) Susp Bridge Secy North Star Lodge. No 15. & O.M.R. & Bro Bahum O.K.L. Post No 9 G.A.R.
44.	January 9. 1884	Phthisis Pulmonalis.	Hospital.	Home Cemetery.	179.	Til & relative William Bath (brother) Nyack. N.Y.
64.	January 25. 1884	Hemiplegia and Apoplexy.	Hospital	Home Cemetery.	180.	Friends notified by Tel & Mail.

U.S. Air Force Historical Research Agency
http://www.au.af.mil/au/afhra/

U.S. Coast Guard Historian's Office (G-CP-4)
http://www.dot.gov/dotinfo/uscg/hq/g-cp/history/collect.html

U.S. Merchant Marine
http://www.usmm.org/

World War II Honor List of Dead and Missing Army and Army Air Forces Personnel, 1946
NAIL: NARA Archival Information Locator
http://www.nara.gov/nara/searchnail.html
(Search hint: select the "NAIL Digital Copies Search Form" and enter "War Casualties" in the first keywords box and "Army" in the second keywords box)

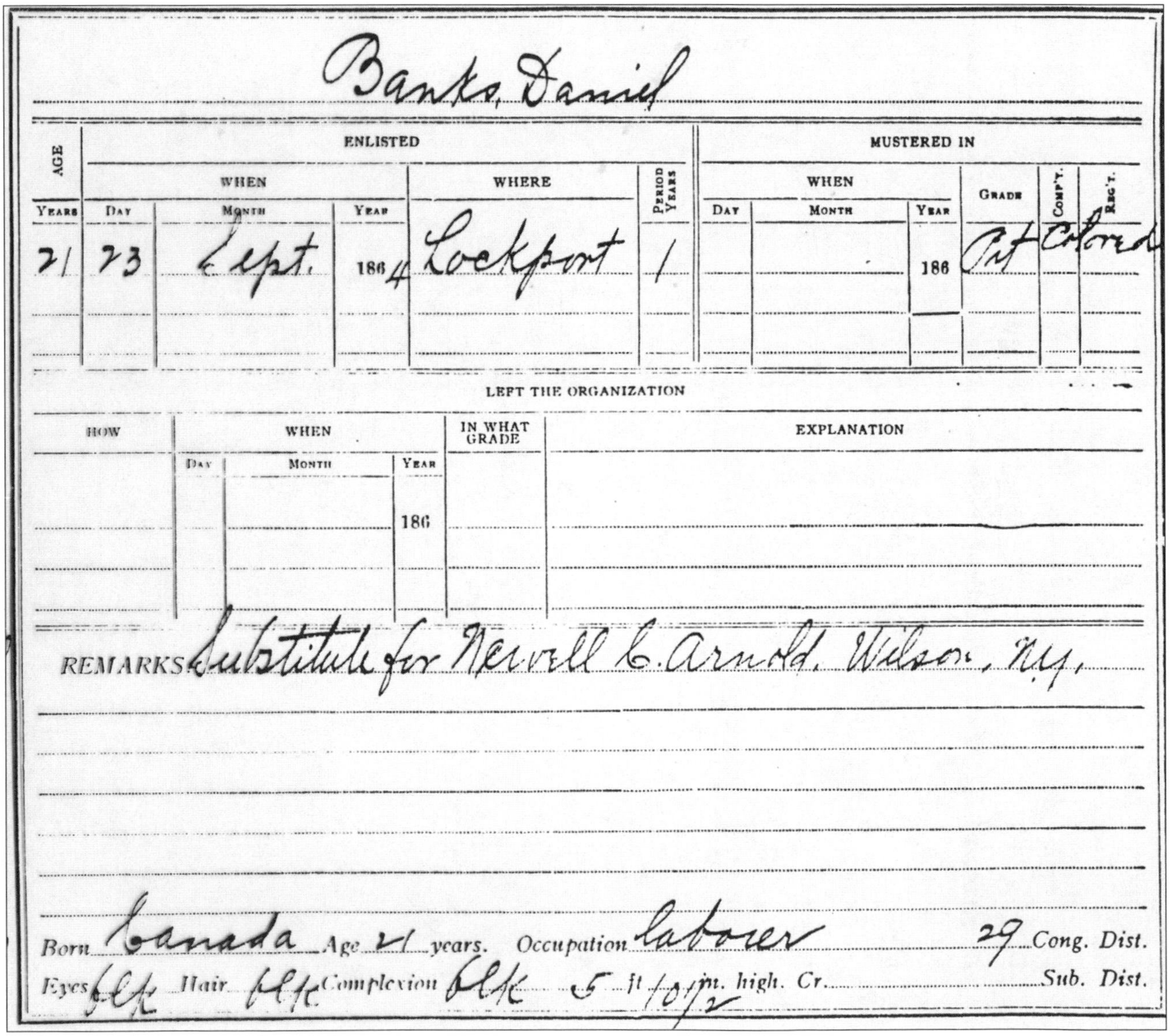

Banks, Daniel

AGE	ENLISTED					MUSTERED IN					
	WHEN			WHERE	PERIOD YEARS	WHEN			GRADE	COMP'T.	REG'T.
YEARS	DAY	MONTH	YEAR			DAY	MONTH	YEAR			
21	23	Sept.	1864	Lockport	1			186	Pvt	Colored	

LEFT THE ORGANIZATION

HOW	WHEN			IN WHAT GRADE	EXPLANATION
	DAY	MONTH	YEAR		
			186		

REMARKS: Substitute for Nevell C. Arnold. Wilson, N.Y.

Born Canada Age 21 years. Occupation laborer 29 Cong. Dist.
Eyes blk Hair blk Complexion blk 5 ft 10 1/2 in. high. Cr. Sub. Dist.

Figure 124
An enlistment form for a substitute for a drafted citizen, Civil War-Union. (Courtesy of the National Archives)

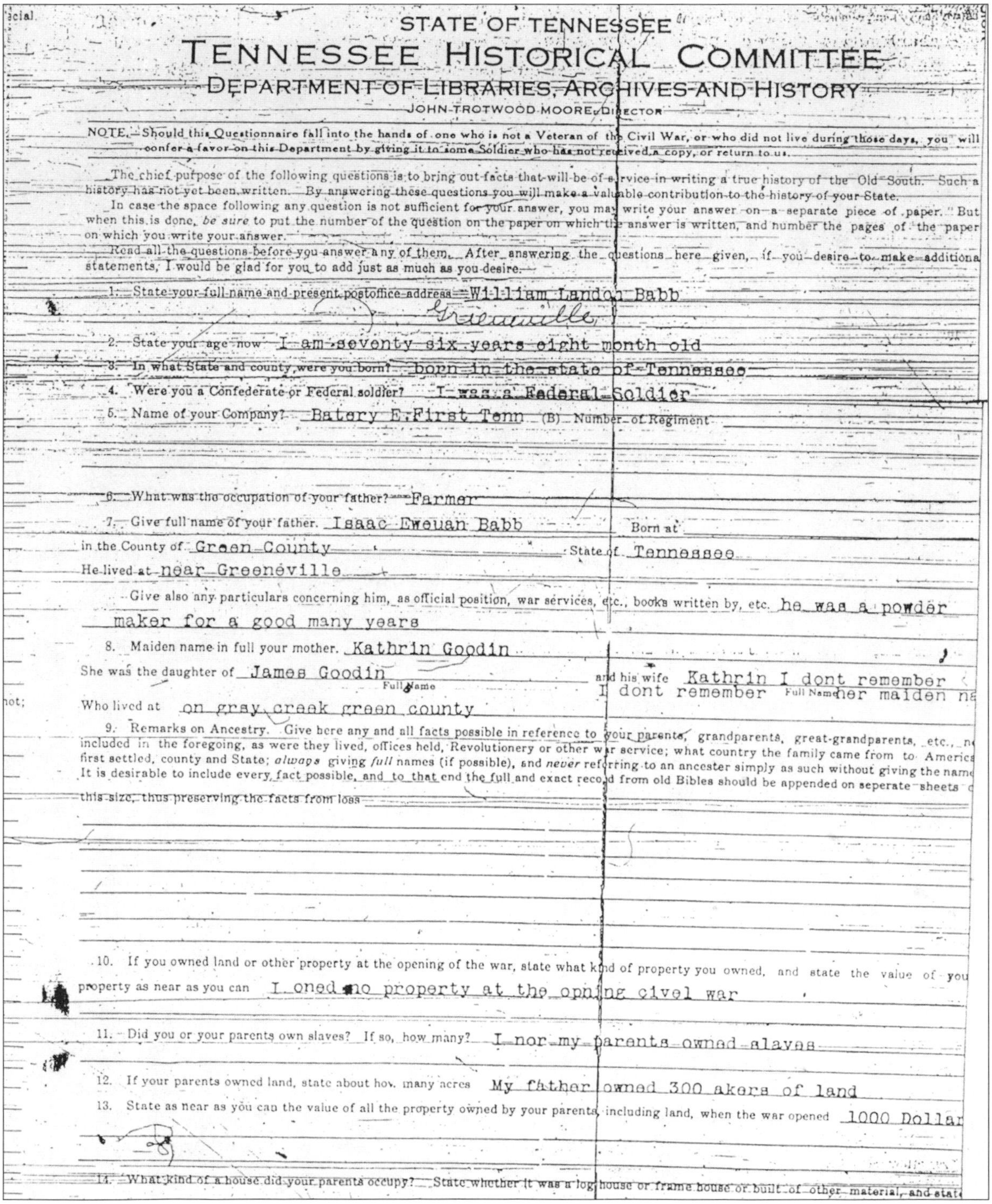

STATE OF TENNESSEE

TENNESSEE HISTORICAL COMMITTEE

DEPARTMENT OF LIBRARIES, ARCHIVES AND HISTORY

JOHN TROTWOOD MOORE, DIRECTOR

NOTE.—Should this Questionnaire fall into the hands of one who is not a Veteran of the Civil War, or who did not live during those days, you will confer a favor on this Department by giving it to some Soldier who has not received a copy, or return to us.

The chief purpose of the following questions is to bring out facts that will be of service in writing a true history of the Old South. Such a history has not yet been written. By answering these questions you will make a valuable contribution to the history of your State.

In case the space following any question is not sufficient for your answer, you may write your answer on a separate piece of paper. But when this is done, *be sure* to put the number of the question on the paper on which the answer is written, and number the pages of the paper on which you write your answer.

Read all the questions before you answer any of them. After answering the questions here given, if you desire to make additional statements, I would be glad for you to add just as much as you desire.

1. State your full name and present postoffice address William Landon Babb Greeneville

2. State your age now I am seventy six years eight month old

3. In what State and county were you born? born in the state of Tennessee

4. Were you a Confederate or Federal soldier? I was a Federal Soldier

5. Name of your Company? Batery E First Tenn (B) Number of Regiment

6. What was the occupation of your father? Farmer

7. Give full name of your father. Isaac Eweuan Babb Born at in the County of Green County State of Tennessee He lived at near Greeneville

Give also any particulars concerning him, as official position, war services, etc., books written by, etc. he was a powder maker for a good many years

8. Maiden name in full your mother. Kathrin Goodin

She was the daughter of James Goodin (Full Name) and his wife Kathrin I dont remember I dont remember her maiden na (Full Name) Who lived at on gray creek green county

9. Remarks on Ancestry. Give here any and all facts possible in reference to your parents, grandparents, great-grandparents, etc., not included in the foregoing, as were they lived, offices held, Revolutionery or other war service; what country the family came from to America; first settled, county and State; *always* giving *full* names (if possible), and *never* referring to an ancester simply as such without giving the name. It is desirable to include every fact possible, and to that end the full and exact record from old Bibles should be appended on seperate sheets of this size, thus preserving the facts from loss

10. If you owned land or other property at the opening of the war, state what kind of property you owned, and state the value of your property as near as you can I oned no property at the opning civel war

11. Did you or your parents own slaves? If so, how many? I nor my parents owned slaves

12. If your parents owned land, state about how many acres My father owned 300 akers of land

13. State as near as you can the value of all the property owned by your parents, including land, when the war opened 1000 Dollar

14. What kind of a house did your parents occupy? State whether it was a log house or frame house or built of other material, and state

Figure 125

In 1914 and 1915, questionnaire forms were sent to all known living Tennessee Civil War soldiers. The questionnaires, such as the one shown here, contain information regarding date and place of birth; date and place of enlistment; war service, including descriptions of battles, prison life, and other war experiences; economic and social status of the soldier and his family; genealogical data; educational and religious data; occupation before and after the war; and some other facts. Veterans were encouraged to write fully of their experiences. The index and the questionnaires, which are housed in the Tennessee State Library and Archives, have been microfilmed and are available at and through the Family History Library.

Mortality Schedules of the Census, 1850-85

Mortality schedules were compiled from inquiries made during the 1850, 1860, 1870, and 1880 censuses about people who had died during the preceding twelve months. As most states had not yet started to record vital statistics, the schedules are an invaluable source of information.

The schedules asked for the following information for all deaths occurring from 1 June to 31 May of 1849-50, 1859-60, 1869-70, 1879-80, and 1884-85: the deceased's name, sex, age, color (white, black, mulatto), whether widowed, place of birth (state, territory, or country), month in which the death occurred, profession/occupation/trade, disease or cause of death, and number of days ill. The birthplaces of the deceased's parents were requested as of 1870, and the length of time the deceased had resided in the area was requested as of 1880.

Copies, indexes, and printed schedules are available in many libraries, including the National Library of the Daughters of the American Revolution and the Family History Library and its Family History Centers™ which have the *United States Census Mortality Schedule Register* on microfiche (an appendix lists where records can be found for the twelve states whose schedules are not at the library).

Selected Readings:

Franklin, W. Neil, comp. *Federal Population and Mortality Census Schedules, 1790-1890 in the National Archives and the States: Outline of a Lecture on Their Availability, Content and Use.*

Special List no. 24. Washington, D.C.: National Archives and Records Service, General Services Administration, 1971. The greater part of this work describes the federal censuses and their availability in 1971. However, a discussion of mortality schedules is still valid. The compiler's bibliography cites some relatively obscure but important finding aids.

Meyerink, Kory L, ed. *Printed Sources: A Guide to Published Genealogical Records.* Salt Lake City: Ancestry, 1998.

National Archives and Records Administration. *Federal Population and Mortality Schedules, 1790-1910, in the National Archives and the States.* Washington, D.C.: National Archives, 1986. Two microfiche.

Volkel, Lowell M. *Illinois Mortality Schedule 1850.* 3 vols. Indianapolis: Heritage House, 1972.

_____. *Illinois Mortality Schedule 1860.* 5 vols. Indianapolis: Heritage House, 1979.

_____. *Illinois Mortality Schedule 1870.* 2 vols. Indianapolis: Heritage House, 1985.

Warren, James W. *Minnesota 1900 Census Mortality Schedules.* St. Paul, Minn.: Warren Research & Marketing, 1991-92.

Internet Sites of Interest:

Ancestry.com
http://www.ancestry.com

National Archives and Records Administration
http://www.nara.gov/publications/microfilm/census/census.html

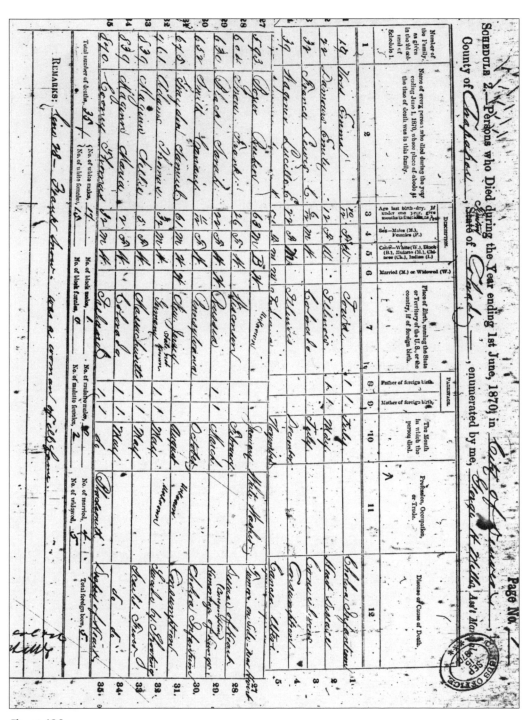

Figure 126

A page from an 1870 mortality schedule for the City of Denver, in the County of Arapahoe, Territory of Colorado, listing the name of the deceased, age, sex, color, whether married or widowed, place of birth, notation if parents were of foreign birth, month in which person died, profession, occupation or trade, and disease or cause of death.

Mortuary Records

Records maintained by mortuaries and funeral homes can be extremely helpful, particularly for the period before vital records were kept. Earlier records contain the name of the deceased, death date, place of death, cause of death, and name of the informant. In some cases, the age, residence, occupation, birthplace, and next of kin of the deceased also are included. Records should also be searched for information that may lead to other avenues of research, such as occupation, service in the armed forces, cemetery, church affiliation, fraternal organizations, and survivors. Contemporary records are more complete; however, these records are not available to the public. Only close relatives of the deceased can obtain them.

The mortician's name will usually be located on the death certificate, in the burial records, or in the obituary. In the absence of that information, if the place of death is known, the annual *National Directory of Morticians* (Youngstown, Ohio: National Directory of Morticians) or *The Yellow Book of Funeral Directors*, which lists the names and addresses of most morticians and funeral directors in the United States, can be used to help locate morticians' records. These directories can be found in the collections of numerous genealogical libraries and in the offices of local mortuaries. Records of mortuaries and funeral homes that are no longer in operation or that have changed proprietorship can often be found in the custody of the town or county clerk, the public library, or the historical society.

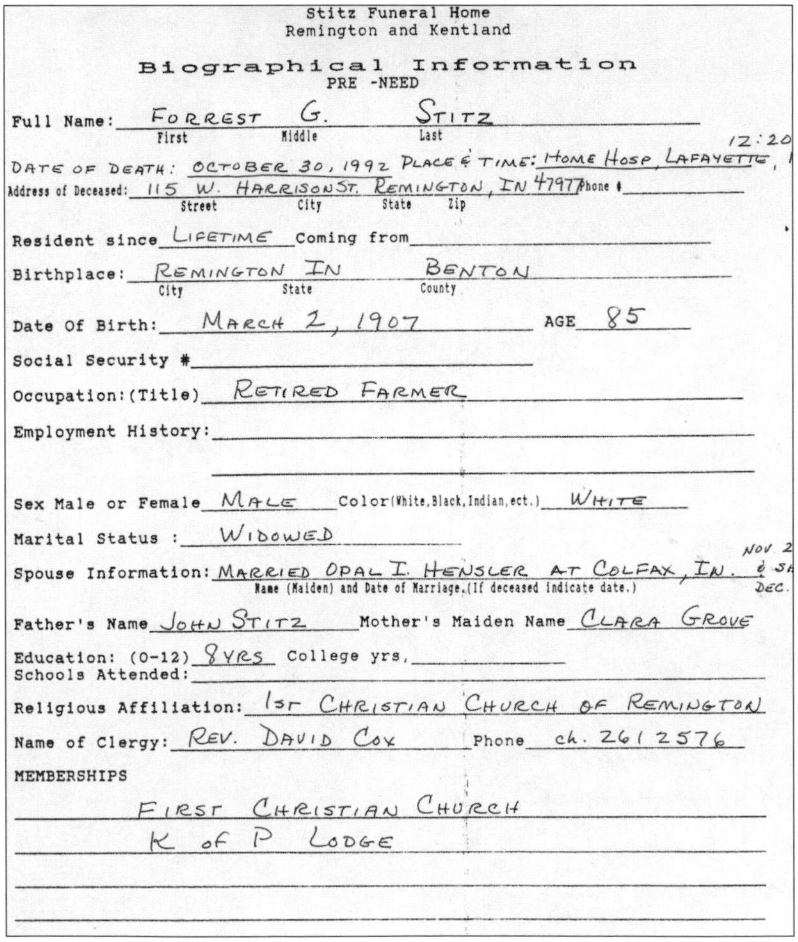
Stitz Funeral Home
Remington and Kentland

Biographical Information
PRE -NEED

Full Name: FORREST G. STITZ
First Middle Last

DATE OF DEATH: OCTOBER 30, 1992 PLACE & TIME: HOME HOSP, LAFAYETTE, 12:20

Address of Deceased: 115 W. HARRISON ST. REMINGTON, IN 47977 Phone #
Street City State Zip

Resident since LIFETIME Coming from

Birthplace: REMINGTON IN BENTON
City State County

Date Of Birth: MARCH 2, 1907 AGE 85

Social Security #

Occupation: (Title) RETIRED FARMER

Employment History:

Sex Male or Female MALE Color (White, Black, Indian, ect.) WHITE

Marital Status : WIDOWED

Spouse Information: MARRIED OPAL I. HENSLER AT COLFAX, IN. NOV. 2 & S DEC.
Name (Maiden) and Date of Marriage. (If deceased indicate date.)

Father's Name JOHN STITZ Mother's Maiden Name CLARA GROVE

Education: (0-12) 8 YRS College yrs,
Schools Attended:

Religious Affiliation: 1ST CHRISTIAN CHURCH OF REMINGTON

Name of Clergy: REV. DAVID COX Phone ch. 261 2576

MEMBERSHIPS

FIRST CHRISTIAN CHURCH

K of P LODGE

Figure 127

A record obtained from Stitz Funeral Home, Remington, Indiana, containing the biographical information of Forrest G. Stitz. (Courtesy of John Stitz)

Selected Readings:

Elder, Charlotte DeVolt. "New Englanders in the Mortuary Records of Savannah, Georgia." *New England Historic and Genealogical Register* 125 (1971): 28–44. (Covers 1803–22)

"Undertakers Records." *Maryland Genealogical Bulletin* 20 (1979), 21 (1980).

Internet Site of Interest:

Funeral Net
http://www.funeralnet.com/index.html

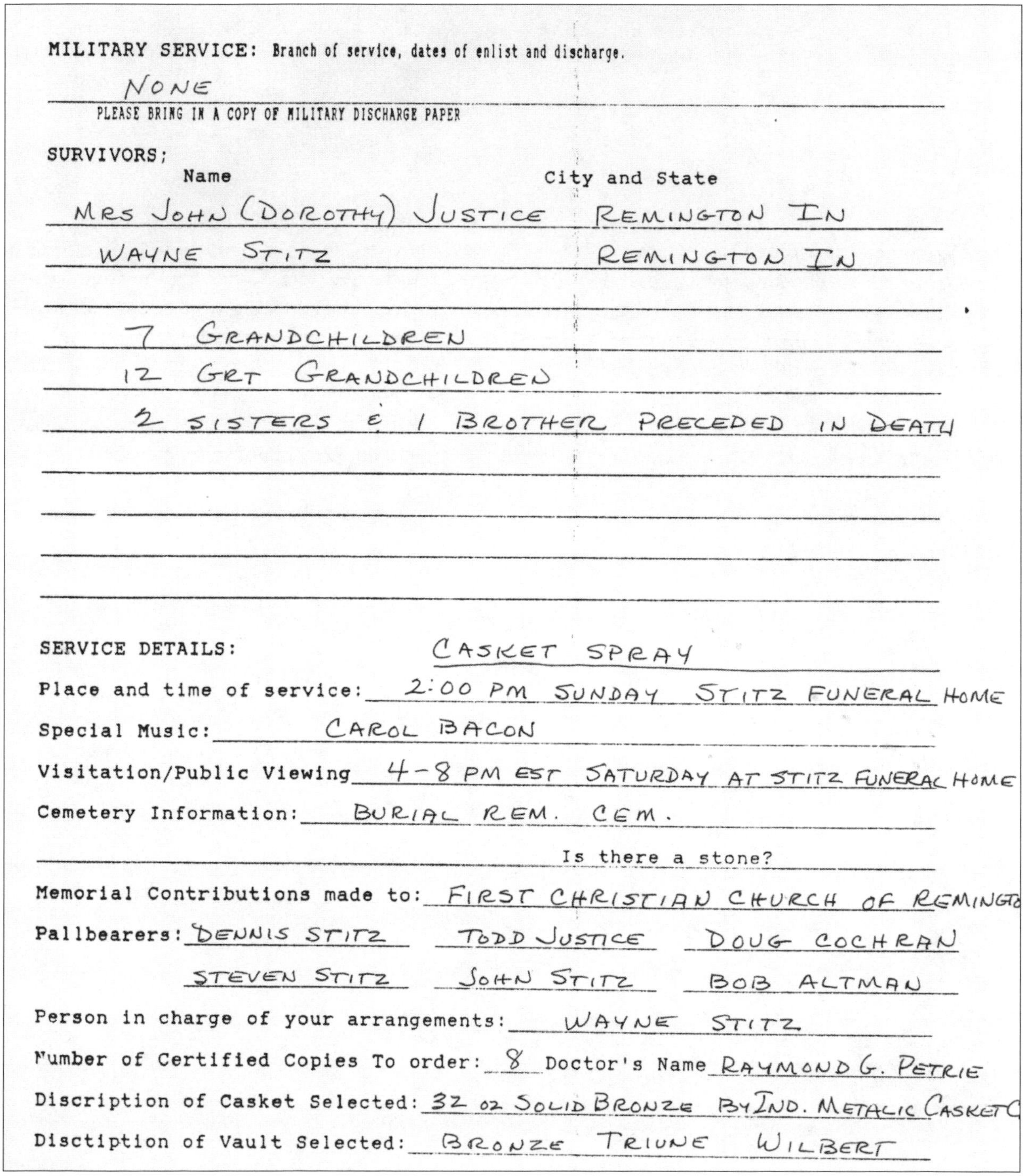

MILITARY SERVICE: Branch of service, dates of enlist and discharge.

NONE

PLEASE BRING IN A COPY OF MILITARY DISCHARGE PAPER

SURVIVORS;

Name	City and State
MRS JOHN (DOROTHY) JUSTICE	REMINGTON IN
WAYNE STITZ	REMINGTON IN

7 GRANDCHILDREN

12 GRT GRANDCHILDREN

2 SISTERS & 1 BROTHER PRECEDED IN DEATH

SERVICE DETAILS: CASKET SPRAY

Place and time of service: 2:00 PM SUNDAY STITZ FUNERAL HOME

Special Music: CAROL BACON

Visitation/Public Viewing 4-8 PM EST SATURDAY AT STITZ FUNERAL HOME

Cemetery Information: BURIAL REM. CEM.

Is there a stone?

Memorial Contributions made to: FIRST CHRISTIAN CHURCH OF REMINGT

Pallbearers: DENNIS STITZ   TODD JUSTICE   DOUG COCHRAN
STEVEN STITZ   JOHN STITZ   BOB ALTMAN

Person in charge of your arrangements: WAYNE STITZ

Number of Certified Copies To order: 8 Doctor's Name RAYMOND G. PETRIE

Discription of Casket Selected: 32 oz SOLID BRONZE BY IND. METALIC CASKET C

Disctiption of Vault Selected: BRONZE TRIUNE WILBERT

Figure 128
The reverse side of the funeral record of Forrest G. Stitz. (Courtesy of John Stitz)

Motor Vehicle Registration Records

The Department of Motor Vehicles may be helpful in locating elusive contemporary relatives. In addition to information pertaining to the vehicle, motor vehicle registration files may provide name, current address, and birth date of the owner of a vehicle.

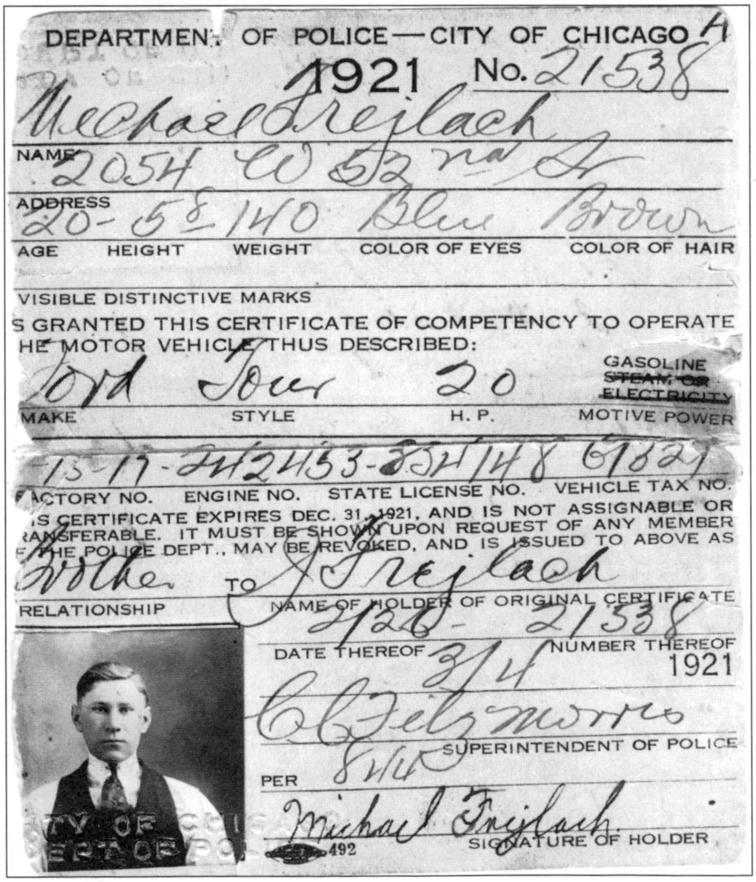
DEPARTMENT OF POLICE—CITY OF CHICAGO A

1921 No. 21538

Michael Frejlach

NAME

2054 W 52nd St

ADDRESS

20 5-8 140 Blue Brown

AGE HEIGHT WEIGHT COLOR OF EYES COLOR OF HAIR

VISIBLE DISTINCTIVE MARKS

IS GRANTED THIS CERTIFICATE OF COMPETENCY TO OPERATE THE MOTOR VEHICLE THUS DESCRIBED:

Ford Tour 20 GASOLINE ~~STEAM, OR~~ ~~ELECTRICITY~~

MAKE STYLE H. P. MOTIVE POWER

FACTORY NO. ENGINE NO. STATE LICENSE NO. VEHICLE TAX NO.

THIS CERTIFICATE EXPIRES DEC. 31, 1921, AND IS NOT ASSIGNABLE OR TRANSFERABLE. IT MUST BE SHOWN UPON REQUEST OF ANY MEMBER OF THE POLICE DEPT., MAY BE REVOKED, AND IS ISSUED TO ABOVE AS

Brother TO J. Frejlach

RELATIONSHIP NAME OF HOLDER OF ORIGINAL CERTIFICATE

DATE THEREOF NUMBER THEREOF

1921

SUPERINTENDENT OF POLICE

PER

Michael Frejlach

SIGNATURE OF HOLDER

Figure 129

The 1921 driver's license of Michael Frejlach, found in an antique store in Lockport, Illinois.

Regulations regarding the availability of records may vary from state to state. Cambridge Statistical Research Associates has made indexes available on CD-ROM for driver's licenses issued during the early and mid–1990s for Maine, Mississippi, Oregon, Texas, South Carolina, and Wisconsin, and for motor vehicle registrations for Colorado, Connecticut, Florida, Ohio, New Hampshire, New York, and Texas.

Selected Readings:

Gunderson, Ted L., and Roger McGovern. *How to Locate Anyone Anywhere*. New York: Penguin, 1996.

Hinckley, Kathleen W. "Tracking Twentieth-Century Ancestors." *The Source: A Guidebook of American Genealogy*. Salt Lake City: Ancestry, 1997.

The MVR Book: A Motor Services Guidebook. Tempe, Ariz.: BRB Publications, 1993.

Museums and Historical Agencies

Museums and historical agencies often house personal collections, artifacts, and manuscript materials donated by local families and businesses. For instance, among items of interest in a museum or located in the basement of a local library were files with old school photographs, newspapers, and scrapbooks of the town, as well as mementos donated by area residents. Also included were files containing old pictures of streets and homes in the town, lists of the original settlers, dissertations based on residents' recollections of the earliest days in the neighborhood, lists of local clubs and organizations, and lists and pictures of veterans from the area. Such a collection can provide a family historian with an idea of what life was like in the town during a particular time period and, quite possibly, a direct reference to the individual being researched. Another local museum, in addition to housing thousands of documents concerning early development of the region, conducts obituary and name searches, with fees going directly to the support of the facility.

A town's library or chamber of commerce should be able to provide the location of museums in the area. The community pages in phone books also list museums of interest in the area, many of them with specialized collections focusing on specific industries, ethnic groups, or historical events. For example, Sacramento lists the California State Railroad Museum Library, Detroit lists the Great Lakes Maritime Institute, and Philadelphia lists the Civil War Library and Museum.

Selected Readings:

Wheeler, Mary Bray, ed. *Directory of Historical Organizations in the United States and Canada.* 14th ed. Nashville: American Association for State and Local History, 1990.

Internet Site of Interest:

Museums in the USA
http://www.museumca.org/usa/misc.html

Figure 130
The Brooklyn Historical Society (originally founded as the Long Island Historical Society) located at Pierrepont and Clinton Streets. (Courtesy of Brooklyn Historical Society)

Name Change Records

Throughout history, individuals have found reasons to change their names. In many cases, names were changed informally and without the benefit of a legal or record-creating procedure. However, there are a number of reliable sources that make it possible to discover name changes.

Every state provides for legal name changes within the court system. Courts having jurisdiction to authorize these changes vary from state to state. Some courts have separately indexed volumes of name changes, and some will be found intermixed with regular court cases.

Amended or revised birth records may also provide information on name changes, such as when birth parents' names are changed to those of the adoptive parents.

Name changes are most common among foreign language-speaking immigrants, often as a result of a conscious choice to become Americanized. In some cases these changes will be recorded in naturalization documents and cross-indexed under both the old and new name.

Selected Readings:

Matakov, Albert. *List of Persons Whose Names Have Been Changed in Massachusetts, 1780-1892.* 2nd ed. 1893. Reprint. Baltimore: Genealogical Publishing Co., 1972.

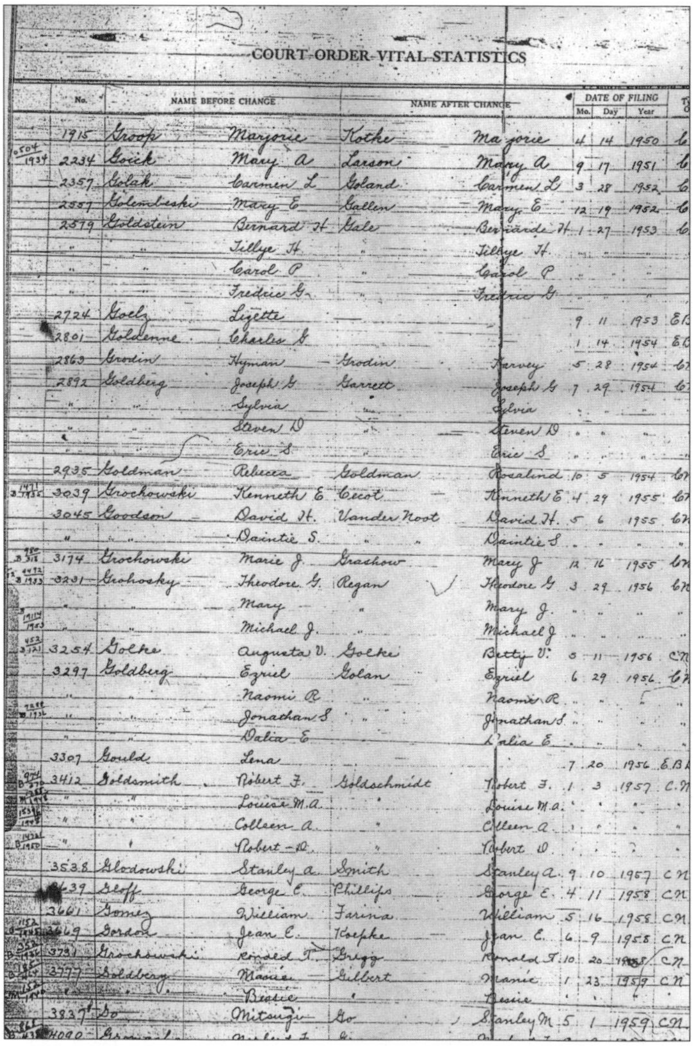
COURT ORDER VITAL STATISTICS

No. | NAME BEFORE CHANGE | NAME AFTER CHANGE | DATE OF FILING (Mo. Day Year)

Figure 131
Copy of a page from "Index to Court Vital Statistics Name Changes 1853-1977" found in Milwaukee County, Wisconsin Register of Deeds Office. The index has been microfilmed and is also available at and through the Family History Library.

Meyer, Mary K. comp. *Divorce and Names Changed in Maryland by Act of the Legislature, 1634-1854.* Pasadena, Md.: the author, 1970.

Rowland, Arthur R. "Names Changed Legally in Georgia, 1800-1856". *National Genealogical Society Quarterly* 55 (1967): 177-210.

CHARLES WILLIAM VODNANSKY)
GENEVIEVE MARY VODNANSKY)
FRANK THOMAS VODNANSKY)   GENERAL NO.
JULIA MARY VODNANSKY)
RAY DONALD VODNANSKY)
GEORGE ROBERT VODNANSKY)
      (a minor))
by his next friend)
BENEDICT FRANCIS VODNANSKY)

<u>PETITION FOR CHANGE OF NAMES</u>

Your petitioners, Benedict Francis Vodnansky, Charles William Vodnansky, Genevieve Mary Vodnansky, Frank Thomas Vodnansky, Julia Mary Vodnansky, Ray Donald Vodnansky, George Robert Vodnansky, (a minor) by his next friend Benedict Francis Vodnansky respectfully show unto the Court the following:

1. That your petitioner Benedict Francis Vodnansky resides at 5027 W. 24th Street, in the Town of Cicero, County of Cook and State of Illinois, having resided in said county and state aforesaid for more than 6 months prior to the filing of this petition; that he desires to change his name according to the provisions of the Statute in such case made and provided.

2. That your petitioners Charles William Vodnansky and Genevieve Mary Vodnansky, his wife, reside at 8001 S. Princeton Avenue, in the City of Chicago, County of Cook and State of Illinois, having resided in said county and state aforesaid for more than 6 months prior to the filing of this petition; that they desire to change their respective names, according to the provisions of the statute in such case made and provided.

3. That your petitioners Frank Thomas Vodnansky and Julia Mary Vodnansky, his wife, reside at 5027 W. 24th Street, in the Town of Cicero, County of Cook and State of Illinois,

Figure 132
The first page of a petition for change of names from a Cook County, Illinois case in which the Vodnansky family members changed their last name to Noel.

National Union Catalog of Manuscript Collections

Many libraries and historical societies have collections of manuscripts. Among the treasures that may be found in a manuscript collection are unpublished letters, diaries, family histories, and records from schools and businesses. Most have been donated by families and businesses in the area. In 1959, the Library of Congress began compiling detailed descriptions of manuscript collections held in 1,369 repositories. These descriptions have been indexed and cross-referenced in twenty-seven volumes of the National Union Catalog of Manuscript Collections (NUCMC) (Washington, D.C.: Library of Congress, 1962–present).

Indexes have been created to help researchers locate information from the 65,325 collections included in *NUCMC*. Among the most helpful are the *Index to Personal Names in the National Union Catalog of Manuscript Collections 1959–1984* (Alexandria, Va.: Chadwyck-Healey, 1988) and *Index to Subjects and Corporate Names in the National Union Catalog of Manuscript Collections 1959–1984* (Alexandria, Va.: Chadwyck-Healey, 1994). Data on manuscript collections from around the country continues to be submitted to the Library of Congress to be included in the *NUCMC*'s online searchable database found at <http://lcweb.loc.gov/coll/nucmc/>.

Selected Readings:

Meyerink, Kory, ed. *Printed Sources: A Guide to Published Genealogical Records*. Salt Lake City: Ancestry, 1998.

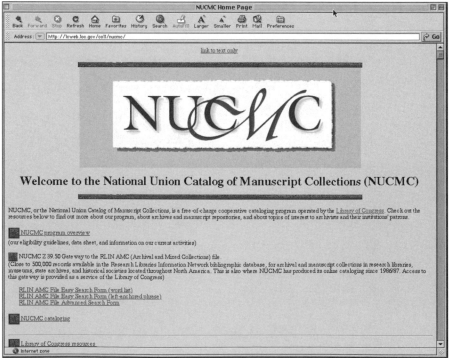

Figure 133

The National Union Catalog of Manuscript Collections page on the Library of Congress Web site.

Naturalization Records

Prior to 1906, an individual could be naturalized in any court of record. Because many of the courts used their own forms, the contents of earlier naturalization records are varied. Standardization of the records came in 1906 with the creation of the Bureau of Immigration and Naturalization and the passing of a new law requiring the use of the same form in all naturalization courts. The new form included an expanded set of questions for the immigrant to answer.

Individuals applying for naturalization after September 1906 provided the following: name, birthplace, age, nationality, country from which emigrated, intended place of settlement, address, occupation, personal description, date of intention, marital status, last foreign residence, port of entry, name of ship, date of entry, and date of document. Most naturalization documents completed before 1906 contain little biographical information, although there are some exceptions.

Figure 134

As a rule, naturalization records before 1906 are scarce on biographical information. However, even the sparse details provided on the 1902 declaration of intention of Mathias Walsch, in Mahoning County, Ohio can be useful. The document places Mathias in a particular place and time. From this document, it is reasonable to assume that he has been in the United States for the required five years before becoming a citizen. The document also states that he is a native of Hungary.

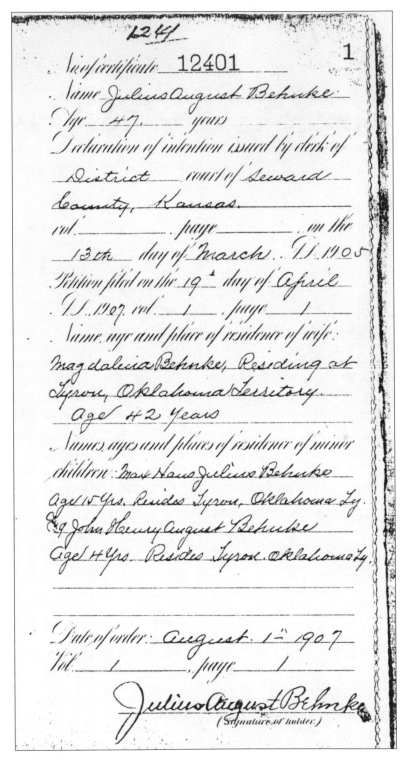

Figure 135

In certain years and in certain courts, naturalization certificates were issued from blank form books. Much like a check book, many of these volumes recorded important information about the person being naturalized on the stub portion before the tear-off naturalization certificate was issued to the new U.S. citizen. Shown is a stub for a certificate issued to Julius August Behnke in the U.S. Court, Northern District of Ohio, Cleveland. The original stub book is now preserved at the National Archives - Great Lakes Region, Chicago.

Earlier records (pre–1906) were frequently filed in county or city offices, and many old court records have been dispersed to archives, historical societies, and libraries. It is best to start the search in the county in which the immigrant was known to reside. Millions of these records have been microfilmed by the Genealogical Society of Utah and are available at the Family History Library. The Works Projects Administration (WPA) created extensive naturalization indexes to aid in the retrieval of records, which requires a petition number; these Soundex indexes, however, are not available for every state. The Immigration and Naturalization Service has duplicate copies of naturalization records from 27 September 1906 to the present.

Selected Readings:

Eichholz, Alice, ed. *Ancestry's Red Book: American State, County and Town Sources.* Rev. ed. Salt Lake City: Ancestry, 1992.

Filby, P. William. *Philadelphia Naturalization Records.* Detroit: Gale Research Co., 1982.

Guide to Genealogical Research in the National Archives. Rev. ed. Washington D.C.: National Archives Trust Fund Board, 1991.

Holcomb, Brent H. *South Carolina Naturalizations, 1783–1850.* Baltimore: Genealogical Publishing Co., 1985.

Meyerink, Kory L., and Loretto Dennis Szucs. "Immigration: Finding Immigrant Origins." *The Source: A Guidebook of American Genealogy.* Rev. ed. Ch. 13: 440–519. Salt Lake City: Ancestry, 1997.

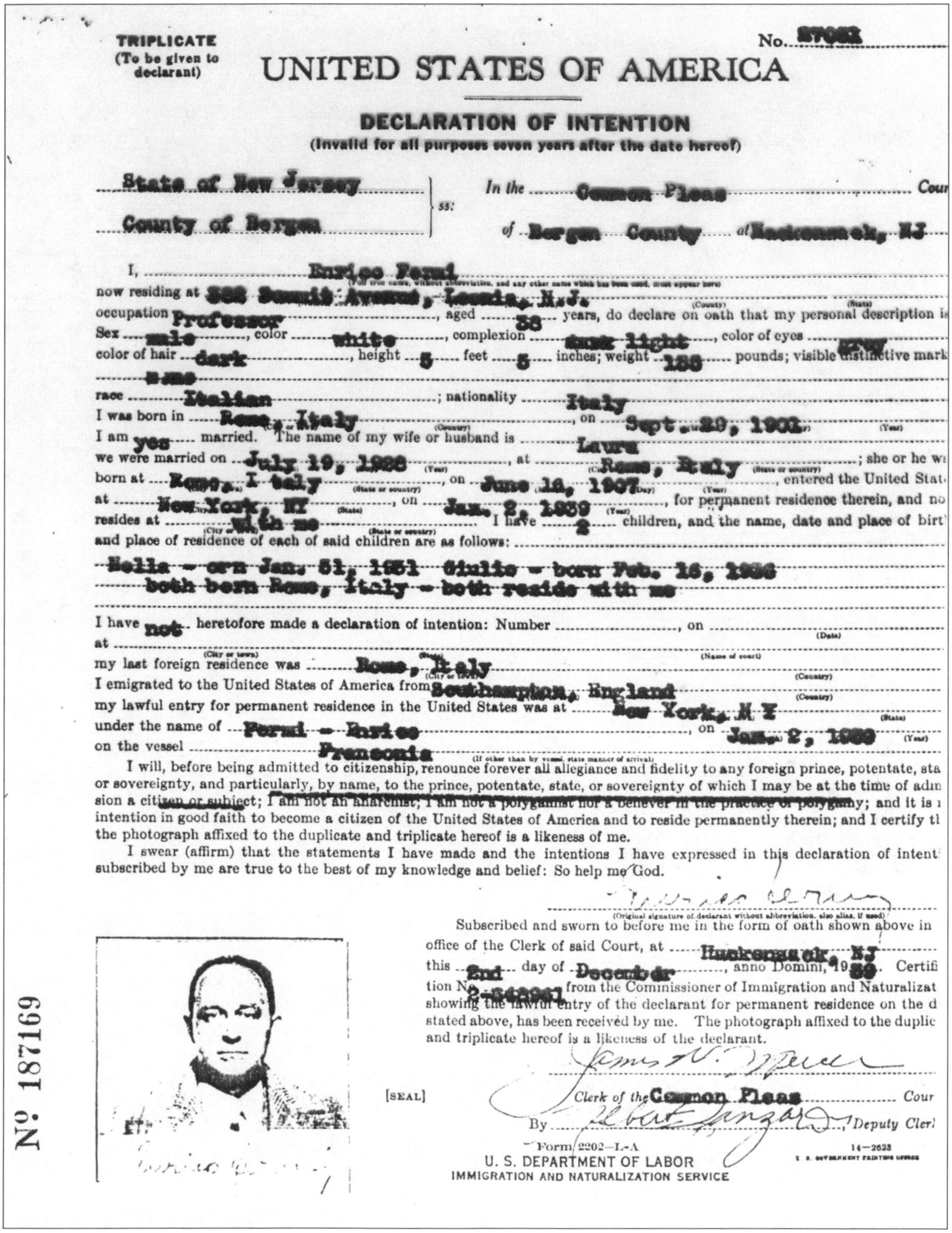

Figure 136

The December 1939 Declaration of Intention of Enrico Fermi sworn in the Court of Common Pleas, Bergan County, New Jersey. The original document is filed with Fermi's final petition and oath at the National Archives - Great Lakes Region, Chicago.

National Archives Trust Fund Board. *Index to Naturalization Petitions of the United States District Court for the Eastern District of New York 1865–1957.* Washington D.C.: National Archives and Records Administration, 1991.

Soundex Index to Naturalization Petitions for the United States District and Circuit Courts, Northern District of Illinois, and Immigration and Naturalization Service District 9, 1840–1950. National Archives Trust Fund Board, 1991.

Scott, Kenneth. *Early New York Naturalizations, 1790–1840.* Baltimore: Genealogical Publishing Co., 1981.

Szucs, Loretto Dennis. *They Became Americans: Finding Naturalization Records and Ethnic Origins.* Salt Lake City: Ancestry, 1998.

Wolfe, Richard J. "The Colonial Naturalization Act of 1740; With a List of Persons Naturalized in New York Colony, 1740–1769." *New York Genealogical and Biographical Record* 94 (1963): 132–47.

Wyand, Jeffrey A., and Florence L. Wyand. *Colonial Maryland Naturalizations.* Baltimore: Genealogical Publishing Co., 1986.

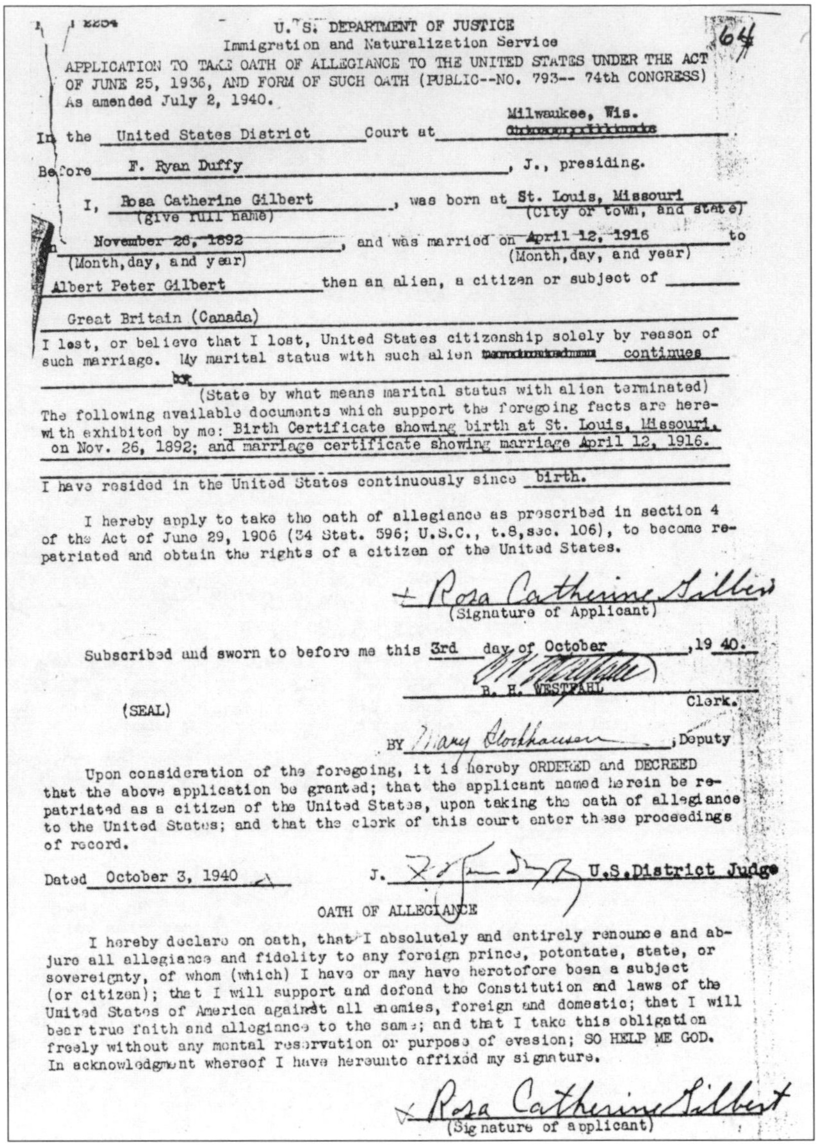

U. S. DEPARTMENT OF JUSTICE
Immigration and Naturalization Service
APPLICATION TO TAKE OATH OF ALLEGIANCE TO THE UNITED STATES UNDER THE ACT OF JUNE 25, 1936, AND FORM OF SUCH OATH (PUBLIC--NO. 793-- 74th CONGRESS) As amended July 2, 1940.

In the United States District Court at Milwaukee, Wis.

Before F. Ryan Duffy, J., presiding.

I, Rosa Catherine Gilbert (give full name), was born at St. Louis, Missouri (City or town, and state) November 26, 1892 (Month, day, and year), and was married on April 12, 1916 (Month, day, and year) to Albert Peter Gilbert then an alien, a citizen or subject of Great Britain (Canada)

I lost, or believe that I lost, United States citizenship solely by reason of such marriage. My marital status with such alien continues (State by what means marital status with alien terminated)

The following available documents which support the foregoing facts are herewith exhibited by me: Birth Certificate showing birth at St. Louis, Missouri, on Nov. 26, 1892; and marriage certificate showing marriage April 12, 1916.

I have resided in the United States continuously since birth.

I hereby apply to take the oath of allegiance as prescribed in section 4 of the Act of June 29, 1906 (34 Stat. 596; U.S.C., t.8, sec. 106), to become repatriated and obtain the rights of a citizen of the United States.

Rosa Catherine Gilbert
(Signature of Applicant)

Subscribed and sworn to before me this 3rd day of October, 1940.

(SEAL)

B. H. WESTFAHL
Clerk.

BY Mary Stockhausen, Deputy

Upon consideration of the foregoing, it is hereby ORDERED and DECREED that the above application be granted; that the applicant named herein be repatriated as a citizen of the United States, upon taking the oath of allegiance to the United States; and that the clerk of this court enter these proceedings of record.

Dated October 3, 1940 J. U.S. District Judge

OATH OF ALLEGIANCE

I hereby declare on oath, that I absolutely and entirely renounce and abjure all allegiance and fidelity to any foreign prince, potentate, state, or sovereignty, of whom (which) I have or may have heretofore been a subject (or citizen); that I will support and defend the Constitution and laws of the United States of America against all enemies, foreign and domestic; that I will bear true faith and allegiance to the same; and that I take this obligation freely without any mental reservation or purpose of evasion; SO HELP ME GOD. In acknowledgment whereof I have hereunto affixed my signature.

Rosa Catherine Gilbert
(Signature of applicant)

Figure 137

During certain periods of history, American-born women lost their U.S. citizenship if they married an individual who was not a natural-born or naturalized U.S. citizen. In order to regain U.S. citizenship, these women had to go before the court, swear allegiance to the United States, and present proof of birth and marriage, as though they were themselves foreign born. Shown is the 1940 application of Rosa Catherine Gilbert. In the U.S. Court at Milwaukee, Wisconsin, Rosa swore that she was born in St. Louis, Missouri on November 26, 1892, and that she was married on April 12, 1916 to Albert Peter Gilbert, a subject of Canada. This record and many like it can be found at the National Archives - Great Lakes Region, Chicago.

Internet Sites of Interest:

Ancestry.com
Guide to Naturalization Records and how to request them
http://www.ancestry.com/research/natrecords.htm

Immigration and Naturalization Service (INS)
http://www.ins.usdoj.gov/

National Archives and Records Administration
Naturalization Records
http://www.nara.gov/genealogy/natural.html

Necrologies

Lists of the recently deceased may be found in a number of publications, especially professional and religious directories, membership publications of organizations, alumnae directories, and yearbooks.

Typically, necrologies list the name of the individual, the last residence, and the date of death. An example is *The Official Catholic Directory* (Wilmette, IL: P.J. Kenedy and Sons, annual since 1846) that traditionally lists 1,500 to 2,000 clergy members who have died during the previous year.

Some necrologies can also be found on the Internet. A search of the word "necrology," for example, yielded over forty possible Web sites that included a Kansas Grand Army of the Republic necrology index; a necrology index to obituaries that appeared in the *South Bend Tribune* for people who died in St. Joseph County, Indiana; a necrology index from the Gaylord Music Library at Washington University, reporting deaths from the music media; necrology reports from the Pioneer Society at the Cass County, Michigan page on U.S. GenWeb; a necrology index of alumni, professors, and officers of Bowdoin College; a necrology of monks and nuns from the English Benedictine Congregation dated back to the 1600s; a necrology list from the Yizkor Book of Gostynin, listing Holocaust victims from that community; and, from the University of Toledo Historic Woodlawn Cemetery Project, the Woodlawn Cemetery Necrology, which includes short biographies of several individuals now resting there.

See also *Obituaries and Obituary Collections.*

Necrology

ARCHBISHOP

✠Noser, Adolph *s.v.d.* Most Rev., Former Archbishop of Madang, New Guinea.—Died April 15, 1981.

BISHOPS

✠Blanchette, Romeo Most Rev., Former Bishop of Joliet.—Died January 11, 1982.
✠Dargin, Edward F. Most Rev., Former Auxiliary Bishop of New York.—Died April 20, 1981.
✠Guilfoyle, Merlin J. Most Rev., Former Bishop of Stockton.—Died November 20, 1981.
✠Leipzig, Francis P. Most Rev., Former Bishop of Baker.—Died January 17, 1981.
✠Mueller, Joseph M., Most Rev. Former Bishop of Sioux City.—Died August 9, 1981.
✠Nold, Wendelin J., Most Rev. Former Bishop of Galveston Houston.—Died October 1, 1981.
✠Rausch, James S., Most Rev. Former Bishop of Phoenix.—Died May 18, 1981.
✠Walsh, James E. *m.m.* Most Rev. Titular Bishop of Sata.—Died July 29, 1981.

PRIESTS

†Adasiewicz, Casimir (MAR) Retired.—Died April 13, 1981.
†Aberle, George P. Msgr. (BIS) Retired.—Died August 23, 1981.
†Adams, Joseph (MOB) Gulf Shores Ala. Our Lady of the Gulf.—Died January 30, 1981.
†Aeschbacher, Thomas *o.f.m.conv.* (IND) Retired.—Died January 1, 1981.
†Ahearn, Joseph D. *s.j.* (BO) Weston MA. Campion Center.—Died September 12, 1981.
†Ahr, Walter (CIN) Retired.—Died December 1, 1981.
†Albiser, Henry *s.s.e.* (BUR) Winooski VT. St. Michael College.—Died December 13, 1981.
†Aleksunas, Joseph (BRK) Brooklyn NY. Annunciation Church.—Died December 9, 1981.
†Allen, William A. *s.j.* (B) Lewiston Idaho St. Stanislaus Church.—Died August 4, 1981.
†Allison, John J. (WH) Shinnston WV. St. Ann Church.—Died June 21, 1981.
†Altman, Peter Msgr. (BRK) Brooklyn N.Y. Our Lady of Angels.—Died May 20, 1981.
†Amodio, Joseph U. *c.s.s.* (BO) Waltham MA. Sacred Heart Church.—Died September 28, 1981.
†Anderson, Thomas M. (MAR) Retired.—Died April 5, 1981.
†Barber, Regis *s.a.* (BO) Brockton Mass. Chapel of Our Savior.—Died October 7, 1981.
†Baraniak, Ignatius *o.f.m.* (BGP) Danbury Conn. Sacred Heart Church.—Died November 27, 1981.
†Barry, Patrick A. Msgr. (BUR) Bellows Falls Vt. St. Charles Parish.—Died December 24, 1981.
†Bartels, James R. (FTW) Columbia City Ind. St. Paul of the Cross.—Died June 27, 1981.
†Beaudry, Albert T. (SPR) Retired.—Died March 30, 1981.
†Becker, Fidelis (SCL) Retired.—Died May 10, 1981.
†Behr, Ignatius *s.d.s.* (RNO) Reno Nev. Bishop Manogue High School.—Died March 7, 1981.
†Bennett, Jerome (IND) Retired.—Died January 10, 1981.
†Benso, Maxim Msgr. (LA) Retired.—Died November 1, 1981.
†Benson, Joachim *s.t.* (MOB) Holy Trinity Ala. St. Joseph Parish.—Died April 21, 1981.
†Berchtold, Walter W. (CAM) Minotola NJ. St. Michael Church.—Died January 31, 1981.
†Berg, Herman *m.s.f.* (CC) Refugio TX. St. James Church.—Died December 14, 1981.
†Bergen, Edward J. *s.j.* (LAF) Grand Coteau LA. St. Charles College.—Died August 4, 1981.
†Berning, Louis H. (CIN) Retired.—Died January 9, 1981.
†Berry, Richard M. (RVC) Uniondale NY. Holly Patterson Home.—Died December 12, 1981.
†Beyer, Gervase *o.f.m.conv.* (L) Louisville KY. Bellarmine College.—Died October 29, 1981.
†Bianchi, Aloysius *s.d.b.* (BO) Ipswich MA. Sacred Heart Retreat House.—Died June 13, 1981.
†Bingham, Thomas M. (BUF) West Valley NY. St. John the Baptist Church.—Died December 27, 1981.
†Birkel, Harold H. (LIN) Steinauer Neb. St. Anthony of Padua.—Died June 17, 1981.
†Biwer, Francis *o.s.c.* (SCL) Onamia MN. Crosier Seminary.—Died October 28, 1981.
†Blesser, John A. (SFD) Retired.—Died March 19, 1981.
†Boeckendorff, Henry *m.s.c.* (IND) Retired.—Died February 12, 1981.
†Boffa, Conrad H. Msgr. (CIN) Cincinnati Ohio Holy Angels Church.—Died June 24, 1981.
†Bogdanski, Augustine *s.a.c.* (WH) Buckhannon WV St. Joseph Hospital.—Died July 16, 1981.
†Bohrer, Raymond S. (DUB) Mason City Iowa Holy Family Church.—Died June 24, 1981.
†Boisvert, Aldor *o.m.i.* (BO) Lowell MA. Oblate Fathers
†Brault, Philip (LAF) New Iberia LA. Our Lady of Perpetual Help.—Died July 12, 1981.
†Brennan, George S. Msgr. (BO) Retired.—Died June 25, 1981.
†Brennan, William E. (NEW) Sick Leave.—Died October 2, 1981.
†Bresnahan, James (STL) St. Louis MO. St. Rita Church.—Died March 27, 1981.
†Breznik, Aloysius (SPK) Davenport, Wash. Immaculate Conception Church.—Died July 16, 1981.
†Britt, Laurence V. *s.j.* (CLV) Cleveland Ohio John Carroll University.—Died November 15, 1980.
†Britt, Patrick *s.s.e.* Coden Ala. St. Rose Parish.—Died November 10, 1980.
†Brody, Thomas V. (CHI) Retired.—Died April 3, 1981.
†Brower, Charles *o.m.i.* (TR) Lyons NJ. V.A. Hospital.—Died July 5, 1981.
†Bruegger, Albert F. (STL) St. Louis MO. Sts. Peter and Paul Church.—Died July 5, 1981.
†Brula, Clifford F. (PIT) McKeesport Pa. St. Peter Church.—Died November 18, 1981.
†Brunelle, Leopold *s.m.* (BO) Lawrence MA. St. Ann Church.—Died June 29, 1981.
†Brzozowski, Jerome J. (CHI) Chicago Ill. St. Pancratius Church.—Died September 3, 1981.
†Buchman, Richard (Y) Orwell Ohio St. Mary Parish.—Died March 5, 1981.
†Buckley, Joseph W. *s.m.* (NO) New Orleans LA. Notre Dame Seminary.—Died September 11, 1981.
†Buckley, Maurice *t.o.r.* (NY) New York NY. St. Veronica Parish.—Died March 6, 1981.
†Buja, Arnold *s.d.b.* (LA) Retired.—Died December 17, 1980.
†Burke, Daniel J. *s.j.* (NY) New York NY. St. Ignatius Residence.—Died October 19, 1981.
†Burke, Leonard B. (SPR) Retired.—Died August 4, 1981.
†Burke, Thomas J. M. *s.j.* (BGP) Fairfield CT. Fairfield University.—Died March 10, 1981.
†Butler, George G. *s.j.* (NY) Bronx NY. Fordham University.—Died October 5, 1981.
†Butler, Henry J. *s.j.* (BAL) Retired.—Died September 2, 1981.
†Buttimer, Edward P. Msgr. (SY) Rome NY. St. Peter Church.—Died February 3, 1981.
†Byers, Farrell *o.f.m.* (CIN) Cincinnati Ohio. St. Francis Church.—Died May 6, 1981.
†Byrne, Thomas P. (CHI) Retired.—Died September 10, 1981.

Figure 138
Entries from the "Necrology" section of *The Official Catholic Directory* (Wilmette, IL: P.J. Kenedy and Sons, 1982).

Neighborhood Collections

Unless an ancestor was prominent enough to be found in a major printed historical source in a city, the most productive search area is typically the neighborhood in which he or she resided. Local histories and neighborhood newspapers are examples of holdings a researcher can expect to find at a local library. It may also be the place to begin a search for school records, which are sometimes dispersed among more than one repository. (See *School Records* for additional information)

City neighborhoods may have their own historical societies and museums (often affiliated with the public library) with information about local residents, community photographs, scrapbooks, and personal mementos. If the neighborhood is no longer in existence, the main branch of the city public library, the municipal library, and the city or county historical library are possible sites for collections pertaining to the area.

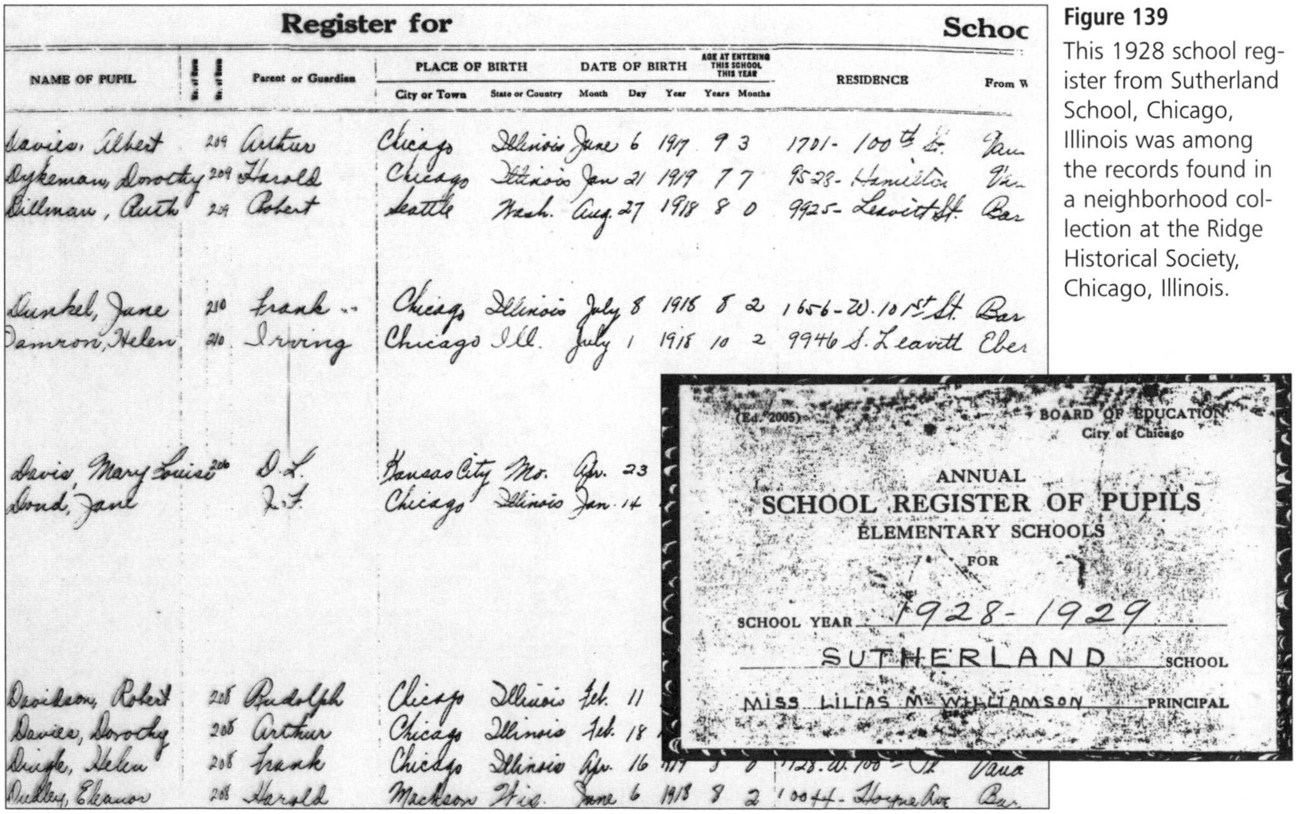
Register for Schoc

NAME OF PUPIL		Parent or Guardian	PLACE OF BIRTH City or Town	State or Country	DATE OF BIRTH Month	Day	Year	AGE AT ENTERING THIS SCHOOL THIS YEAR Years	Months	RESIDENCE	From W
Davies, Albert	209	Arthur	Chicago	Illinois	June	6	1917	9	3	1701- 100th St.	
Dykeman, Dorothy	209	Harold	Chicago	Illinois	Jan	21	1919	7	7	9528- Hamilton	
Dillman, Ruth	209	Robert	Seattle	Wash.	Aug.	27	1918	8	0	9925- Leavitt St.	
Dunkel, Jane	210	Frank	Chicago	Illinois	July	8	1918	8	2	1656- W. 101st St.	
Damron, Helen	210	Irving	Chicago	Ill.	July	1	1918	10	2	9946 S. Leavitt	
Davis, Mary Louise	206	D.L.	Kansas City	Mo.	Apr.	23					
Dond, Jane		R.F.	Chicago	Illinois	Jan.	14					
Davidson, Robert	208	Rudolph	Chicago	Illinois	Feb.	11					
Davies, Dorothy	208	Arthur	Chicago	Illinois	Feb.	18					
Dingle, Helen	208	Frank	Chicago	Illinois	Apr.	16					
Dudley, Eleanor	208	Harold	Madison	Wis.	June	6	1918	8	2	10044- Hoyne Ave	

(Ed. 2005) BOARD OF EDUCATION City of Chicago

ANNUAL
SCHOOL REGISTER OF PUPILS
ELEMENTARY SCHOOLS
FOR
SCHOOL YEAR 1928-1929
SUTHERLAND SCHOOL
MISS LILLIAS McWILLIAMSON PRINCIPAL

Figure 139
This 1928 school register from Sutherland School, Chicago, Illinois was among the records found in a neighborhood collection at the Ridge Historical Society, Chicago, Illinois.

NEIGHBORHOOD HISTORICAL COLLECTIONS

UNDER

DR. SCHOLL FOUNDATION GRANT

(Processed March 1982-March 1983)

The following twenty-one historical collections from three CPL branch libraries were organized, preserved and descriptive finding guides written for:

Dr. Scholl Foundation - Final Report

Collections conserved processed and descriptive finding guides written for:

HILD REGIONAL LIBRARY:

The Stephen Bedell Clark Papers, 1971-1974 (3/4 linear foot)

The John Drury Collection, 1935-1953, (½ linear foot)

The Helen G. Kinsella Drama Collection, 1931-1961, (½ linear foot)

The Lake View High School Collection, 1874-1974, (5½ linear feet)

The Mrs. Frank W. Little Scrapbook of Ravenwood, 1874-1888 (1 scrapbook)

Papers of the Ravenswood Congregational Church, 1870-1969, (1 linear foot)

The Ravenswood-Lake View Community Collection, 1844-1981, (11 linear feet)
        (include 60 artifacts & 1300 photographs)

Papers of the Ravenswood-Lake View Historical Association, 1872-1931
        (predominately 1935-1931), (1 linear foot & 3 scrapbooks)

Papers of the Ravenswood Women's Club, 1894-1974, (2 linear feet)

PULLMAN BRANCH LIBRARY

The George A. Brenna Papers. 1915-1934, (10 file folders)

Papers of the Calumet Pioneers Historical Society, 1935-1967 (½ linear foot)

The Calumet Region Community Collection, 1850-1975, (3 linear feet,
        2 scrapbooks) (includes 342 photographs)

The Fenger High School Collection, 1925-1965, (2½ linear feet)

Mr. & Mrs. William Fernstemacher Scrapbooks of Fernwood
        Methodist Church, 1953-1971, (2 scrapbooks)

The Historic Pullman Collection, 1882-1979, (4 linear feet, 1 scrapbook)
        (include 97 photographs),

Figure 140

Examples of neighborhood collections housed at the Chicago Public Library, Chicago, Illinois.

Newspapers

Newspapers can be an excellent source of data for the determined researcher. Among the local news items, a family historian may find vital statistics information in birth notices, marriage notices, and obituaries. These are particularly useful for the periods predating public record keeping of vital statistics, or when the public records have been lost or destroyed. Also noteworthy are the social columns that give attention to news of a personal nature, such as anniversaries, graduations, promotions, and reunions; legal notices concerning probate proceedings, divorce cases, and estate or tax sales; advertisements, or wanted notices for missing persons, which often include personal details, last known whereabouts, and the intended destination; and special editions or columns commemorating local historical events. It is important to keep in mind, however, that newspapers are a secondary source of information, and details are sometimes inaccurate.

A search of newspapers should encompass community, ethnic, and religious newspapers as well as multiple editions of the major daily newspapers, if the ancestor was a city dweller. While early newspapers can be difficult to locate, sources such as Clarence Brigham's *History and Bibliography of American Newspapers, 1690–1820*, 2 vols. (Worcester, Mass.: American Antiquarian Society, 1947) and

Winifred Gregory's *American Newspapers, 1821–1936: A Union List of Files Available in the United States and Canada* (1937. Reprint. New York: Kraus, 1967) can provide information needed to begin a search.

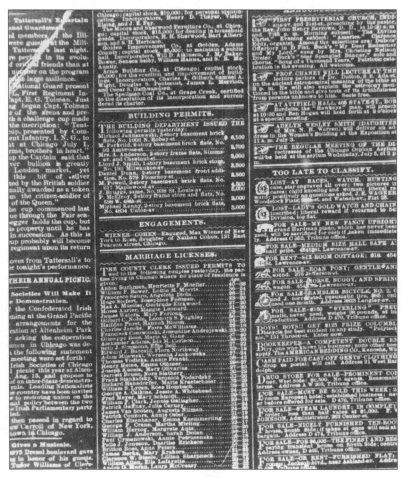

Figure 141

Announcements from a 2 July 1893 issue of the *Chicago Tribune*.

164

Newspapers, or microforms of them, are often located in libraries and historical societies. The Library of Congress has an outstanding newspaper collection and publishes *The Checklist of American 18th Century Newspapers* and *Newspapers in Microform*. Also available through the Library of Congress are indexes created by the Work Projects Administration. Another exceptional collection is located at the State Historical Society of Wisconsin. James L. Hansen's *Wisconsin Newspapers, 1833–1850: An Analytical Bibliography* (Madison, Wis.: State Historical Society, 1979) describes this collection.

PAGE 8   THE C

HARRY L. VAIL IS DEAD AT 76

Former Newspaperman and Public Official Was Ardent Republican

Mr. Vail

Harry L. Vail, former newspaperman, county clerk, county commissioner and attorney, died today in his home at 8319 Carnegie avenue following a short illness. He was 76.

Mr. Vail was the father of Herman L. Vail, member of the law firm of Spring, Sayre & Vail. Funeral plans were to be announced later in the day.

Born in Cleveland, the son of Judge Isaac C. Vail, Mr. Vail was educated in Cleveland public schools and graduated from Ohio Wesleyan University in 1879.

He started his newspaper career as reporter for the old Cleveland Voice. He became city editor of the paper. He also was a member of the staff of the Cleveland Herald.

While he was following the newspaper profession he began the study of law in the office of Judge Stevenson Burke. Later he was admitted to the Ohio bar.

He served two terms as county clerk, from 1894 to 1900, and two terms as county commissioner, from 1908 to 1912. It was during his commissionership that High Level Bridge was built.

An ardent Republican, he was associated in politics with Mark Hanna, Myron T. Herrick, President McKinley, Theodore Burton and other notable Republicans.

was a 32d degree Mason, member of Tyrian Lodge No. 370. Surviving are his widow, Sarah; his son, and a sister, Mrs. Iza Fowler of Delaware, O.

"SECRET SEVEN" PLAN RECEPTION

Chamber Mystery Group Will Entertain Congressman Charles Kramer

The Secret Seven announced

Civil War Vet and Wife Mark 68th Anniversary of Wedding

Mr. and Mrs. Nicholas Weidenkopf

NICHOLAS WEIDENKOPF, president of the board of the Soldiers' and Sailors' Commission, and his wife, Kate, today were receiving congratulations on the 68th anniversary of their marriage.

Mr. Weidenkopf is 92. His wife is 88. They were observing the event quietly at their residence, 1223 Summit avenue, Lakewood. During the day Mr. Weidenkopf put in the usual amount of time working at his office.

Besides being active in the veterans' organizations, Mr. Weidenkopf is president of the Commercial Travelers' Association and served as fire commissioner from 1861 to 1865. They have one son, Burton R. Weidenkopf, former city surveyor.

"I am the only living member of the First Ohio Light Artillery," he confided. "We were on our way to battle 12 days after Ft. Sumpter was fired on and we took part in the Battle of Philippi, the first land battle of the war."

STATE CUTS PRICES ON LIQUOR BRANDS

Reductions Range From 10 to 50 Cents at Stores

Press State Service
COLUMBUS, Feb. 27—New prices for 12 brands of liquor sold in state stores will be in effect Monday. Prices of 10 brands were reduced and two were increased.

The reductions ranged from 10 cents a pint to 50 cents a quart; increases were 15 and 20 cents a fifth.

Reductions were:

	Old Price	New Price
M. R. Vermouth (bottle)	$2.00	$1.80

GERMANY PREPARES TO NAZIFY THE SAAR

Rapid Introduction of New Laws Planned by Cabinet

By United Press
BERLIN, Feb. 27—The cabinet last night approved a series of decrees for swift and thorough Nazification of the Saar basin, when it is taken over by the Reich on Saturday.

The government approved all agreements with France relative to purchase of the rich Saar mines and on the Saar territory's debts. In all, 40 decrees were gazetted covering the introduction of German law in the Saar the moment it returns to the Fatherland.

A "Foot-note"

MISSION NEEDS

Children's Aid Group M peal to Replace Old Ins

An appeal for a piano f day School was made too Metropolitan Mission at 45th street.

The mission, which is

For a Bad Better

Quicker, Lasting
Big Saving! No C

Here's an old home r mother knew, but, for rea is still the best thing ever severe coughs. Try it onc swear by it.

It's no trouble at all syrup by stirring 2 cups of sugar and one cup of wate ments, until dissolved. N needed—a child could do i Now put 2½ ounces of pint bottle, and add your s

FAIRM

Michiga

Fairmount Special

$5 50 TON

LUMP or EGG

HIGH GI RUN....
OHIO LU SLACK..
PENNSY M-R....
W. VA. SLACK..
COARSE SLACK..

The W

"Cream of Kentucky"
Reg. U. S. Pat. Off.

CRI
KEN
...the
straigl

Figure 142

In earlier times, newspapers devoted more space to events in the lives of ordinary people, as this example from the 27 February 1935 edition of the *Cleveland Plain Dealer* shows.

Selected Readings:

American Newspaper Directory (annual), 1869–1908. New York: George P. Rowell and Co.

Brigham, Clarence. *History and Bibliography of American Newspapers, 1690–1820.* 2 vols. Worcester, Mass.: American Antiquarian Society, 1947.

Gale Directory of Publications and Broadcast Media (annual) 1880–. Detroit: Gale Research Co.

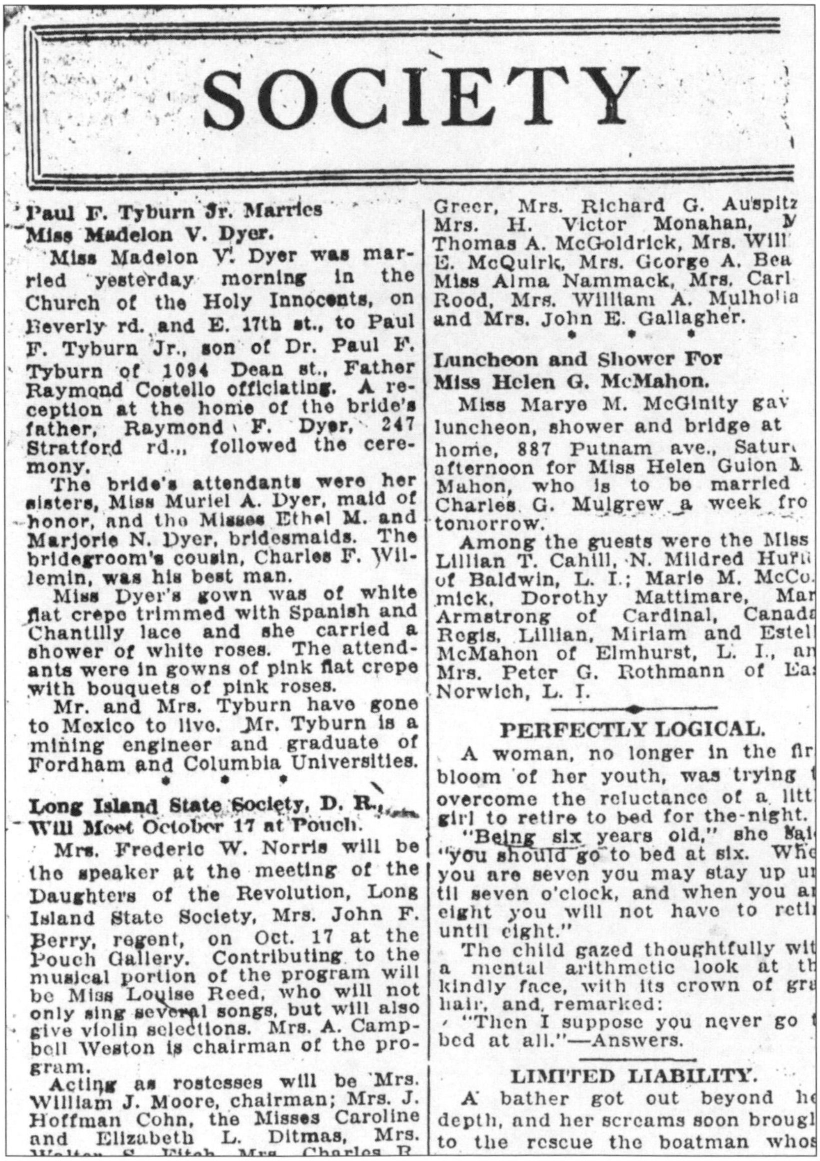

SOCIETY

Paul F. Tyburn Jr. Marries Miss Madelon V. Dyer.

Miss Madelon V. Dyer was married yesterday morning in the Church of the Holy Innocents, on Beverly rd. and E. 17th st., to Paul F. Tyburn Jr., son of Dr. Paul F. Tyburn of 1094 Dean st., Father Raymond Costello officiating. A reception at the home of the bride's father, Raymond F. Dyer, 247 Stratford rd.,, followed the ceremony.

The bride's attendants were her sisters, Miss Muriel A. Dyer, maid of honor, and the Misses Ethel M. and Marjorie N. Dyer, bridesmaids. The bridegroom's cousin, Charles F. Willemin, was his best man.

Miss Dyer's gown was of white flat crepe trimmed with Spanish and Chantilly lace and she carried a shower of white roses. The attendants were in gowns of pink flat crepe with bouquets of pink roses.

Mr. and Mrs. Tyburn have gone to Mexico to live. Mr. Tyburn is a mining engineer and graduate of Fordham and Columbia Universities.

* * *

Long Island State Society, D. R., Will Meet October 17 at Pouch.

Mrs. Frederic W. Norris will be the speaker at the meeting of the Daughters of the Revolution, Long Island State Society, Mrs. John F. Berry, regent, on Oct. 17 at the Pouch Gallery. Contributing to the musical portion of the program will be Miss Louise Reed, who will not only sing several songs, but will also give violin selections. Mrs. A. Campbell Weston is chairman of the program.

Acting as rostesses will be Mrs. William J. Moore, chairman; Mrs. J. Hoffman Cohn, the Misses Caroline and Elizabeth L. Ditmas, Mrs.

Greer, Mrs. Richard G. Auspitz Mrs. H. Victor Monahan, M Thomas A. McGoldrick, Mrs. Will E. McQuirk, Mrs. George A. Bea Miss Alma Nammack, Mrs. Carl Rood, Mrs. William A. Mulholla and Mrs. John E. Gallagher.

* * *

Luncheon and Shower For Miss Helen G. McMahon.

Miss Marye M. McGinity gav luncheon, shower and bridge at home, 887 Putnam ave., Satur afternoon for Miss Helen Guion M Mahon, who is to be married Charles G. Mulgrew a week fro tomorrow.

Among the guests were the Miss Lillian T. Cahill, N. Mildred Huff of Baldwin, L. I.; Marie M. McCo mick, Dorothy Mattimare, Mar Armstrong of Cardinal, Canada Regis, Lillian, Miriam and Estell McMahon of Elmhurst, L. I., an Mrs. Peter G. Rothmann of Ea Norwich, L. I.

PERFECTLY LOGICAL.

A woman, no longer in the fir bloom of her youth, was trying t overcome the reluctance of a litt girl to retire to bed for the night.

"Being six years old," she sai "you should go to bed at six. Whe you are seven you may stay up un til seven o'clock, and when you ar eight you will not have to reti until eight."

The child gazed thoughtfully wit a mental arithmetic look at th kindly face, with its crown of gra hair, and, remarked:

"Then I suppose you never go t bed at all."—Answers.

LIMITED LIABILITY.

A bather got out beyond he depth, and her screams soon brough to the rescue the boatman whos

Figure 143

Local society columns are often rich in biographical information, as shown in this marriage announcement in the *Brooklyn Eagle*. Spelling errors can make a search through indexes difficult, however. In this announcement, for example, the groom's last name Pyburn is incorrectly given as Tyburn.

Gregory, Winifred. *American Newspapers, 1821–1936: A Union List of Files Available in the United States and Canada.* 1937. Reprint. New York: Kraus, 1967.

Hansen, James L. "Research in Newspapers." *The Source: A Guidebook of American Genealogy.* Rev. ed. Ch. 12: 412–38. Salt Lake City: Ancestry, 1997. (This chapter devoted to newspaper research discusses what can be found in newspapers, gives tips on locating newspapers, and includes a large bibliography with sections on ethnic newspapers, religious newspapers, specialty newspapers, and newspaper sources arranged by state).

________. *Wisconsin Newspapers, 1833–1850: An Analytical Bibliography.* Madison, Wis.: State Historical Society, 1979.

Hoornstra, Jean, and Trudy Heath. *American Periodicals, 1741–1900: An Index to the Microfilm Collections—American Periodicals 18th Century, American Periodicals, 1800–1850, American Periodicals, 1850–1900, Civil War and Reconstruction.* Ann Arbor, Mich.: University Microfilms International, 1979.

Library of Congress. Catalog Management and Publication Division. *Newspapers in Microform: United States, 1848–1983.* 2 vols. Washington, D.C.: Library of Congress, 1984.

Parch, Grace D. *Directory of Newspaper Libraries in the U.S. and Canada.* New York: Special Libraries Association, 1976.

Internet Site of Interest:

The U.S. Newspaper Program
http://www.neh.gov/html/usnp.html

Obituaries and Obituary Collections

While early obituaries were typically limited in detail, by the end of the nineteenth century, they had become excellent sources of biographical information. Obituaries usually include dates and places of birth, marriage, and death, along with the names of surviving relatives and their relationship to the deceased. References may also be made to military service, memberships in organizations, and employment.

The search for an ancestor's obituary usually begins with local newspapers. The *Gale Directory of Publications and Broadcast Media* (Detroit: Gale Research Co., annual) is a helpful tool that provides names and addresses of newspapers that are currently published in a particular area. Researchers should be aware that newspaper indexing and abstracting projects have been undertaken by libraries and historical and genealogical societies, and have done much to facilitate the search for obituaries. The American Antiquarian Society, for example, indexed marriage and death notices for several newspapers in the Boston area and has circulated copies of the indexes to the Library of Congress and the New York Public Library. Alphabetized card files of obituaries are also maintained by many libraries, some of which are available on microfilm at the Family History Library. Betty M. Jarboe's *Obituaries: A Guide to Sources*, 2d ed. (Boston: G.K. Hall, 1989) is a valuable resource that provides the locations of many of

"Thomas **MURPHY** of 319 Illinois St., father of Joseph H, William, Thomas M., Frank G., John S, James R, Mrs. Fleming, Mrs. R. Fullen, died Feb. 28 after a brief illness of one week with la-grippe, age 72 years. Mr. Murphy was of Trim, County Meath, Ireland and came to America in 1849 and had been a resident of Chicago and the Cathedral Parish since 1853. He was engaged for a number of years in the ice business and won for himself hosts of friends in social and business circles. He retired from active business a few years ago. A peculiar incident in connection with Mr. Murphy's death was the fact that he died on the same day, date and hour that his wife died eleven years ago. The funeral took place at the Holy Name Cathedral Wednesday morning March 2, at 10:30 o'clock where Solemn High Mass of Requiem was celebrated by the Reverend J.M. Scanlan; Reverend J.P. Dorr, deacon; and Reverend F.J. Barry, subdeacon. The eulogy over the remains was delivered by the Rev. J.M. Scanlan who paid a well merited tribute to the departed and revered father. The remains were laid to rest in the family lot in Calvary, Reverend J.P. Dorr officiating at the grave. The pall-bearers were: Messrs. James Healy, William Walsh, Thomas Duggan, Martin Cooney, Thomas Drurry, and William Spain. May he rest in peace."

Figure 144

The 1898 obituary of Thomas Murphy, published in *The New World*, a Chicago Catholic newspaper.

these card files and, in total, identifies over 3,500 published collections and indexes to death notices and cemetery listings throughout the United States. One entry indicates that the New Orleans Public Library has a file of approximately 523,000 obituary cards, which is expanding by 25,000 new cards per year. An increasing number of obituaries can be found on the Internet. Ancestry.com, for example, offers selected UMI and other obituary databases.

Selected Readings:

Jarboe, Betty M. *Obituaries: A Guide to Sources.* 2d ed. Boston: G.K. Hall, 1989.

Milner, Anita. *Newspaper Indexes: A Location and Subject Guide for Researchers.* 3 vols. Metuchen, N.J.: Scarecrow Press, 1977–82.

Sittner, Kathi. "Obituaries." *Ancestry* 13 (6) (November/December 1995): 26–7.

Szucs, Loretto Dennis, and Sandra Hargreaves Luebking, eds. *The Source: A Guidebook of American Genealogy.* Rev. ed. Salt Lake City: Ancestry, 1997.

Internet Sites of Interest:

Ancestry.com UMI Obituary Index
http://www.ancestry.com

The U.S. Newspaper Program
http://www.geocities.com/heartland/bluffs/7748/obit/obituary.htm

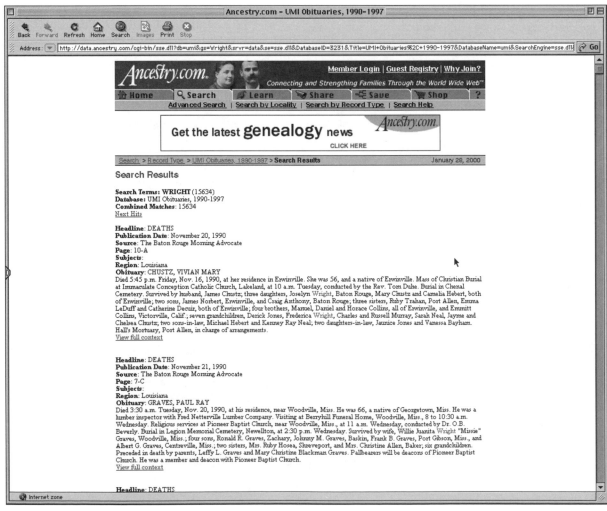

Figure 145
Results from a UMI Obituary search at Ancestry.com.

Occupational Records

Occupational records, such as trade or professional licenses, personnel records, or Union membership records, though difficult to locate, can be useful for the genealogical information they may contain. The American Medical Association, for example, keeps files on its members. Private associations printed directories, almanacs, company histories, and collective biographies with information on their members. And the regulating of business practices has also created records that may be of interest to family historians.

If you can associate an ancestor with a specific company or business, you may be able to search the records of that business, if it is still in existence or if the records have been deposited in a society or corporate archive. Because of their importance in the development of the United States, the records of many transportation companies have survived and can be located in libraries, archives, and historical societies. Wayne State University in Detroit is the site of the Archives of Labor History and holds manuscripts from unions all over the country. In fact, unions still hold many membership records. Two publications, *Directories in Print* (Detroit: Gale Research Co.) and the *Encyclopedia of Associations* (Detroit: Gale Research Co.), are helpful tools for locating trade association publications. Business directories like Dun and Bradstreet's *America's Corporate Families* (Skokie: Ill.: National Register Publishing Co.) and *Ward's Business Directory of U.S. Private and Public Companies* (Petaluma, Calif.: Baldwin H. Ward) can be extremely helpful in locating businesses. From 1816 to 1959, the federal government issued an annual or biennial list of its employees, civilian and military. Although the title of the publication varied, it is most often referred to as the *Official Register* and is located at the National Archives and in other large libraries.

Figure 146
Several members of the female workforce take a rare break for a photograph in an early twentieth century knitting mill.

See also *American Medical Association Records; Applications, Appointment Papers, and Commisions; Apprenticeship Records; Biographies; Insurance Records; Maritime Records; Railroad Records;* and *Pension Records.*

Selected Readings:

Benedict, Karen M. *A Select Bibliography on Business Archives and Records Management.* Chicago: Society of American Archivists.

Directories in Print. Detroit: Gale Research Co., annual.

Directory of Business Archives in the United States and Canada. Chicago: Society of American Archivists, 1975.

Dun and Bradstreet. *America's Corporate Families.* Skokie: Ill.: National Register Publishing Co., annual. (Provides information on mergers, acquisitions, name changes, and affiliations of major American corporations)

Encyclopedia of Associations. Detroit: Gale Research Co., bi-annual.

Guide to Genealogical Research in the National Archives. Washington, D.C.: National Archives Trust Fund Board, 1985.

Lewinson, Paul, and Morris Rieger. "Labor Union Records in the United States." *American Archivist* 25 (January 1963): 46–57.

Meyerink, Kory L., and Johni Cerny. "Research in Business, Employment, and Institutional Records." *The Source: A Guidebook of American Genealogy.* Rev. ed. Ch. 10: 336–83. Salt Lake City: Ancestry, 1997.

Figure 147
An 1893 photograph of the Alex Banet family, taken in front of the family-owned saloon in Fort Wayne, Indiana.

EDUCATIONAL BACKGROUND

NAMES AND LOCATIONS OF HIGH SCHOOLS, COLLEGES UNIVERSITIES, SPEC. PROGRAMS	FACULTY REFERENCE	DATES FROM	TO	DEGREE EARNED	GRAD. DATE	COLLEGE MAJOR	GRADE POINT AVERAGE A 4.0	CHECK CLASS RANK
H.S. FOREMAN H.S. CHICAGO, ILL.	?	9/40	6/44	High School Diploma	?			
1. QUINCY COLLEGE QUINCY, ILL.	FR. JULIAN	9/48	2/49	NA	NA	PRE-ENGRG.	3.5	✓
2. NO. ILL. U. DEKALB, ILL.	DR. EATON	2/49	6/50	NA	NA	PRE-ENGRG.	3.5	✓
3.								
4.								

COLLEGE HONORS, PUBLICATIONS, PROFESSIONAL SOCIETIES, FRATERNITIES, ATHLETICS AND OTHER EXTRA-CURRICULAR ACTIVITIES (Indicate positions held)

% COLLEGE EXPENSES EARNED G.I. BILL
AVERAGE NO. OF HOURS WORKED PER WEEK WHILE IN COLLEGE

SELECTIVE SERVICE CLASSIFICATION 5A
HIGHEST RANK OBTAINED ELECTRICIAN

BUSINESS EXPERIENCE

Please start with your present or most recent position. If there are references or prior employers whom you do not want us to contact without your permission, please circle their name. If you were ever in business for yourself, either as sole or part owner or if you were ever employed by a member of your family, please indicate under REMARKS.

COMPANY (1) AUTOMATIC ELECTRIC CO.   ADDRESS 400 N. WOLF RD., NORTHLAKE, ILL.
KIND OF BUSINESS MFR. OF COMMUNICATIONS EQPT.   EMPLOYED FROM: 7-9-62   TO: PRESENT
POSITION TTY & DATA SVC. FACILITY   COMPENSATION: WEEKLY / ANNUAL $12,700.0
NATURE TTY & DATA EQPT. FOR GEN. TEL. SYSTEM   NUMBER SUPERVISED 5
POSITION OF SUPERVISOR MANAGER

... WITH THE GREAT GEOGRAPHICAL SPREAD OF OUR CUSTOMERS
...EST DEVELOPMENTS IN THE STATE OF THE ART. SECONDLY I
...ITH THE ENGRG. & PURCH. DEPTS. OF THE MANY COS. SERVED
...R DEPT. REPRESENT LESS THAN 1% OF THE COMPANY. 79TH
...UNCONCERNED MAKING IT VERY DIFFICULT TO RECEIV
...ing to change from this position? I THINK WE HAVE JUST SCRATCHED
...OICE & PARTICULARLY DATA COMMUNICATIONS. I WOUL
...MPANY INTERESTED IN MAINTAINING AN EFFICIENT

ADDRESS 400 N. PULASKI RD. CHICAGO, ILL.
...QPT.   EMPLOYED FROM: FEB. 1960   TO: 7-8-62
...ITAL DATA.   COMPENSATION: WEEKLY $165.00 / ANNUAL   NUMBER SUPERVISED 3
For SAGE, 465L & CRITICOMM PROJ.
POSITION OF SUPERVISOR MANAGER
...JECTS WORKED ON AFFORDED ME A
...DIFFERENT TYPES OF EQUIPMENT WHICH
...S. GOVERNMENT & MILITARY FOR SALES.
...COMPANY WAS INVOLVED LARGELY IN
...T COMPLETED AND NOTHING NEW.

...WASHINGTON CHICAGO, ILL.
...OYED FROM: ...6. 1950   TO: FEB. 1960.
...SATION: WEEKLY $125.50
...HILIGER

APPLICATION FOR EMPLOYMENT

PERSONAL BACKGROUND

PLEASE PRINT IN BLACK INK

FIRST NAME EDWARD   MIDDLE INITIAL F.   IF MARRIED WOMAN—MAIDEN NAME NA
DATE AVAILABLE FOR EMPLOYMENT NOW   FROM (MO. & YR.) JUNE 1964   FROM (MO. & YR.) TO: JUNE 57 TO JUNE 64   JUNE 54 TO JUNE 57
NAME: LAST PFEIFFER
SOCIAL SECURITY NUMBER 345-14-9701   TELEPHONE NUMBER 312-543-4510   STATE & ZIP CODE ILL. 60101
PRESENT ADDRESS: STREET, RFD, BOX 451 SIXTH AVE.   CITY ADDISON   STATE ILL.   IF U.S. VISA, TYPE & DATE NA
PRIOR ADDRESS: STREET, RFD, BOX 5406 S. MAY ST.   CITY CHICAGO   STATE ILL.
1) 4532 S. RICHMOND   CITY CHICAGO   COUNTRY OF CITIZENSHIP U.S.A.   FIRST NAME OF SPOUSE CAROL
HEIGHT 6'-1"   WEIGHT 205
SEX ☒ Male ☐ Female   ☐ French ☐ Spanish ☐ German ☐ Other ☐ Divorced ☐ Separated ☐ Engaged
WILLING TO MOVE? ☒ Yes ☐ No
BIRTH DATE DEC. 3, 1926   AGE 42
LANGUAGE SPOKEN ☒ English
MARITAL STATUS ☒ Married ☐ Single
OTHER DEPENDENTS IN HOME & RELATIONSHIP NONE
AGES OF CHILDREN 13, 12, TWINS 8, 3
MAJOR FIELD OF EMPLOYMENT INTEREST OR POSITION DESIRED 1) TELECOMMUNICATIONS COORDINATOR
GEOGRAPHIC PREFERENCE(S) 1) CHICAGO AREA
SALARY REQUIREMENT NEGOTIABLE
PROFESSIONAL LICENSES AND CERTIFICATES NONE
HOW DO YOU FEEL ABOUT WORKING EVENINGS, WEEKENDS, OR HOLIDAYS IF REQUIRED BY THE NATURE OF THE WORK? AGREEABLE IF NECESSARY
LICENSE EVER RESTRICTED, SUSPENDED, REVOKED? (If Yes, explain) ☐ Yes ☒ No
POSSESS A VALID DRIVER'S LICENSE? ☒ Yes ☐ No   STATE ILLINOIS   WHERE WERE YOU RAISED? CHICAGO   PHONE 543-4510
RELATIONSHIP WIFE
WHAT WAS YOUR FATHER'S OCCUPATION BREWER   ADDRESS 451 6TH AVE. ADDISON   NA
RELATIONSHIP NA
In event of emergency, notify: NAME CAROL PFEIFFER   LOCATION
Friends or relatives employed by Weyerhaeuser Company: NAME NONE KNOWN   LOCATION NA   DATE NA
POSITION
I have previously ☐ applied for employment ☐ been employed by the Weyerhaeuser Company: LOCATION NA   MR. P. ACKINS
From whom did you receive this application?

...N WITH
...SITIONS.
...IN MY
...RATE
...Y
...EN.
...I ALWAYS
...BACK AS A SEVENTH
...VERED, IN PART, MAGNETISM
...S MY MAIN SCHOLASTIC INTEREST.
...HOOL, COLLEGE, & MY EMPLOYMENT.
...ULD BE A SUCCESSFUL WEYERHAEUSER COMPANY EMPLOYEE IN YOUR CHOSEN FIELD? I FEEL MY TECHNICAL
...AND EXPERIENCE GIVE ME AN EXCELLENT KNOWLEDGE OF THE EQPT.
...D IN THE WEYERHAEUSER NETWORK. I AM ABLE TO TALK WITH PEOPLE AND
REACH AMICABLE AGREEMENTS WITHOUT DIFFICULTY. I HAVE AN APPRECIATION
FOR AN OPERATORS OR MANAGERS FEELINGS WHEN THEY ARE OUT OF SERVICE OR
EXPERIENCING DIFFICULTY. I BELIEVE HONESTY IS THE BEST POLICY AND REALIZE
THERE ARE TIMES TO TALK AND TIMES TO LISTEN. IF I AM CORRECT IN MY INTERPRETATION
OF THE SCOPE OF THE POSITION OF TELECOMMUNICATIONS COORDINATOR, THEN I FEEL

COMPANY (4) ROSENAU M...
KIND OF BUSINESS BRICK & ST...
POSITION APPRENTICE
NATURE OF WORK BRICKLAYING

COMPANY SPENCER'S 20TH CEN...
KIND OF BUSINESS BOWLING ALLE...
POSITION COUNTERMAN (W...
NATURE OF WORK TAKE CARE OF COU...
OUT ALLEYS, COLLECT FOR GAMES & KEEP RECORD.

Fill in if you have ever been unemployed. Include college w... opportunity to explain any gaps in your employment record.

FROM MO	YR	TO MO	YR	HOW DID YOU SPE...

ORGANIZATIONAL

TYPE OF ORGANIZATION	NAME
Business, Scientific, Professional	
Athletics or Sports	ADDISON RECREATION CLUB
Civic or Community	
Luncheon or Men's Clubs	
Other	

What are your hobbies or avocations? BOYS SPORTS AS PRESCRIBED ABOVE. AND...

What books have you read in the past six months? 1000 PAGES

What special reading interests do you pursue regularly? TELEPHONY MAG.; TELEPHONE E... MANAGEMENT... COMMUNICATION NEWS. READERS DIGEST.

Figure 148

In addition to biographical data, this application for employment provides information on hobbies, reading interests, short-term and long-term goals, and other details that may otherwise be lost to future generations.

National Union Catalog of Manuscript Collections. Washington, D.C.: Library of Congress, annual since 1962.

Pfugll, Warner. *A Guide to the Archives of Labor History and Urban Affairs.* Detroit: Wayne State University Press, 1974.

Prechtel-Kluskens, Claire. "Documenting the Career of Federal Employees." *Prologue* 26 (Fall 1994): 180-85.

Ward, Baldwin H., ed. *Ward's Business Directory of U.S. Private and Public Companies.* Petaluma, Calif.: Baldwin H. Ward Publications, annual.

Internet Sites of Interest:

Bowling Green State University —Center for Archival Collections, Records of the International Association of Bridge, Structural, and Ornamental Ironworkers http://www.bgsu.edu/colleges/library/cac/ms0077.html

University of Missouri/State Historical Society of Missouri Labor
http://www.system.missouri.edu/whmc/labor.htm

Western Historical Manuscript Collection
http://www.umsl.edu/~whmc/whmlabor/index.html

146   *HISTORY OF CHICAGO, AND SOUVENIR OF THE LIQUOR INTEREST.*

ONE of the gems of Chicago's liquor saloons is found at No. 136 S. Halsted Street, at the southeast corner of Adams Street, where Mr. W. F. Fitzgerald conducts his sample room. This place is well known, and conceded to be the handsomest saloon on the West Side of Chicago. The business was established by a Mr. Tierney, who was a wholesaler. In 1878 Mr. Fitzgerald secured the place and reopened it as a retail store and sample room. In 1885 the proprietor had the place refitted throughout in the most elegant and expensive style, making it, indeed, a polished gem. The ground floor covers space 25x50 feet in extent, while overhead are three large and convenient lodge halls, occupying two entire floors, 40x92. In the saloon, the bar, thirty feet in length, and, in fact, all the wood work about the room, is solid mahogany, highly polished and artistically hand-carved in the most curious and beautiful patterns; delicate frescoes and stucco work form the ceiling, whilst upon the floor one treads upon fine German tiling, and around the walls are arranged the most expensive French plate mirrors.

Mr. W. F. Fitzgerald is a native of New York State, and in the prime of life. He is the financial secretary of the Chicago Liquor Dealers' Protective Association, and is connected with the Independent Brewing Association. He is the vice-president of the association, and was one of the prime originators of this large corporation, being one of the five gentlemen who met and formed the plan upon which it is now conducted.

PROMINENT among the places worthy of mention in this historical work of Chicago is the sample room of P. F. Maloney, corresponding secretary of the Chicago Liquor Dealers' Association, 161 Michigan Street. This saloon was established in 1871 by M. J. Casey, and was successfully conducted by him until his death, in 1888. In this year Mr. Maloney purchased the business and refitted and thoroughly renovated the premises, and made the saloon one of the handsomest in the city. The place is artistically and elegantly finished in cherry, contains a twenty-foot bar, hand carved and marble covered, has an attractively furnished reading room connected, and also a cozy private office. His saloon is a recognized headquarters for prominent politicians, lawyers and the officials of the Criminal Court Building, and it is likewise much frequented by financial and commercial men. Mr. P. F. Maloney is a gentleman in his thirty-eighth year, and was born in Dunkirk, N. Y. He came to Chicago in the year 1868, where he has since remained and become a prominent and influential citizen. He is a stanch and energetic Democrat, and takes an active interest in politics. He was elected County Commissioner in 1888, and filled that responsible position with credit to himself and in a most satisfactory manner to the general public and his constituency. Prior to establishing himself in his present location he conducted a sample room at 238 E. Chicago Avenue, and has been engaged in the liquor business since 1881. From 1884 to 1888 he was the efficient secretary of the Liquor Dealers & Manufacturers' State Protective Association, and for three terms filled the same position in the First District Association. Mr. Maloney has been identified with measures beneficial to the liquor interests of the city. He is also a member in high standing of the Independent Order of Foresters, Red Men, and D. Molay, Knights of Pythias. Mr. Maloney is well and favorably known as a gentleman of sound business integrity and commercial veracity.

Figure 149

In some cases, published biographical histories of specific occupations and trades can be enlightening. Pictured here is a page from *History of Chicago and Souvenir of the Liquor Interest* (Chicago: Belgravia Publishing Co., 1891). In addition to flattering descriptions of the liquor establishments, the book contains biographical data on a significant number of owners.

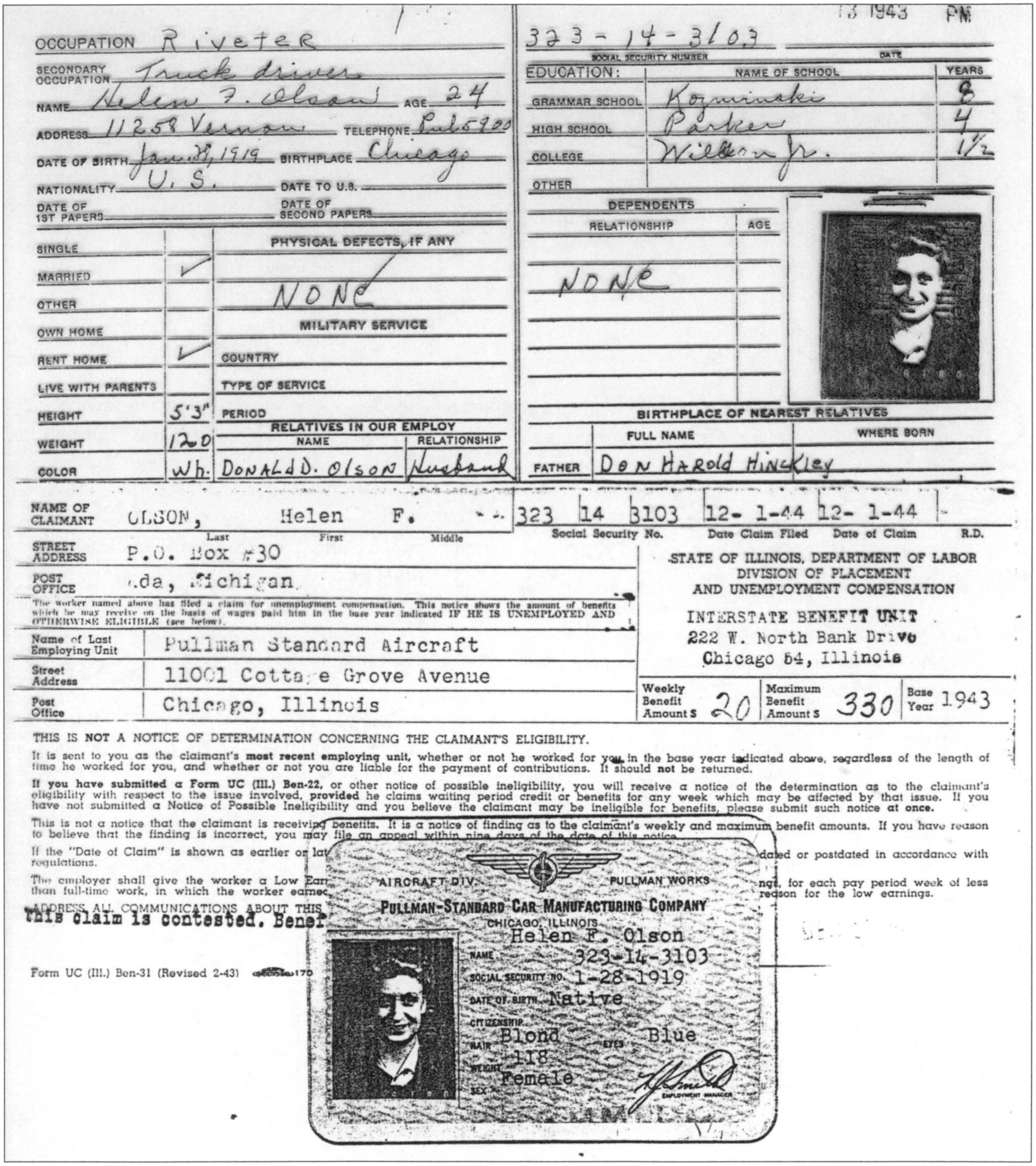

13 1943 PM

OCCUPATION Riveter
SECONDARY OCCUPATION Truck driver
NAME Helen F. Olson AGE 24
ADDRESS 11258 Vernon TELEPHONE Pul 5900
DATE OF BIRTH Jan. 28, 1919 BIRTHPLACE Chicago
NATIONALITY U. S. DATE TO U.S.
DATE OF 1ST PAPERS DATE OF SECOND PAPERS

		PHYSICAL DEFECTS, IF ANY
SINGLE		
MARRIED	✓	NONE
OTHER		
OWN HOME		MILITARY SERVICE
RENT HOME	✓	COUNTRY
LIVE WITH PARENTS		TYPE OF SERVICE
HEIGHT	5'3"	PERIOD
WEIGHT	120	RELATIONS IN OUR EMPLOY — NAME / RELATIONSHIP
COLOR	Wh.	DONALD D. OLSON / Husband

323-14-3103
SOCIAL SECURITY NUMBER DATE

EDUCATION:	NAME OF SCHOOL	YEARS
GRAMMAR SCHOOL	Kozminski	8
HIGH SCHOOL	Parker	4
COLLEGE	Wilson Jr.	1½
OTHER		

DEPENDENTS

RELATIONSHIP	AGE
NONE	

BIRTHPLACE OF NEAREST RELATIVES

	FULL NAME	WHERE BORN
FATHER	Don Harold Hinckley	

NAME OF CLAIMANT	OLSON, Last	Helen First	F. Middle	323 14 3103 Social Security No.	12- 1-44 Date Claim Filed	12- 1-44 Date of Claim	R.D.

STREET ADDRESS P.O. Box #30
POST OFFICE .da, Michigan

The worker named above has filed a claim for unemployment compensation. This notice shows the amount of benefits which he may receive on the basis of wages paid him in the base year indicated IF HE IS UNEMPLOYED AND OTHERWISE ELIGIBLE (see below).

Name of Last Employing Unit Pullman Standard Aircraft
Street Address 11001 Cottage Grove Avenue
Post Office Chicago, Illinois

STATE OF ILLINOIS, DEPARTMENT OF LABOR
DIVISION OF PLACEMENT
AND UNEMPLOYMENT COMPENSATION

INTERSTATE BENEFIT UNIT
222 W. North Bank Drive
Chicago 54, Illinois

Weekly Benefit Amount $	Maximum Benefit Amount $	Base Year
20	330	1943

THIS IS **NOT** A NOTICE OF DETERMINATION CONCERNING THE CLAIMANT'S ELIGIBILITY.

It is sent to you as the claimant's **most recent employing unit**, whether or not he worked for you in the base year indicated above, regardless of the length of time he worked for you, and whether or not you are liable for the payment of contributions. It should **not** be returned.

If you have submitted a Form UC (Ill.) Ben-22, or other notice of possible ineligibility, you will receive a notice of the determination as to the claimant's eligibility with respect to the issue involved, **provided** he claims waiting period credit or benefits for any week which may be affected by that issue. If you have not submitted a Notice of Possible Ineligibility and you believe the claimant may be ineligible for benefits, please submit such notice **at once.**

This is not a notice that the claimant is receiving benefits. It is a notice of finding as to the claimant's weekly and maximum benefit amounts. If you have reason to believe that the finding is incorrect, you may file an appeal within nine days of the date of this notice.

If the "Date of Claim" is shown as earlier or lat... dated or postdated in accordance with regulations.

The employer shall give the worker a Low Earn... ng, for each pay period week of less than full-time work, in which the worker earned... reason for the low earnings.

ADDRESS ALL COMMUNICATIONS ABOUT THIS...

This claim is contested. Benef...

Form UC (Ill.) Ben-31 (Revised 2-43)

AIRCRAFT DIV. PULLMAN WORKS
PULLMAN-STANDARD CAR MANUFACTURING COMPANY
CHICAGO, ILLINOIS

NAME Helen F. Olson
SOCIAL SECURITY NO. 323-14-3103
DATE OF BIRTH 1-28-1919
CITIZENSHIP Native
HAIR Blond EYES Blue
WEIGHT 118
SEX Female
EMPLOYMENT MANAGER

Figure 150

Employment records from Pullman-Standard Car Manufacturing Co. from a collection held by the South Suburban Genealogical and Historical Society in South Holland, Illinois.

Orphan Asylum Records

Children too young to be indentured or bound out in apprenticeships were sent to orphanages. Records from these institutions can provide a child's name, age or birth date, names of parents, birthplaces of parents, name and residence of nearest kin, and information pertaining to the admission to and discharge from the orphanage.

The location and content of the records will vary according to whether the institution was operated by a state or local government, religious organization, or private benefactor. If the orphanage is no longer in existence, places to search include state archives, state agencies responsible for child welfare, historical societies, and local and university libraries. Religious organizations often maintain archives and may hold records of orphanages run by their order.

Selected Readings:

Allen, Desmond Walls. "Paupers at the Turn of the Century." *Professional Genealogists of Arkansas, Inc. Newsletter* 6 (6) (November 1993).

Fink, Arthur E. "Changing Philosophies and Practices in North Carolina Orphanages." *North Carolina Historical Review* 48 (1971).

Greenwood, Peggy Thomson. "City's House of Refuge; Orphanages 1827–1870" and "Orphanages (Part 2) 1870–1900." *St. Louis Genealogical Quarterly* 24 (1) (Fall 1990).

Speare, Jean E., and Dorothy Paul. *Admission Record Indianapolis Asylum for Friendless Colored Children, 1871– 1900.* Indianapolis: Family History and Genealogy Section, Indiana Historical Society, 1978.

Teeters, Negley K. "The Early Days of the Philadelphia House of Refuge." *Pennsylvania History* 27 (1960): 165–87.

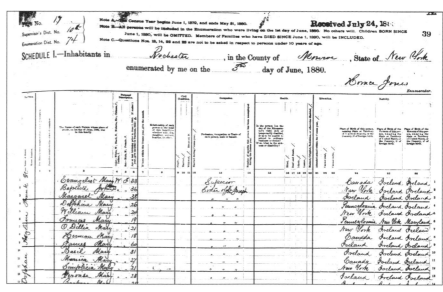

Figure 151

One way to discover names of orphans, along with other identifying information, is to locate them in census records. Shown is an 1880 federal census schedule for St. Patrick's Orphans Asylum, Rochester, New York.

Orphan Train Records, 1853-1929

The practice of relocating homeless children, via train, from large cities to towns and farms in rural areas began with a small trial group in the 1850s and was deemed successful enough to continue until approximately 200,000 orphans had been placed in new surroundings. County court records document adoptions and apprenticeship agreements resulting from the relocation. The orphanage from which the children left may also have a record of the orphans' depar- ture (See the addresses on the following page for a few of the orphanages that participated in the Orphan Train Program.) The Orphan Train Heritage Society of America, 614 E. Emma, #115, Springdale, Arkansas 72764, is a national clearinghouse of information about individuals and institutions that took part in the orphan train program and is another source to con- sider if a search of county records proves unsuccessful.

Figure 152
The Orphan Train, ca. 1900. (Courtesy of the Kansas State Historical Society, Topeka, Kansas)

New England Home for Little Wanderers
850 Boylston Street, Suite 201
Chestnut Hill, MA 02167

New York Children's Aid Society
105 East 22nd Street
New York, NY 10021

New York Foundling Hospital Dept. of Closed Records
590 Avenue of the Americas
New York, NY 10001

New York Juvenile Asylum Alumni Affairs
Children's Village
Dobbs Ferry, NY 10007

See also *Adoption Records.*

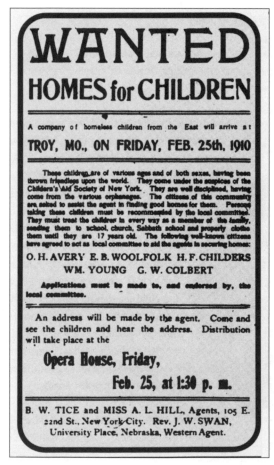

Figure 153
A newspaper advertisement advising readers of a planned orphan train stop in Troy, Missouri. (Courtesy of State Historical Society of Missouri)

Selected Readings:

Charlotte County (Florida) Genealogical Society. "Orphan Train Children." *Geneagram* 24 (1) (June 1991): 44–46.

Coble, Janet. "They Came to Our Town: A Story of Orphan Train Children." *Illinois State Genealogical Society Quarterly* 24 (2) (Summer 1992): 102–04.

Gilbert, Meredith. "Orphan Trains." *Polish Genealogical Society of Texas News* 10 (3) (Fall 1993): 26–28.

Holt, Marilyn Irvin. "Orphan Train Genealogy." *Ancestry* 13 (1) (January/February 1995): 5–7.

Illinois State Genealogical Society. *Children of Orphan Trains From NY to IL, and Beyond.* Springfield, Ill.: Illinois State Genealogical Society, 1995.

Internet Sites of Interest:

Orphan Train Adoptees
http://www.system.missouri.edu/shs/orphan.html

Orphan Trains
Illinois State Genealogical Society
http://www.tbox.com/isgs/projects/orphan-train.html

Orphan Trains of Kansas
http://kuhttp.cc.ukans.edu/carrie/kancoll/articles/orphans/index.html

Orphan Train Riders Heritage Society of America, Inc.
http://pda.republic.net/othsa/

Orphan Train Riders Research Center
http://www.angelfire.com/sd/OrphanTrainRiders/

Passenger Lists

An ancestor's arrival in the United States may be documented by passenger lists. Although lists were not kept for every ship and the contents of those in existence vary, they are among the most desirable of immigration sources. Earlier U.S. passenger arrival lists usually included the immigrant's name, age, and country of origin or the ship's last port of call. It wasn't until the 1880s that more detailed information, such as the place of origin, was included in the lists. By 1893, federal law mandated that immigration passenger lists also contain the following information: a passenger's sex; marital status; occupation; nationality; last residence; final destination; and whether going to join a relative, and if so, the relative's name, address, and relationship to the passenger. Changes in subsequent years added race, personal description, birthplace, and name and address of the

Figure 154
During the peak years of immigration, from about 1900 to 1914, as many as five thousand people a day were processed at Ellis Island.

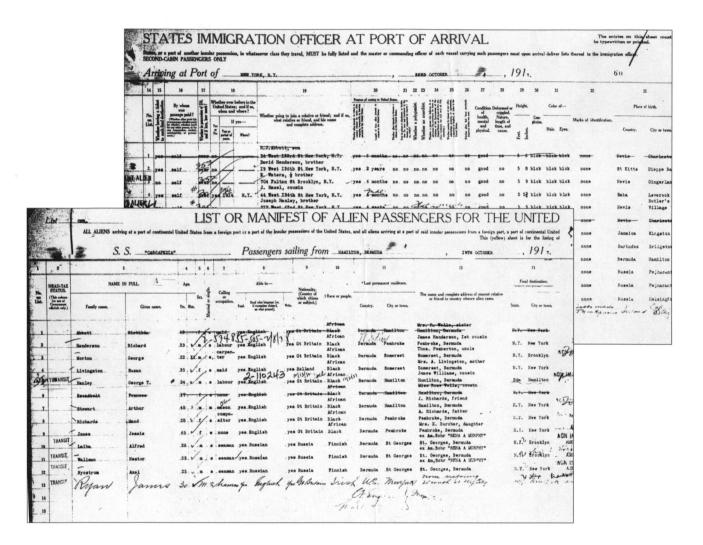

Figure 155

After 1906, the Immigration and Naturalization Service asked thirty-three questions of passengers coming into the United States. Shown is a section of a list of aliens who arrived on the *S.S. Cascapedia*, sailing from Hamilton, Bermuda, on 19 October 1917 and arriving at the Port of New York on the 22nd of October 1917. Information about each passenger runs across two pages in a bound volume. Passenger lists such as this have been microfilmed and are available at the National Archives and at and through the Family History Library.

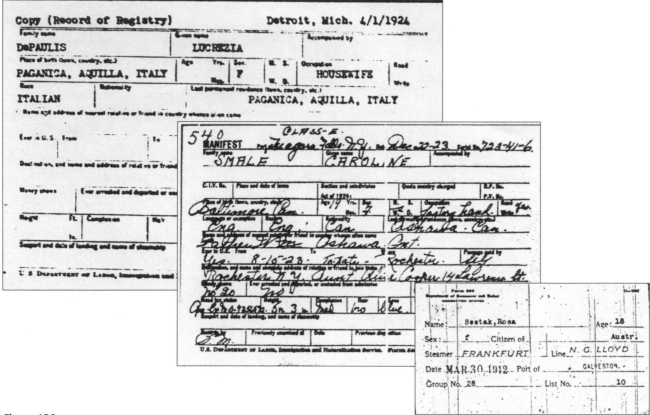

Figure 156

While New York was by far the most used landing point for immigrants coming to the United States, many entered this country through other immigration stations. When the arrival date for an individual and/or the port of arrival are uncertain, it may be necessary to search the passenger list indexes for several ports. Extant passenger list indexes have been microfilmed and are available at the National Archives and some of its regional branches, in some libraries with genealogical collections, and at and through the Family History Library. Shown here are samples of passenger list cards for Caroline Smale, who entered the United States through the Port of New York in 1923; Lucrezia DaPaulis, who entered through the Port of Detroit in 1924; and Rosa Sestak, who entered the Port of Galveston in 1912.

nearest relative in the immigrant's home country. Researchers should be aware that passenger lists were also created and filed with the port of embarkation, ports of call during the voyage, and newspapers at the both the port of departure and port of arrival. A list was kept with the ship's manifest, and notations of the passengers were made in the ship's log.

Knowing the port of entry, the name of the vessel, and the approximate date of arrival greatly improves a researcher's chances of finding the record of a particular immigrant. A search of naturalization records may reveal these key pieces of information. Official U.S. government passenger lists for the period 1820 through 1945 are available for most ports in the United States that have customs houses. The National Archives has a significant collection, most of which has been indexed. The Family History Library has microfilm copies of many of the lists held by the National Archives. Selected passenger lists are also available at some public libraries. For the period prior to 1820, copies of ship cargo manifests may be the only way to document an ancestor's arrival in the United States. *Passenger and Immigration Lists Index* (Detroit: Gale Research Co., 1981–) is an index to the manifests that have been published. As is the case with passenger arrival lists, the information pertaining to each passenger varies.

See also *Foreign Records of Emigration to the United States* and *Naturalization Records*.

Selected Readings:

Colletta, John P. *They Came in Ships: A Guide to Finding Your Immigrant Ancestor's Arrival Record.* Rev. ed. Salt Lake City: Ancestry, 1993.

Filby, P. William, Mary K. Meyer, and Dorothy M. Lower. *Passenger and Immigration Lists Index.* Detroit: Gale Research Co., 1981– (including supplements).

_____, and Mary K. Meyer, eds. *Passenger and Immigration Lists Index: A Guide to Published Arrival Records of More Than 1,775,000 Passengers Who Came to the New World Between the Sixteenth, Seventeenth, and Eighteenth Centuries.* Detroit: Gale Research Co., 1981. Supplements 1982–.

_____. *Passenger and Immigration Lists Bibliography, 1538–1900: Being a Guide to Published Lists of Arrivals in the United States and Canada.* 2d ed. Detroit: Gale Research Co., 1988.

Immigration Information Bureau. *Morton Allen Directory of European Passenger Steamship Arrivals.* 1931. Reprint. Baltimore: Genealogical Publishing Co., 1993.

Lancour, Harold. *Bibliography of Passenger Lists.* New York: New York Public Library, 1937.

Meyerink, Kory L., and Loretto Dennis Szucs. "Immigration: Finding Immigrant Origins." *The Source: A Guidebook of American Genealogy.* Rev. ed. Salt Lake City: Ancestry, 1997.

National Archives Trust Fund Board. *Immigrant and Passenger Arrivals: A Select Catalog of National Archives Publications.* Revised. Washington, D.C., 1992.

Szucs, Loretto Dennis. *They Became Americans: Finding Naturalization Records and Ethnic Origins.* Salt Lake City: Ancestry, 1998.

Tepper, Michael. *American Passenger Arrival Records: A Guide to the Records of Immigrants Arriving at American Ports by Sail and Steam.* 2d ed. Baltimore: Genealogical Publishing Co., 1993.

Internet Sites of Interest:

Immigrant Ship Transcribers Guild
http://istg.rootsweb.com/

Sites with Genealogical Source Material - Emigrants
http://freespace.virgin.net/alan.tupman/sites/index.htm

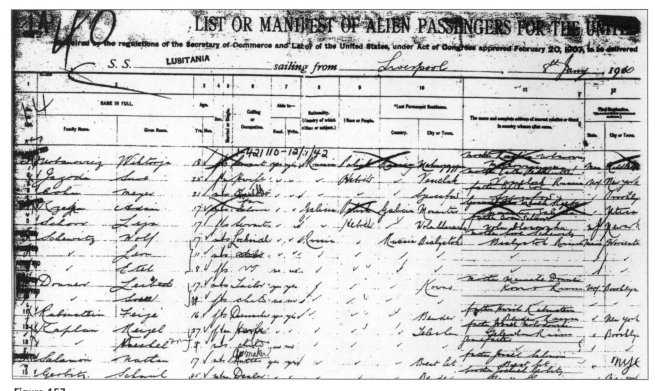

Figure 157
List or Manifest of Alien Passengers for the United States sailing on the *S.S. Lusitania* from Liverpool, England to New York City, dated 8 January 1910.

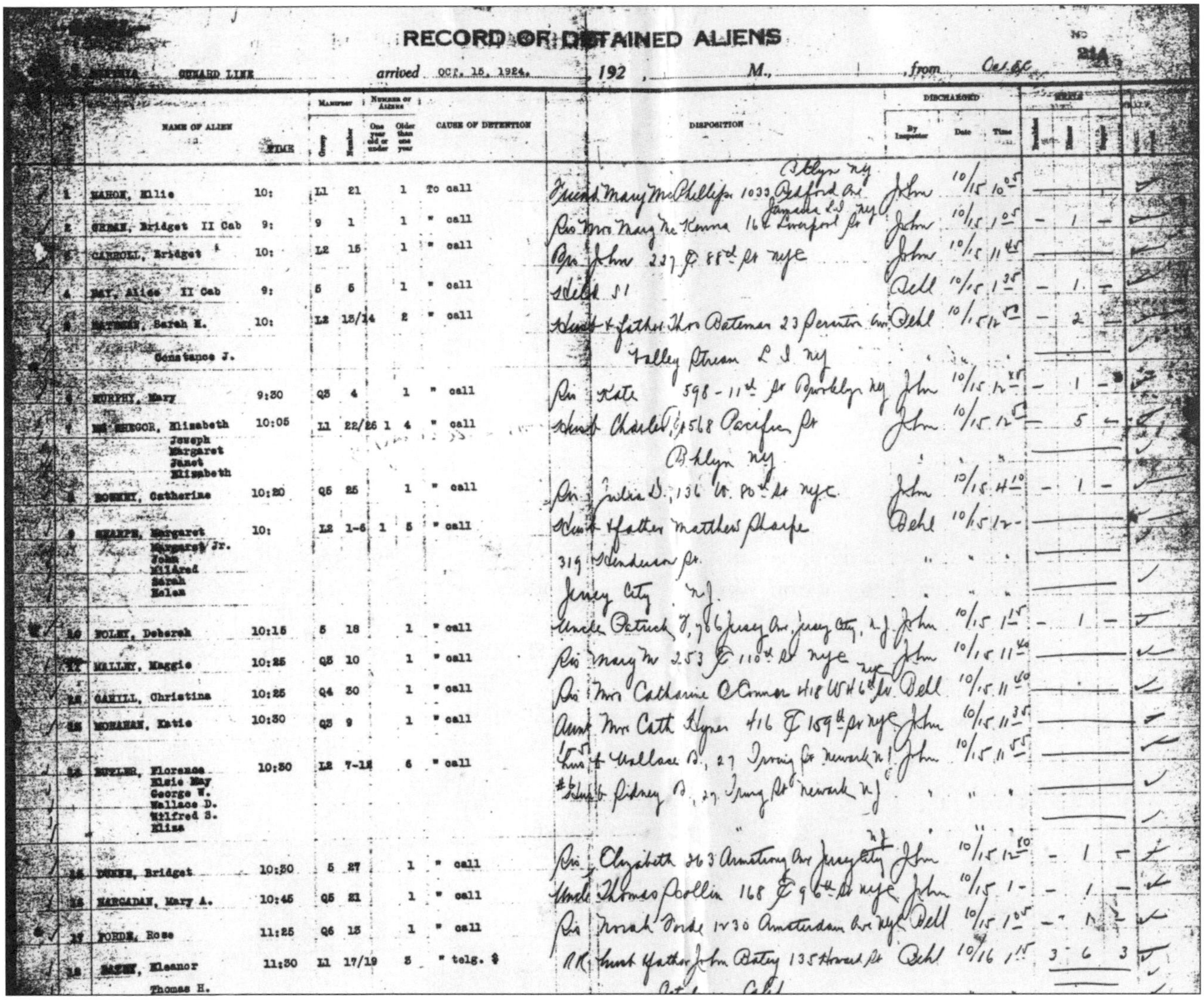

RECORD OF DETAINED ALIENS

SCYTHIA CUNARD LINE arrived OCT. 15, 1924, 192 , M., from Cobh

	NAME OF ALIEN	TIME	Manifest Group	Manifest Number	Number of Aliens: One year old or under	Number of Aliens: Older than one year	CAUSE OF DETENTION	DISPOSITION	Discharged By Inspector	Discharged Date	Discharged Time
1	MAHON, Ellie	10:	L1	21		1	To call	Friend Mary McPhillips 1033 Bedford Av. Bklyn NY	John	10/15	10:05
2	Bridget II Cab	9:	9	1		1	" call	Sis Mrs Mary McKenna 16 Liverpool St Jamaica L.I. NY	John	10/15	1:05
3	CARROLL, Bridget	10:	L2	15		1	" call	Bro John 237 E 88th St NYC	John	10/15	11:45
4	Alice II Cab	9:	6	6		1	" call		Dell	10/15	1:35
5	Sarah E. / Constance J.	10:	L2	15/14		2	" call	Husb & father Thos Bateman 23 ... Valley Stream L.I. NY	Dell	10/15	12
6	MURPHY, Mary	9:30	Q3	4		1	" call	Sis Kate 598 - 11th St Brooklyn NY	John	10/15	12
7	McGREGOR, Elizabeth / Joseph / Margaret / Janet / Elizabeth	10:05	L1	22/26	1	4	" call	Husb Charles 568 Pacific St Bklyn NY	John	10/15	12
8	Catherine	10:20	Q5	25		1	" call	Sis Julia D. 136 W. 80th St NYC	John	10/15	4:10
9	SHARPE, Margaret / Margaret Jr. / John / Mildred / Sarah / Helen	10:	L2	1-6	1	5	" call	Husb & father Matthew Sharpe 319 Henderson St Jersey City NJ	Dell	10/15	12
10	FOLEY, Deborah	10:15	5	18		1	" call	Uncle Patrick 786 Jersey Av. Jersey City NJ	John	10/15	1:15
11	MALLEY, Maggie	10:25	Q5	10		1	" call	Sis Mary W 253 E 110th St NYC	John	10/15	11:40
12	CAHILL, Christina	10:25	Q4	30		1	" call	Sis Mrs Catherine O'Connor 418 W 46th St	Dell	10/15	11:40
13	MONAHAN, Katie	10:30	Q5	9		1	" call	Aunt Mrs Cath Flynn 416 E 159th St NYC	John	10/15	11:35
14	BUTLER, Florence / Elsie May / George W. / Wallace D. / Wilfred S. / Eliza	10:30	L2	7-12		6	" call	Husb & Wallace D. 27 Spring St Newark NJ / Husb & Sidney D. 27 Spring St Newark NJ	John	10/15	11:55
15	Bridget	10:30	5	27		1	" call	Sis Elizabeth 363 Armstrong Av Jersey City	John	10/15	12:10
16	MARGADAN, Mary A.	10:45	Q5	21		1	" call	Uncle Thomas Collin 168 E 96th St NYC	John	10/15	1
17	FORDE, Rose	11:25	Q6	13		1	" call	Sis Norah Forde 1230 Amsterdam Av NYC	Dell	10/15	1:05
18	Eleanor / Thomas H.	11:30	L1	17/19		3	" telg.	Aunt & father John Batey 135 Howard St	Dell	10/16	1:15

Figure 158

For various reasons, many aliens were detained at immigration stations. Often the newcomers were kept at Ellis Island until a relative or friend would accept financial responsibility and come to take them home with them. An often overlooked source, alien detention records can provide additional insights into immigration and family history. Shown here is a list of detained aliens who had arrived on the *S.S. Soythia* on Oct. 15, 1924. These records have been microfilmed and are available at the National Archives and at and through the Family History Library.

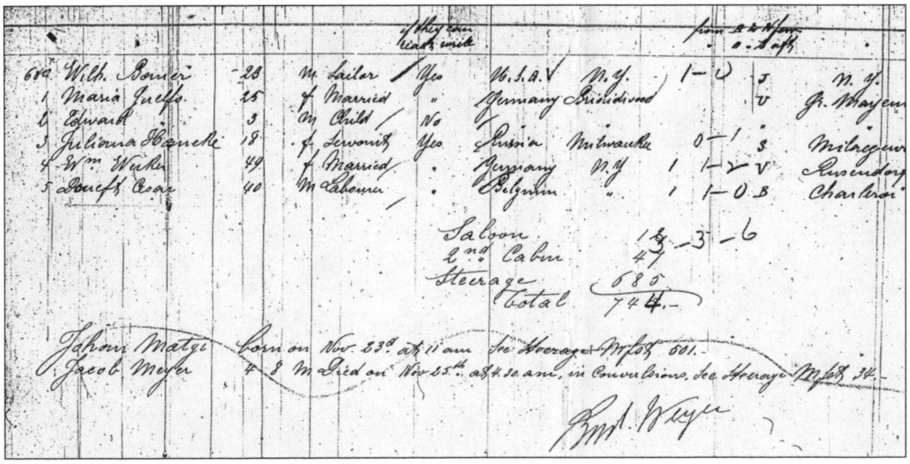

690	Wilh. Bower	23	m	Sailor	Yes	U.S.A.	N.Y.	N.Y.
1	Maria Juchs	25	f	Married	"	Germany		
2	Edward	3	m	Child	No			
3	Juliana Hanecke	18	f	Servant	Yes	Prussia	Milwaukee	Milwaukee
4	Wm Wake	44	f	Married	"	Germany	N.Y.	
5	Joseph Cesar	40	m	Labourer	"	Belgium	"	Charleroi

Saloon 13-3-6
2nd Cabin 47
Steerage 685
total 744.

Johann Matzi born on Nov. 23d at 11 am See Steerage Mfst 501.
Jacob Meyer 48 m Died on Nov 25th at 4.30 am, in Convulsions. See Steerage Mfst 34.

Figure 159

Beyond the expected list of names of individuals and the accompanying identifying information on passenger lists, it was necessary to list the births and deaths that occurred on the voyage. Ship masters had to account for all passengers as they arrived in port, thus vital statistics are often found at the end of passenger lists. Shown here is the last page of a manifest indicating the birth of a baby and the death of a 48-year-old man of convulsions.

Passport Records

Although the United States did not require passports for international travel before World War I (except for a brief period during the Civil War), travelers often obtained them for identification and to document citizenship. Individuals applying for a U.S. passport had to submit an application with their name, signature, place of residence, age, and personal description; names or number of persons in the family intending to travel; the date of travel; and, if applicable, the date and court of naturalization. In some cases, the date and place of birth of the applicant, spouse, and any minor children accompanying the applicant is included. If the applicant was a

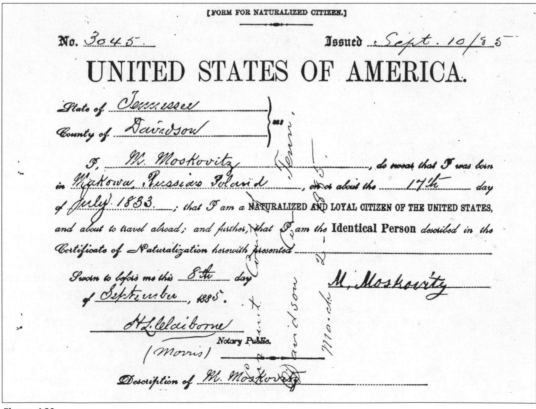

Figure 160
An 1885 passport application affidavit for M. Moskovitz, who, in Davidson County, Tennessee, swore that he was a naturalized citizen of the United States, born in Makova, Russia Poland on or about the 17th day of July 1833.

naturalized citizen, the date and port of arrival in the United States, name of vessel on which the applicant arrived, and date and court of naturalization may also be found. A number of applications were submitted with letters verifying U.S. citizenship and the reason for travel as well.

Passport records for the years 1791 through 1925 are located at the National Archives and have been microfilmed by the Family History Library. Later applications are held by the Passport Office, Department of State, 1425 K St. N. W., Washington, DC 20520, and, due to privacy laws, can be obtained only with written permission from the applicant or a copy of the death certificate if the applicant is deceased.

Selected Readings:

Guide to Genealogical Research in the National Archives. Rev. ed. Washington, D.C.: National Archives Trust Fund Board, 1991.

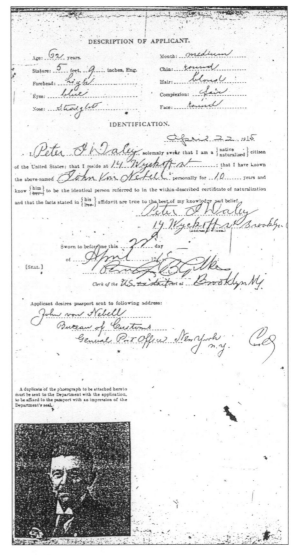

Figure 161

A passport application for John von Nebell, filed in 1915 in Kings County, New York, reveals the applicant's birthplace, month, and year of emigration, the name of the ship, and date and location of his naturalization.

Patent Records

A patent is a grant of a property right by the U.S. government to the inventor "to exclude others from making, using, or selling the invention." President George Washington signed the first patent bill, "An Act to Promote the Useful Arts," on 10 April 1790, and since then, patent applications, drawings, and specifications have poured into the Patent Office. Accessible records exist for more than 4.5 million inventions and inventors.

Two notable national collections are found in the Washington, D.C. area in the Arts and Industries building of the Smithsonian, which opened in 1881. The patent application files in the National Archives usually contain original correspondence from the inventor to the Patent Office, letters from the patent examiner to the inventor, copies of patent drawings, and other documents, some of which have been microfilmed.

A system of more than fifty Patent and Trademark Depository Libraries (PTDLs) has been established throughout the United States where collections of patents and patent-related materials may be examined. The PTDLs receive current issues of U.S. patents and maintain collections of earlier-issued patents. The scope of such collections varies from library to library. For locations of patent depository libraries, consult the reference librarian at a local library. The Patent and Trademark Depository Library Program Web site listed below also provides addresses for PTDLs.

Selected Readings:

Jones, Stacy V. *The Inventor's Patent Handbook*. New York: The Dial Press, 1966.

Szucs, Loretto Dennis. "Patently Useful." *Ancestry* 14 (1) (Jan/Feb 1996): 21–23.

Internet Sites of Interest:

U.S. Patent and Trademark Office Searchable Patent Databases
http://www.uspto.gov/patft/

Patent and Trademark Depository Library Program
http://www.uspto.gov/web/offices/ac/ido/ptdl/index.html

Figure 162

A page from the *Official Gazette of Patentees*, showing name, locality, what was patented, the patent number, and the date the patent was issued.

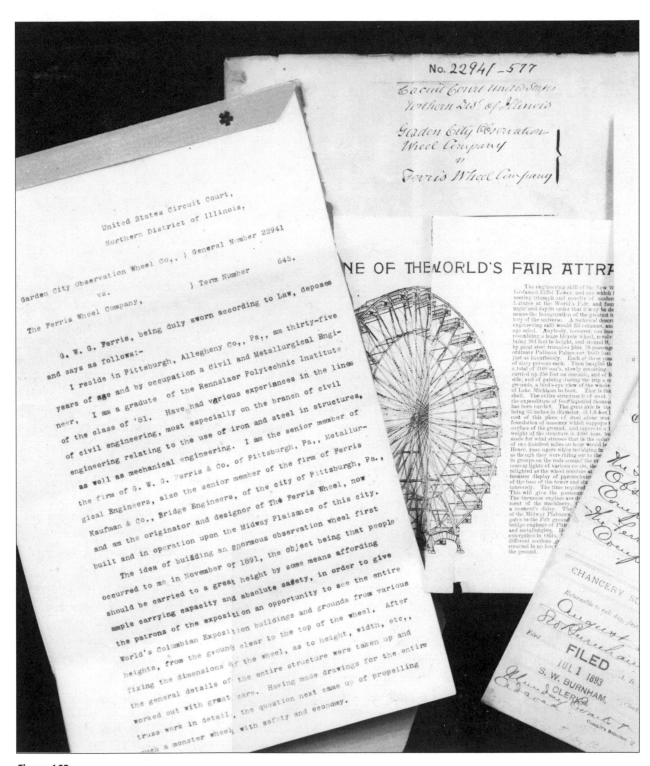

Figure 163

Patent infringement lawsuit files are numerous in all the regions of the National Archives. Above are drawings and testimony from a patent infringement case concerning the Ferris Wheel, found in the U.S. District Court records in the National Archives - Great Lakes Region, Chicago.

Pension Records

Pension records contain valuable information, in many cases including the pensioner's full name, date and place of birth, place of residence, names of spouse and children, if any, and death and beneficiary information. Employers and municipalities often keep records of their pensioners and may release them if the pensioner is deceased. (Privacy laws prohibit them from releasing any information on a former employee that is still living.) Municipal archives and reference libraries are good sources for locating police and firefighter pension records.

If an ancestor worked in the railroad industry and began taking a pension after 1936, the U.S. Railroad Retirement Board, the national pensioning agency for railworkers located in Chicago, Illinois, should have a record of them. The records, which are filed by Social Security number, include: employee's death certificate, application for employee annuity under the retirement act, description and certification as to eligibility of evidence submitted, certification in support of employer service for which no records are available, employee's statement of compensated service rendered, employee's prior service, employee registration, and employee's certificate of termination of service and relinquishment of rights. For a fee, the board will search for information on deceased persons. Railroad records are often found in archives, museums, and historical societies.

A number of indexes have been compiled and published to help locate records for United States military pensioners, which, in addition to basic information, typically include details of military service, maiden name of spouse, information of subsequent marriages, and the veteran's residences after discharge. Many of the pension files, which are held by the National Archives, have been microfilmed and are available through the regional branches of the National Archives, the Family History Library and its Family History Centers, and major libraries.

Additional Sources Covering Military Pensions:

Census of Pensioners for Revolutionary or Military Service. Baltimore: Genealogical Publishing Co., 1967.

Index to Revolutionary War Pension Applications in the National Archives. Arlington, Va.: National Genealogical Society, 1976.

List of Pensioners on the Roll January 1, 1883 Giving the Name of Each Pensioner, the Cause for Which Pensioned, the Post Office Address, the Rate of Pension per Month, and the Date of Original Allowance as Called for by Senate Resolution of December 8, 1882. 5 vols. Baltimore: Genealogical Publishing Co., 1970.

Neagles, James C. *U.S. Military Records: A Guide to Federal & State Sources, Colonial America to the Present.* Salt Lake City: Ancestry, 1994.

White, Virgil D. *Index to Old Wars Pension Files 1815–1926.* 2 vols. Waynesboro, Tenn.: National Historical Publishing Co., 1987.

_______. *Genealogical Abstracts of Revolutionary War Pension Files*. Waynesboro, Tenn.: National Historical Publishing Co., 1990–92.

Additional Sources Covering Railroad Pensions:

Elliott, Wendy. "Railroad Records for Genealogical Research." *National Genealogical Society Quarterly (NSGQ)* 75 (December 1987): 271–77.

Hinckley, Kathleen W. "Tracking Twentieth-Century Ancestors." *The Source: A Guidebook of American Genealogy.* Rev. ed.: 646–47. Salt Lake City: Ancestry, 1997.

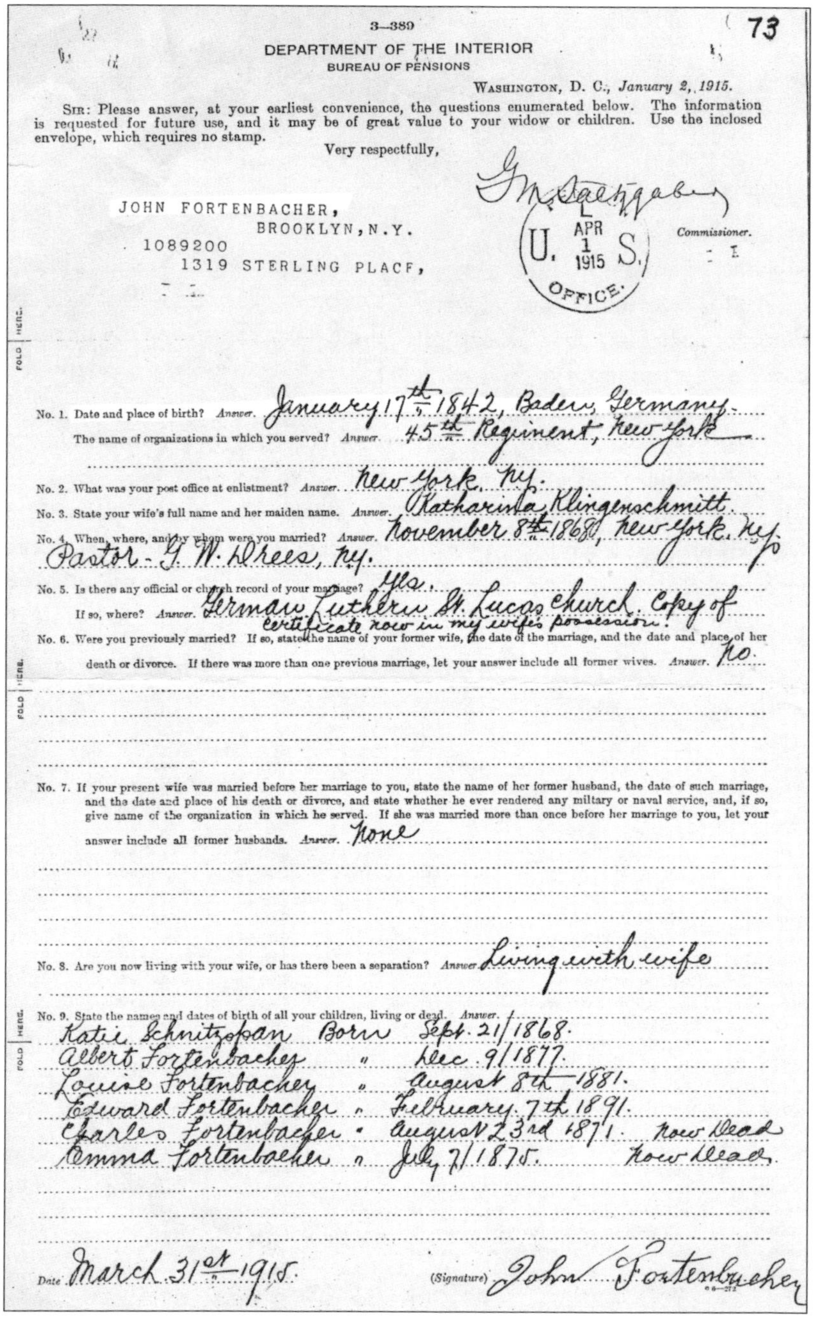

3—389 73

DEPARTMENT OF THE INTERIOR
BUREAU OF PENSIONS

WASHINGTON, D. C., *January 2, 1915.*

SIR: Please answer, at your earliest convenience, the questions enumerated below. The information is requested for future use, and it may be of great value to your widow or children. Use the inclosed envelope, which requires no stamp.

Very respectfully,

G. M. Saltzgaber
Commissioner.

JOHN FORTENBACHER,
BROOKLYN, N.Y.
1089200
1319 STERLING PLACF,

U. S. APR 1 1915 OFFICE

No. 1. Date and place of birth? Answer. January 17th 1842, Baden, Germany.
The name of organizations in which you served? Answer. 45th Regiment, New York

No. 2. What was your post office at enlistment? Answer. New York, ny.

No. 3. State your wife's full name and her maiden name. Answer. Katharina Klingenschmitt.

No. 4. When, where, and by whom were you married? Answer. November 8th 1868, New York, ny. Pastor - G. W. Drees, ny.

No. 5. Is there any official or church record of your marriage? Yes.
If so, where? Answer. German Lutheran St. Lucas church. Copy of certificate now in my wife's possession.

No. 6. Were you previously married? If so, state the name of your former wife, the date of the marriage, and the date and place of her death or divorce. If there was more than one previous marriage, let your answer include all former wives. Answer. No.

No. 7. If your present wife was married before her marriage to you, state the name of her former husband, the date of such marriage, and the date and place of his death or divorce, and state whether he ever rendered any military or naval service, and, if so, give name of the organization in which he served. If she was married more than once before her marriage to you, let your answer include all former husbands. Answer. None

No. 8. Are you now living with your wife, or has there been a separation? Answer. Living with wife

No. 9. State the names and dates of birth of all your children, living or dead. Answer.
Katie Schnitzspan Born Sept. 21/1868.
Albert Fortenbacher " Dec. 9/1877.
Louise Fortenbacher " August 8th 1881.
Edward Fortenbacher " February 7th 1891.
Charles Fortenbacher " August 23rd 1871. Now Dead
Emma Fortenbacher " July 7/1875. Now Dead

Date March 31st 1915. (Signature) John Fortenbacher

Figure 164

A document from the pension file of John Fortenbacher, dated 31 March 1915. (Courtesy of Linda Lamberty)

PERSI

The Allen County Public Library in Fort Wayne, Indiana is well-known for its extensive genealogical collection. The *Periodical Source Index*, or *PERSI*, is an indexing project undertaken by the library's Historical Genealogy Department and is gaining notoriety for its usefulness to family historians. Alphabetically arranged under five different categories, the publication indexes genealogical and local historical periodicals by subject. The category "U.S. Places" is broken down first by state, then county, and again by the record type. Another category, "Family Records," provides a listing by surname. Periodicals under "Research Methodology" are arranged by record type (e.g., cemeteries, vital records, etc.). The final two categories, "Canada Places" and "Foreign Places," are arranged similarly to "U.S. Places."

After the first of its annual volumes covering materials published during 1986, *PERSI* compiled and published a sixteen-volume retrospective index of periodicals dating back to 1847. Both the annual and the retrospective volumes can be found at most major genealogical libraries. *PERSI* is also available on CD-ROM, and subscribers to Ancestry.com's Web site can search the index online.

PERiodical Source Index
07/01/88 pg 129

STATE	COUNTY	RECORD TYPE	TITLE OF ARTICLE	JOURNAL	VOL	NUM	MON	YEAR
CO	Boulder	History	First fire department of Boulder	COBQ	3	1-2	Feb	1971
CO	Boulder	History	First governmental organization of Boulder	COBQ	3	3	Aug	1971
CO	Boulder	History	First water works of Boulder	COBQ	3	1-2	Feb	1971
CO	Boulder	History	Origins of Caribou	COBQ	5	2	May	1973
CO	Boulder	History	Origins of Eldora	COBQ	6	1	Feb	1974
CO	Boulder	History	Origins of Erie	COBQ	6	3	Aug	1974
CO	Boulder	History	Origins of Jamestown	COBQ	5	4	Nov	1973
CO	Boulder	History	Origins of Lafayette	COBQ	4	3	Aug	1972
CO	Boulder	History	Origins of Longmont	COBQ	4	2	May	1972
CO	Boulder	History	Origins of Lyons	COBQ	5	3	Aug	1973
CO	Boulder	History	Origins of Nederland	COBQ	4	4	Nov	1972
CO	Boulder	History	Origins of Sugar Loaf district	COBQ	7	1	Feb	1975
CO	Boulder	History	Origins of Sunshine	COBQ	5	1	Feb	1973
CO	Boulder	History	Origins of Ward	COBQ	6	2	May	1974
CO	Boulder	Institutions	Early fraternal societies in Boulder, 1869, 1875	COBQ	4	3	Aug	1972
CO	Boulder	Institutions	First Odd Fellows' building in Boulder	COBQ	7	2	May	1975
CO	Boulder	Institutions	Lodges, IOOF	COBQ	15	2	May	1983
CO	Boulder	Institutions	Masonic lodges in Boulder co.	COBQ	11	4	Nov	1979
CO	Boulder	Land	Land claims in Boulder co, 1859	COBQ	5	3	Aug	1973
CO	Boulder	Maps	Map of Boulder co	COBQ	5	2	May	1973
CO	Boulder	Military	Lower Boulder & St. Vrain Valley Home Guards	COBQ	17	1	Feb	1985
CO	Boulder	Military	Military personnel buried in Columbia Cemetery	COBQ	3	1-2	Feb	1971
CO	Boulder	Military	Military personnel buried in Green Mtn. Cemetery	COBQ	3	3	Aug	1971
CO	Boulder	Military	Organization of ex-Union soldiers formed in 1881	COBQ	7	2	May	1975
CO	Boulder	Military	Participation in Spanish-American War, 1898-99	COBQ	5	1	Feb	1973
CO	Boulder	Military	Veterans buried in Valmont cemetery	COBQ	17	1	Feb	1985
CO	Boulder	Naturalization	Boulder co naturalization records J-K	COBQ	14	2	May	1982

Figure 165

A sample page from *PERSI*, showing some of what has been indexed from genealogical and historical periodicals from Boulder County, CO, covering subjects such as the first fire department of Boulder, 1859 land claims, military interred in local cemeteries, and naturalizations.

Selected Readings:

Meyerink, Kory L. "Databases, Indexes, and Other Finding Aids." *The Source: A Guidebook of American Genealogy.* Rev. ed. Ch. 2: 34–56. Salt Lake City: Ancestry, 1987.

Thackery, David T. "Periodical Sources." *Ancestry* 12 (2) (March/April 1994): 18–20.

Photographs, Postcards and Other Graphic Materials

In themselves, photographs, drawings, paintings, postcards, and other graphics generally do not provide biographical information. Their usefulness, however, should not be overlooked for their power to provide a better understanding of people, places, and lifestyles of days gone by. Photographs, postcards, and illustrations can connect individuals, families, buildings, landscapes, and events to a certain place and a certain time. Whether they are artistic renderings or photographs, illustrations are also capable of providing critical clues to other record sources.

A lithograph or drawing can provide a glimpse of the neighborhood as ancestors probably saw it. Clothing worn by the subjects of photographs can reveal social status, ethnic and religious origins, and important clues to personalities. Even the name of studio photographers stamped on old photographs or their backings can place the subject in a particular place at a particular time. By locating the name and address of the photographer in directories for the time period, and by tracing the years in which a studio was in business, it is possible to approximate the time in which the photograph was taken. Karen Frisch-Ripley describes dating photographs in detail in *Unlocking the Secrets in Old Photographs* (1991).

Postcards are yet another important source of illustrations. From big cities like New York to small towns like Attalla, Alabama (Figure 166), postcards have been a

Figure 166
Attalla, Alabama, 1908.

189

popular and inexpensive way to send greetings for over a century. Each of the city scenes is a closeup look at a world that no longer exists. Like the postcard of the milkman in Belgium (Figure 167) these pieces of history are all the more valuable when addresses, messages, postage stamps, and postal dates are included on the reverse side.

Used in connection with other sources, illustrations can recreate the past in a special way. They transcend time and offer unique windows to the past. Best of all, they are becoming increasingly available through a number of sources, including the Internet. As in all other phases of family history, home sources are the first places to look for pictures, photographs, and postcards. Distant relatives are often in possession of these personal items. In the case of Figure 168, of the four generations captured in the photograph, only one copy of the photo was known to exist. When the images of family members are not available, it is usually possible to find some kind of visual images of the places where they lived. Almost every place in the world has been the subject of an artist or a camera lens, and the results can often be found in original formats and in published works, in local histories, or in travel books. Libraries, museums, archives, genealogical societies, historical agencies, and even antique stores are good places to look for visual materials.

An extraordinary collection of New York City photographs is available at The Municipal Archives. The Tax Photograph Collection, taken by the Department of Taxes, 1939-41 includes pictures that were taken of every building in the five New York City boroughs. Photographs can be ordered by visiting The Municipal Archives (31 Chambers Street, Room 103, New York, NY 10007), or by downloading an order form from its Web site at <www.ci.nyc.ny.us/html/doris/html/index.html>.

The Library of Congress Web site (http://memory.loc.gov.amem/amhome.html) is a valuable tool for family historians that includes thousands of photographs arranged by various American subjects and regions. The subjects can be searched or browsed, and reproductions can be ordered from the site. The National Archives lists photographs in its collection at <www.nara.gov/research>.

Figure 167
Belgian Milkman, 1927.

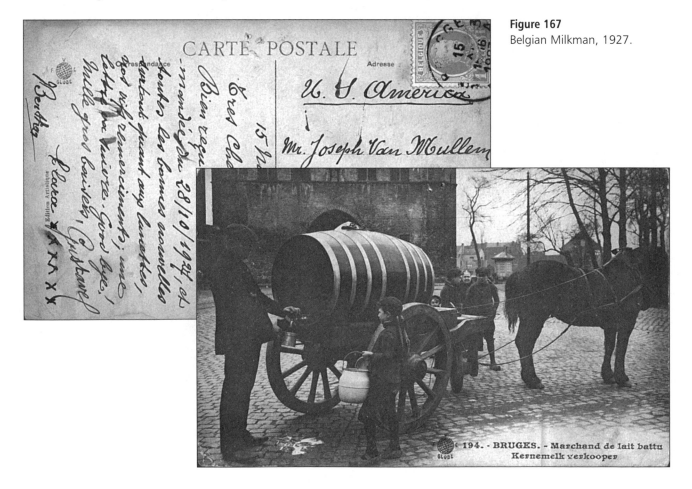

The Steamship Historical Society of America Collection contains approximately 200,000 photographs of passenger liners, cruise ships, lake and coastal ships, river steamboats, tugboats, cargo vessels, military transports, and work boats, covering a date span of the mid-1800s to the present. All ship photograph requests must be made in writing. Direct inquiries should be sent to the Steamship Historical Society Collection, Langsdale Library, University of Baltimore, 1420 Maryland Avenue, Baltimore, MD 21201. Further information can be obtained from the Society Web site at <www.ubalt.edu//archives/ship.htm>.

In addition to the picture collections listed above, an Internet search for the words "photographs," "pictures," and "postcards," as well as the names of specific places, can turn up interesting results.

Selected Readings:

Frisch-Ripley, Karen. *Unlocking the Secrets in Old Photographs*. Salt Lake City: Ancestry, 1991.

Prucha, Francis Paul. *Handbook for Research in American History: A Guide to Bibliographies and Other Reference Works*. 2nd ed. Lincoln: University of Nebraska Press, 1994.

Robl, Ernest H. *Picture Sources*. 4th ed. New York: Special Libraries Association, 1983.

Internet Sites of Interest:

Library of Congress
http://memory.loc.gov.amem/amhome.html

Municipal Archives of the City of New York
http://www.ci.nyc.ny.us/html/doris/html/index.html

National Archives and Records Center
http://www.nara.gov/research/

Steamship Historical Society of America Collection
http://www.ubalt.edu/archives/ship.htm.

Figure 168
In 1900, four generations of the Banet family gathered at the matriarch's home in Fort Wayne, Indiana to celebrate the First Communion day of several of the Banet grandchildren. Despite the large number of people in the photograph, only one of the descendants is known to have a copy.

Figure 169

Research into fashions of the period and traditional eth-
nic clothing can help match an individual to a picture.
For example, this 1893 photograph of four-year-old Paul
F. Pyburn, at first glance, would appear to be a girl.

Figure 170

Photographs can also reveal something about family traditions. This 1902 backyard birthday, noted on the back as
"Madelon's Fifth Birthday," shows not only the proud hostess,
but the food on the table and its elaborate setting, including
flowers in crystal vases.

Figure 171
This photograph of the village of Paricutin (Mexico) can be dated by the size of the volcano in the background, and by the fact that the volcano was only active from 1943 until 1952.

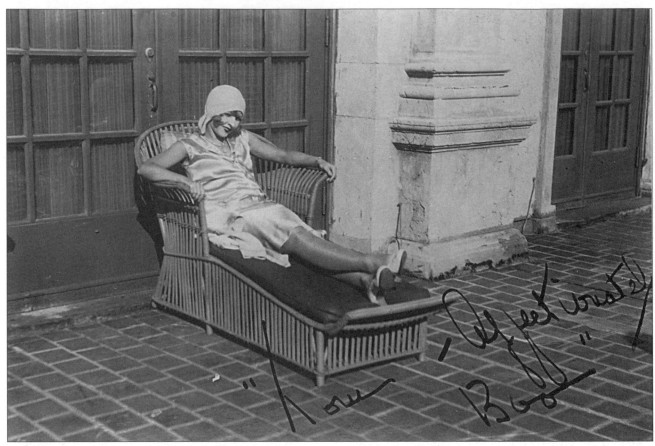

Figure 172
The flapper-era dress and hat of Theodora Fleming in this photograph help place her in an approximate time and locality. (Courtesy of Thomas J. Fleming)

Figure 173
Stitz wagon, Lafayette, Indiana, 1900. The wagon-making business that had been the Stitz family's livelihood might easily have been forgotten were it not for a picture that was passed down in the family.

Figure 174
The apparel of this young family helps to date this photograph to the late nineteenth century. (From the Franklin family collection; reproduced by Sunny Nash)

Figure 175

Two radios, clothing styles, the newspaper, and the photograph in the background help to date the 1947 photograph of Muriel Dennis (above), and the 1920 photograph of her mother, Muriel Dyer (at left). The two photographs, taken when mother and daughter were nearly the same age, reveal strong family resemblances, another fascinating facet of research that can be captured in photographs.

Figure 176

Details in the background of photographs should be studied as carefully as the subjects. The dated Chicago license plate in this photo, together with a family photo known to have been taken the same day, was the key to putting a group of people in a certain time and place.

Figure 177
Finding the photograph of these two sisters with a street number was key to matching the family with its address in a Cleveland city directory. This was a crucial link because the family had changed its last name, and linking the photograph to the name published in the city directory made it possible to know when the name change went into effect and to later track down land ownership records.

Figure 178
New York City, ca. 1900.

Figure 179
This lithograph, depicting the Five Points District of New York City in 1859, was found in a family collection. Though not offering any real proof that it was so, the lithograph lends some credibility to the story of a family-owned business in the district. By consulting a New York City directory for 1859, a map of the city for the time period, and the lithograph, it was possible to determine the exact location of the family business on the map and lithograph, and to identify neighbors and their businesses as well.

Post Office Guides, Directories, and Records

Postal guides and directories were created and published by the United States Post Office to aid in the delivery of mail in a country that was changing and expanding daily. Such records can be helpful to a researcher in circumstances where only the street address of an ancestor is known, or in determining the location of a town that no longer exists. Listings of post offices, arranged by state, can be found in postal guides printed during the nineteenth century, now housed in the National Archives. Some of these guides are also available on microfilm at the Family History Library and its Family History Centers™. *The Street Directory of the Principal Cities of the United States Embracing Letter-Carrier Offices Established to April 30, 1908, 5th ed.* (Washington, D.C.: published by order of the postmaster general, 1908) lists the name of the state or states in which each street, avenue, court, place, lane, and road was located.

Researchers of ancestors known to be postmasters should search appointment registers that date from 1789 through 1971 and that have been microfilmed and are available at the National Archives and the Family History Library, and through their respective research centers.

See also *Street Indexes.*

Selected Readings:

Abridged United States Official Postal Guide. Washington, D.C.: U.S. Government Printing Office, 1934.

Postmaster appointment registers, dating from 1789 through 1971, are available at the National Archives and the Family History Library, and through their respective research centers.

Bowen, Eli. *The United States Post-Office Guide.* New York: D. Appleton, 1851. Reprint. New York: Arno Press, 1976.

Hecht, Arthur, and William J. Heynen, comps. *Records and Policies of the Post Office Department Relating to Place-Names.* Reference Information Paper no. 72. Washington, D.C.: National Archives and Records Service, 1975.

_____. Frank J. Nivert, Fred W. Warriner, Jr., and Charlotte M. Ashby, comps. Revised by Forrest R. Holdcamper. *Records of the Post Office Department.* Preliminary Inventory 168. Washington, D.C.: National Archives and Records Service, 1967.

_____. Fred W. Warriner, Jr., and Charlotte M. Ashby, comps. *Records of the Bureaus of the Third and Fourth Assistant Postmasters General...* Preliminary Inventory 114. Washington, D.C.: National Archives and Records Service, 1955.

Prechtel-Kluskens, Claire. "Post Office Records Deliver." *The Record: News from the National Archives and Records Administration* 3 (1) (September 1996): 21-22.

Schiffman, Carol Mehr. "Geographic Tools: Maps, Atlases, and Gazetteers." *Printed Sources: A Guide to Published Genealogical Sources.* Ch. 3: 94–144.

Simmons, Don. *Post Offices in the United States.* Melber, Ky.: Simmons Historical Publications, 1991.

(Provides a listing of post offices in the United States dating back to 1893)

Street Directory of the Principal Cities of the United States Embracing Letter-Carrier Offices Established to April 30, 1908, 5th ed. Washington, D.C.: published by order of the postmaster general, 1908.

United States Official Postal Guide. Published annually from 1874 through 1954 at the direction of the Post Office Department.

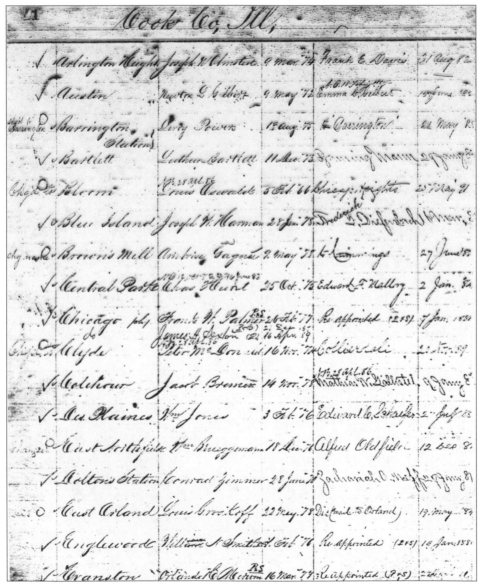

Figure 180

Appointments of Postmasters, Cook County, Illinois ca. 1870s.

Prison Records

Admission and discharge books, biographical registers, descriptive registers, and registers of prisoners are among the types of records that were kept by early penal institutions. Information contained in admission records includes the name of the inmate, date of admission, race, age, sex, physical and mental health, temperament, marital status, immunizations, family diseases, number of convictions, length of sentence, birthplace, and occupation. In addition to basic information about the prisoner, the biographical register may include details about the inmate's family and addresses of correspondents. The registers of prisoners may be helpful in locating court records, as they list the court and date of sentencing.

Privacy laws protect prison records from the mid–1920s to the present. The correctional facility, if still in existence, or the state department of corrections may have earlier prison records. State and local archives are a good place to begin a search.

Selected Readings:

Carter, Kent. "The Hanging Judge's Records." *The Record* 1 (1) (September 1994).

Cerny, Johni. "Institutional Records" *The Source: A Guidebook of American Genealogy* Rev. ed. p. 359–69. Salt Lake City: Ancestry, 1997. (Provides a state-by-state listing of correctional institutions before 1900 and contemporary federal/state agencies)

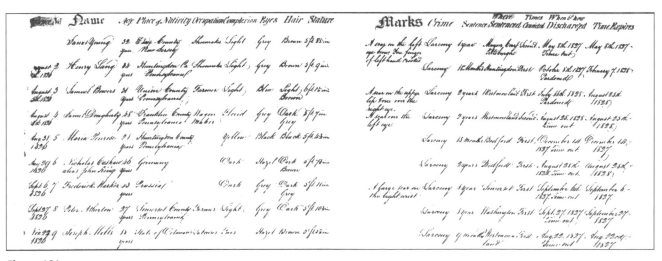

Figure 181
From the Descriptive Register, May 1826-February 1827, Pennsylvania Western State Penitentiary, p. 1. (FHL 1,032,653)

Probate Records

Probate records typically deal with the validation of a decedent's will or the distribution of a decedent's assets in the absence of a will (intestate). The contents of a probate file usually include a will (if applicable), a list of assets, receipts, and some form of documentation of the distribution of assets from the executor or administrator of the estate. These records are public and can provide insight as to the financial state and lifestyle of an ancestor. Beneficiaries named in a will or surviving relatives named in the records of those who died intestate may lead a researcher to previously unknown relations. Probate courts may also handle petitions for guardianship of minors or disabled persons.

See also *Guardianship Records.*

Selected Readings:

Devine, Donn. "Probate Records: An Underutilized Source." *Ancestry* 12 (3) (May/June 1994): 14–15.

Eakle, Arlene H. "Research in Court Records." *The Source: A Guidebook of American Genealogy.* Rev. ed. Salt Lake City: Ancestry, 1997.

Greenwood, Val D. *The Researcher's Guide to American Genealogy.* 2d ed. Baltimore, Md.: Genealogical Publishing Co., Inc., 1990.

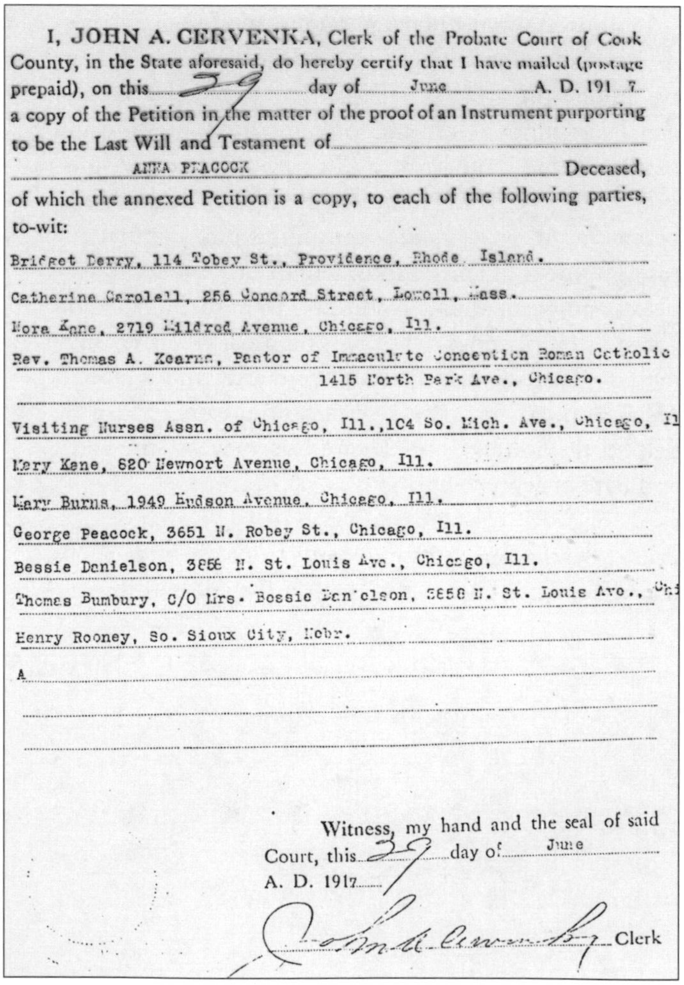

I, JOHN A. CERVENKA, Clerk of the Probate Court of Cook County, in the State aforesaid, do hereby certify that I have mailed (postage prepaid), on this 29 day of June A. D. 1917 a copy of the Petition in the matter of the proof of an Instrument purporting to be the Last Will and Testament of ANNA PEACOCK Deceased, of which the annexed Petition is a copy, to each of the following parties, to-wit:

Bridget Derry, 114 Tobey St., Providence, Rhode Island.

Catherine Caroleil, 256 Concord Street, Lowell, Mass.

Nora Kane, 2719 Mildred Avenue, Chicago, Ill.

Rev. Thomas A. Kearns, Pastor of Immaculate Conception Roman Catholic 1415 North Park Ave., Chicago.

Visiting Nurses Assn. of Chicago, Ill., 104 So. Mich. Ave., Chicago, Il

Mary Kane, 820 Newport Avenue, Chicago, Ill.

Mary Burns, 1949 Hudson Avenue, Chicago, Ill.

George Peacock, 3651 N. Robey St., Chicago, Ill.

Bessie Danielson, 3856 N. St. Louis Ave., Chicago, Ill.

Thomas Bumbury, C/O Mrs. Bessie Danielson, 3858 N. St. Louis Ave., Chi

Henry Rooney, So. Sioux City, Nebr.

A

Witness, my hand and the seal of said Court, this 29 day of June A. D. 1917

John A. Cervenka Clerk

Figure 182

Probate records are especially valuable in that they usually identify next of kin, close friends, and sometimes provide addresses of distant relatives. The paper shown from the probate file of Anna Peacock identifies relatives and addresses in Providence, Rhode Island; Lowell, Massachusetts; Chicago, Illinois; and South Sioux City, Nebraska.

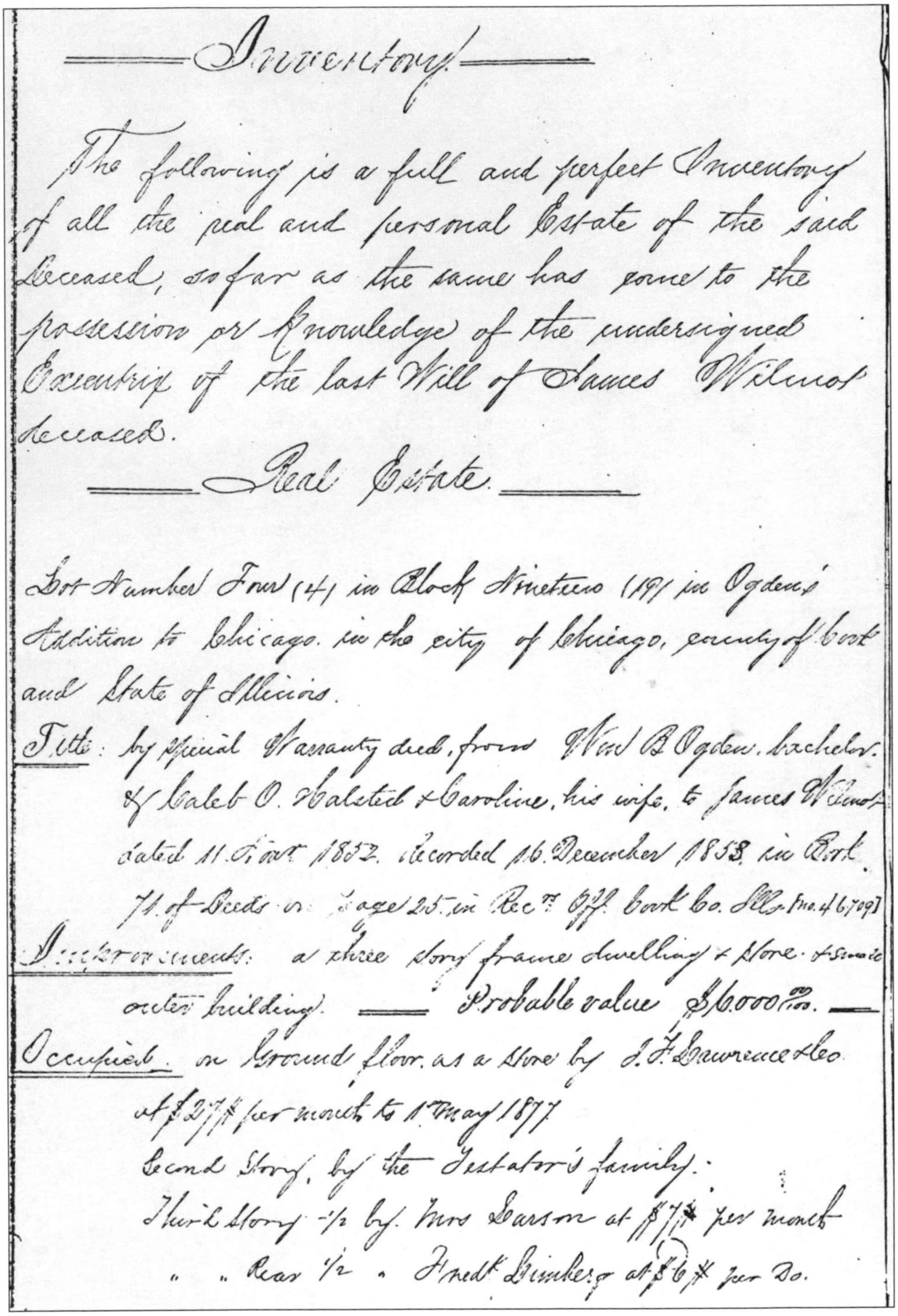

Inventory.

The following is a full and perfect Inventory of all the real and personal Estate of the said Deceased, so far as the same has come to the possession or Knowledge of the undersigned Executrix of the last Will of James Wilmot deceased.

Real Estate.

Lot Number Four (4) in Block Nineteen (19) in Ogden's Addition to Chicago. in the city of Chicago, County of Cook and State of Illinois.

Title: by special Warranty deed, from Wm B Ogden. bachelor. & Caleb O. Halsted & Caroline, his wife, to James Wilmot dated 11. Oct 1852. Recorded 16. December 1853. in Book 71. of Deeds on Page 25. in Rec. Off. Cook Co. Ills. [No. 46709]

Improvements: a three story frame dwelling & store. & small outer building. — Probable value $6000 00/100. —

Occupied on Ground floor. as a store by J. F. Lawrence & Co. at $27 per month to 1 May 1877

Second Story, by the Testator's family.

Third Story ½ by Mrs Larson at $7 per month

" " Rear ½ " Fredk Dimberg at $6 per do.

Figure 183

In addition to a last will and testament, documents from the 1879 probate file of James Wilmot, deceased (Cook County, Illinois), include an inventory of assets.

TESTIMONY TAKEN IN THE PROBATE COURT OF COOK COUNTY, ON APRIL 2, 1879, IN THE MATTER OF HEIR-SHIP IN THE ESTATE OF JAMES WILMOT, DECEASED.

EL~~O~~~~U~~ISA WILMOT BEING FIRST DULY SWORN, TESTIFIED IN OPEN COURT AS FOLLOWS:

EXAMINED BY JUDGE KNICKERBOCKER.

Q. WHAT IS YOUR NAME? A. LOUISE WILMOT.

Q. DID YOU KNOW JAMES WILMOT IN HIS LIFETIME? A. YES, NOT ALL HIS LIFE.

Q. WELL HOW OLD WAS HE WHEN YOU FIRST BECAME ACQUAINTED WITH HIM? A. I GUESS HE WAS --- I COULD NOT HARDLY SAY. HE WAS OVER TWENTY SOME.

Q. WAS HE MARRIED AT THAT TIME WHEN YOU FIRST KNEW HIM? A. NO, HE WAS A YOUNG MAN.

Q. HAD HE EVER BEEN MARRIED WHEN YOU FIRST KNEW HIM? A NO.

Q. DID YOU MARRY HIM? A. YES.

Q. DID YOU LIVE WITH HIM FROM THE TIME OF HIS MARRIAGE UNTIL HIS DEATH? A. YES.

Q. WERE THERE ANY CHILDREN BORN OF THAT MARRIAGE? A. TWELVE.

Q. GIVE ME THEIR NAMES, COMMENCING WITH THE OLDEST? A. SOME OF THEM DIED YOUNG.

Q. I DO NOT CARE, --- GIVE ME THE NAMES OF ALL, COMMENCING WITH THE OLDEST? A. THE OLDEST WAS NOT BAPTIZED.

Q. WAS'NT NAMED? A. NO.

Q. DIED BEFORE MR. WILMOT? A. OH YES, DIED YEARS BEFORE.

Q. NOW THE NEXT? A. THEN THE E WAS MARY.

Q. IS SHE LIVING? A. NO, SHE IS DEAD.

Q. SHE DIED BEFORE YOUR HUSBAND DIED? A. SHE DIED WHEN SHE WAS THREE YEARS OLD.

County Probate
RAL # 6-839
ET E Page 280

Figure 184

In addition to a last will and testament, documents from the 1879 probate file of James Wilmot, deceased (Cook County, Illinois), include a testimony from Elisa Wilmot, his widow.

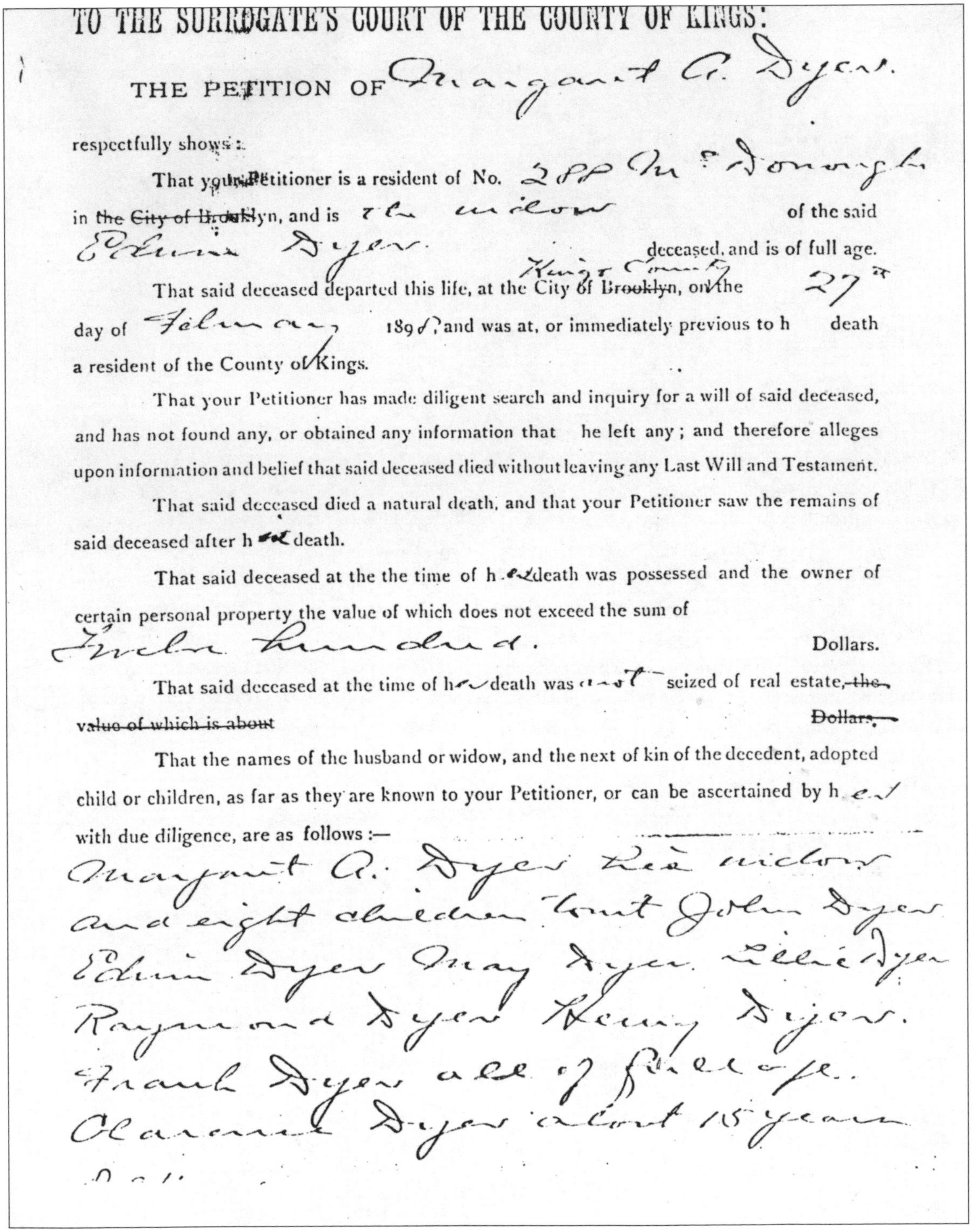

TO THE SURROGATE'S COURT OF THE COUNTY OF KINGS:

THE PETITION OF Margaret A. Dyer.

respectfully shows:

That your Petitioner is a resident of No. 288 McDonough in ~~the City of Brook~~lyn, and is the widow of the said Edwin Dyer. deceased, and is of full age.

That said deceased departed this life, at the City of ~~Brooklyn~~ Kings County, on the 27th day of February 1898, and was at, or immediately previous to his death a resident of the County of Kings.

That your Petitioner has made diligent search and inquiry for a will of said deceased, and has not found any, or obtained any information that he left any; and therefore alleges upon information and belief that said deceased died without leaving any Last Will and Testament.

That said deceased died a natural death, and that your Petitioner saw the remains of said deceased after his death.

That said deceased at the the time of his death was possessed and the owner of certain personal property the value of which does not exceed the sum of twelve hundred. Dollars.

That said deceased at the time of his death was not seized of real estate, ~~the value of which is about Dollars.~~

That the names of the husband or widow, and the next of kin of the decedent, adopted child or children, as far as they are known to your Petitioner, or can be ascertained by her with due diligence, are as follows:—

Margaret A. Dyer the widow and eight children —— John Dyer Edwin Dyer May Dyer Lillie Dyer Raymond Dyer Henry Dyer. Frank Dyer all of full age. Clarence Dyer about 15 years old

Figure 185

It is often possible to find records in Probate Court, even if an individual died intestate (without a will), as is the case of Edwin Dyer in this 1898 petition.

Railroad Records

The railroads played a vital role in the development of the United States and employed as many as two and a quarter million people at their peak in the early 1900s. Many of the records pertaining to the industry have been preserved. Information that can be found among railroad records includes employment files, which may contain employment applications; pension files (see *Pension Records*); land acquisition schedules that list the landowner, the date and cost of the acquisition, and the parcel of land involved; land field notes that include the names of the owners of properties adjacent to the railroad right-of-way and the land's value; life insurance claims of employees; and claims related to services on military railroads from 1861 to 1870.

The National Archives houses the land acquisition schedules and the land field notes described above. Publications containing railroad maps, such as *Cram's Standard American Railway System Atlas of the World: Accompanied by a Complete and Simple Index of the United States Showing the True Locations of All Railroads,* *Towns, Villages and Post Offices . . .*(Chicago: George F. Cram, 1895), can help a researcher determine if an ancestor's property may be noted in these records. Also at the National Archives are the claims related to services on military railroads and 113 volumes of material relating to railroad transportation accounts. Many of the other records can be found in museums, research libraries, and historical societies. For example, the Newberry Library in Chicago has manuscripts from the Chicago, Burlington, and Quincy Railroads and some

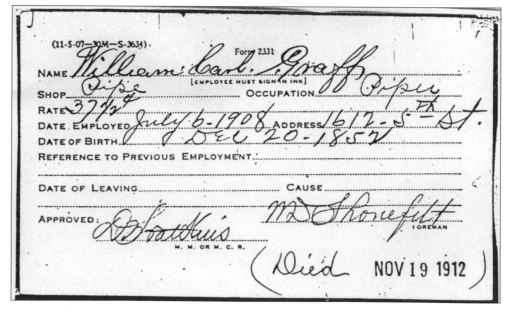

Figure 186
A Southern Pacific Railroad employment card for William Carl Graff, identifying the shop in which he worked, his occupation, date employed, home address, and dates of birth and death. This card was microfilmed and is available at and through the Family History Library.

from the Pullman Standard Car Company. The South Suburban Genealogical Society in South Holland, Illinois has indexed nearly a million Pullman Company records that are on file at the society. The Chicago Historical Society has acquired some files of the Brotherhood of Sleeping Car Porters. Records available through the Family History Library include life insurance records filed by Union Pacific employees and some employee records from the Southern Pacific Railroad.

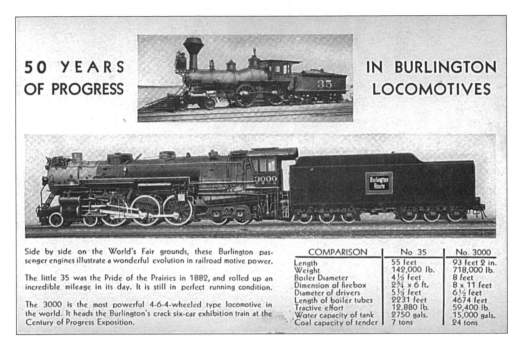

50 YEARS OF PROGRESS — **IN BURLINGTON LOCOMOTIVES**

Side by side on the World's Fair grounds, these Burlington passenger engines illustrate a wonderful evolution in railroad motive power.

The little 35 was the Pride of the Prairies in 1882, and rolled up an incredible mileage in its day. It is still in perfect running condition.

The 3000 is the most powerful 4-6-4-wheeled type locomotive in the world. It heads the Burlington's crack six-car exhibition train at the Century of Progress Exposition.

COMPARISON	No 35	No. 3000
Length	55 feet	93 feet 2 in.
Weight	142,000 lb.	718,000 lb.
Boiler Diameter	4½ feet	8 feet
Dimension of firebox	2¾ x 6 ft.	8 x 11 feet
Diameter of drivers	5⅓ feet	6¼ feet
Length of boiler tubes	2231 feet	4674 feet
Tractive effort	12,880 lb.	59,400 lb.
Water capacity of tank	2750 gals.	15,000 gals.
Coal capacity of tender	7 tons	24 tons

Figure 187
A postcard extoling the virtues of the latest in locomotive technology from Burlington.

Selected Readings:

Biographical Directory of the Railway Officials of America. New York: Simmons-Boardman Publishing Co., irregular since 1885. (Later editions titled *Who's Who in Railroading in North America*)

Cochran, Thomas. *Railroad Leaders, 1845-1890: The Business Mind in Action.* Cambridge: Harvard University Press, 1953. (Based on letters of sixty-one railroad officials)

Cram's Standard American Railway System Atlas of the World: Accompanied by a Complete and Simple Index of the United States Showing the True Locations of All Railroads, Towns, Villages and Post Offices . . . Chicago: George F. Cram, 1895.

Elliott, Wendy. "Railroad Records for Genealogical Research." *National Genealogical Society Quarterly (NSGQ)* 75 (Dec. 1987): 271-77.

Hinckley, Kathleen W. "Tracking Twentieth-Century Ancestors." *The Source: A Guidebook of American Genealogy.* Rev. ed. Ch. 18: 628-53. Salt Lake City: Ancestry, 1997.

Modelski, Andrew M., comp. *Railroad Maps of the United States: A Selective Annotated Bibliography of Original 19th-Century Maps in the Geography and Map Division of the Library of Congress.* Washington, D.C.: Library of Congress, 1975.

Pfeiffer, David A. "Riding the Rails Up Paper Mountain: Researching Railroad Records in the National Archives." *Prologue* 29 (1) (Spring 1997): 52-61.

Internet Sites of Interest:

Railroad Historical Information
www.rrhistorical.com

Railroad Retirement Board
http://www.rrb.gov/

Religious Records

Though sometimes difficult to locate, religious records are a valuable source because they often predate civil records and frequently contain information not found elsewhere. Many congregations keep lists of parishioners or members and records of the religious ceremonies officiated at that parish. Christian ceremonies typically include baptisms, confirmations, marriages, and burials. Information found in the records may include the date of the event, date and place of birth, names of parents, date and age of death, date of burial, and place of internment. Some records also include dates and locations (sometimes in the old country) of previous registrations if the individual had transferred from another church. For various reasons, vital records were not often kept in the Jewish religion; however, some helpful guides have been written to help locate the records that do exist. Two such guides are listed in the bibliography section.

Challenges that a researcher might face in trying to locate reli-

gious records include the varying practices of record keeping among denominations (some transfer records when members move), the closing and consolidation of churches as neighborhoods changed, and the fact that an ancestor may have traveled outside of the community to attend a church that worshiped in a native tongue. A tool that may help you overcome some of the obstacles in searching for church records is the Historical Records Survey of the WPA, in which WPA workers inventoried church and public records extant in

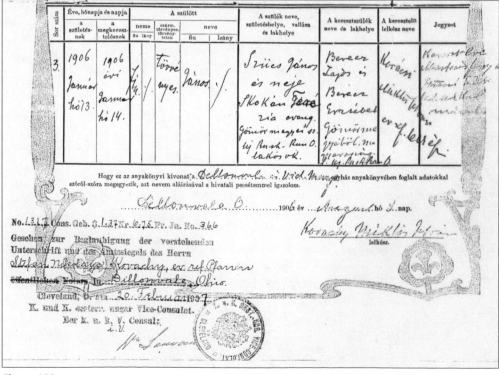

Figure 188
A baptismal document from the Hungarian Reformed Church in Dillonvale, Ohio.

206

the 1930s for many areas in the United States. A typical entry for church vital records would contain the name and address of the institution at the time of publication, ethnic orientation, if any, and comprehensive dates for each type of vital record. If the organization housed documents from other congregations, the survey noted that fact and included a range of dates. While the records may have been moved since the survey, an overview of the years for which records were kept is provided. For information on additional WPA projects, see *Works Progress Administration*.

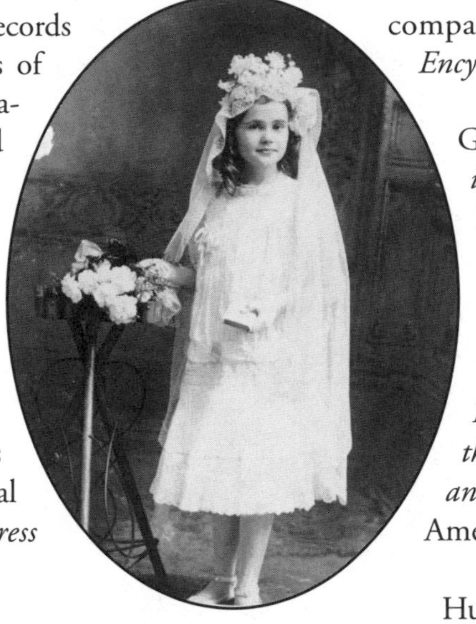

Figure 189
First Communion

Church records are sometimes available in book form or microform. Large genealogical libraries, such as the Family History Library and the Newberry Library in Chicago, and some historical societies have collections of church records. Early city or county histories, biographical sketches, and anniversary (jubilee) books sometimes provide background on religious institutions in the area that could aid in the search as well.

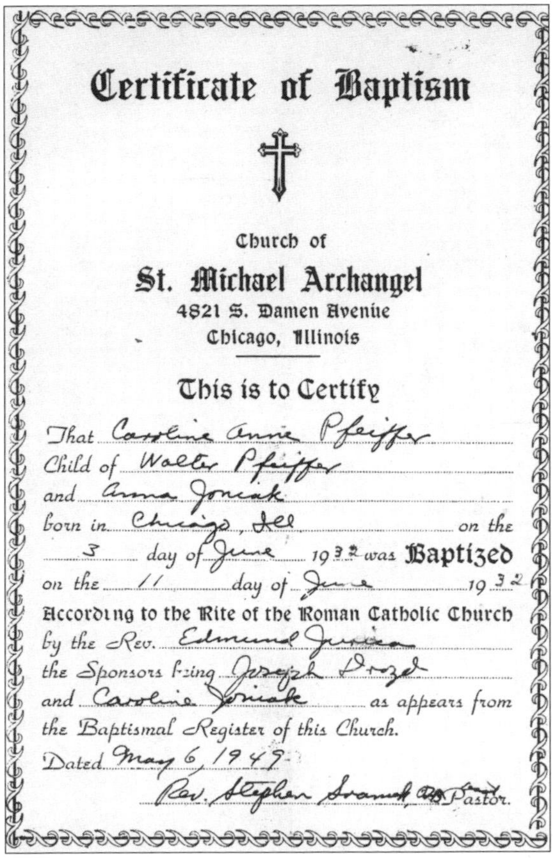

Certificate of Baptism

Church of
St. Michael Archangel
4821 S. Damen Avenue
Chicago, Illinois

This is to Certify
That Caroline Annie Pfeiffer
Child of Walter Pfeiffer
and Anna Joniak
born in Chicago, Ill on the 3 day of June 1932 was Baptized
on the 11 day of June 1932
According to the Rite of the Roman Catholic Church
by the Rev. Edmund [illegible]
the Sponsors being Joseph Drozd
and Caroline Joniak as appears from
the Baptismal Register of this Church.
Dated May 6, 1949
Rev. Stephen [illegible], Pastor.

Figure 190
With all record types, it is important to verify dates against other sources. This baptismal certificate states the year of birth as 1932, when it should be 1933.

Selected Readings:

Bochar, Jack. *Locations of Chicago Roman Catholic Churches, 1850-1990.* Geneva, Ill.: the author, 1990.

Child, Sargent B., and Dorothy P. Holmes. *Bibliography of Research Project Reports.* WPA Technical Series no. 7. 1943. Reprint. Bountiful, Utah: Faisal, 1979.

Encyclopedia of American Religions: Religious Creeds. Detroit: Gale Research Co., 1995. (A companion to J. Gordon Melton's *Encyclopedia of American Religions*)

Guzik, Estelle, ed. *Genealogical Sources in the New York Metropolitan Area.* New York: Jewish Genealogical Society, 1989. (Contains specific addresses for Jewish material)

Hefner, Loretta L. *The WPA Historical Records Survey: A Guide to the Unpublished Inventories, Indexes, and Transcripts.* Chicago: Society of American Archivists, 1980.

Humling, Virginia. *U.S. Catholic Sources: A Diocesan Guide.* Salt Lake City: Ancestry, 1995.

Kurzweil, Arthur, and Miriam Weiner, eds. *The Encyclopedia of Jewish Genealogy.* Northvale, N.J., and London: Jason Aronson, 1991.

Melton, J. Gordon. *The Encyclopedia of American Religions.* 2d ed. Detroit: Gale Research Co., 1987.

National Directory of Churches, Synagogues and Other Houses of Worship. Detroit: Gale Research Co., 1995.

Rehkopf, Charles F. "Using Records in the Archives of Religious Organizations." *Ancestry* 12 (4) (July/August 1994): 5-9. (Partial listing of national church repositories with addresses)

Works Progress Admin. *A Guide to Church Vital Statistics Records in California.* San Francisco: N. California Historical Records Survey, 1940.

Internet Sites of Interest:

Archidiocese of the Evangelical Lutheran
Church in America
http://www.elca.org/os/archives/intro.html

The Church of Jesus Christ of Latter-day Saints
http://www.lds.org/

JewishGen: The Official Home of Jewish
Genealogy
http://www.jewishgen.org

Local Catholic Church History and Genealogy
Research Guide
http://home.att.net/~Local_Catholic/

Figure 191

A certificate of marriage for Gary Mokotoff and Ruth Lois Auerbach. (Courtesy of Gary Mokotoff)

Lutheran Roots Genealogy Exchange
http://www.aal.org/LutheransOnline/Gene_Ex/

United Methodist Archives Center
http://www.drew.edu/infosys/library/uma.html

Mennonite Heritage Center
http://www.mhep.org/

U.S. Roman Catholic Historical Society
http://www.catholic.org/uschs/

Presbyterian Historical Society
http://www.libertynet.org/pacscl/phs/

```
VOGEL, Philipp              oo 1/23/1883    Elisabeth Stadter
   +Frantz Anton Vogel oo Elisabeth Kuntz, Steinfeld
   +Johann Georg Stadter oo Elisabeth Lorenz, Ruelzheim
   T:Philipp Woock, Martin Vogel

VOGEL, Philipp              oo 6/30/1908    Magdalene Vogel
   +Johann Vogel oo Anna Maria Pfeiffer (defs) Schaid
   *1878 +Johann (def) Vogel oo Catharine Kornmann, Steinfeld
   T:Johann Thomas, Philipp Braun

VOGEL, Rudolph             oo 1/16/1910    Emilia Dillmann
   +Jacob Vogel oo Margaret Georger, Schaid
   *1886 +Martin Dillmann oo Maria Anna Ott, Steinfeld
   Marriage performed at Schaid, Rev. Brenner, pastor

VOGEL, Johann Theobald     oo 11/19/1804   Anna Maria Burckbuchler
   +Joseph (def) Vogel oo Catharine Flick, farmer, Steinfeld
   widow Johann Kornmann (+Frantz Joseph Bürckbüchler oo Eva Catharine Vogel)
   Dispensation 3rd degree consanguinity, equal lines
   T:Paul Bürckbüchler, Wilhelm Muster, Martin Vogel, Jacob Guckert

VOGEL, Johann Theobald     oo 9/12/1808    Magdalene Burkhart
   +widower (Anna Maria Burckbuchler), farmer, Steinfeld
   +Johann (def) Matthias Burckart oo Eva Catharine Nist, Steinfeld
   Dispensation 3rd degree collateral lines consanguinity
   T:Johann Matthias Nist (Maire, id est Propositus, in Steinfeld)
      Nepomucene Beck, Michael Oster, Wilhelm Moster

VOGEL, Theobald            oo 2/26/1816    Maria Magdalene Hirtz
   widower (Magdalene Burckhart), farmer, Steinfeld
   +Jacob Hirtz oo Anna Maria (def) Schwoebel, farmer, Steinfeld
   T: Joseph Hirtz, Wilhelm Moster, Martin Vogel, Johann Burkhart

VOGEL, Theobald           oo 9/9/1817     Maria Elisabeth Vogel
   widower (Magdalene Hirtz), farmer, Steinfeld
   +Martin Vogel oo Eva Catharine Moock, sutor, Steinfeld, *ca 1792
   "nullo detecto impedimento"
   T:Lorentz Flick, Wilhelm Moster, Johann Matthias Michel, Martin Vogel

VOGEL, Theobald           oo 9/5/1820     Catharine Schopp
   widower             Steinfeld
   +Georg Heinrich Schopp oo Barbara Hoff, pastor ovium, Altenstadt
   T:Martin Vogel, Wilhelm Moster, Joseph Fischer (Kapsweyer) Michael Schopp (Kpswyr
```

Figure 192

Although rare, it is possible that a church may have a published index of its registers. This illustration shows a page from an index of marriage registers for the Catholic parish, St. Leodegar, at Steinfeld, Germany for the period 1692-1911, translated, indexed and edited in 1978 by Reverend Charles Banet, C.PP.S. This index, in addition to other indexing projects by Fr. Banet, can be found at <www.ancestry.com>.

School Censuses

School censuses are taken to insure that local facilities and teachers are adequate, as well as to plan for future appropriations. The schedules count the children of school age. Some school censuses are arranged in family units with parents' names included, and others are simply lists of children's names with their ages. Unfortunately, not all school census records have been preserved, but when they do exist, they can be rich sources of biographical information. Information was often collected on form file cards that asked the name and address of the child, race, date of birth, age, sex, school grade, names, and addresses of parents or guardians, and the school district. Parental information might include names, occupation, and whether living or dead. In some cases, school censuses have been taken for private and segregated schools.

The timing of these special school censuses can make them especially valuable as supplements to the missing 1890 federal census. For example, in *Kentucky Ancestry: A Guide to Genealogical and Historical Research*, Dr. Hogan states: "The General Assembly of Kentucky required a school census to be kept beginning in 1888. Census reports of children between the ages of six and eighteen were prepared annually." (Hogan, 1992, p. 121)

While not all school census records were kept, they are worth investigation. They may be found in local boards of education, county clerks' offices, historical societies, and local and state archives. In some cases, school censuses have been microfilmed by the Genealogical Society of Utah, and these will be found in the catalog under the appropriate state- and county-level headings.

See also *School Records*.

Selected Readings:

Hogan, Roseann Reinemuth. *Kentucky Ancestry: A Guide to Genealogical and Historical Research*. Salt Lake City: Ancestry, 1992.

White, Clifford. *Texas Scholastics 1854-1855: A State Census of School Children*. Bowie, MD: Heritage Books, 1991.

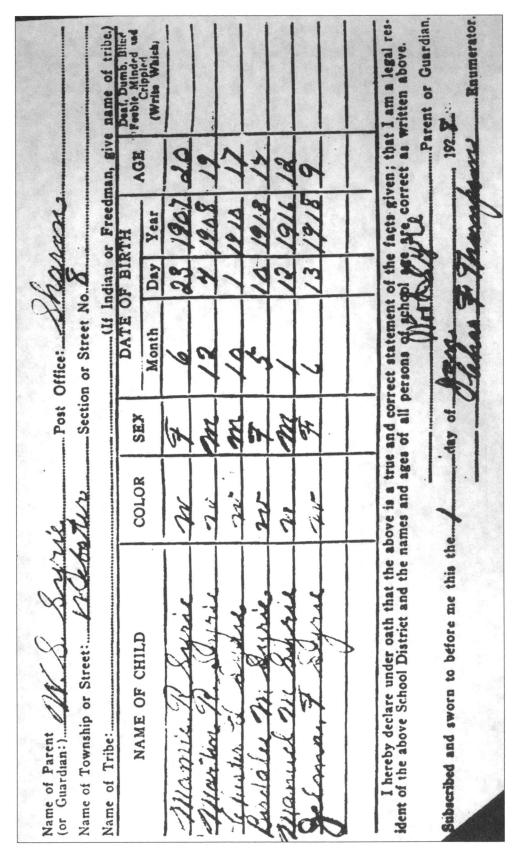

Figure 193

School census taken in 1928 for Sharon, Woodward County, Oklahoma, showing the school-age children of the Syrie family.

School Records

Educational records can play a very important role in family history research. School histories, class lists, report cards, student profiles, and photographs can add a new dimension to an ancestor known previously by name and vital statistics alone. In addition to class photos, yearbooks, which are produced by most colleges, universities, high schools, and even some grade schools, reveal nicknames, club memberships, sports and music participation, and general interests. Alumni directories typically indicate year of graduation and current address, and sometimes include maiden name, spouse's name, children's names, occupation, and employer's name. Fraternities and sororities often publish directories of members as well. Reunion booklets, printed for class reunions, can also provide a wealth of genealogical information.

School districts or archives of the institutions that created the records are most likely to have the types of records that are valuable to family historians. If an

Figure 194
Cathedral School, Ft. Wayne, Indiana. (Courtesy of Rev. Charles Banet)

ancestor attended a military school (the Military Academy at West Point and the Naval Academy at Annapolis have the largest collections), records such as applications for admission, grades earned, and lists of demerits may be housed in the academy's archives. Some of these records are also available at the National Archives. Yearbooks, directories, and reunion books can often be obtained through the school where they originated, but used-book, antique, and memorabilia stores should not be overlooked in a search for these publications. Local libraries, historical societies, museums, and genealogical societies and state, local, and federal archives are often the recipients of records of long-closed schools.

See also *College and University Records.*

Selected Readings:

Neagles, James C. *U.S. Military Records: A Guide to Federal & State Sources, Colonial America to the Present.* Salt Lake City: Ancestry, 1994.

ECHOES OF REUNION

Having specialized in Latin, she took the examination for teacher of Latin in the Chicago high schools and was fortunate enough to begin her work as substitute the following Fall. Her permanent appointment soon followed at Medill where she is now teaching both Latin and Spanish. At one time, while serving as substitute for Mrs. Dracass, Elsie had charge of old "Room 6" (Mr. Comstock's room) in which she had been enrolled and where she had recited English to Mrs. **Dracass.**

Esie was unable to attend the reunion on account of sickness, which has also kept her away from her schoolroom du.ies part of the Winter.

Harry R. Gill, 1544 Post St., Jacksonville, Florida.

Laura A. Goodwin, 1742½ New England Ave., Los Angeles, Calif.

Guy P. Goodwin was married to Jeanne **Foulks** June 15th, 1909, at Los Angeles and now lives in that city, 1742½ New England Ave. Many of us remember Guy not only as a good student but also as a very clever artist, and we learn that his main occupation and principal interest since graduating with the Class of '99 has been along the line of Art. After leaving Englewood he worked for the Rock Island R. R. and attended the Chicago Academy of Fine Arts, and later

12 years of age. Th
Hazel St., Texarkan
Mr. Willett is worki
machinist. They live
City for eight years
Maud was greatly in
work. Was Presider
nightly Study Club an
of that city.

Laura C. Griff
(Mrs. J. F. S

Ida
class at
when sh
After cad
taught at th
years. On A
Dr. Y. J. R
daughters and n
ren Ave., Chicag
tist with offices in
Annex and 1759
They enjoyed a plea
weeks in the Rockies.

Richard S. Hickey t
course at the Chicago
but he taught only o
now salesmanager of
Mortgage Co. of Detro
ous to July 1st of last y
eling through the mid
years and from Denve
Canada to Mexico for
finally joined the ran

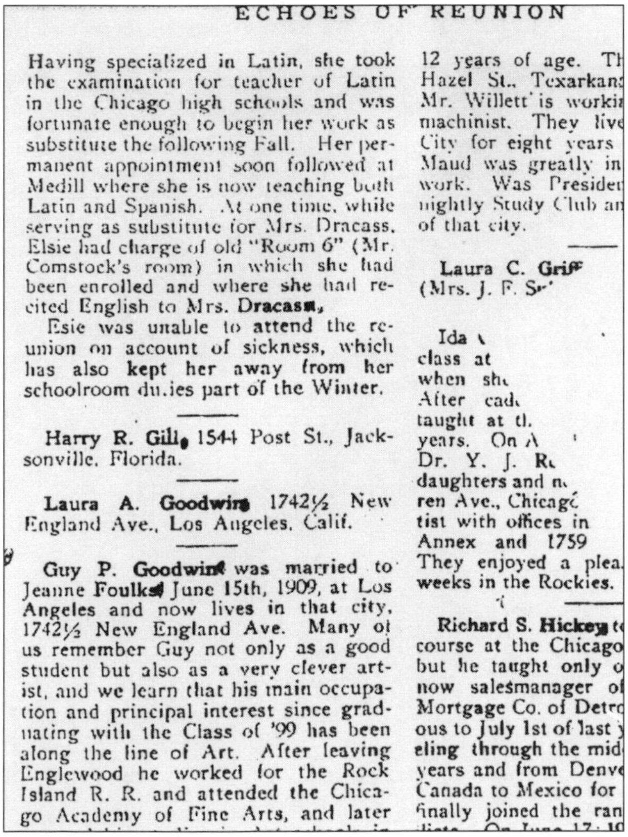

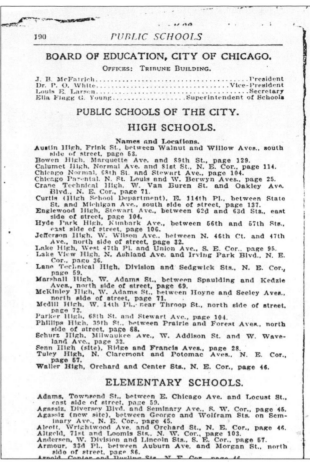

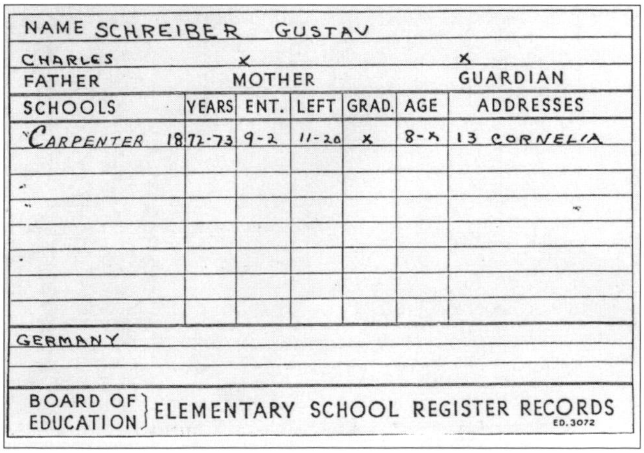

Figure 195

A page from a reunion book published in 1917, containing biographical sketches for the graduating class of 1899 from Englewood High School in Chicago, Illinois.

190 PUBLIC SCHOOLS

BOARD OF EDUCATION, CITY OF CHICAGO.

OFFICES: TRIBUNE BUILDING.

J. B. McFatrich........President
Dr. P. O. White........Vice-President
Louis E. Larsen........Secretary
Ella Flagg G. Young........Superintendent of Schools

PUBLIC SCHOOLS OF THE CITY.

HIGH SCHOOLS.

Names and Locations.

Austin High, Frink St., between Walnut and Willow Aves., south side of street, page 53.
Bowen High, Marquette Ave. and 89th St., page 129.
Calumet High, Normal Ave. and 81st St., N. E. Cor., page 114.
Chicago Normal, 68th St. and Stewart Ave., page 104.
Chicago Parental, N. St. Louis and W. Berwyn Aves., page 25.
Crane Technical High, W. Van Buren St. and Oakley Ave. Blvd., N. E. Cor., page 71.
Curtis (High School Department), E. 114th Pl., between State St. and Michigan Ave., south side of street, page 137.
Englewood High, Stewart Ave., between 62d and 63d Sts., east side of street, page 104.
Hyde Park High, Kimbark Ave., between 56th and 57th Sts., east side of street, page 106.
Jefferson High, W. Wilson Ave., between N. 46th Ct. and 47th Ave., north side of street, page 32.
Lake High, West 47th Pl. and Union Ave., S. E. Cor., page 95.
Lake View High, N. Ashland Ave. and Irving Park Blvd., N. E. Cor., page 36.
Lane Technical High, Division and Sedgwick Sts., N. E. Cor., page 59.
Marshall High, W. Adams St., between Spaulding and Kedzie Aves., north side of street, page 69.
McKinley High, W. Adams St., between Hoyne and Seeley Aves., north side of street, page 71.
Medill High, W. 14th Pl., near Throop St., north side of street, page 72.
Parker High, 68th St. and Stewart Ave., page 104.
Phillips High, 39th St., between Prairie and Forest Aves., north side of street, page 88.
Schurz High, Milwaukee Ave., W. Addison St. and W. Waveland Ave., page 32.
Senn High (site), Ridge and Francis Aves., page 28.
Tuley High, N. Claremont and Potomac Aves., N. E. Cor., page 67.
Waller High, Orchard and Center Sts., N. E. Cor., page 46.

ELEMENTARY SCHOOLS.

Adams, Townsend St., between E. Chicago Ave. and Locust St., east side of street, page 59.
Agassiz, Diversey Blvd. and Seminary Ave., S. W. Cor., page 45.
Agassiz (new site), between George and Wolfram Sts. on Seminary Ave., N. E. Cor., page 45.
Alcott, Wrightwood Ave. and Orchard St., N. E. Cor., page 46.
Altgeld, 71st and Loomis Sts., N. W. Cor., page 103.
Andersen, W. Division and Lincoln Sts., S. E. Cor., page 57.
Armour, 33d Pl., between Auburn Ave. and Morgan St., north side of street, page 86.

Figure 196

Without the specific name and address of a school, locating old records in a big city can be difficult. Public school directories, such as this one published in 1912 for Chicago schools, are useful for narrowing the search. Similar directories can be found in school board offices, historical societies, and archives.

NAME SCHREIBER GUSTAV

CHARLES	X	X
FATHER	MOTHER	GUARDIAN

SCHOOLS	YEARS	ENT.	LEFT	GRAD.	AGE	ADDRESSES
CARPENTER	1872-73	9-2	11-20	X	8-X	13 CORNELIA

GERMANY

BOARD OF EDUCATION } ELEMENTARY SCHOOL REGISTER RECORDS ED.3072

Figure 197

An example of a record received from the Chicago Public School system for Gustav Schreiber, who attended Carpenter School during the 1872-73 school year. The document provides a street address and implies that his family was from Germany.

Slave Schedules of the Census, 1850-60

Slaves were enumerated separately during the 1850 and 1860 censuses, though, unfortunately, most schedules do not provide personal names. Usually, individuals are not named, but simply numbered, and can be distinguished only by age, sex, and color; the names of the owners are recorded as well. Because of the limited amount of information in these schedules, they are most often used to support information found in other documents.

Ancestry.com has made available the AIS Indexes to these schedules for a number of states at its Web site at <www.Ancestry.com>.

Selected Readings:

Jackson, Ronald Vern, ed. *Delaware 1850/1860 Slave Schedules.* Salt Lake City: Accelerated Indexing Systems International, 1986.

_____. *Texas 1850 Slave Schedules.* North Salt Lake, Utah: Accelerated Indexing Systems International, 1988.

Meyerink, Kory L, ed. *Printed Sources: A Guide to Published Genealogical Records.* Salt Lake City: Ancestry, 1998.

Szucs, Loretto Dennis, and Sandra Hargreaves Luebking, eds. *The Source: A Guidebook of American Genealogy.* Rev. ed. Salt Lake City: Ancestry, 1997.

Internet Sites of Interest:

Ancestry.com
http://www.ancestry.com

National Archives and Records Administration
http://www.nara.gov/publications/microfilm/census/census.html

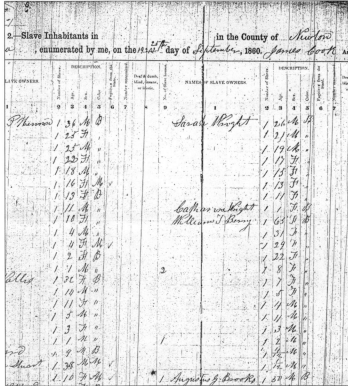

Figure 198

A slave schedule from the 1860 Census for Newton County, Georgia, listing the name of the slave owner, number of slaves, and each slave's age, sex, and color.

Slavery Records

Researching African American lineage prior to 1870 can be very difficult, since a large number of African Americans were slaves who had no legal rights, and therefore are not found in many of the record sources available for that period. References to ancestors, however, can sometimes be found in records pertaining to their owners. Census schedules listed slaves, usually anonymously with age, gender, racial identity (black or mulatto), and sometimes occupation, under the name of the owner. County records can also turn up information pertaining to slaves. A county deed book may contain, in addition to real estate transactions, documentation of slave sales, and tax records often include listings of slaves among the property for which the owner was taxed. For a period of time in the 1850s the states of Virginia and Kentucky required the registration of births and deaths. The births of children born to slave mothers are included in these records and provide the date and place of birth, sex, and name of owner. Probate records should also be searched, as slaves were sometimes named in the description and disposition of a slave owner's estate. If an ancestor attempted to escape, it is possible that an advertise-

DATE	NAME	SEX	FATHER OR SLAVE OWNER	PLACE	DISEASE OR CAUSE	AGE	BIRTH	OCCUPATION
Mar	NOT NAMED	F	Malvina Hinkle	Pulaski	Cold	2	Mont.	
Jun	NOT NAMED (S)	F	James Hoge	"	Unknown	3	Pulaski	
7-11	SARAH J. HARROLD	F	H. & S. Harrold	"	Scarlet Fever	3-10		"
9-17	CHARLOTTE E. HOGE	F	J. & C. Trollinger	"	Unknown	23		"
12-29	MARY (S)	F	William Hoge	"	Pneumonia	20		
Oct	LUCINDA HILL	F	A. & S. Odell	"	Consumption	35		"
Aug	JOHN H. HILL	M	H. & L. Hill	"	Diarria	11		"
Feb	PETER (S)	M	James N. Hoge	"	Old Age	70		"
12-22	JAMES S. HOWARD	M	J.D. & A. Howard	"	Dropsey of Heart	13-01-18		"
4-15	JAMES M. HOLMES	M		"			1-02	"
Mar	HARRISON (S)	M	Joseph Graham	"			4	
Feb	HARRIET (S)	F	Harvey Shepherd	"	Scarlet Fever			
Oct	NOT NAMED (S)	F	Elizabeth Kent	"	Not Known		18	
8-8	MARY F. LITTLE	F	S. & A. Little	"	Scarlet Fever	3-01-25		"
8-13	WALTER C. LITTLE	M	"	"	"		6-15	"
Oct	NOT NAMED (S)	F	F.A. Morgan	"	Unknown	6		"
Oct	NOT NAMED (S)	F	"	"	"	3		"
4-5	SARAH E. MARTIN	F	W. & M. Martin	"	"	3		"
2-22	WILLIAM MARTIN	M	C. & M. Martin	"	Old Age	84		"
12-31	DOLLY ODEL	F	R. & S. Day	"	Unknown	35-06		"
12-23	RICHARD (S)	M	James N. Pierce	"	Smothered	5		"
Jan	BALLARD QUESENBERRY	M	Crockett E. Quesenberry	"	Fever	5		"
Feb	MARINDA QUESENBERRY	F	"	"	"	8		"
12-7	JOHN SUTTON	M	Unknown	"	"	64		Farmer

Figure 199

A portion of a slavery record found in *Births and Deaths 1853-1871 on Record in Pulaski County Court House, Pulaski Virginia* (n.p., n.d.).

ment containing a physical description and sometimes biographical information may have been placed by the owner. Many of these advertisements have been transcribed and published.

The National Union Catalog of Manuscript Collections (NUCMC), containing descriptions of manuscript collections held by libraries throughout the United States, can aid in finding the papers of plantation owners. Information pertaining to slaves, particularly documentation of births, can often be found in these personal records. An extensive microfilm collection, Kenneth Stampp, ed. *Records of the Ante-Bellum Southern Plantations From the Revolution Through the Civil War* (Frederick, Md.: University Publications of America, 1985-), is another place to look for these records. As is the case with all of those records mentioned above, the name of the slaveholder must be known.

Other potential sources are records of military service that may exist for an ancestor who was a slave. During the War of 1812, some owners donated slaves for service, and during the Civil War, slave owners from border states that had not seceded were known to exchange their slaves for the bounty that was normally paid to volunteers. The National Archives has an index to the Civil War service records of the United States Colored Troops (USCT) and other African American servicemen.

See also *Slave Schedules of the Census 1850-60* and *Freedmen's Bureau Records.*

Selected Readings:

Cornish, Dudley Taylor. *The Sable Arm: Black Troops in the Union Army, 1861-1865.* Lawrence: University Press of Kansas, 1956.

Hawbaker, Gary T. *Runaways, Rascals, And Rogues: Missing Spouses, Servants and Slaves. Abstracts from Lancaster County Pennsylvania Newspapers.* Hershey, Penn.: the author, 1987.

Headley, Robert K. *Genealogical Abstracts From the 18th Century Virginia Newspapers.* Baltimore: Genealogical Publishing Co., 1987.

The National Union Catalog of Manuscript Collections. Washington, D.C.: Library of Congress, 1962-present.

Stampp, Kenneth, ed. *Records of the Ante-Bellum Southern Plantations From the Revolution Through the Civil War.* Frederick, Md.: University Publications of America, 1985-.

Streets, David H. *Slave Genealogy: A Research Guide with Case Studies.* Bowie, Md.: Heritage, 1986.

Thackery, David T. "African American Family History." *The Source: A Guidebook of American Genealogy.* Rev. ed. Salt Lake City: Ancestry, 1997.

Townsend, Stephen. "Slave Ancestral Research, Part I: Resources." *Forum* 9 (3) (Fall 1997).

Windley, Lathan A. *Runaway Slave Advertisements: A Documentary History From the 1730s to 1790.* 4 vols. Westport, Conn.: Greenwood, 1983. (Contains transcribed advertisements for the states of Virginia, North Carolina, Maryland, South Carolina, and Georgia)

Internet Sites of Interest:

African American Census Schedules Online
http://www.prairiebluff.com/aacensus/

African American Genealogy Sources in the Louisiana Division of the New Orleans Public Library
http://home.gnofn.org/~nopl/guides/black.htm

African American Slave Narratives
www.ancestry.com

Database of Servitude & Emancipation Records (1722-1863)
http://www.sos.state.il.us/depts/archives/servant.html

Mississippi Genealogy Project
Index to Wills Containing Slave Information
http://www.rootsweb.com/~msmadiso/abstract/slaveindex.htm

National Park Service Database on United States Colored Troops (USCT)
http://www.itd.nps.gov/cwss/usct.html

Slavery in Pennsylvania
Central Pennsylvania Slaveowners and Slaves
http://www.geocities.com/Athens/Parthenon/6329/

Social Security Death Index

The Freedom of Information Act has made it possible to order copies of Social Security files for deceased persons from the Social Security Administration. Included in the file is the application for a Social Security Number, which requests birth date and place, parents' names, and place of residence at the time of application. Subsequent addresses may also be noted in the file.

The Social Security Death Index (SSDI), a listing of individuals who died between the years of 1962 and the present and whose deaths were reported to the Social Security Administration, is now available at the Family History Library and can be searched free of charge on the Internet at <www.ancestry.com> (updated quarterly), or can be purchased on CD-ROM. If an individual is included in the SSDI, a search by surname will yield the month and year of birth, the Social Security Number, the state where the Social Security Number was issued, the year of death, and the last state where the person resided.

With the Social Security Number of the deceased, a copy of the Social Security file can be requested from: Social Security Administration, Office of Central Records Operations, FOIA Workgroup, P.O. Box 17772, 300 N. Greene Street, Baltimore, MD 21290.

See also *Social Security Records.*

Selected Readings:

Sittner, Kathi. "U.S. Social Security Death Index." *Ancestry* 14 (1) (January/February 1996): 26-27.

Internet Sites of Interest:

Ancestry.com
Social Security Death Index
http://www.ancestry.com/ssdi/advanced.htm

Social Security Administration's Guide to Freedom of Information Act Requests
http://www.ssa.gov/foia/foia_guide.htm

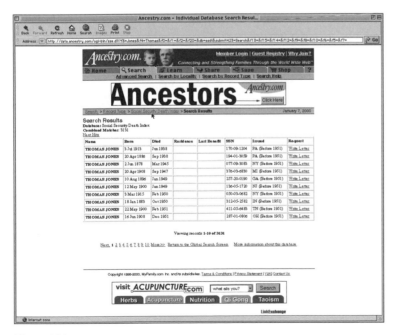

Figure 200

Results from a Social Security Death Index search for Thomas Jones, conducted at Ancestry.com.

Social Security Records

The Freedom of Information Act has made it possible for researchers to obtain information from the Social Security files of deceased persons. Even though the Social Security Administration was not formed until 1936, people born as early as 1850 may have a file. In that file is an application for a Social Security Number, which requests information including full name, address, employer name and address, age, date of birth, place of birth, father's full name, mother's full maiden name, sex, and color. The file may also contain original documents, such as a birth certificate, alien registration card, or naturalization record.

All applications are microfilmed, and copies may be requested from: Social Security Administration, Office of Central Records Operations, FOIA Workgroup, P.O. Box 17772, Baltimore, MD 21290. As Kathleen W. Hinckley suggests in *The Source: A Guidebook of American Genealogy* (page 639), a microprint from the microfilmed original should be requested as opposed to a printout from the database, which includes only five of the sixteen questions asked on the form. A copy of the death certificate should be included with the request. While supporting documents (like the original application for Social Security) are usually destroyed due to the tremendous volume of records created by the administration, there are some exceptions, so it is wise to request the entire file if one exists.

See also *Social Security Death Index*.

Selected Readings:

Szucs, Loretto Dennis, and Sandra Hargreaves Luebking, eds. *The Source: A Guidebook of American Genealogy*. Rev. ed. Salt Lake City: Ancestry, 1997.

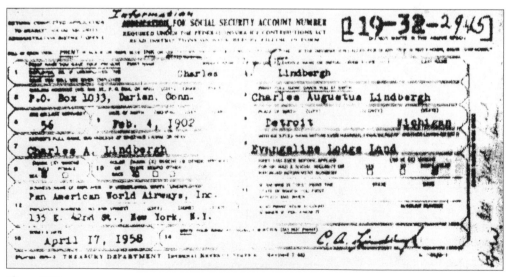

Figure 201

A copy of the Social Security application filed by Charles Lindbergh in 1958 was obtained by writing to the Social Security Administration.

Social Statistics of the Census, 1850-80

Social statistics schedules compiled from 1850 to 1880 contain three items of specific interest for the family historian: (1) The schedules list cemetery facilities within city boundaries, including maps with cemeteries marked; name, addresses, and general description of all cemeteries; procedures for internment; and cemeteries no longer functioning, along with the reasons for their closing. (2) The schedules also list trade societies,

Church records are especially helpful for researching immigrants, and the census of social statistics is a valuable finding tool to locate the records of a specific religious group.

lodges, clubs, and other groups with addresses, major branches, names of executive officers, and statistics showing members, meetings, and financial worth. (3) The schedules list churches with a brief history, a statement of doctrine and policy, and a statistical summary of membership by county. The 1880 schedules were printed by the Government Printing Office, and most government document sections of public and university libraries have them. Those for 1906, 1916, and 1926 are printed; the originals were destroyed by order of Congress. Church records are especially helpful for researching immigrants, and the census of social statistics is a finding tool to locate the records of a specific group.

Selected Readings:

Meyerink, Kory L, ed. *Printed Sources: A Guide to Published Genealogical Records.* Salt Lake City: Ancestry, 1998.

Szucs, Loretto Dennis, and Sandra Hargreaves Luebking, eds. *The Source: A Guidebook of American Genealogy.* Rev. ed. Salt Lake City: Ancestry, 1997.

Internet Sites of Interest:

Ancestry.com
http://www.ancestry.com

National Archives and Records Administration
http://www.nara.gov/publications/microfilm/census/census.html

State Censuses

In order to collect more specific data, such as the financial needs and strengths of communities, state censuses were often taken in years between the federal censuses. As noted by Ann Lainhart in her comprehensive study *State Census Records* (Baltimore: Genealogical Publishing Co., 1992), tallies taken at the state level take on special importance for researchers attempting to fill in gaps left by missing censuses. For example, state and territorial censuses taken in Colorado, Florida, Iowa, Kansas, Nebraska, New Jersey, New Mexico, New York, North Dakota, and Wisconsin in years between 1885 and 1895 can partially compensate for the missing 1890 census schedules.

The New York state census, for example, is actually more useful to family historians than is the federal census of the same time period. The New York census that was taken in June and July 1855 gives for each household: the value of the dwelling, and the material of which it is built; number of families in the dwelling; all members of the household by name, age, sex, and relation to the head of family; in what county of New York or in what other state or foreign country born; marital status; profession, trade, or occupation; number of years resident in the city; whether native voter, naturalized voter, or alien; and whether adults listed could read or write.

Probably no other state enumeration surpasses the 1925 Iowa state census in terms of genealogical value. In that year, Iowa asked for the names of all residents and their relationship to the head of that household; place of abode (including house number and street in cities and towns); sex; color or race; age at last birthday; place of birth; marital status; if foreign born, year naturalized;

A state census takes on a special importance for any researcher attempting to fill gaps left by missing censuses. For example, censuses taken in many states between 1885 and 1895 can partially compensate for the missing 1890 census schedules.

number of years in the United States; number of years in Iowa; level of education; names of parents (including mother's maiden name); places of birth, age if living, and place of marriage of parents; nine specific questions relating to military service; nine questions regarding occupation; church affiliation; and six questions related to real estate, including the amount for which each listed property owner's house was insured.

Unlike the federal censuses, most state census manuscripts are not indexed; they are alphabetically arranged by county, and then geographically by election precincts. In most state censuses, users must obtain election precinct numbers to expedite a search.

A useful indication of what the Family History Library has on state and other censuses is "U.S. State and Special Census Register: A Listing of Family History Library Microfilm Numbers." It is an inventory, arranged by state and census year, describing the contents of each census and providing microfilm numbers for most known existing state censuses. The unpublished listing, compiled by G. Eileen Buckway and Fred Adams, was revised in 1992 and is available at and through the Family History Library and its centers. State censuses are often found in state archives and historical agencies as well.

Selected Reading:

Lainhart, Ann S. *State Census Records*. Baltimore: Genealogical Publishing Co., 1992.

Szucs, Loretto Dennis, and Sandra Hargreaves Luebking, eds. *The Source: A Guidebook of American Genealogy*. Salt Lake City: Ancestry, 1997.

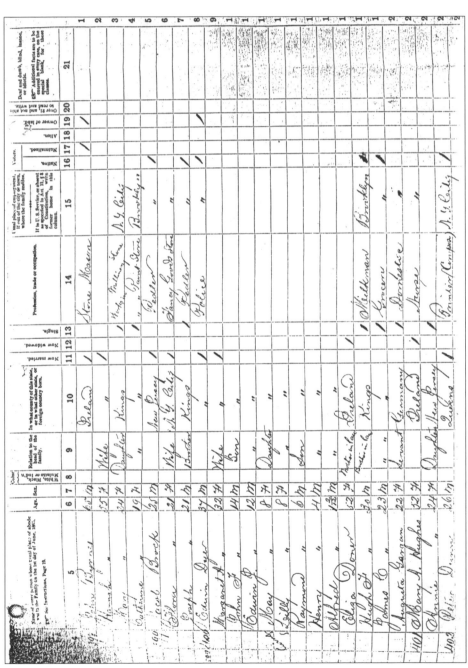

Figure 202

1875 New York State Census showing a page from Brooklyn, Kings County.

Statewide Collections and Indexes

State historical societies and libraries are often involved in the cataloging of rural, city, and state collections and, as a result, are a major source for research materials. The California State Library, for example, holds approximately 640,000 index cards covering 1.2 million items from sources such as newspapers, manuscripts, periodicals, and county histories in the California Information File. The Connecticut State Library holds most of the state's probate estate papers from before 1850 and state census records, including a 1917 Connecticut military census that included males ages ten to thirty along with automobile owners, aliens, and nurses. Also at the Connecticut State Library is a master index of individual names compiled by the WPA from tombstones in more than 2,000 cemeteries in Connecticut.

Statewide projects are ongoing in almost every state. Hundreds of thousands of marriages have been entered in a pre-1900 Illinois Statewide Marriage Index, a continuing project of the Illinois State Archives and the Illinois State Genealogical Society. In an effort to replace the missing 1890 federal census, genealogists in California have launched a statewide project to transcribe and computerize names from the voting lists for California for 1890. Most state genealogical and historical societies are aware of (and possibly involved in) such projects and can provide researchers with information about them.

Selected Readings:

American Library Directory: A Classified List of Libraries in the United States and Canada, With Personnel and Statistical Data. New York: R.R. Bowker, annual.

Buenker, John D., Gerald Michael Greenfield, and William J. Murin. *Urban History: A Guide to Information Sources.* Detroit: Gale Research Co., 1981.

Kirkham, E.K. *A Handy Guide to Searching in the Larger Cities of the United States.* Logan, Utah: The Everton Publishers, 1974.

Meyers, Mary K., ed. *Meyer's Directory of Genealogical Societies in the U.S.A. and Canada.* Mt. Airy, Md.: the editor (updated and reissued in even-numbered years).

Street Indexes

It is not uncommon for a researcher to come across a photograph or letter that has a street address noted without mention of a city or town. A street directory or index may provide insight as to where to continue a search and may turn what might have otherwise been useless information into an important find. *The Street Directory of the Principal Cities of the United States* (Detroit: Gale Research Co., 1973), originally published by order of the postmaster general in 1908, is one such directory that provides an alphabetical listing of streets, avenues, courts, places, lanes, roads, and wharves to which mail was delivered, with references to all the cities and towns where these street names appear. City directories frequently included street guides, as well, which may be helpful in confirming a suspected location.

An index to city streets and census enumeration districts for thirty-nine cities in the 1910 federal census is widely available on fifty sheets of microfiche. Used in conjunction with a known 1910 address or one found in a city directory, the index enables users of the census schedules to translate specific addresses into appropriate district number and volume number on the microfilmed census. These street indexes are available in most places where the 1910 census is available.

STREET NAME CHANGES

OLD NAME	NEW NAME
Abbott Ct. N.	Orchard St. N.
Airdrie Pl. W.	Gordon Ter. W.
Alaska St. W.	Weed St. W.
Albert St. S.	Bishop St. S.
Aldine Sq. E.	De Sable Sq. E.
Allee Pl. W.	Concord Pl. W.
Aubert Av. W.	Hutchinson St. W.
Austin Av. E.	Hubbard St. E.
Austin Av. W.	Hubbard St. W.
Ayers Ct. N.	Willard Ct. N.
Ballou St. N.	St. Louis Av. N.
Barton Av. N.	Claremont Av. N.
Beethoven Pl. W.	Scott St. W.
Belknap St. W.	Grenshaw St. W.
Best Av. N.	Wilton Av. N.
Bickerdike St. N.	Bishop St. N.
Binzo St. N.	Wolcott Av. N.
Birch St. W.	Arthington St. W.
Bixby Ct. N.	Bishop St. N.
Blackwell St. S.	Wells St. S.
Blaine Pl. W.	Gunnison St. W.
Blair St. S.	Clinton St. S.
Blanche St. W.	LeMoyne St. W.
Blucher St. W.	Potomac Av. W.
Boston Av. W.	Gladys Av. W.
Bradley St. W.	Potomac Av. W.
Brand St. N.	Wolcott Av. N.
Brigham St. W.	Beach Av. W.
Buena Park Ter. W.	Cullom Av. W.
Bunker St. W.	Grenshaw St. W.
Burlington St. S.	Clinton St. S.

OLD NAME	NEW NAME
Gardner St. W.	Goethe St. W.
Garfield Av. W.	Dickens Av. W.
Gary Pl. W.	Patterson Av. W.
Gilpin Pl. W.	Cabrini St. W.
Girard St. N.	Honore St. N.
Glengyle Pl. W.	Carmen Av. W.
Glenlake Av. N. (Bet. Peterson & Kilpatrick Avs.)	Hiawatha Av. N.
Gloy Pl. N.	Honore St. N.
Good St. W.	Cabrini St. W.
Gormont Av. N.	Lakewood Av. N.
Granville Av. N. (Bet. Kostner & Keene Avs.)	Ionia Av. N.
Graves Ct. S.	St. Lawrence Av. S.
Green St. S. (On the line of Canal St.)	Canal St. S.
Greenwich St. W.	Moffat St. W.
Grimm Av. W.	Ainslie St. W.
Gross Av. S.	McDowell Av. S.
Grove Av. S.	Perry Av. S.
Hammond St. N.	Orleans St. N.
Hancock St. N.	Drake Av. N.
Hein Pl. W.	Goethe St. W.
Herndon St. N.	Lakewood Av. N.
Hervey St. W.	Dickens Av. W.
Heyden St. W.	Thorndale Av. W
High St. N.	Janssen Av. N.
Hilldale Av. N.	Wolcott Av. N.
Holt St. N.	Greenview Av. N.

OLD NAME	NEW NAME
Nebraska Av. N.	Whipple St. N.
Nevada St. W.	Deming Pl. W.
Newell Av. W.	Highland Av. W.
Newell Av. N.	Sayre Av. N.
Newton St. N.	Honore St. N.
Nieman Av. W.	Devon Av. W.
North Park Av. N. (Bet. Menomonee and Clark Sts.)	Lincoln Park West
Oak Grove Av. W.	Patterson Av. W.
Oliver Pl. W.	17th Place W.
O'Neil St. W.	23rd Street W.
Oregon Av. W.	Flournoy St. W.
Osborn St. N.	Hermitage Av. N.
Osgood St. N.	Kenmore Av. N.
Otis St. N.	Howe St. N.
Otto St. W.	Henderson St. W.
Park Av. S.	Eggleston Av. S.
Parkhurst Av. N.	Winchester Av. N.
Peck Ct. W.	Thorndale Av. W.
Penn St. N.	Orchard St. N.
Philadelphia Pl. W.	Carroll Av. W.
Photo Pl. W.	Arcade Pl. W.
Pingree St. N.	Bell Av. N.
Plaisance Ct. E.	60th Place E.
Potwyne Pl. W.	Agatite Av. W.
Powell Av. N.	Campbell Av. N.
Putnam St. N.	Union Av. N.
Raleigh Ct. S.	Claremont Av. S.
Rawson St. W.	Concord Pl. W.

Figure 203
Many street names have changed over the years, some more than once. Most cities have published or unpublished guides to street name changes, such as this one taken from "Kirk's Map of Chicago and Suburbs" (Chicago: Fred W. Kirk, 1917). Municipal archives and libraries with local collections are logical places to look for these guides.

Tax Records

Dating back to colonial times, local, state, and federal governments have imposed taxes on citizens and various personal assets. If an ancestor was a free male between the ages of twenty-one (or as young as sixteen in some areas) and sixty, it is likely that he can be found in poll tax lists for the county of residence. Some name lists survive from the federal direct taxes, which were used to bolster military forces in 1798, and for the War of 1812 and the Civil War. Records of taxes collected or owed on land holdings, slaves, livestock, and even windows may also be available.

From tax records, a researcher may get an idea of a family's financial status or may be able to link family members by checking for others in the area with the same surname. In searching them, it is important to keep in mind that the ages of individuals subject to the poll tax changed periodically, and that certain groups

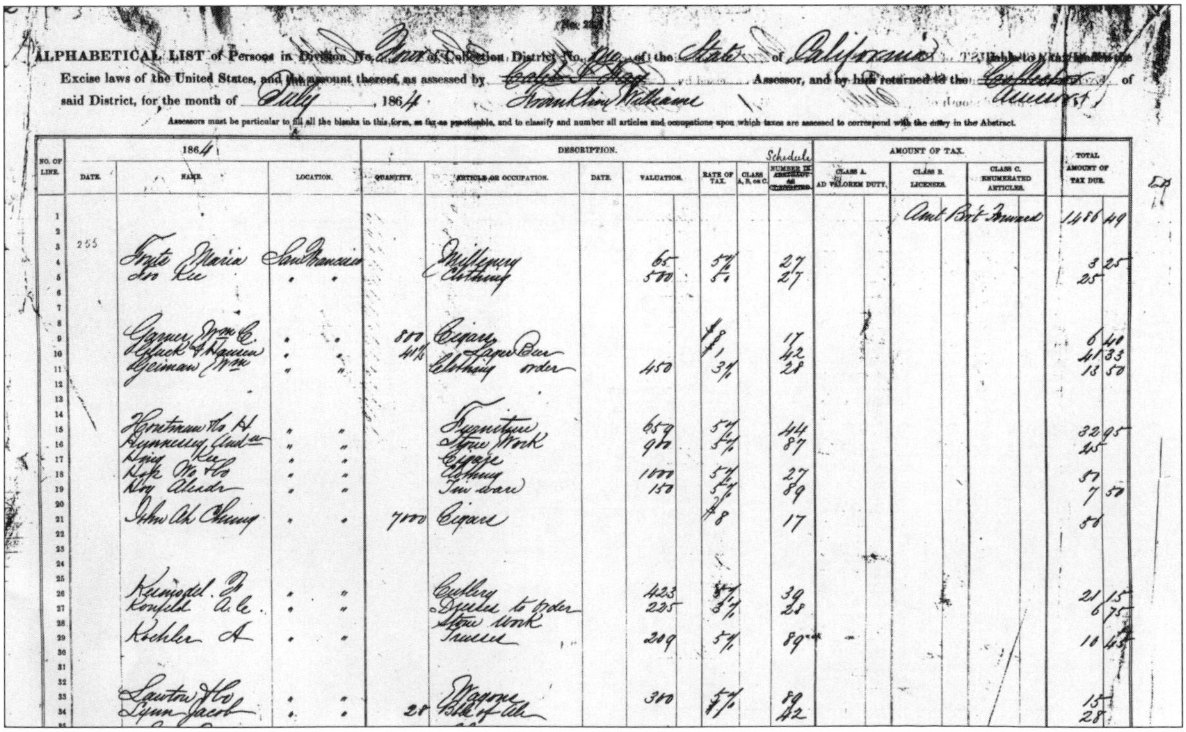
ALPHABETICAL LIST of Persons in Division No. Four of Collection District No. One of the State of California ... Excise laws of the United States, and the amount thereof, as assessed by ... Assessor, and by him returned to the Collector ... of said District, for the month of July, 1864

Figure 204

An 1864 Bureau of Internal Revenue tax assessment list for Division No. Four, of Collection District No. One (San Francisco), California. Lists are arranged alphabetically by surname of those assessed for each period and include names, locations, taxable article or occupation, valuation, tax rates, and total amount of tax due.

of individuals were exempt from the tax. These groups include ministers, justices of the peace, militia officers, tax assessors, and in some cases, veterans of war. Children, slaves, and indentured servants were usually left off the lists as well.

Federal direct tax lists from the Civil War can be found on microfilm at the National Archives. Earlier direct tax lists are likely to be found in state historical societies and state archives. County courthouses or archives are the best place to begin a search for taxes levied on the county level, such as poll and property taxes.

Selected Readings:

Dilts, G. David. "Censuses and Tax Lists." *Printed Sources: A Guide to Published Genealogical Sources.* Ch. 9: 300-52. Salt Lake City: Ancestry, 1998.

Eakle, Arlene H. *Tax Records: A Common Source with an Uncommon Value.* Salt Lake City: Family History World, 1978.

Pompey, Sherman Lee. *Indexes to American and Western Canada Census and Tax Records, 1800-1900.* Salt Lake City: Genealogical Society of Utah, 1967. Microfilmed typescript.

Sittner, Kathi. "Tax Records." *Ancestry* 13 (3) (May/June 1995): 26-7.

Stemmons, John D. *The United States Census Compendium: A Directory of Census Records, Tax Lists, Poll Lists, Petitions, Directories, etc. Which Can Be Used as a Census.* Logan, Utah: Everton Publishers, 1973.

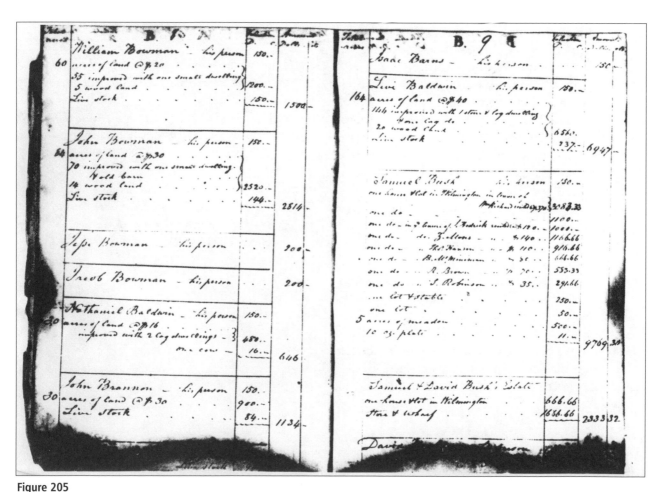

Figure 205
New Castle County, Delaware, Tax Assessment Records, 1816-17. Microfiche copy published by the Delaware State Archives; used with permission. (Courtesy of Donn Devine, CG, CGI, JD)

Territorial Records

At the time the United States acquired the Northwest Territory (1787), a policy of territorial government was established for the sparsely populated areas until statehood was achieved. The records produced by the territories was edited by Clarence Edwin Carter and published in a twenty-six volume set titled *Territorial Papers of the United States* (Washington, D.C.: Government Printing Office, 1934-78). Published in the Carter work are the activities of the territorial governments, including correspondence relating to land and court proceedings. Frequently included are early settler lists and petitions to the government by these early residents. While the bulk of the public land papers deal with plans and policies, a significant number of them deal with land claims of individual settlers, e.g., lists of appointments to county and local offices and licenses approved for certain trades, such as keeping a tavern or operating a ferry. Territories included in the set are the oldest territories, including northwest of the Ohio River, south of the Ohio River, Mississippi, Indiana, Orleans, Michigan, Louisiana, Illinois, Alabama, Florida, and Wisconsin.

Published territorial papers may be found in libraries with government document collections. There are also many original territorial records in the regions of the National Archives.

See also *American State Papers, Deeds, Homestead Records, Land Grants,* and *Patents.*

Selected Readings:

Carter, Clarence, 1949. "The Territorial Papers as a Source for the Genealogist." *National Genealogical Society Quarterly* 37 (December): 93-94.

Hone, E. Wade. *Land and Property Research in the United States.* Salt Lake City: Ancestry, 1997.

Meyerink, Kory L. *Printed Sources: A Guide to Published Genealogical Records.* Salt Lake City: Ancestry, 1998.

Szucs, Loretto Dennis, and Sandra Hargreaves Luebking. *The Archives: A Guide to the National Archives Field Branches.* Salt Lake City: Ancestry, 1998.

Tombstone and Monument Inscriptions

In an effort to preserve valuable historical information, volunteers from local and state genealogical and historical societies have journeyed through thousands of cemeteries, transcribing the inscriptions on weathered and deteriorating tombstones. These volunteers have provided a valuable service to family historians by saving names and vital and biographical information from periods predating the official registration of vital statistics. The work has taken on added importance in a time when history often loses out to progress and cemeteries are moved to make space for a new development. Completed transcriptions are often indexed and published as articles in society newsletters.

The Daughters of the American Revolution have donated the results of their cemetery transcriptions to selected libraries, including the DAR's national library in Washington, D.C. In addition to the collection of transcriptions from every state that was compiled by its own volunteers, the Family History Library has also microfilmed those of the DAR and has made them available through its Family History Centers™.

Figure 206

A monument in a cemetery in Las Cruces, New Mexico. (Photo courtesy of James Otto Bombach)

Records of cemetery gravestones in the form of card files can sometimes be found at historical societies, state and local archives, and libraries, as is the case of indexes created by a WPA study. To determine if a published cemetery inscription exists for a particular cemetery, consult the Family History Library's *Index to United States Cemeteries* (Salt Lake City: Family History Library, 1988). Available on microfilm through the Library and its centers, this listing of cemeteries, arranged by state and county, identifies transcription projects completed through 1985.

Researchers who aren't sure where an ancestor is buried can consult one of several cemetery directories available to find out which cemeteries were in the area of the individual's last residence. One such index is Deborah M. Burek, ed., *Cemeteries of the U.S.: A Guide to Contact Information for U.S. Cemeteries and Their Records* (Detroit: Gale Research, 1994). Once the burial site is located, the cemetery, if still in existence, can be contacted to request copies of burial records. For American veterans buried overseas, the American Battle Monuments Commission can provide information on the time of death, military unit, place of internment, and photographs of headstones. [American Battle Monuments Commission, Pulaski Building (Room 5119-5120), Twenty Massachusetts Avenue, NW, Washington, D.C. 20314-0300, (202) 475-1329].

Whenever possible, a visit should be made to the burial plot. Frequently, historians rely heavily on published cemetery records and correspondence from cemetery offices, thereby missing other important information that is found on the stone, for example relationship, birth and death dates, birth places, military service information, fraternal lodge or other organizational memberships, religious affiliation, and even photos affixed to the stone. Important clues can also be gleaned from other stones nearby, as family members were often buried in nearby plots.

See also *Cemetery Records*.

Selected Readings:

Burek, Deborah M., ed. *Cemeteries of the U.S.: A Guide to Contact Information for U.S. Cemeteries and Their Records*. Detroit: Gale Research, 1994.

Kot, Elizabeth G., and James D. Kot. *United States Cemetery Address Book: 1994-1995*. Vallejo, Calif.: Indices Publishing, 1994.

McKay, Douglas B., and Kory L. Meyerink. *American Genealogical Gazetteer*. CD-ROM. Salt Lake City: Ancestry.

Meyerink, Kory L. "Cemetery Inscriptions." *Printed Sources: A Guide to Published Genealogical Sources*. Salt Lake City: Ancestry, 1998, 244-50.

Stemmons, John "D," and E. Diane Stemmons, comps. *The Cemetery Record Compendium: Comprising a Directory of Cemetery Records and Where They May Be Located*. Logan, Utah: Everton Publishers, 1978.

Internet Sites of Interest:

Internment.net
Cemetery Records & Tombstone Inscriptions
http://www.interment.net/

USGenWeb
The Tombstone Transcription Project
http://www.rootsweb.com/~cemetery/

Commonwealth War Graves Commission
http://www.cwgc.org

Figure 207
Cemetery monuments can sometimes be the key to finding ethnic origins. A monument in a cemetery in Lansing, Illinois indicates that the deceased were born in the Netherlands.

Figure 208
A plot in Lafayette Cemetery, located in New Orleans, Louisiana, lists the names of several family members.

Urban Guides

A number of genealogical and historical guides for specific cities have been published over the past few years. Such guides are invaluable, especially to researchers looking for records in a distant city. Typically identified in the publications are the archives serving the metropolitan area, bureaus of vital records, city clerks' offices, civil, county, and federal courts, genealogical and historical societies, and libraries with genealogical holdings and special collections. Additional information may include addresses, phone numbers, and hours of operation for these and other sources. Historical events that affect the availability of records in the area are sometimes noted as well. Researchers may also find that the details pertaining to records maintained by public agencies may be helpful in other cities or counties.

Cities covered by urban guides include New York City, in Estelle Guzik, ed., *Genealogical Resources in the New York Metropolitan Area* (New York: Jewish Genealogical Society, 1989); Chicago, in Loretto Dennis Szucs, *Chicago and Cook County: A Guide to Research* (Salt Lake City: Ancestry, 1996); and Baltimore, in Robert W. Barnes, *Guide to Research in Baltimore City and County* (Westminster, Md.: Family Line Publications, 1989). Individuals unable to locate a guide for a specific city may find a statewide compilation to be helpful.

Selected Readings:

Bailey, Rosalie F. *Guide to Genealogical and Biographical Sources for New York City, 1783-1898*. New York: the author, 1954. Reprinted by New York Genealogical & Biographical Society, 1998.

Barnes, Robert W. *Guide to Research in Baltimore City and County*. Westminster, Md.: Family Line Publications, 1989.

Bell, Carol Willsey. *Ohio Guide to Genealogical Sources*. Baltimore: Genealogical Publishing Co., 1988.

Davis, Robert Scott, Jr. *Research in Georgia*. Easley, S.C.: Southern Historical Press, 1981.

Eichholz, Alice, ed. *Ancestry's Red Book: American State, County and Town Sources*. Rev. ed. Salt Lake City: Ancestry, 1992. (This multi-state reference covers all U.S. states and cities)

Guzik, Estelle, ed. *Genealogical Resources in the New York Metropolitan Area*. New York: Jewish Genealogical Society, 1989.

Hogan, Roseann Reinmuth. *Kentucky Ancestry: A Guide to Genealogical and Historical Research*. Salt Lake City: Ancestry, 1993.

Leary, Helen F.M., ed. *North Carolina Research: Genealogy and Local History*. Raleigh, N.C.: North Carolina Genealogical Society, 1996.

Steele, Edward E. *A Guide to Genealogical Research in St. Louis*. 2d ed. St. Louis, Mo.: St. Louis Genealogical Society, n.d.

Szucs, Loretto Dennis. *Chicago and Cook County: A Guide to Research*. Salt Lake City: Ancestry, 1996.

U.S. Government Documents and Publications

Millions of documents have been created by the United States Government Printing Office, and while these records were not created or preserved for the purpose of genealogical research, they can be rich sources of information. Just a few examples of the fascinating things that can be found in a government document depository are: the United States Serial Set (*see* U.S. Serial Set), the 130-volume set *War of the Rebellion: Official Records of the Union and Confederate Armies* containing detailed reports and eyewitness accounts to events that changed lives and the nation during the Civil War; army, navy and air force registers dating from 1789 to 1950; the *Historic Resource Study of the Jean Lafitte, Chalmette Unit/Louisiana* (129.58/3:J34) with a list of named slaves, including age and job description, conveyed in an 1805 sale of land to Jean Baptiste Prevost; *Inhabitants of the Parish of St. Mary, Louisiana, Praying Repeal of Tariff of 1846*; and from the Department of the Treasury, *Table Showing Arrivals of Alien Passengers and Immigrants in U.S. from 1820-1888 [by country, origin, sex, age, occupation, and customs district...]*.

There are congressionally designated government document repositories in college, university, and public libraries in every part of the country. *A Directory of U.S. Government Depository Libraries* (Washington, D.C.: Joint Committee on Printing, U.S. Government Printing Office, 1990) lists alphabetically by state, and then city, the addresses and telephone numbers of these official repositories. Not all will have exactly the same collections, but most will have the examples cited above and are arranged according to the Superintendent of Documents Classification System with a number preceded by a letter designating the department or agency that issued the document.

See also *American State Papers*.

Selected Readings:

A Directory of U.S. Government Depository Libraries. Washington, D.C.: Joint Committee on Printing, U.S. Government Printing Office, 1990.

Checklist of United States Public Documents, 1789-1909. Washington, D.C.: Government Printing Office, 1911. 3d ed. (Arranged by government agency, this publication provides a listing of documents that have been printed)

		Age
Jean-Baptiste	digger	17
(Fandango)	digger	35
(Douilha)	digger	25
Jupiter	builder	30
Sans Chargrin	builder	30
Fazau	blacksmith	40
Elie Toussaint		45
Francois		50
Lucie	mulatta	45
Polidon	laborer	40
Remy	foreman	45
Lubin		40
Banadarme	digger	35
Jean	digger	30
Antoine	digger	30
Ret ( )	blacksmith's aid	30
Lucielle		20
Cupidon	digger	30
Laurent	builder	30
Augustine	gardener	30

Figure 209

Slaves conveyed in an 1805 sale of land to Jean Baptiste Provost (P. Pedesclaux, June 12, 1805, NONA) from the Historic Resource Study of Jean Lafitte Chalmette Unit, National Historical Park and Preserve/Louisiana (I 29.58/3:J34).

U.S. Serial Set

The *United States Serial Set* is a collection of 14,000 volumes of bound government publications compiled under the direction of Congress. Documents in the set date from 1789 to 1969 and include detailed information on a wide variety of subjects. Congressional journals, reports on public and private legislation, commission investigations, federal agency reports, statistical reports, and selected special reports of non-governmental agencies are organized in rough chronological order. Information that can be found among this collection includes lists of names and addresses of individuals who have applied for patents and descriptions of the invention; lists of army and navy pensioners with their rank, residence, and amount of pension; individual claims for damages; lists of mail carriers; and annual reports on immigration, sometimes providing names and other personal details about passengers.

As with other government documents (*see* U.S. Government Documents), the U.S. Serial Set can be located in most government document repositories. The *CIS U.S. Serial Set Index*, a twelve-volume set in thirty-six parts, was created to facilitate use of the set and is usually available, along with *The User Handbook for the CIS Serial Set Index 1769-1969,* where the sets are located. A copy of the handbook can also be obtained through Congressional Information Service, Inc., 4520 East West Highway, Suite 800, Bethesda, MD 20814, (301) 654-1550.

See also *American State Papers*.

Selected Readings:

CIS U.S. Serial Set Index. 12 vols. Washington, D.C.: Congressional Information Service, 1975-79.

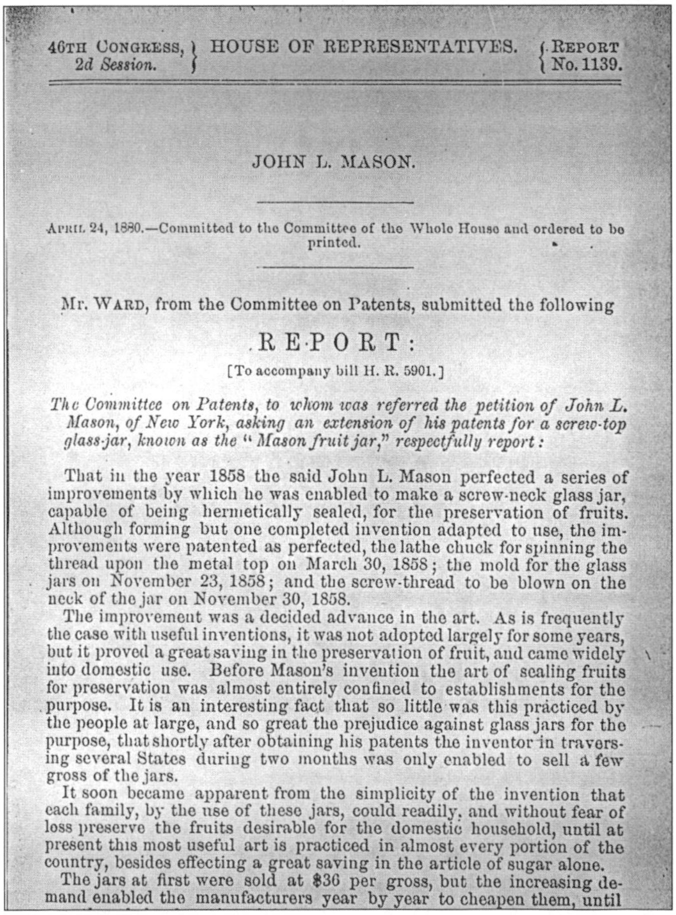

46TH CONGRESS, 2d Session. } HOUSE OF REPRESENTATIVES. { REPORT No. 1139.

JOHN L. MASON.

APRIL 24, 1880.—Committed to the Committee of the Whole House and ordered to be printed.

MR. WARD, from the Committee on Patents, submitted the following

REPORT:

[To accompany bill H. R. 5901.]

The Committee on Patents, to whom was referred the petition of John L. Mason, of New York, asking an extension of his patents for a screw-top glass-jar, known as the "Mason fruit jar," respectfully report:

That in the year 1858 the said John L. Mason perfected a series of improvements by which he was enabled to make a screw-neck glass jar, capable of being hermetically sealed, for the preservation of fruits. Although forming but one completed invention adapted to use, the improvements were patented as perfected, the lathe chuck for spinning the thread upon the metal top on March 30, 1858; the mold for the glass jars on November 23, 1858; and the screw-thread to be blown on the neck of the jar on November 30, 1858.

The improvement was a decided advance in the art. As is frequently the case with useful inventions, it was not adopted largely for some years, but it proved a great saving in the preservation of fruit, and came widely into domestic use. Before Mason's invention the art of sealing fruits for preservation was almost entirely confined to establishments for the purpose. It is an interesting fact that so little was this practiced by the people at large, and so great the prejudice against glass jars for the purpose, that shortly after obtaining his patents the inventor in traversing several States during two months was only enabled to sell a few gross of the jars.

It soon became apparent from the simplicity of the invention that each family, by the use of these jars, could readily, and without fear of loss preserve the fruits desirable for the domestic household, until at present this most useful art is practiced in almost every portion of the country, besides effecting a great saving in the article of sugar alone.

The jars at first were sold at $36 per gross, but the increasing demand enabled the manufacturers year by year to cheapen them, until

Figure 210
This petition of John L. Mason for extension of his patent on the screw-top glass jar (known as a Mason fruit jar) was found in the U.S. Serial Set Index for the 46th-50th Congresses (1879-1889).

Veterans' Schedules of the Census

In 1840, Revolutionary War pensioners were recorded on the reverse of each page of the 1840 population schedules. By government order, these names were published in a volume called *A Census of Pensioners for Revolutionary or Military Services* (1841, various years. Reprint. Baltimore: Genealogical Publishing Co., 1996). The names of some men who had received state or Congressional pensions were inadvertently included with the Revolutionary War veterans. The Genealogical Society of Utah indexed the volume in *A General Index to a Census of Pensioners...1840* (Baltimore: Genealogical Publishing Co., 1965). Both of these volumes are available in most libraries with genealogical collections.

In 1890, a special census of Union veterans and widows of veterans was taken. Each entry in the schedule shows the name of a Union veteran; the name of his widow, if appropriate; the veteran's rank, company, regiment, or vessel; dates of enlistment and discharge, and length of service in years, months, and days; post office address; nature of any disability; and remarks. In some areas, Confederate veterans were mistakenly listed as well.

The National Archives has the surviving 1890 schedules on microfilm, which include those for Washington, D.C., approximately half of Kentucky, and Louisiana, Maine, Maryland, Massachusetts, Michigan, Minnesota, Mississippi, Missouri, Montana, Nebraska, Nevada, New Hampshire, New Jersey, New Mexico, New York, North Carolina, North Dakota, Ohio, Oklahoma, Oregon, Pennsylvania, Rhode Island, South Carolina, South Dakota, Tennessee, Texas, Utah, Vermont, Virginia, Washington, West Virginia, Wisconsin, Wyoming, Indian territories, and U.S. ships and Navy yards. Schedules for other states were destroyed in the 1921 fire that also destroyed population schedules. Printed indexes are available for most of the 1890 census at the Family History Library and larger genealogical libraries.

It should also be mentioned that in 1911, a census of veterans of the Confederate army was taken. See *Selected Readings* for indexes available.

Ancestry.com has made AIS Indexes to these schedules for a number of states available at its Web site at <www.Ancestry.com>.

Selected Readings:

A Census of Pensioners for Revolutionary or Military Services. 1841, various years. Reprint. Baltimore: Genealogical Publishing Co., 1996.

Dilts, Bryan Lee. *1890 Maine Census Index of Civil War Veterans or Their Widows.* Salt Lake City: Index Publishing, 1984.

Dilts, G. David. "Censuses and Tax Lists." *Printed Sources: A Guide to Published Genealogical Records.* Chapter 9: 300-52. Salt Lake City: Ancestry, 1998.

_____. *1890 New York Census Index of Civil War Veterans or Their Widows.* Salt Lake City: Index Publishing, 1984.

_____. *1890 West Virginia Census Index of Civil War Veterans or Their Widows.* Salt Lake City: Index Publishing, 1986.

Jenks, Houston C. *An Index to the [Louisiana] Census of 1911 of Confederate Veterans or Their Widows.* [Baton Rouge, La.: Jenks], 1989.

McLane, Bobbie Jones. *An Index to the Three Volumes, Arkansas 1911 Census of Confederate Veterans.* Hot Springs, Ark.: Arkansas Ancestors, 1988.

Prechtel-Kluskens, Claire. "The 1890 Census." *The Record: News from the National Archives and Records Administration* 3 (4) (March 1997): 24-25.

Thurber, Evangeline. "The 1890 Census Records of the Veterans of the Union Army," *National Genealogical Society Quarterly* 34 (March 1946): 7-9.

U.S. Library of Congress. Census Library Project. *Special Schedules of the Eleventh Census (1890) Enumerating Union Veterans and Widows of Union Veterans of the Civil War.* National Archives Microfilm Publication M-123 (118 rolls).

Internet Sites of Interest:

Ancestry.com
http://www.ancestry.com

National Archives and Records Administration
http://www.nara.gov/publications/microfilm/census/census.html

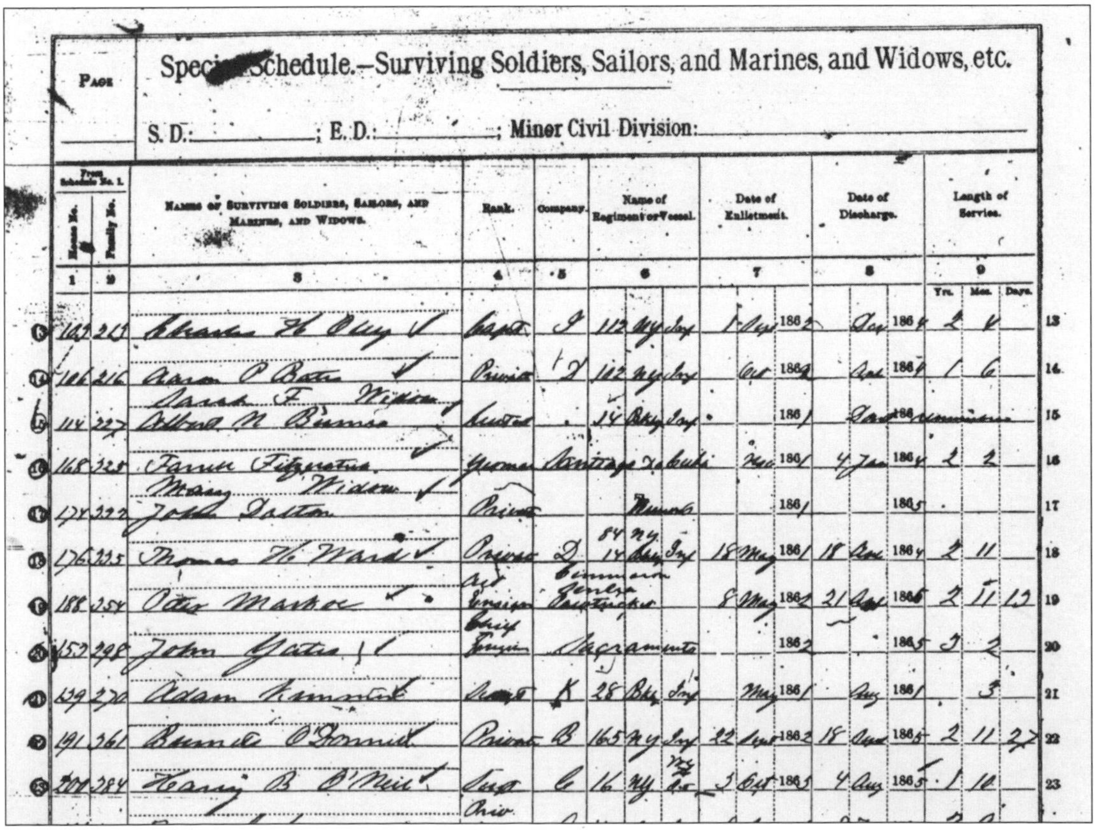

Figure 211
A page from an 1890 veterans schedule from Kings County, New York, showing names of surviving soldiers, sailors, and marines, and widows; rank; company; name of regiment or vessel; date of enlistment; date of discharge; length of service; street address; disability incurred; and remarks, if any.

Voter Registration Records

A number of cities and counties maintain voter registration records, which can provide valuable information about an ancestor. Usually included on the voter registration card is the individual's full name, address, birth date, birthplace, and, for naturalized citizens, the naturalization court and date. In some cases, the port, ship, and date of arrival may be listed.

Voter registration records can sometimes be located in county offices and state archives.

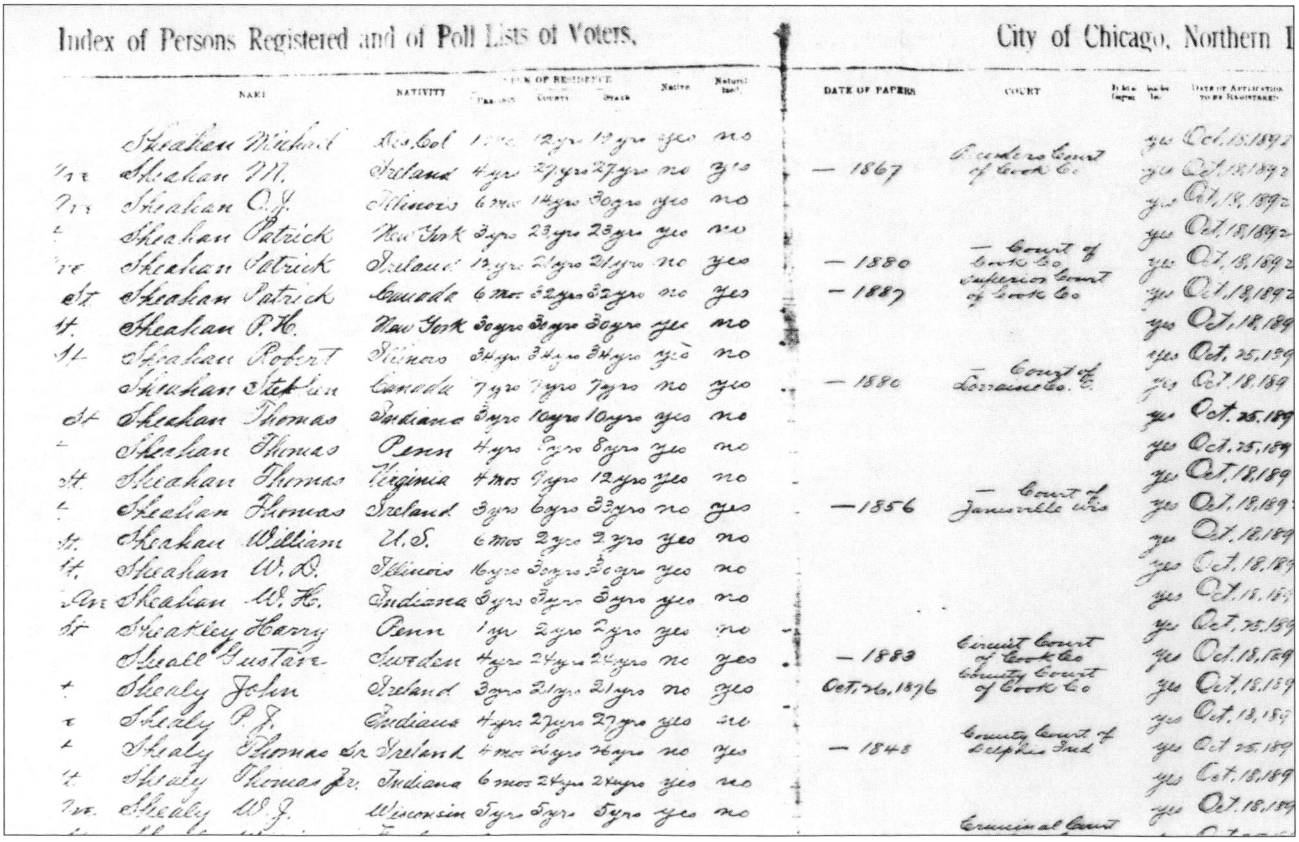

Index of Persons Registered and of Poll Lists of Voters. City of Chicago, Northern I

Name	Nativity	Precinct	County	State	Native	Natural'd	Date of Papers	Court		Date of Application to be Registered
Sheahan Michael	[illegible]	[illegible]	12 yrs	12 yrs	yes	no			yes	Oct. 18, 1892
Sheahan M.	Ireland	4 yrs	27 yrs	27 yrs	no	yes	— 1867	Recorder's Court of Cook Co.	yes	Oct. 18, 1892
Sheahan O. J.	Illinois	6 mos	14 yrs	30 yrs	yes	no			yes	Oct. 18, 1892
Sheahan Patrick	New York	3 yrs	23 yrs	23 yrs	yes	no			yes	Oct. 18, 1892
Sheahan Patrick	Ireland	13 yrs	21 yrs	21 yrs	no	yes	— 1880	— Court of Cook Co	yes	Oct. 18, 1892
Sheahan Patrick	Canada	6 mos	32 yrs	32 yrs	no	yes	— 1887	Superior Court of Cook Co	yes	Oct. 18, 1892
Sheahan P. H.	New York	30 yrs	30 yrs	30 yrs	yes	no			yes	Oct. 18, 189
Sheahan Robert	Illinois	34 yrs	34 yrs	34 yrs	yes	no			yes	Oct. 25, 189
Sheahan Stephen	Canada	7 yrs	7 yrs	7 yrs	no	yes	— 1880	— Court of Lorraine Co. O.	yes	Oct. 18, 189
Sheahan Thomas	Indiana	3 yrs	10 yrs	10 yrs	yes	no			yes	Oct. 25, 189
Sheahan Thomas	Penn	4 yrs	8 yrs	8 yrs	yes	no			yes	Oct. 25, 189
Sheahan Thomas	Virginia	4 mos	9 yrs	12 yrs	yes	no			yes	Oct. 18, 189
Sheahan Thomas	Ireland	3 yrs	6 yrs	33 yrs	no	yes	— 1856	— Court of Janesville Wis	yes	Oct. 18, 189
Sheahan William	U.S.	6 mos	2 yrs	2 yrs	yes	no			yes	Oct. 18, 189
Sheahan W. D.	Illinois	16 yrs	30 yrs	30 yrs	yes	no			yes	Oct. 18, 189
Sheahan W. H.	Indiana	3 yrs	3 yrs	3 yrs	yes	no			yes	Oct. 18, 189
Sheakley Harry	Penn	1 yr	2 yrs	2 yrs	yes	no			yes	Oct. 25, 189
Sheall Gustave	Sweden	4 yrs	24 yrs	24 yrs	no	yes	— 1883	Circuit Court of Cook Co	yes	Oct. 18, 189
Shealy John	Ireland	3 yrs	21 yrs	21 yrs	no	yes	Oct. 26, 1876	County Court of Cook Co	yes	Oct. 18, 189
Shealy P. J.	Indiana	4 yrs	27 yrs	27 yrs	yes	no			yes	Oct. 18, 189
Shealy Thomas Sr.	Ireland	4 mos	26 yrs	26 yrs	no	yes	— 1848	County Court of Delphi Ind	yes	Oct. 25, 189
Shealy Thomas Jr.	Indiana	6 mos	24 yrs	24 yrs	yes	no			yes	Oct. 18, 189
Shealy W. J.	Wisconsin	5 yrs	5 yrs	5 yrs	yes	no		Criminal Court	yes	Oct. 18, 189

Figure 212

An index of persons registered and of poll lists of voters from Chicago, Cook County, Illinois, listing voter's name; nativity; term of residence in precinct, county, and state; and date and court of naturalization.

Women's Collections

Tracing females in early American history can be difficult because of the change in surnames when they married and because many documents do not contain references to women, particularly married women. Documents related to the payment of taxes and the purchase of property were typically filed under the name of the male head of household and, with the exception of those residing in states that passed woman's suffrage before the ratification of the Nineteenth Amendment, women did not appear in voter registration records until 1920. Furthermore, prior to 1922, a woman's citizenship status was considered to be the same as that of her husband or father, and therefore was not required to apply for naturalization.

Figure 213

Portrait of Muriel Dyer, ca. 1922.

Records from women's schools and organizations are other potential sources. An invaluable guide to collections of these records is Andrea Hinding, ed., *Women's History Sources: A Guide to Archives and Manuscript Collections in the United States* (New York: R.R. Bowker Company, 1979). A couple of examples pulled from the more than 18,000 entries that are indexed and arranged alphabetically by state include: a collection of papers relating to women's educational institutions and to women as teachers at the Chicago Historical Society, containing records from the Chicago Board of Education, records of the Dearborn Seminary in Chicago for the period 1856 to 1899, and lists of teachers, pupils, and attendance from the Grant Collegiate Institute from 1869 to 1896; a collection at the Maine State Archives with correspondence to the Adjutant General's Department during the Civil War, including letters of application with biographical information from women seeking appointment as nurses; and a collection of materials, including membership records, from the Woman's Christian Temperance Union of Rhode Island, covering the years 1880 to 1960, at the Rhode Island Historical Society Library.

A significant source of information exists for widows of military veterans in the pension application files held by the National Archives. Filed under the name of the veteran on whose service the application is based, the record typically includes the widow's name, age, residence, maiden name, marriage date and place, husband's name, death date and place, his rank, military unit, period of service, residence, birthplace, and date of birth or age.

Selected Readings:

Carmack, Sharon DeBartolo. *A Genealogist's Guide to Discovering Your Female Ancestors*. Cincinnati: Betterway Books, 1998.

Goodfriend, Joyce D., comp. *The Published Diaries and Letters of American Women: An Annotated Bibliography*. Boston: G.K. Hall and Co., 1987.

Hinding, Andrea. *Women's History Sources: A Guide to Archives and Manuscripts Collections in the United States*. New York: R.R. Bowker, 1979.

Hogan, Roseann R. "Female Ancestry." *Ancestry* 12 (2) (March/April 1994): 26-28.

Purdy, Virginia C., and Robert Gruber. *American Women and the U.S. Armed Forces: A Guide to the Records of Military Agencies in the National Archives Relating to American Women*. Rev. ed. Washington, D.C.: National Archives Trust Fund Board, 1992.

Schulz, Constance B. "Daughters of Liberty: The History of Women in the Revolutionary War Pension Records." *Prologue* (Fall 1984): 140-53.

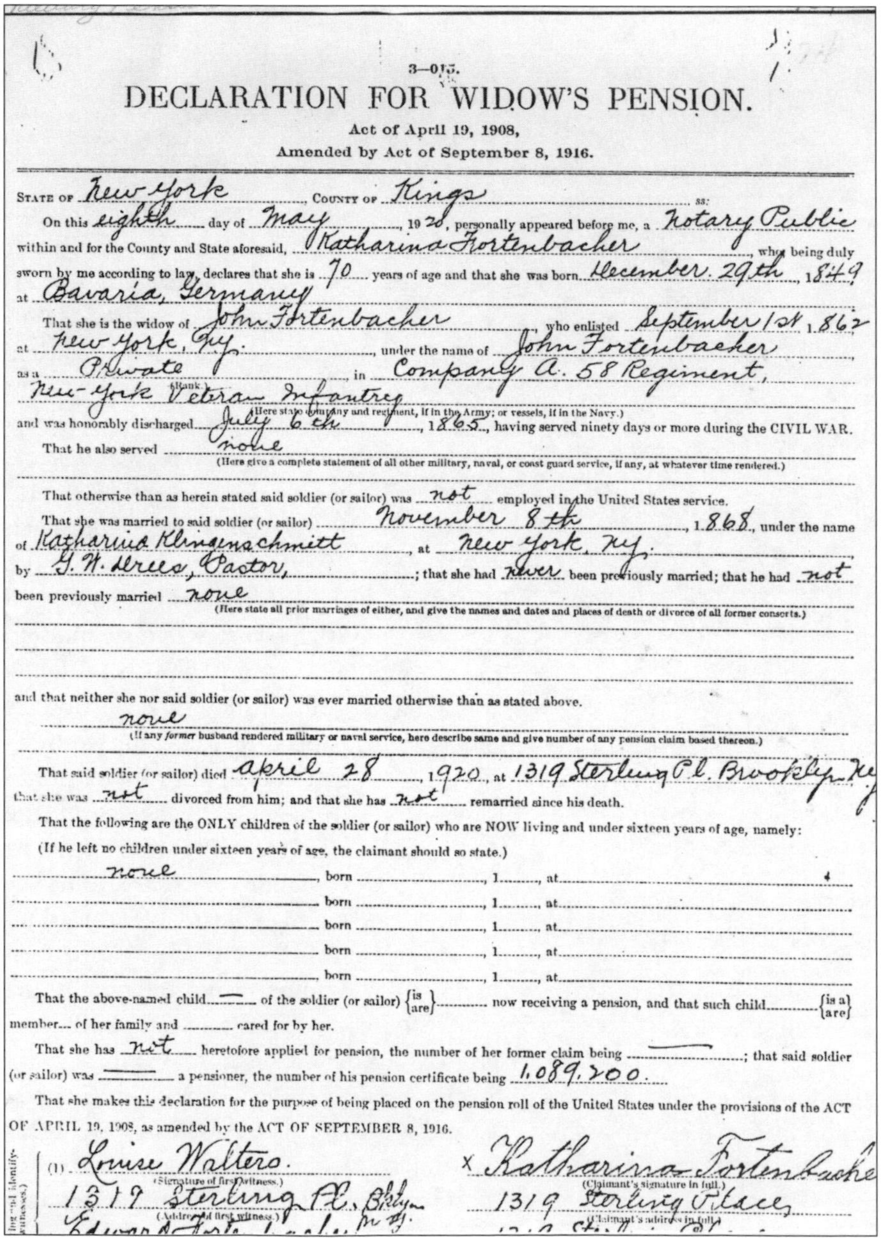

3—015.

DECLARATION FOR WIDOW'S PENSION.

Act of April 19, 1908,
Amended by Act of September 8, 1916.

STATE OF New York, COUNTY OF Kings ss:

On this eighth day of May, 1920, personally appeared before me, a Notary Public within and for the County and State aforesaid, Katharina Fortenbacher, who being duly sworn by me according to law, declares that she is 70 years of age and that she was born December 29th, 1849 at Bavaria, Germany.

That she is the widow of John Fortenbacher, who enlisted September 1st, 1862 at New York, Ny., under the name of John Fortenbacher, as a Private (Rank.) in Company A. 58 Regiment, New-York Veteran Infantry (Here state company and regiment, if in the Army; or vessels, if in the Navy.) and was honorably discharged July 6th, 1865, having served ninety days or more during the CIVIL WAR.

That he also served none (Here give a complete statement of all other military, naval, or coast guard service, if any, at whatever time rendered.)

That otherwise than as herein stated said soldier (or sailor) was not employed in the United States service.

That she was married to said soldier (or sailor) November 8th, 1868, under the name of Katharina Klingenschmitt, at New York, Ny. by G. W. Drees, Pastor; that she had never been previously married; that he had not been previously married none (Here state all prior marriages of either, and give the names and dates and places of death or divorce of all former consorts.)

and that neither she nor said soldier (or sailor) was ever married otherwise than as stated above.

none (If any former husband rendered military or naval service, here describe same and give number of any pension claim based thereon.)

That said soldier (or sailor) died April 28, 1920, at 1319 Sterling Pl. Brooklyn Ny

that she was not divorced from him; and that she has not remarried since his death.

That the following are the ONLY children of the soldier (or sailor) who are NOW living and under sixteen years of age, namely:

(If he left no children under sixteen years of age, the claimant should so state.)

none, born ......, 1...., at ......

......, born ......, 1...., at ......

......, born ......, 1...., at ......

......, born ......, 1...., at ......

......, born ......, 1...., at ......

That the above-named child — of the soldier (or sailor) {is / are} ...... now receiving a pension, and that such child ...... {is a / are} member... of her family and ...... cared for by her.

That she has not heretofore applied for pension, the number of her former claim being ——; that said soldier (or sailor) was —— a pensioner, the number of his pension certificate being 1,089,200.

That she makes this declaration for the purpose of being placed on the pension roll of the United States under the provisions of the ACT OF APRIL 19, 1908, as amended by the ACT OF SEPTEMBER 8, 1916.

(1) Louise Walters. (Signature of first witness.) x Katharina Fortenbacher (Claimant's signature in full.)

1319 Sterling Pl. Bklyn (Address of first witness.) 1319 Sterling Place, (Claimant's address in full.)

Figure 214

A declaration for widow's pension filed by Katharina Fortenbacher on 8 May 1920. (Courtesy of Linda Lamberty)

Internet Sites of Interest:

General Federation of Women's Clubs
http://www.gfwc.org/

National Women's History Project
http://www.nwhp.org/

Women's History and Resource Center
http://www.gfwc.org/whrc.htm

Works Progress Administration

The Works Progress Administration (WPA) was created to provide jobs for the millions of people left unemployed by the Depression. Established by executive order in 1935, it became the biggest relief program in U.S. history.

The Historical Records Survey Program represents the efforts undertaken by the WPA. The intent of the program was to organize historical materials, particularly the unpublished government documents and records that are basic in the administration of local government and which provide invaluable data for students of political, economic, and social history. Out of work historians, lawyers, teachers, researchers, and clerical workers prepared massive bibliographies, inventories, indexes, and other historical materials.

Useful WPA sources include the Soundex indexes to the 1880, 1900, 1910, and 1920 U.S. population censuses on microfilm at the National Archives, the Soundex indexes

NAME	ADDRESS		DATE OF DEATH MO. - DAY - YEAR			REGISTER NUMBER	
FLEMING TIMOTHY 5400 PRINCETON			9	20	27	35747	20
FLEMING TIMOTHY J 1718 N ROCKWELL			1	7	14	653	7
FLEMING ULARGAN 27 SANGER		E	1	28	77	175	3
FLEMING VALENTINE P 3230 OSGOOD			10	11	12	28087	5
FLEMING VERNE 4131 WABASH			8	19	17	25908	10
FLEMING VERONICA 1214 COTTAGE GROVE			8	21	10	21705	3
FLEMING VIOLA M 3589 PRAIRIE		J	4	26	82	21	28
FLEMING WALTER EUGENE 518T AND MORGAN		N 1	3	9	98	113	33
FLEMING WALTER S EVANSVILLE WIS		OT	12	10	19	760	11
FLEMING WARREN W 6645 YALE			7	8	13	19689	6
FLEMING WILBERT J 1733 ESTES			3	18	18	7603	11
FLEMING WILBUR F 1948 EVERGREEN			3	13	28	8074	21
FLEMING WILLARD 5001 STATE		HP	10	2	85	48	5
FLEMING WILLIAM MERCY HOSP		R 1	2	5	00	120	43
FLEMING WILLIAM 741 ESTES		Z 1	5	29	04	139	35
FLEMING WILLIAM 10409 HOXIE		1	11	4	04	137	5
FLEMING WILLIAM 1581 GRENSHAW		4	4	3	06	137	13
FLEMING WILLIAM PATROL WAGON			2	4	12	4843	5
FLEMING WILLIAM 492 LASALLE			8	4	14	22140	7
FLEMING WILLIAM DUNNING ILL		OT	3	1	18	1610	10
FLEMING WILLIAM U S GOVT OVERSEAS		OT	10	6	18	4459	10
FLEMING WILLIAM 2552 S WESTERN			12	30	23	33432	16
FLEMING WILLIAM 900 TOWNSEND			10	8	25	27800	18
FLEMING WILLIAM 3340 S MICHIGAN			4	22	26	12809	19
FLEMING WILLIAM 7637 CHAMPLAIN			4	23	28	13317	21
FLEMING WILLIAM RIVER GROVE ILL			12	3	32	32813	25
FLEMING WILLIAM A 3702 PRAIRIE		I	10	24	81	160	10
FLEMING WILLIAM B 311 S RACINE			12	30	26	34359	19
FLEMING WILLIAM B 5015 WILSON			1	28	33	2635	26
FLEMING WILLIAM E MADISON AND CARPENTER		1	10	30	04	126	22
FLEMING WILLIAM E 3708 LOWE			6	1	16	16376	9

Figure 215
A portion of a WPA Chicago death index covering 1871-1933. This record was found on microfilm at the Family History Library.

to naturalization petitions available through the National Archives and through the Family History Library, a compilation of church records for many areas in the United States, and the indexing of vital and court records in various parts of the country. The WPA created cemetery listings and indexes and newspaper indexes as well.

Internet Sites of Interest:

American Life Histories—Manuscripts from the Federal Writers' Project, 1936-1940
http://rs6.loc.gov/ammem/wpaquery.html

Cass County, Indiana WPA Birth, Marriage and Death Records, 1882-1920
U.S. GenWeb Project
http://www.rootsweb.com/~incass/county.html

Florida WPA Inventories
http://www.rootsweb.com/~flsgs/fhswpa.htm

Illinois State Archives
Illinois Historical Records Survey of the Works Progress Administration
http://www.sos.state.il.us/depts/archives/di/954__002.htm

Indiana WPA Vital Records Microfilm Index - Tri-State Genealogical Society
http://www.rootsweb.com/~intsgs/wpa.html

NARA: RG69 - Records of the Works Projects Administration
gopher://gopher.nara.gov:70/00/inform/guide/10s/rg069.txt

Pioneer Biography Files
State Historical Society of North Dakota
http://www.state.nd.us/hist/infwpa.htm

Tennessee State Library and Archives Records
http://www.state.tn.us/sos/statelib/techsvs/rglistd/rg107.htm

The Works Progress Administration Index to Texas Naturalizations, Texas State District and County Courts, 1846-1939
http://sparc.hpl.lib.tx.us/hpl/tx005.html

American Slave Narratives: An Online Anthology
http://xroads.virginia.edu/~hyper/wpa/wpahome.html

```
Roman Catholic Church                                    Entries 409-425


409.     MOST HOLY REDEEMER, 1844--.        417.     HOLY CROSS, 1852--.
             165 E. 3d St.                               331 W. 42d St.
Baptisms 1844--, 11 vols.                    Baptisms 1852--, 7 vols.
Marriages 1844--, 6 vols.                    Marriages 1852--, 5 vols.
Deaths 1887--, 2 vols.                       Deaths 1932--, 1 vol.

410.     ST. FRANCIS OF ASSISI, 1844---.    418.     ST. ANN'S, 1852--.
             135 W. 31st St.                             112 E. 12th St.
Baptisms 1844-90, 5 vols.                    Baptisms 1852--, 4 vols.
Marriages 1844--, 5 vols.                    Marriages 1852--, 3 vols.
Baptisms, marriages, 1864--, 7 vols.
                                             419.     ANNUNCIATION, 1853--.
411.     ST. COLUMBA'S, 1845--.                          131st St. and Convent Ave.
             331 W. 25th St.                 Baptisms 1853--, 7 vols.
Baptisms 1845--, 9 vols.                     Marriages 1853--, 5 vols.
Marriages 1846--, 5 vols.                    Deaths 1853--, 3 vols.
Deaths 1928--, 1 vol.
                                             420.     IMMACULATE CONCEPTION, 1855--.
412.     ST. ALPHONSUS', 1847--.                         505 E. 14th St.
             312 W. Broadway                 Baptisms 1855--, 7 vols.
Baptisms 1847--, 14 vols.                    Marriages 1855--, 2 vols.
Marriages 1848--, 5 vols.
```

Figure 216

This WPA survey of church records for New York City, New York is available in many major libraries.

HIDDEN SOURCES

Family History in Unlikely Places

Appendixes

National Archives and Records Administration

National Archives and Records Administration (NARA)
Archives I
8th & Pennsylvania Avenues
Washington, DC 20408
Tel: 202-501-5410 (Genealogical Staff)
    202-501-5400 (Record Availability)
Fax: 301-713-6905 (Fax-on-Demand Information)
E-mail: inquire@arch1.nara.gov
URL: http://www.nara.gov/nara/dc/Archives1_info.html

National Archives and Records Administration (NARA)
Archives II
8601 Adelphi Road
College Park, MD 20740
Tel: 202-501-5400 (Record Availability)
    301-713-6800 (General Reference)
    301-713-7040 (Cartographic Reference)
Fax: 301-713-6905 (Fax-on-Demand Information)
E-mail: inquire@arch2.nara.gov
URL: http://www.nara.gov/nara/dc/
Archives1_info.html

NATIONAL RECORDS CENTERS

National Personnel Records Centers, NARA
http://www.nara.gov/nara/frc/nprc.html

Civilian Records Facility
111 Winnebago Street
St. Louis, MO 63118-4199
Tel: 314-425-5761

Fax: 314-425-5719
E-mail: center@cpr.nara.gov
URL: http://www.nara.gov/nara/frc/cpr.html

Military Records Facility
9700 Page Avenue
St. Louis, MO 63132-5100
Recorded Information Lines
314-538-4243 Air Force
314-538-4261 Army
314-538-4141 Navy/Marine/Coast Guard
Fax: 314-538-4175
E-mail: center@stlouis.nara.gov
URL: http://www.nara.gov/nara/frc/mpr.html

Pittsfield Federal Records Center, NARA
100 Dan Fox Drive
Pittsfield, MA 01201-8230
Tel: 413-445-6885
Fax: 413-445-7305
E-mail: center@pittsfield.nara.gov
URL: http://www.nara.gov/nara/frc/1ncloc.html

Washington National Records Center, NARA
Shipping Address:
4205 Suitland Road
Suitland, MD 20746-2042
Mailing Address:
4205 Suitland Road
Washington, DC 20409-0002
Tel: 301-457-7000
Fax: 301-457-7117
E-mail: center@suitland.nara.gov
URL: http://www.nara.gov/nara/frc/ncwbloc.html

REGIONAL ARCHIVES

National Archives – Alaska Region
654 W. 3rd Avenue
Anchorage, AK 99501-2145
Tel: 907-271-2441
Fax: 907-271-2442
E-mail: archives@alaska.nara.gov
URL: http://www.nara.gov/nara/regional/
11nsgil.html
(Alaska)

National Archives – Central Plains Region
2312 East Bannister Road
Kansas City, MO 64131
Tel: 816-926-6272
Fax: 816-926-6982
E-mail: archives@kansascity.nara.gov
URL: http://www.nara.gov/nara/regional/
06nsgil.html
(Iowa, Kansas, Minnesota, Missouri, Nebraska,
North Dakota, and South Dakota)

National Archives – Great Lakes Region
7358 Pulaski Road
Chicago, IL 60629
Tel: 773-581-7816
Fax: 312-353-1294
E-mail: archives@chicago.nara.gov
URL: http://www.nara.gov/nara/regional/05nsgil.htm
(Illinois, Indiana, Michigan, Minnesota, Ohio, and
Wisconsin)

National Archives – Mid-Atlantic Region
Ninth and Market Streets
Philadelphia, PA 19107
Tel: 215-597-3000
Fax: 215-597-2303
E-mail: archives@philarch.nara.gov
URL: http://www.nara.gov/nara/regional/
03nsgil.html
(Delaware, Maryland, Pennsylvania, Virginia,
and West Virginia)

National Archives – New England Region
380 Trapelo Road
Waltham, MA 02154-8104
Tel: 617-647-8100
Fax: 617-647-8460
E-mail: archives@waltham.nara.gov

URL: http://www.nara.gov/nara/regional/
01nsbgil.html
(Connecticut, Maine, Massachusetts, New
Hampshire, Rhode Island, and Vermont)

National Archives – Northeast Region
201 Varick Street
New York, NY 10014
Tel: 212-337-1300
Fax: 212-337-1306
E-mail: archives@newyork.nara.gov
URL: http://www.nara.gov/nara/regional/
02nsgil.html
(New Jersey, New York, Puerto Rico, and
U.S. Virgin Islands)

National Archives – Pacific Northwest Region
6125 Sand Point Way, NE
Seattle, WA 98115
Tel: 206-526-6507
Fax: 206-526-4344
E-mail: archives@seattle.nara.gov
URL: http://www.nara.gov/nara/regional/
10nsgil.html
(Idaho, Oregon, and Washington)

National Archives – Pacific Sierra Region
1000 Commodore Drive
San Bruno, CA 94066
Tel: 415-876-9009
Fax: 415-876-9233
E-mail: archives@sanbruno.nara.gov
URL: http://www.nara.gov/nara/regional/
09nssgil.html
(Northern California, Hawaii, Nevada—except Clark
County, Guam, American Samoa, and the Trust
Territory of the Pacific Islands)

National Archives – Pacific Southwest Region
24000 Avila Rd., First Floor-East Entrance
P.O. Box 6719
Laguna Niguel, CA 92607-6719
Tel: 714-360-2641
Fax: 714-360-2644
E-mail: archives@laguna.nara.gov
URL: http://www.nara.gov/nara/regional/
09nslgil.html
(Arizona, Southern California, and
Clark County, NV)

National Archives – Rocky Mountain Region
Denver Federal Center, Building 48
P.O. Box 25307
Denver, CO 80225-0307
Tel: 303-236-0817
Fax: 303-236-9354
E-mail: archives@denver.nara.gov
URL: http://www.nara.gov/nara/regional/
08nsgil.html
(Colorado, Montana, New Mexico, North Dakota,
South Dakota, Utah, and Wyoming)

National Archives – Southeast Region
1557 St. Joseph Avenue
East Point, GA 30344-2593
Tel: 404-763-7477
Fax: 404-763-7033
E-mail: archives@atlanta.nara.gov
URL: http://www.nara.gov/nara/regional/
04nsgil.html
(Alabama, Florida, Georgia, Kentucky, Mississippi,
North Carolina, South Carolina, and Tennessee)

National Archives – Southwest Region
501 W. Felix Street, Building 1
P.O. Box 6216
Fort Worth, TX 76115-0216
Tel: 817-334-5525
Fax: 817-334-5621
E-mail: archives@ftworth.nara.gov
URL: http://www.nara.gov/nara/regional/
07nsgil.html
(Arkansas, Oklahoma, Louisiana, and Texas)

HELPFUL NARA WEB SITES

American Indians
http://www.nara.gov/publications/microfilm/
amerindians/indians.html

Black Studies
http://www.nara.gov/publications/microfilm/
blackstudies/blackstd.html

Census Records
http://www.nara.gov/publications/microfilm/
census.html

**Federal Court Records —A Select Catalog of
NARA Microfilm Publ.**
http://www.nara.gov/publications/microfilm/
courts/fedcourt.html

Genealogical and Biographical Research
http://www.nara.gov/publications/microfilm/
biographical/genbio.html

Genealogical Searchable Database—NAIL
http://www.nara.gov/nara/nail/nailgen.html

Genealogy Page
http://www.nara.gov/genealogy/genindex.html

Immigrant and Passenger Arrivals
http://www.nara.gov/publications/microfilm/
immigrant/immpass.html

Microfilm Resources for Research
http://www.nara.gov/publications/microfilm/
comprehensive/compcat.html

Military Service Records
http://www.nara.gov/publications/microfilm/military/
service.html

Naturalization Records
http://www.nara.gov/genealogy/natural.html

Post Office Records
http://www.nara.gov/genealogy/postal.html

State Archives

This list was compiled by Linda S. McCleary, MLS Public Library Development Consultant, Library Extension Division, Department of Library, Archives and Public Records Phoenix, Arizona. For additional information regarding the full holdings and unique collections within each archive division, contact the state you are researching.

Alabama Department of Archives and History
624 Washington Ave.
Montgomery, AL 36130
(205) 242-4441
Fax: (205) 240-3433

**Alaska State Archives
and Records Management Services**
141 Willoughby Ave.
Juneau, AK 99802-1720
(907) 465-2275
Fax: (907) 465-2465

Arizona State Archives
Department of Library, Archives, and Public Records
1700 W. Washington St.
Phoenix, AZ 85007
(602) 542-4159
Fax: (602) 542-4402

Arkansas History Commission
One Capitol Mall
Little Rock, AR 72201
(501) 682-6900

California State Archives
201 N. Sunrise Ave.
Sacramento, CA 95561
(916) 773-3000
Fax: (916) 773-8249

Colorado Department of Administration
Division of State Archives and Public Records
1313 Sherman St., I-B20
Denver, CO 80203
(303) 866-2055
Fax: (303) 866-2257

Connecticut State Archives
Connecticut State Library
231 Capitol Ave.
Hartford, CT 06106
(203) 566-5650
Fax: (203) 566-2133

**Delaware Bureau of Archives
and Records Management**
Hall of Records
Dover, DE 19901
(302) 739-5318
Fax: (302) 739-6711

Florida State Archives
R. A. Gray Building (M.S. 9A)
Tallahassee, FL 32399-0250
(904) 487-2073
Fax: (904) 488-4894

Georgia Department of Archives and History
Box RPM
330 Capitol Ave., S.E.
Atlanta, GA 30334
(404) 656-5486
Fax: (404) 656-2940

Hawaii State Archives
Iolani Palace Grounds
Honolulu, Hawaii 96813
(808) 586-0310
Fax: (808) 586-0330

Idaho Library and Archives
210 Main St.
Boise, ID 83702
(208) 334-3890
Fax: (208) 334-3198

Illinois State Archives
Archives Building
Springfield, IL 62756
(217) 782-4682
Fax (217) 524-3930

Indiana State Archives
Commission on Public Records
State Office Bldg., Rm. W472
Indianapolis, IN 46204-2215
(317) 232-3373
Fax: (317) 232-3154

State Archives of Iowa
State Historical Society of Iowa
Capitol Complex
600 E. Locust
Des Moines, IA 50319
(515) 281-8837
Fax: (515) 282-0502

Kansas State Historical Society
120 W. Tenth St.
Topeka, KS 66612-1291
(913) 296-3251
Fax: (913) 296-1005

Kentucky Dept. for Lib/Arch.
Public Records Division
Archives Research Room
P.O. Box 537

Frankfort, KY 40602-0537
(502) 875-7000 Ext. 173
Fax: (502) 564-5773

State of Louisiana
Secretary of State
Division of Archives, Records Management,
and History
P.O. Box 94125
Baton Rouge, LA 70804-9125
(504) 922-1206
Fax: (504) 925-4726

Maine State Archives
Capitol—Station House 84
Augusta, ME 04333-0084
(207) 289-5790
Fax: (207) 289-8598

Maryland State Archives
350 Rowe Blvd.
Annapolis, MD 21401
(301) 974-3915

Massachusetts Archives
Office of Secretary of State
Boston, MA 02125
(617) 727-2816
Fax: (617) 727-2826

Michigan State History Bureau
State Archives
Lansing, MI 48906
(517) 373-1401
Fax: (517) 373-0851

Minnesota Historical Society
345 Kellogg Blvd. W.
St. Paul, MN 55102-1906
(612) 297-4502
Fax: (612) 296-9961

Mississippi Department of Archives and History
100 S. State St.
Jackson, MS 39205-0571
(601) 359-6850
Fax: (601) 359-6905

Missouri State Archives
600 W. Main St.

Jefferson City, MO 65102
(314) 751-4717

Montana Historical Society
Division of Library and Archives
225 N. Roberts St.
Helena, MT 59620
(406) 444-4775
Fax: (406) 444-2696

Nebraska State Historical Society
1500 R St.
Box 82554
Lincoln, NE 68501
(402) 471-4785
Fax: (402) 471-3100

Nevada State Library and Archives
100 Stewart Street
Carson City, NV 89710
(702) 687-5210

New Hampshire State Archives
71 S. Fruit St.
Concord, NH 03301-2410
(603) 271-2236
Fax: (603) 271-2272

New Jersey State Archives
CN 307, 2300 Stuyvesant Ave.
Trenton, NJ 08625
(609) 530-3203
Fax: (609) 530-6121

New Mexico Commission of Public Records
New Mexico Records and Archives
404 Montezuma Ave.
Santa Fe, NM 87503
(505) 827-7332
Fax: (505) 827-7331

New York State Archives
State Education Department
Albany, NY 12230
(518) 474-1195

North Carolina State Archives
Department of Cultural Resource
109 E. Jones St.
Raleigh, NC 27601-2807

(919) 733-7305
Fax: (919) 733-5679

North Dakota State Archives and Historical Research Library
612 E. Blvd. Ave.
Bismarck, ND 58505-0830
(701) 224-2668
Fax: (701) 224-3000

Ohio Historical Society
Archives/Library Division
1982 Velma Ave.
Columbus, OH 43211-2497
(614) 297-2510
Fax: (614) 297-2411

Oklahoma Department of Libraries
200 North East Eighteenth St.
Oklahoma City, OK 73105-3298
(405) 521-2502
WATS 1-800-522-8116
Fax: (405) 525-7804

Oregon Secretary of State
Archives Division
800 Summer N.E.
Salem, OR 97310
(503) 373-0701
Fax: (503) 373-0659

Pennsylvania State Archives
P.O. Box 1026
Harrisburg, PA 17108-1026
(717) 787-2891

Rhode Island State Archives
337 Westminister St.
Providence, RI 02903-3302
(401) 277-2353
Fax: (401) 277-3199

South Carolina Department of Archives and History
1430 Senate St.
Columbia, SC 29211
(803) 734-8577
Fax: (803) 734-8820

South Dakota Historical Society/State Archives
900 Governors Dr.
Pierre, SD 57501-2217
(605) 773-3458
Fax: (605) 773-6041

Tennessee State Library and Archives
403 Seventh Ave. N.
Nashville, TN 37219-1411
(615) 741-7996
Fax: (615) 741-6471

Texas State Archives Division
Lorenzo de Zavala State Archives
and Library Building
P.O. Box 12927
Austin, TX 78711-2927
(512) 463-5480
Fax: (512) 463-5436

Utah State Archives and Records Service
Archives Building, State Capitol
Salt Lake City, UT 84114
(801) 538-3012
Fax: (801) 538-3354

State of Vermont Archives
Secretary of State's Office
26 Terrace Street
Montpelier, VT 05633-1103
(802) 828-2369
Fax: (802) 828-2496

Commonwealth of Virginia
Virginia State Library and Archives
11th St. at Capitol Square
Richmond, VA 23219-3491
(804) 786-2332
Fax: (804) 786-5855

Washington Secretary of State Office
Division of Archives and Records Management
1120 Wash St., S.E.
P.O. Box 40238
Olympia, WA 98504-0238
(206) 753-5485
Fax: (206) 586-5629

West Virginia Archives
Division on Culture and History
1900 Kanawha Blvd. E.
Charleston, WV 25305-0300
(304) 558-0230
Fax: (304) 558-2779

The State Historical Society of Wisconsin
816 State St.
Madison, WI 53706-1488
(608) 264-6480
Fax: (608) 264-6472
Wyoming Archives

Parks and Cultural Resources Division
Barrett Building
Cheyenne, WY 82002
(307) 777-7013
Fax: (307) 777-6289

Historical Societies

Alabama Historical Association
P.O. Box 2877
Tuscaloosa, AL 35486

Alaska Historical Library and Museum
P.O. Box G
Eighth Floor, State Office Building
Juneau, AK 99811
Phone: (907) 465-2925

Alaska Historical Society
524 W. Fourth Ave., Suite 208
Anchorage, AK 99501

Arizona Historical Society
Century House Museum
240 Madison Ave.
Yuma, AZ 85364
Phone: (602) 782-1841

Arkansas Historical Association
History Department
Ozark Hall, 12, University of Arkansas
Fayetteville, AR 72701
Phone: (501) 575-5884

Arkansas Historical Society
422 S. Sixth St.
Van Buren, AR 72956

Arkansas History Commission
1 Capitol Mall
Little Rock, AR 72201
Phone: (501) 682-6900

California Historical Society
2090 Jackson St.
San Francisco, CA 94109

Colorado Historical Society
Stephen H. Hart Library
1300 Broadway
Denver, CO 80203
Phone: (303) 866-2305

Connecticut Historical Commission
59 S. Prospect St.
Hartford, CT 06106

Connecticut Historical Society
1 Elizabeth St. at Asylum Ave.
Hartford, CT 06105
Phone: (203) 236-5621

Connecticut League of Historical Societies
P.O. Box 906
Darien, CT 06820

Historical Society of Delaware
Town Hall
505 Market St.
Wilmington, DE 19801
Phone: (302) 655-7161

Florida Historical Society
P.O. Box 3645, University Station
Gainesville, FL 32601

Georgia Historical Society
501 Whittaker St.
Savannah, GA 31499
Phone: (912) 651-2128

Hawaiian Historical Society
560 Kawaiahao St.
Honolulu, HI 96813
Phone: (808) 537-6271

Idaho Historical Society
610 N. Julia Davis Dr.
Boise, ID 83706
Phone: (208) 384-2120
        (208) 334-3356

Illinois State Historical Library
Old State Capitol
Springfield, IL 62701
Phone: (217) 782-4836

Indiana Historical Society
State Library and Historical Building
Family History Section
315 W. Ohio St.
P.O. Box 88255
Indianapolis, IN 46202
Phone: (317) 232-1879

State Historical Society of Iowa
Headquarters
Centennial Building
402 Iowa Avenue
Iowa City, IA 52240
Phone: (319) 335-3916

State Historical Society of Iowa
Museum
State of Iowa Historical Building
600 E. Locust
Des Moines, IA 50319
Phone: (515) 281-5111

Kansas State Historical Society
Archives Division
Memorial Building
120 W. Tenth St.
Topeka, KS 66612
Phone: (913) 296-4776
        (913) 296-3251

Kentucky Historical Society
300 Broadway
Old Capitol Annex
P.O. Box H
Frankfort, KY 40602
Phone: (502) 564-3016

Louisiana Genealogical and Historical Society
P.O. Box 3454
Baton Rouge, LA 70821
Phone: (504) 343-2608

Maine Historical Society
485 Congress St.
Portland, ME 04111
Phone: (207) 774-1822

Maryland Historical Society
201 W. Monument St.
Baltimore, MD 21201
Phone: (301) 685-3750, ext. 359

Massachusetts Historical Society
1154 Boylston St.
Boston, MA 02215
Phone: (617) 536-1608

Historical Society of Michigan
2117 Washtenaw Ave.
Ann Arbor, MI 48104

Michigan Historical Commission
505 State Office Building
Lansing, MI 48913

Minnesota Historical Society
690 Cedar St.
Saint Paul, MN 55101
Phone: (612) 296-2143

Historical and Genealogical Association of Mississippi
618 Avalon Rd.
Jackson, MS 39206

Missouri Historical Society
Research Library and Archives
Jefferson Memorial Building Forest Park
Saint Louis, MO 63112-1099
Phone: (314) 361-1424

State Historical Society of Missouri
1020 Lowry St.
Columbia, MO 65201
Phone: (314) 882-7083

Nebraska State Historical Society
State Archives Division
1500 R St.
P.O. Box 82554
Lincoln, NE 68501
Phone: (402) 471-4771
          (402) 471-4751

Nebraska State Historical Society Room
Chadron State College
Chadron State Library
Chadron, NE 69337

Nevada State Historical Society
1650 N. Virginia St.
Reno, NV 89503
Phone: (702) 789-0190

Nevada State Museum and Historical Society
700 Twin Lakes Dr.
Las Vegas, NV 89107
Phone: (702) 486-5205

Association of Historical Societies of New Hampshire
Maple St.
Plaistow, NH 03865

New Hampshire Historical Society
30 Park St.
Concord, NH 03301
Phone: (603) 225-3381

New Jersey Historical Society
230 Broadway
Newark, NJ 07104
Phone: (201) 483-3939

Historical Society of New Mexico
P.O. Box 4638
Santa Fe, NM 87501

History Library Museum of New Mexico
Palace of the Governors
Santa Fe, NM 87501

The New York Historical Society
170 Central Park W.
New York, NY 10024-5194
Phone: (212) 873-3400

North Carolina Society of County and Local Historians
1209 Hill St.
Greensboro, NC 27408

State Historical Society of North Dakota
State Archives and Historical Research Library
Heritage Center
612 E. Blvd. Ave.
Bismarck, ND 58505
Phone: (701) 224-2668—Division Office
          (701) 224-2091—Reference Desk

Ohio Historical Society
Archives-Library Division
Interstate Route 71 and 17th Ave./1985 Velma Ave.
Columbus, OH 43211
Phone: (614) 297-2510
          (614) 297-2300

Oklahoma Historical Society
Library Resources Division
Wiley Post Historical Building
2100 N. Lincoln Blvd.
Oklahoma City, OK 73105
Phone: (405) 521-2491

Oregon Historical Society
1230 S.W. Park Ave.
Portland, OR 97268
Phone: (503) 222-1741

Heritage Society of Pennsylvania
P.O. Box 146
Laughlintown, PA 15655

Historical Society of Pennsylvania
1300 Locust St.
Philadelphia, PA 19107
Phone: (215) 545-0391

Rhode Island State Historical Society
121 Hope St.
Providence, RI 02909
Phone: (401) 331-8575

South Carolina Historical Society
100 Meeting St.
Charleston, SC 29401
Phone: (803) 723-3225

South Dakota State Historical Society
South Dakota Archives
Cultural Heritage Center
900 Governors Dr.
Pierre, SD 57501
Phone: (605) 773-3804

Tennessee Historical Society
Ground Floor
War Memorial Building
300 Capital Blvd.
Nashville, TN 37243-0084
Phone: (615) 242-1796

Tennessee Historical Commission
Conservation Department
701 Broadway
Nashville, TN 37203
Phone: (615) 742-6717

Texas State Historical Association
2.306 SRH, University Station
Austin, TX 78712

Utah State Historical Society
300 Rio Grande
Salt Lake City, UT 84101
Phone: (801) 533-5808

Virginia Historical Society
428 N. Blvd.
P.O. Box 7311
Richmond, VA 23211
Phone: (804) 342-9677

Washington State Historical Society
Hewitt Library
State Historical Building
315 N. Stadium Way
Tacoma, WA 98403
Phone: (206) 593-2830

West Virginia Historical Society
Division of Archives and History
Department of Culture and History
Science and Cultural Center
Capitol Complex
Charleston, WV 25305
Phone: (304) 348-2277
        (304) 348-0230

The State Historical Society of Wisconsin
816 State St.
Madison, WI 53706
Phone: (608) 262-9590—Reference Librarian
        (608) 262-3338—Reference Archivist

Wyoming State Archives
Barrett Building
2301 Central Ave.
Cheyenne, WY 82002
Phone: (307) 777-7826

The Family History Library
and Its Centers

compiled by Kory L. Meyerink

The Family History Library is the largest library in the world specializing in collecting genealogical or family history material. Sometimes called the "mecca" of genealogy, the Family History Library attracts many family historians who plan trips and vacation time to come to Salt Lake City, Utah, to use the worldwide collections housed in the library's five-story building.

Because of the scope of the library's collections, as well as the easy access provided by its thousands of branch libraries, it is useful for every family historian to know about the library. Its history dates back to 1894, when the Genealogical Society of Utah was founded to gather and preserve the various records that help people trace their ancestry. Shortly after its founding, the society opened a library, which later became the Family History Library. In 1938, the society began preserving records on microfilm. Today, about 250 microfilm camera operators microfilm birth, marriage, death, probate, immigration, military, and many other records in more than fifty countries. Through this microfilming activity, as well as a carefully planned purchasing program, the library has acquired the world's largest collection of genealogical information.

Since 1944, the library (as well as the Genealogical Society of Utah) has been wholly owned and operated by The Church of Jesus Christ of Latter-day Saints. Also known as the LDS church or "Mormon" church, it teaches its members to "seek out their kindred dead" in preparation for the afterlife. However, while the library is maintained as a resource to LDS church members, all persons, regardless of race, creed, or religion, are welcome to visit the library and use its collections and services at no charge. In 1964, a system of branch libraries, now called Family History Centers™, was established to

give more people access to the library's resources. These are described further below.

The Family History Library is located at 35 N. West Temple St., Salt Lake City, UT 84150 (phone: 801-240-2331). The library is open Tuesday through Saturday from 7:30 a.m. until 10:00 p.m. and on Mondays from 7:30 a.m. until 6:00 p.m. It is closed on the following holidays each year: New Year's Day, Independence Day, Pioneer Day (a state holiday on or near 24 July), Thanksgiving, Christmas Eve, and Christmas.

MICROFORM COLLECTIONS

The heart of the library's collection is approximately 2 million rolls of microfilmed records (equal to more than 6 million written volumes) and more than 500,000 microfiche. The collection includes records kept by governments, churches of many denominations, other organizations, and individuals. These records include copies of church registers, census records, passenger lists, military records, land records, and probate records. Most of the records date from about 1550 to about 1920. Various "rights of privacy" regulations mean that the library has few records of living persons. Also, the library does not have a record of everyone who has ever lived. However, the library does have a substantial collection of records for many areas of the world, particularly countries from which North Americans have ancestors.

North America

The library's largest collection covers the United States. More than half a million microfilm rolls represent every state. At least 100,000 of those rolls are federal records (including census, military, and immigration records). These records come from more than 2,300 archives, county courthouses, and other repositories, particularly from the states east of the Mississippi River. With at least 35,000 rolls for Canada, almost all Quebec church records and many civil records from Ontario and other provinces are included.

British Areas

The more than 155,000 rolls for Great Britain include a comprehensive collection of Scottish records, as well as a very large collection of records from England. The library also has significant collections for Ireland and Wales, with many records also available for Australia and New Zealand.

Europe

With more than half a million rolls of microfilm, the European microfilms form the second-largest collection at the library. They include church and civil records for many areas of Germany and France (more than 100,000 rolls each). Virtually all major genealogical records are available for the Netherlands (90,000 rolls), Belgium (66,000 rolls), Hungary (12,000 rolls), and Luxembourg. The fastest growth in the European collection is for the countries of Italy, Poland, Portugal, Spain, and Switzerland.

Scandinavia

The library's collection of more than 200,000 microfilms for Denmark (95,000 rolls), Sweden (79,000 rolls), Norway (12,000 rolls), and Finland (15,000 rolls) provides virtually comprehensive coverage for these countries.

Latin America

Most church parish records are included in the collections for Mexico (140,000 rolls), Chile (8,000 rolls), and Uruguay. Another 50,000 rolls provide growing, but still incomplete coverage for the other Latin countries, most notably Argentina, Brazil, and Guatemala (each with at least 8,000 rolls).

Other Areas

Other countries for which the library has comprehensive collections include the Philippines (51,000 rolls),

Sri Lanka, many Pacific islands, and many smaller countries. There are partial collections for South Africa and many other countries. The library has a growing collection of family histories for China, Japan, and Korea.

BOOK AND OTHER COLLECTIONS

The library also has more than a quarter of a million volumes of books, including published family histories, local histories, indexes, periodicals, and other research aids. More than half of this collection is also available on microfilm or microfiche. Many thousands of the library's microfilms are reproductions of books that are not available (as books) at the library. Often these are obscure books not easily found in other libraries and which may have been out of print for decades.

The library also has a very useful collection of maps to help place ancestors in geographic perspective and to aid the research process. Several hundred manuscript pedigrees represent the research of previous family historians. Microfilm copies of most of these are also available.

The library's Automated Resource Center houses electronic materials the library has collected and also provides access to the major online services, such as CompuServe and America Online. The collection of compact discs represents virtually every title available that pertains to local or family history.

FamilySearch®

FamilySearch is a computerized collection of genealogical information created by The Church of Jesus Christ of Latter-day Saints. It is available throughout the library. The collection uses compact disc technology to store and retrieve massive amounts of genealogical data. However, it is not available through modem or Internet use (as of 1996). FamilySearch is described in chapter 2, *Databases, Indexes, and Other Finding Aids*. The following files and programs are part of FamilySearch:

- Ancestral File™
- Family History Library Catalog™
- International Genealogical Index™
- U.S. Social Security Death Index

- U.S. Military Index
- Scottish Church Records
- TempleReady™
- Personal Ancestral File®

FAMILY HISTORY LIBRARY CATALOG™

The *Family History Library Catalog™* lists and describes each of the microfilms, microfiche, books, compact discs, manuscripts, and all other records in the library. It is the key to understanding the growing collection of the library and to having success in your research. Each year almost 100 million new pages of historical documents are preserved and cataloged (about 50,000 rolls). The catalog is available on compact disc and on microfiche, both of which are updated, usually annually. Individuals or institutions may purchase the microfiche version of the catalog, or portions of it. With the catalog, researchers can find records by author, title, subject, locality, or surname. The compact disc version of the catalog allows searches by microfilm or microfiche number or by computer number, but not by author, title, or subject (as of 1996).

LIBRARY SERVICES

Guided tours of the Family History Library are not provided. However, library volunteers provide a short orientation for persons new to the library. Orientation classes can be provided for groups of fifteen to sixty people. Contact the library in advance so that the staff will be prepared to meet the group's needs.

The library staff does not do research for patrons. However, they will help all library users to understand how to use the facilities. The staff is very friendly and will answer brief reference questions, help locate a town, or determine what records are available for a specific locality. The staff will answer questions received by mail, telephone, fax, e-mail (fhl@byu.edu), and online services (CompuServe, America Online, etc.).

The library has "open stacks" so that patrons can retrieve and use virtually any of the materials personally. Copies of most of the microfilms are immediately available in the library and can be used at any of the more than seven hundred microfilm readers and dozens of microfiche readers. Patrons can photocopy selected portions of books, microfilms, and microfiche inexpensively. Copy machines are available on each floor.

The library also holds classes on the use of the library, its collections, and its computer systems, as well as basic research procedures. Classes are often repeated every week or month. Contact the library for a copy of the current month's schedule. Most of the library's microfilms and microfiche can be lent for use at one of the Family History Centers. There is a small postage and duplication fee, and this service can only be requested in person at a local Family History Center. (See below.)

PREPARING TO VISIT THE LIBRARY

Family historians are more successful when they visit the library if they are prepared to effectively use its resources. To do this, gather all the background information you can beforehand, and familiarize yourself with the records you will need to access in your research. Where possible, visit a local family history center before you visit the library. Also note that, while most of the microfilms you will want to use are kept at the library, some are housed in a different location. If you are planning to use recent (new) films, films of obscure sources, or films for countries outside western Europe and Great Britain, contact the library to check on film availability or write the library at least two weeks in advance and request the films you need.

The library has records from many governments, churches, and organizations. Most documents are written in the language of the country where they were made. While you may not need to know the foreign language to use the records, it would be useful to learn a few key words. Most original records are handwritten and in chronological order. Also, they are not indexed, so allow plenty of time at the library to search these records carefully.

You may want to read more about the library when preparing for a visit. A thorough treatment of the library's collection, including a description of many major reference sources for each country or state, is Johni Cerny and Wendy Elliott, *The Library: A Guide to the LDS Family History Library* (Salt Lake City: Ancestry, 1988). For a more recent and more brief guide see Carlyle Parker, *Going to Salt Lake City to Do Family History Research*, 2nd ed. (Turlock, Calif.: Marietta Publishing Co., 1993).

If you wish to share your family information with the library and its patrons while preserving it for future generations, contact the Acquisitions Unit on the third floor of the library for more information (telephone: 801-240-2337).

FAMILY HISTORY CENTERS™

The Family History Library currently supports more than 2,500 "branch libraries," called Family History Centers, throughout the world. As branches of the Family History Library, they can provide access to almost all of the microfilm and microfiche maintained at the main library. Because of the LDS church's interest in genealogical research, these centers have been provided as a way for their members and the entire public to use the resources of the Family History Library (at no charge) without having to travel to Salt Lake City.

Family History Centers have been established in most LDS stakes. (A stake is a group of six to twelve "wards," or congregations.) Through them, microfilm and microfiche copies of the records at the Family History Library can be borrowed for a small handling fee. The books at the main library do not circulate, but more than half of them are available on microfilm. Many published sources are under copyright, and in most such cases the Family History Library cannot microfilm them.

Family History Centers are found in LDS Church buildings throughout the United States and in dozens of foreign countries, generally in or near large population centers. Areas of greater LDS population, such as the western United States, have more family history centers. Usually these centers are about the size of a classroom, and they are equipped with microfilm and microfiche reading machines, computers with the FamilySearch® program, a copy of the Family History Library Catalog™, and other major sources, such as Ancestral File™, the International Genealogy Index, and the Accelerated Indexing System's census indexes. The staff are all volunteers with varying experience in genealogical research. Nonetheless, you will generally find them to be quite helpful. In these centers, patrons can use the library resources and request copies of sources not immediately available.

While most centers have a small collection of general reference books, centers do not collect records of the area where they are located. However, because of the size of the Family History Library's collection and the fact that many of the sources are public domain documents and books, most sources that the researcher is seeking are available on microfilm or microfiche and can be sent to any center. Most films are only kept at the centers for a short period of time while patrons use them for their immediate research.

Do not be concerned that these centers are sponsored by a church. Proselyting is not allowed in Family History Centers. Furthermore, studies have shown that, on average, more than half of their patrons are not members of the LDS Church. For more information on family history centers, see pages 2-3 of *The Library* (cited earlier).

Some of the older, larger Family History Centers have collected several thousand books and hundreds of rolls of microfilm. Some of these "regional" libraries are in or near the cities of San Diego, Los Angeles, Oakland, Sacramento, Phoenix, Provo and Logan, Utah, Las Vegas, Calgary (Alberta), and Pocatello and Rexburg, Idaho.

The following list identifies the cities in each state and Canadian province where major Family History Centers can be found. This list does not include smaller centers, most of which are open for very few hours, do not have the staff to serve public patrons, and usually do not have microfilm circulation available. When using this list to locate centers near large cities, such as Chicago or Boston, look for surrounding suburban towns. To locate the center in one of the towns listed below, contact a local congregation of The Church of Jesus Christ of Latter-day Saints (see the white pages of a telephone directory) or a local genealogical society. In addition, a list of Family History Centers in your state can be obtained from the Family History Library.

UNITED STATES

Alabama

Anniston, Birmingham, Cullman, Decatur, Dothan, Eufaula, Florence, Huntsville, Mobile, Montgomery, Tuscaloosa

Alaska

Anchorage, Bethell, Fairbanks, Juneau, Ketchikan, Sitka, Soldotna, Wasilla

Arizona

Benson, Buckeye, Casa Grande, Cottonwood, Duncan, Eagar, Flagstaff, Globe, Holbrook, Kingman, Mesa, Nogales, Page, Payson, Peoria, Phoenix (7), Prescott, Safford, Scottsdale, Show Low, Sierra Vista, Snowflake, St. Johns, Sun City, Tucson (2), Willcox, Winslow, Yuma

Arkansas

Fort Smith, Hot Springs, Jacksonville, Little Rock, Rogers, Russelville, Springdale

California

Northern California: Anderson, Chico, Eureka, Gridley, Miranda, Mt. Shasta, Quincy, Redding, Susanville, Ukiah, Vacaville, Weaverville, Yuba City, Bay Area, Antioch, Concord, Fairfield, Fremont (2), Los Altos, Menlo Park, Napa, Oakland, Pacifica, San Bruno, San Jose (2), Santa Clara, Santa Cruz, Santa Rosa, Central California, Auburn, Clovis (2), Fresno (2), Hanford, Manteca, Merced, Modesto (2), Placerville, Sacramento (2), Seaside, Sonora, Stockton, Sutter Creek, Turlock, Visalia, Woodland

Los Angeles County: Burbank, Canoga Park, Carson, Cerritos, Chatsworth, Covina (Spanish), Glendale, Hacienda Heights, Huntington Park, La Crescenta, Lancaster (2), Los Alamitos, Los Angeles, Monterey Park (Spanish), Northridge, Norwalk, Palmdale, Pasadena, Rancho Palos Verdes, Torrance, Valencia, Whittier

Southern California (outside Los Angeles County): Anaheim, Bakersfield (3), Barstow, Blythe, Buena Park, Camarillo, Carlsbad, Chino, Corona, El Cajon, El Centro, Escondido (2), Fontana, Hemet, Huntington Beach, Lake Elsinore, Lompoc, Mission Viejo, Moreno Valley, Needles, Newbury Park, North Edwards, Orange, Palm Desert, Redlands, Ridgecrest, Riverside (3), San Bernardino, San Diego (3), San Luis Obispo, Santa Barbara, Santa Maria, Simi Valley, Thousand Oaks, Upland, Ventura, Victorville, Vista, Westminster

Colorado

Alamosa, Arvada, Aurora, Colorado Springs, Cortez, Craig, Denver, Durango, Fort Collins, Frisco, Grand Junction, Greeley, La Jara, Lakewood, Littleton (2), Longmont, Louisville, Montrose, Northglenn, Paonia, Pueblo, Sterling

Connecticut

Bloomfield, Madison, Mystic, New Canaan, Woodbridge

Delaware

Dover, Wilmington

District of Columbia

(See Maryland)

Florida

Arcadia, Belle Glade, Boca Raton, Bradenton, Ft. Myers, Gainsville, Homestead, Jacksonville, Key West, Lake City, Lake Mary, Largo, Lecanto, Miami, New Port Richey, Orange Park, Orlando, Palm Beach Gardens, Palm City, Panama City, Pensacola, Plantation, Port Charlotte, Rockledge, Tallahassee, Tampa, Winter Haven

Georgia

Albany, Brunswick, Columbus, Douglas, Evans, Jonesboro, Macon, Marietta, Powder Springs, Rome, Roswell, Savannah, Suwanee, Tucker

Hawaii

Hilo, Hawaii; Kailua-Kona, Hawaii; Lihue, Kauai; Kahului, Maui; Honolulu, Oahu (2); Kaneohe, Oahu; Laie, Oahu; Mililani, Oahu; Waipahu, Oahu

Idaho

Arimo, Basalt, Blackfoot (2), Boise (3), Burley, Caldwell, Coeur D'Alene, Driggs, Eagle, Emmett, Grangeville, Hailey, Idaho Falls (3), Lewiston, McCammon, Malad, Montpelier, Moore, Moscow, Mountain Home, Nampa, Pocatello, Preston, Rexburg, Rigby (2), Salmon, Sandpoint, Shelley, Soda Springs, Terreton, Twin Falls, Weiser

Illinois

Buffalo Grove, Champaign, Chicago Heights, Naperville, Nauvoo, O'Fallon, Peoria, Rockford, Schaumburg, Wilmette

Indiana

Bloomington, Columbus, Evansville, Fort Wayne, Indianapolis, Kokomo, Muncie, New Albany, Noblesville, South Bend, Terre Haute, West Lafayette

Iowa

Ames, Cedar Falls, Cedar Rapids, Davenport, Mason City, Sioux City, West Des Moines

Kansas

Dodge City, Emporia, Hutchinson, Olathe, Salina, Topeka, Wichita

Kentucky

Corbin, Hopkinsville, Lexington, Louisville, Martin, Morgantown, Owingsville, Paducah

Louisiana

Alexandria, Baton Rouge, Denham Springs, Monroe, Metairie, Shreveport, Slidell

Maine

Bangor, Cape Elizabeth, Caribou, Farmingdale

Maryland

Annapolis, Ellicott City, Frederick, Germantown, Kensington, Lutherville, Suitland

Massachusetts

Foxboro, Weston, Worcester

Michigan

Ann Arbor, Bloomfield Hills, East Lansing, Escanaba, Grand Blanc, Grand Rapids, Harvey, Hastings, Kalamazoo, Ludington, Midland, Muskegon, Traverse City, Westland

Minnesota

Bemidji, Brooklyn Park, Duluth, Minneapolis, Rochester, St. Paul

Mississippi

Booneville, Clinton, Columbus, Gulfport, Hattiesburg

Missouri

Cape Girardeau, Columbia, Farmington, Frontenac, Hazelwood, Independence, Joplin, Kansas City, Liberty, Springfield, St. Joseph

Montana

Billings (2), Bozeman, Butte, Glasgow, Glendive, Great Falls (2), Havre, Helena, Kalispell, Lewiston, Missoula, Stevensville

Nebraska

Gordon, Grand Island, Lincoln, Omaha, Papillion

Nevada

Ely, Elko, Fallon, Henderson, Las Vegas, Logandale, Mesquite, Reno, Tonapah, Winnemucca

New Hampshire

Concord, Nashua, Portsmouth

New Jersey

Cherry Hill, East Brunswick, Morristown, North Caldwell, Short Hills

New Mexico

Alamogordo, Albuquerque (3), Carlsbad, Clovis, Farmington, Gallup, Grants, Las Cruces, Los Alamos, Roswell, Santa Fe, Silver City

New York

Brooklyn, Elmhurst (Spanish), Ithaca, Jamestown, Lake Placid, Liverpool, Loudonville, New York City, Pittsford, Plainview, Rochester, Scarsdale, Vestal, Williamsville, Yorktown

North Carolina

Chapel Hill, Charlotte (2), Durham, Fayetteville, Goldsboro, Greensboro, Hickory, Kinston, Raleigh, Skyland, Wilmington, Winston-Salem

North Dakota

Bismarck, Fargo, Grand Forks, Minot

Ohio

Cincinnati (2), Dayton, Dublin, Fairborn, Kirtland, Perrysburg, Reynoldsburg, Tallmadge, Westlake, Wintersville

Oklahoma

Ardmore, Enid, Lawton, Muskogee, Norman, Oklahoma City (2), Stillwater, Tulsa (2), Woodward

Oregon

Baker City, Beaverton, Bend, Brookings, Central Point, Corvallis, Eugene, Grants Pass, Gresham, Hermiston, Hillsboro, John Day, Klamath Falls, La Grande, Lake Oswego, Lebanon, McMinnville, Medford, Milwaukie, Newport, Northbend, Nyssa, Ontario, Oregon City, Portland (2), Prineville, Roseburg, Scio, St. Helens, Salem (2), Sandy, The Dalles, Tualatin

Pennsylvania

Broomall, Clarks Summit, Erie, Johnstown, Kane, Lancaster, Meridian, Philadelphia, Pittsburgh, Reading, State College, York

Rhode Island

Warwick

South Carolina

Charleston, Columbia, Florence, Greer

South Dakota

Gettysburg, Pierre, Rapid City, Rosebud, Sioux Falls

Tennessee

Bartlett, Chattanooga, Cordova, Franklin, Kingsport, Knoxville, Madison, McMinnville

Texas

Abilene, Amarillo, Austin (2), Bay City, Bryan, Conroe, Coppell, Corpus Christi, Dallas, Denton, Duncanville, El Paso (2), Fort Worth (2), Friendswood, Gilmer, Harlingen, Houston (2), Katy, Kileen, Kingwood,

Longview, Lubbock, McAllen, Midland, Odessa, Orange, Pasadena, Plano, Port Arthur, San Antonio (2), Spring, Sugarland, The Colony, Tyler, Victoria, Wichita Falls

Utah (except Davis, Salt Lake, and Utah counties)

Altamont, Beaver, Blanding, Brigham City, Castle Dale, Cedar City, Delta, Duchesne, Enterprise, Escalante, Eureka, Ferron, Fillmore, Goshen, Helper, Huntington, Hurricane, Hyrum, Kanab, Laketown, Loa, Logan (2), Manti, Marion, Midway, Moab, Monticello, Morgan, Moroni, Mt. Pleasant, Nephi, Ogden, Panguitch, Park City, Parowan, Price, Richfield, Roosevelt, St. George, Tooele, Tremonton, Tropic, Vernal, Wellington, Wendover

Davis County: Bountiful, Farmington (3), Kaysville (2), Layton, Syracuse

Salt Lake County: Bluffdale, Draper, Kearns (3), Magna (2), Midvale, Murray (4), Salt Lake City (13), Sandy (9), South Jordan, West Jordan (3), West Valley City (6)

Utah County: American Fork (2), Lehi, Lindon, Mapleton, Orem (5), Payson, Pleasant Grove (2), Provo (8), Santaquin, Spanish Fork, Springville

Vermont

Berlin

Virginia

Alexandria, Annandale, Bassett, Centreville, Charlottesville, Chesapeake, Dale City, Falls Church, Fredericksburg, Hamilton, Harrisonburg, Midlothian, Newport News, Oakton, Pembroke, Richmond, Salem, Virginia Beach, Waynesboro, Winchester

Washington

Auburn, Bellevue, Bellingham, Bremerton (2), Centralia, Chehalis, Colville, Ellensburg, Elma, Ephrata, Everett, Federal Way, Kirkland, Lake Stevens, Longview, Moses Lake, Mountlake Terrace, Mount Vernon, North Bend, Olympia, Omak, Othello, Port Angeles, Puyallup, Quincy, Richland, Seattle (2), Spokane (4), Sumner, Tacoma, Vancouver (3), Walla Walla, Wenatchee, Yakima

West Virginia

Charleston, Fairmont, Huntington

Wisconsin

Appleton, Eau Claire, Hales Corner, Kenosha, Madison, Shawano, Wausau

Wyoming

Afton, Casper, Cheyenne, Cody, Diamondville, Evanston, Gillette, Green River, Jackson Hole, Laramie, Lovell, Lyman, Rawlins, Riverton, Rock Springs, Sheridan, Worland

CANADA

Alberta

Calgary, Cardston, Edmonton, Fort Macleod, Grande Prairie, Lethbridge, Magrath, Medicine Hat, Raymond, Red Deer, Taber

British Columbia

Burnaby, Courtenay, Cranbrook, Fort St. John, Kamloops, Kelowna, Prince George, Surrey, Terrace, Vernon, Victoria

Manitoba

Brandon, Winnipeg

New Brunswick

St. John

Newfoundland

St. John's

Nova Scotia

Dartmouth

Ontario

Brampton, Chatham, Etobicoke, Fort Frances, Glenburnie, Hamilton, Kitchener, London, Oshawa, Ottawa, Sarnia, Sault St. Marie, St. Thomas, Thunder Bay, Timmins, Windsor

Quebec

La Salle, Montreal (French)

Saskatchewan

Regina, Saskatoon

Genealogical Societies

compiled by Carol Yocom

The following is a sampling of the hundreds of national, state, regional, and ethnic genealogical societies and umbrella organizations in the United States. For a more comprehensive and current listing, see Mary K. Meyer, *Directory of Genealogical Societies in the USA and Canada*, 10th ed. (Maryland: the compiler, 1994), and *Federation of Genealogical Societies 1996 Membership Directory* (Richardson, Tex.: Federation of Genealogical Societies, 1996).

NATIONAL SOCIETIES

Afro-American Historical and Genealogical Society
P.O. Box 73086
Washington, DC 20056-3086

American-Canadian Genealogical Society
P.O. Box 668
Manchester, NH 03105

American Family Records Association (AFRA)
P.O. Box 15505
Kansas City, MO 64106

American-French Genealogical Society
P.O. Box 2113
Pawtucket, RI 02861

Association of Jewish Genealogical Societies
1485 Teaneck Rd.
Teaneck, NJ 07666

The Belgian Researchers, Inc.
62073 Fruitdale Lane
La Grande, OR 97850

Czechoslovak Genealogical Society
P.O. Box 16225
St. Paul, MN 55116-0225

Federation of Genealogical Societies
P.O. Box 830220
Richardson, TX 75083-0220

German Genealogical Society of America
P.O. Box 291818
Los Angeles, CA 90029

Hispanic Genealogical Society
P.O. Box 810561
Houston, TX 77281-0561

International Genealogy Fellowship of Rotarians
c/o Charles D. Townsend
5721 Antietam Dr.
Sarasota, FL 34231

Irish Genealogical Society
P.O. Box 16585
St. Paul, MN 55116-0585

Irish Family History Forum
P.O. Box 351
Rockville Centre, NY 11571

Italian Genealogy Group
7 Grayson Dr.
Dix Hills, NY 11746

Jewish Genealogical Society, Inc.
P.O. Box 6398
New York, NY 10128

National Genealogical Society
4527 Seventeenth St. N.
Arlington, VA 22207-2399

National Society, Daughters of the American Revolution
Library
1776 D St. N.W.
Washington, DC 20006

New England Historic Genealogical Society
101 Newbury St.
Boston, MA 02116

Northwest Territory Canadian and French Heritage Center
P.O. Box 29397
Brooklyn Center, MN 55429

Orphan Train Heritage Society of America
4912 Trout Farm Rd.
Springdale, AR 72764

Palatines To America
Capital University, Box 101G4
Columbus, OH 43209-1294

POINT [Pursuing Our Italian Names Together]
P.O. Box 2977
Palos Verdes, CA 90274

Polish Genealogical Society of Michigan
Burton Collection
Detroit Public Library
5201 Woodward Ave.
Detroit, MI 48202

Polish Genealogical Society
984 N. Milwaukee Ave.
Chicago, IL 60622

Puerto Rican Hispanic Genealogical Society
25 Ralph Ave.
Brentwood, NY 11717-2424

Scandinavian-American Genealogical Society
P.O. Box 16069
St. Paul, MN 55116-0069

TIARA [The Irish Ancestral Research Association]
P.O. Box 619
Sudbury, MA 01776

ALABAMA
Alabama Genealogical Society
Samford University Library
Box 2296
800 Lakeshore Dr.
Birmingham, AL 35229

Natchez Trace Genealogical Society
P.O. Box 420
Florence, AL 35631-0420

Tuscaloosa Genealogical Society
1439 Forty-Ninth Ave.
East Tuscaloosa, AL 35404

ALASKA
Alaska Genealogical Society
7030 Dickerson Dr.
Anchorage, AK 99504

ARIZONA
Arizona Genealogical Advisory Board
P.O. Box 5641
Mesa, AZ 85211
Arizona State Genealogical Society
P.O. Box 42075
Tucson, AZ 85733

ARKANSAS
Arkansas Genealogical Society
P.O. Box 908
Hot Springs, AR 71902-0908

CALIFORNIA
California Genealogical Society
P.O. Box 77105
San Francisco, CA 94107-0105

California State Genealogical Alliance
c/o Wendy Elliott
4808 E. Garland St.
Anaheim, CA 92807

Conejo Valley Genealogical Society
P.O. Box 1228
Thousand Oaks, CA 91358

Contra Costa Genealogical Society
P.O. Box 910
Concord, CA 94522

Los Angeles Westside Genealogical Society
P.O. Box 10447
Marina del Rey, CA 90295

San Diego Genealogical Society
1050 Pioneer Way
Suite E
El Cajon, CA 92020-1943

Questing Heirs GenSoc, Inc.
P.O. Box 15102
Long Beach, CA 90815-0102

COLORADO
Colorado Genealogical Society
P.O. Box 9218
Denver, CO 80209
Colorado Council of Genealogical Societies
P.O. Box 24379
Denver, CO 80224-0379
The council can provide a list of all genealogical societies in the state if a self-addressed stamped envelope is included with the request.

Columbine Genealogical Society
P.O. Box 2074
Littleton, CO 80161

CONNECTICUT
Connecticut Society of Genealogists
P.O. Box 435
Glastonbury, CT 06033

The Connecticut Ancestry Society
P.O. Box 249
Stamford, CT 06940-0249

DELAWARE
Delaware Genealogical Society
505 Market St. Mall
Wilmington, DE 19801-3091

FLORIDA
Central Florida Genealogical Society
P.O. Box 177
Orlando, FL 32802-0177

Florida Genealogical Society, Inc.
P.O. Box 18624
Tampa, FL 33679-8624

Florida State Genealogical Society
P.O. Box 10249
Tallahassee, FL 32302-2249

Genealogical Society of North Brevard
P.O. Box 897
Titusville, FL 32781

GEORGIA
Georgia Genealogical Society
P.O. Box 54575
Atlanta, GA 30308-0575

HAWAII
Hawaii County Genealogical Society
P.O. Box 831
Keaau, HI 96749

The Sandwich Islands Genealogical Society
Hawaii State Library
478 S. King St.
Honolulu, HI 96813

IDAHO
Idaho Genealogical Society
4620 Overland Rd. No. 204
Boise, ID 83705-2867

ILLINOIS
Chicago Genealogical Society
P.O. Box 1160
Chicago, IL 60690

**Fulton County Historical
and Genealogical Society**
45 N. Park Dr.
Canton, Il 61520-1126

Illinois State Genealogical Society
P.O. Box 10195
Springfield, IL 62791

**Jacksonville Area Genealogical
and Historical Society**
P.O. Box 21
Jacksonville, IL 62651-0021

McLean County Genealogical Society
P.O. Box 488
Normal, IL 61761-0488

Madison County Genealogical Society
P.O. Box 631
Edwardsville, IL 62025

**South Suburban Genealogical
and Historical Society**
P.O. Box 96
South Holland, IL 60473

Genealogical Society of Southern Illinois
John A. Logan College
Route 2 Box 145
Carterville, IL 62918

INDIANA

Allen County Genealogical Society
P.O. Box 12003
Fort Wayne, IN 46862

Indiana Genealogical Society, Inc.
P.O. Box 10507
Fort Wayne, IN 46852-0507

Southern Indiana Genealogical Society
P.O. Box 665
New Albany, IN 47151-0665

Tippecanoe County Area Genealogical Society
909 S. St.
Lafayette, IN 47901

IOWA

Iowa Genealogical Society
P.O. Box 7735
Des Moines, IA 50322-7735

Northeast Iowa Genealogical Society
503 S. St.
Waterloo, IA 50701

Northwest Iowa Genealogical Society
46 First St. S.W.
Le Mars, IA 51031

KANSAS

Kansas Genealogical Society
P.O. Box 103
Dodge City, KS 67801

Kansas Council of Genealogical Societies
P.O. Box 3858
Topeka, KS 66604-6858

Reno County Genealogical Society
P.O. Box 5
Hutchinson, KS 67504-0005

Topeka Genealogical Society
P.O. Box 4048
Topeka, KS 66604-0048

KENTUCKY

Eastern Kentucky Genealogical Society
P.O. Box 1544
Ashland, KY 41105-1544

Kentucky Genealogical Society
P.O. Box 153
Frankfort, KY 40602

Louisville Genealogical Society
P.O. Box 5164 DGS
Louisville, KY 40255-0164

**West-Central Kentucky
Family Research Association**
P.O. Box 1932
Owensboro, KY 42302

LOUISIANA

Baton Rouge Genealogical Society
P.O. Box 80565
SE Station
Baton Rouge, LA 70898

Louisiana Genealogical and Historical Society
P.O. Box 3454
Baton Rouge, LA 70821

MAINE

Maine Genealogical Society
P.O. Box 221
Farmington, ME 04938

MARYLAND

Baltimore County Genealogical Society
P.O. Box 10085
Towson, MD 21204

Historical Society of Charles County
P.O. Box 261
Port Tobacco, MD 20677

Maryland Genealogical Society
201 W. Monument St.
Baltimore, MD 21201

Prince George's County Genealogical Society
P.O. Box 819
Bowie, MD 20718-0819

MASSACHUSETTS

Berkshire Family History Association, Inc.
P.O. Box 1437
Pittsfield, MA 01201

Essex Society of Genealogists
P.O. Box 313
Lynnfield, MA 01940

Massachusetts Genealogical Council
P.O. Box 5393
Cochituate, MA 01778

The Massachusetts Society of Genealogists, Inc.
P.O. Box 215
Ashland, MA 01721-0215

MICHIGAN

The Detroit Society for Genealogical Research
Detroit Public Library
5201 Woodward Ave.
Detroit, MI 48202

Genealogical Society of Washtenaw County, Michigan
P.O. Box 7155
Ann Arbor, MI 48107

Kalamazoo Valley Genealogical Society
P.O. Box 405
Comstock, MI 49041

Michigan Genealogical Council
P.O. Box 80953
Lansing, MI 48908-0593

MINNESOTA

Minnesota Genealogy Society
P.O. Box 16069
St. Paul, MN 55116-0069

MISSISSIPPI

Mississippi Genealogical Society
P.O. Box 5301
Jackson, MS 39216-5301

MISSOURI

Missouri State Genealogical Association
P.O. Box 833
Columbia, MO 65205-0833

Northwest Missouri Genealogical Society
P.O. Box 382
St. Joseph, MO 64502-0382

Ozarks Genealogical Society
P.O. box 3945
Springfield, MO 65808-3945

St. Louis Genealogical Society
9011 Manchester Rd.
Suite No. 3
Brentwood, MO 63144

MONTANA

Montana State Genealogical Society
P.O. Box 555
Chester, MT 59522

Great Falls Genealogy Society
Paris Gibson Square
1400 First Ave.N., Room 30
Great Falls, MT 59401-3299

NEBRASKA

Greater Omaha Genealogical Society
P.O. Box 4011
Omaha, NE 68104

Lincoln-Lancaster Genealogical Society
P.O. Box 30055
Lincoln, NE 68503-0055

Nebraska State Genealogical Society
P.O. Box 5608
Lincoln, NE 68505-0608

NEVADA

Nevada State Genealogical Society
P.O. Box 20666
Reno, NV 89515-0066

Clark County Genealogical Society
P.O. Box 1929
Las Vegas, NV 89125-1929

NEW HAMPSHIRE

New Hampshire Society of Genealogists
P.O. Box 2316
Concord, NH 03302-2316

NEW JERSEY

Gloucester County Historical Society
17 Hunter St.
P.O. Box 409
Woodbury, NJ 08096-0409

Genealogical Society of New Jersey
P.O. Box 1291
New Brunswick, NJ 08903-1291

Monmouth County Genealogy Club
Monmouth County Historical Association
70 Court St.
Freehold, NJ 07728

Morris Area Genealogy Society
P.O. Box 105
Convent Station, NJ 07961

Genealogical Society of the West Fields
550 E. Broad St.
Westfield, NJ 07090

NEW MEXICO

Genealogy Club of the Albuquerque
Public Library
423 Central Ave. N.E.
Albuquerque, NM 87102

New Mexico Genealogical Society
P.O. Box 8283
Albuquerque, NM 87198-8283

Southern New Mexico Genealogical Society
1840 Amis Ave.
Las Cruces, NM 88005-1652

NEW YORK

Capital District Genealogical Society
P.O. Box 2175
Empire State Plaza
Albany, NY 12220-0175

Central New York Genealogical Society
P.O. Box 104, Colvin Station
Syracuse, NY 13205

Dutchess County Genealogical Society
P.O. Box 708
Poughkeepsie, NY 12603

New York State Council of Genealogical
Organizations
P.O. Box 2593
Syracuse, NY 13220-2593

New York Genealogical and Biographical Society
122 E. 58th St.
New York, NY 10022-1939

Western New York Genealogical Society
P.O. Box 338
Hamburg, NY 14075-0338

NORTH CAROLINA
Carolinas Genealogical Society
P.O. Box 397
Monroe, NC 28111

Forsyth County Genealogical Society
P.O. Box 5715
Winston-Salem, NC 27113-5715

Johnson County Genealogical Society
c/o Public Library of Johnson County
Smithfield, NC 27577

North Carolina Genealogical Society
P.O. Box 1492
Raleigh, NC 27602

Wilkes Genealogical Society
P.O. Box 1629
North Wilkesboro, NC 28659

NORTH DAKOTA
Bismark-Mandan Historical and Genealogical Soc.
P.O. Box 485
North Wilkesboro, NC 28659

Red River Valley Genealogical Society
P.O. Box 9284
Fargo, ND 58106

OHIO
The Greater Cleveland Genealogical Society
P.O. Box 40254
Cleveland, OH 44140

Ohio Genealogical Society
34 Sturges Ave.
P.O. Box 2625
Mansfield, OH 44906

OKLAHOMA
Federation of Oklahoma Genealogical Societies
P.O. Box 26151
Oklahoma City, OK 73126

Oklahoma Genealogical Society
P.O. Box 12986
Oklahoma City, OK 73157-2986

OREGON
Genealogical Council of Oregon, Inc.
P.O. Box 15169
Portland, OR 97215

Genealogical Forum of Oregon
2130 S.W. 5th Ave.
Suite 220
Portland, OR 97201-4934

Oregon Genealogical Society, Inc.
P.O. Box 10306
Eugene, OR 97440-2306

PENNSYLVANIA
Blair County Genealogical Society
P.O. Box 855
Altoona, PA 16603

Cornerstone Genealogical Society
P.O. Box 547
Waynesburg, PA 15370

Genealogy Society of Pennsylvania
1305 Locust St.
Philadelphia, PA 19107

Historical Society of Western Pennsylvania and Western Pennsylvania Genealogical Society
4338 Bigelow Blvd.
P.O. Box 8530
Pittsburgh, PA 15220-0530

South Central Pennsylvania Genealogical Society
P.O. Box 1824
York, PA 17405-1824

RHODE ISLAND
Rhode Island Genealogical Society
507 Clark's Row
Bristol, RI 02809-1481

SOUTH CAROLINA

Chester District Genealogical Society
P.O. Box 336
Richburg, SC 29729

South Carolina Genealogical Society
P.O. Box 16355
Greenville, SC 29606

SOUTH DAKOTA

Sioux Valley Genealogical Society
200 W. Sixth St.
Sioux Falls, SD 57104-6881

South Dakota Genealogical Society
P.O. Box 490
Winner, SD 57580

TENNESSEE

Jefferson County Genealogical Society
P.O. Box 267
Jefferson City, TN 37760

Middle Tennessee Genealogical Society
P.O. Box 190625
Nashville, TN 37219-0625

Tennessee Genealogical Society
P.O. Box 111249
Memphis, TN 38111-1249

TEXAS

Austin Genealogical Society
P.O. Box 1507
Austin, TX 78767-1507

Dallas Genealogical Society
P.O. Box 12648
Dallas, TX 75225-0648

Houston Area Genealogical Association
2507 Tannehill
Houston, TX 77008-3052

Texas State Genealogical Society
Route 4, Box 56
Sulphur Springs, TX 75482

Tip O' Texas Genealogical Society
410 76 Dr.
Harlingen, TX 78550

UTAH

Utah Genealogical Association
P.O. Box 1144
Salt Lake City, UT 84110

VERMONT

Vermont Genealogical Society
P.O. Box 422
Pittsford, VT 05763

VIRGINIA

Genealogical Research Institute of Virginia
P.O. Box 29178
Richmond, VA 23242-0178

Tidewater Virginia Genealogical Society
P.O. Box 7650
Hampton, VA 23666

Virginia Genealogical Society
5001 W. Broad St. No. 115
Richmond, VA 23230-3023

WASHINGTON

Clark County Genealogical Society
P.O. Box 2728
Vancouver, WA
98668-2728

Eastside Genealogical Society
P.O. Box 374
Bellevue, WA 98009

Washington State Genealogical Society
P.O. Box 1422
Olympia, WA 98507

WEST VIRGINIA

Kanawha Valley Genealogical Society
P.O. Box 8555
South Charleston, WV 25303

West Virginia Genealogical Society
P.O. Box 249
Elkview, WV 25071

WISCONSIN

Milwaukee County Genealogical Society
P.O. Box 27326
Milwaukee, WI 53227-0326

Wisconsin Genealogical Council
6083 Co. Trk. S.
Wisconsin Rapids, WI 54495

Wisconsin State Genealogical Society
2109 Twentieth Ave.
Monroe, WI 53566-3426

WYOMING

Fremont County Genealogical Society
Riverton Branch Library
1330 W. Park Ave.
Riverton, WY 82501

Major U.S. Genealogical Libraries

This appendix identifies three types of genealogical libraries in the United States: major public and private libraries with significant genealogical collections, state libraries, and genealogical rental libraries. For additional addresses of other useful libraries, see *The Ancestry Family Historian's Address Book* (Salt Lake City: Ancestry, 1998), compiled by Juliana Szucs Smith, which contains the most extensive list of genealogical addresses, URLs, and e-mail addresses in print today.

LIBRARIES WITH NATIONAL OR REGIONAL COLLECTIONS

The following libraries have excellent collections that cover much more than just the state where they are located. These are often considered "destination" libraries—major collections around which entire trips may be planned. The list is arranged by region of the country. Within each region, libraries with the largest genealogical collections are listed first. An asterisk (*) indicates that the library is a private, not public, institution and therefore may have some usage restrictions or limited hours.

Eastern States

American Antiquarian Society*
185 Salisbury Street
Worcester, MA 01609-1634
Tel.: 508-755-5221

Godfrey Memorial Library*
134 Newfield Street
Middletown, CT 06457
Tel.: 860-346-4375

Fax: 860-347-9874
E-mail: godfrey@connix.com
http://www.godfrey.org

Historical Society of Pennsylvania
1300 Locust Street
Philadelphia, PA 19107
Tel.: 215-732-6201
Fax: 215-732-2680
E-mail: hsppr@aol.com
http://www.libertynet.ort/~pahist

New England Historic Genealogical Society Library*
99-101 Newbury Street
Boston, MA 02116-3007
Tel.: 616-536-5740
Fax: 617-536-7307
E-mail: nehgs@nehgs.org
http://www.nehgs.org

New York Genealogical and Biographical Society Library*
122 East Fifty-Eighth Street
New York, NY 10022-1939
Tel.: 212-755-8532
http://www.tnp.com/nycgenweb/NYG&BS.htm

New York Public Library
Local History and Genealogy Division
5th Avenue and 42nd Street
New York, NY 10016
Tel.: 212-340-0849
http://www.nypl.org

Southern States and Washington, D.C.

Dallas Public Library
Genealogy Section
1515 Young Street
Dallas, TX 75202
Tel.: 214-670-1400
Fax: 214-670-7839
http://central4.lib.ci.dallas.tx.us

Ellen Payne Odom Genealogical Library
204 Fifth Street, SE
P.O. Box 1110
Moultrie, GA 31776-1110
Tel.: 912-985-6540
Fax: 912-985-0936
E-mail: jenkinsm@mail.colquitt.public.lib.ga.us
http://www.firstct.com/fv/EPO.html

Houston Public Library
Clayton Library Center for Genealogical Research
5300 Caroline
Houston, TX 77004-6896
Tel.: 713-524-0101
http://sparc.hpl.lib.tx.us/hpl/clayton.html

L. W. Anderson Genealogical Library*
William Carey College, Hwy. 90
P.O. Box 1647
Gulfport, MS 39502
Tel.: 601-865-1554

Library of Congress
Local History and Genealogy Division
101 Independence Avenue, S.E.
Washington, D.C. 20540
Tel.: 202-287-5537
E-mail: lcweb@loc.gov
http://www.lcweb.loc.gov

National Genealogical Society Library*
4527 Seventeenth Avenue North
Arlington, VA 22207-2363
Tel.: 703-525-0050
Fax: 703-525-0052
E-mail: 76702.2417@compuserv.com
http://www.genealogy.org/~ngs

National Society, Daughters of the American Revolution Library*
1776 D Street, N.W.

Washington, D.C. 20006-5392
Tel.: 202-879-3229

National Society of the Sons of the American Revolution Library*
1000 South Fourth Street
Louisville, KY 40203
Tel.: 502-589-1776
Tel.: 505-589-1776
http://www.sar.org

University of Texas at Austin
The Center for American History
Sid Richardson Hall, Unit 2
Austin, TX 78713
Tel.: 512-495-4250
http://www.lib.utexas.edu

Midwestern States

Allen County Public Library Reynolds Historical Genealogy Department
900 Webster Street
P.O. Box 2270
Fort Wayne, IN 46802
Tel.: 219-424-7241
http://www.acpl.lib.in.us

Detroit Public Library
Burton Historical Collection
5201 Woodward Avenue
Detroit, MI 48202
Tel.: 313-833-1480
Fax: 313-832-0877
E-mail: nvangor@cms.cc.wayne.edu
http://www.detroit.lib.mi.us

Mid-Continent Public Library
North Independence Branch
Genealogy and Local History Department
15616 East 24 Highway
Independence, MO 64050
Tel.: 816-252-0950
E-mail: ge@mcpl.lib.mo.us
http://www.mcpl.lib.mo.us/gen.htm

Minnesota Historical Society
345 Kellog Boulevard
St. Paul, MN 55102-1906
Tel.: 612-296-0332
http://www.mnhs.org

Newberry Library*
Local and Family History Section
Sixty West Walton Street
Chicago, IL 60610-3305
Tel.: 312-255-3512
E-mail: furmans@newberry.org
http://www.newberry.org

**Public Library of Cincinnati
and Hamilton County**
800 Vine Street, Library Square
Cincinnati, OH 45202-2071
Tel.: 513-369-6905
Fax: 513-369-6067
E-mail: comments@plch.lib.oh.us
http://plch.lib.oh.us

St. Louis Public Library
History and Genealogy Department
1301 Olive Street
St. Louis, MO 63103
Tel.: 314-241-2288
Fax: 314-539-0393
E-mail: webmaster@slpl.lib.mo.us
http://www.slpl.lib.mo.us

State Historical Society of Wisconsin
Genealogy Section
816 State Street
Madison, WI 53706
Tel.: 608-264-6535
http://www.shsw.wisc.edu

Western Reserve Historical Society Library
Case Western Reserve University
10825 East Boulevard
Cleveland, OH 44106-1788
Tel.: 216-721-5722
http://www.cwru/edu

Western States
Brigham Young University
Harold B. Lee Library
Provo, UT 84602
Tel.: 801-378-6200
http://www.lib.byu.edu

Denver Public Library
Genealogy Division
Western History Collection

1357 Broadway
Denver, CO 80203-2165
Tel.: 303-571-2190

Family History Library*
Thirty-Five North West Temple Street
Salt Lake City, UT 84150
Tel.: 801-240-2331
http://www.lds.org/Family_History/How_Do_
I_Begin.html

Family History Library*
Thirty-Five North West Temple Street
Salt Lake City, UT 84150
Tel.: 801-240-2331
http://www.lds.org/Family_History/How_Do_
I_Begin.html

Los Angeles Public Library
History and Genealogy Department
630 West Fifth Street
Los Angeles, CA 90071
Tel.: 213-228-7400
Fax: 213-228-7409
E-mail: history@lapl.org
http://www.lapl.org/central/hihp.html

Ricks College
McKay Library
525 South Center
Rexburg, ID 83440
Tel.: 208-356-2377
http://www.ricks.edu

Seattle Public Library
Genealogy Section
1000 Fourth Avenue
Seattle, WA 98104
Tel.: 206-386-4625
http://www.spl.lib.wa.us/contents.html

STATE LIBRARIES

Every state has a state library or a related government department that functions as a state library. However, not every state library has a large collection of books about the state; some state libraries are only administrative offices that direct library services throughout the state. This list identifies the state library or similarly responsible department for every state, regardless of the nature of its collection. Even those without research collections can direct the researcher to the most useful libraries and collections in the state. State historical societies, which often have the best genealogical collection in a state, are not listed here unless they also serve as the state library. For a full list of state historical societies, see appendix C in *The Source: A Guidebook of American Genealogy*, rev. ed.

Alabama Department of Archives and History
624 Washington Avenue
Montgomery, Al 36130-3601
Tel.: 205-242-4435

Alaska State Library
State Office Building, Eighth Floor
Juneau, AK 99801
Tel.: 907-465-2921

**Arizona Department of Library,
Archives and Public Records**
State Capitol
1700 West Washington
Phoenix, AZ 85007
Tel.: 602-542-3942

Arkansas State Library
Department of Education
1 Capitol Mall
Little Rock, AR 72201
Tel.: 501-682-1527

California State Library
California Section
914 Capitol Mall
P.O. Box 942837
Sacramento, CA 95814
Tel.: 916-654-0176

Colorado State Library
201 East Colfax Avenue
Denver, CO 80203
Tel.: 303-866-6728

Connecticut State Library
History and Genealogy Unit
231 Capitol Avenue
Hartford, CT 06106
Tel.: 203-566-3690

Delaware Division of Libraries
Department of Community Affairs
43 South Dupont Highway
Dover, DE 19901
Tel.: 302-736-4748

State Library of Florida
Florida Collection
Division of Library and Information Services
R.A. Gray Building, Second Floor
500 South Bronough Street
Tallahassee, FL 323990-0250
Tel.: 904-487-2073

Georgia Department of Archives and History
Office of Secretary of State
330 Capitol Avenue, S.E.
Atlanta, GA 30334
Tel.: 404-656-2350

Hawaii State Library
Hawaii and Pacific Section
478 South King Street
Honolulu, HI 96813
Tel.: 808-586-3535

Idaho State Historical Society
Genealogical Library
325 West State Street
Boise, ID 83702
Tel.: 208-334-2305

Illinois State Library
300 South Second Street
Springfield, IL 62701
Tel.: 217-782-5430

Indiana State Library
Indiana Division
140 North Senate Avenue
Indianapolis, IN 46204
Tel.: 317-232-3689

State Historical Society of Iowa
Library/Archives Bureau
600 East Locust, Capitol Complex
Des Moines, IA 50319
Tel.: 515-281-6200

Kansas State Library
Third Floor, Statehouse
Topeka, KS 66612
Tel.: 913-296-3296

Kentucky State Archives
Kentucky Department for Libraries and Archives
300 Coffee Tree Road
P.O. Box 537
Frankfort, KY 40602-0537
Tel.: 502-875-7000

State Library of Louisiana
760 North Third Street
P.O. Box 131
Baston Rouge, LA 70804-9125
Tel.: 504-922-1206

Maine State Library
State House Station, Number 64
Augusta, ME 04333
Tel.: 207-287-5600

Maryland State Archives
Hall of Records Building
350 Rowe Boulevard
Annapolis, MD 21401
Tel.: 410-974-3914

State Library of Massachusetts
George Fingold Library
341 State House
Beacon Street
Boston, MA 02133
Tel.: 617-727-2590

Library of Michigan
717 West Allegan Street
P.O. Box 30007
Lansing, MI 48909
Tel.: 517-373-1300

Minnesota Historical Society Research Center
345 Kellog Boulevard, West
Saint Paul, MN 55102-1906
Tel.: 612-296-2143

Mississippi Department of Archives and History
100 South State Street
P.O. Box 571

Jackson, MS 39205-0571
Tel.: 601-359-6850

Missouri State Library
301 West High Street
P.O. Box 387
Jefferson City, MO 65102
Tel.: 314-751-3615

Montana State Library
1515 East Sixth Avenue
Helena, MT 59620
Tel.: 406-444-3004

Nebraska State Historical Society
1500 R Street, Lincoln, NE 68508
P.O. Box 82554
Lincoln, NE 68501-2554
Tel.: 402-471-4771

Nevada State Library and Archives
Division of Archives and Records
100 Stewart Street
Carson City, NV 89710
Tel.: 702-687-5210

New Hampshire State Library
20 Park Street
Cconcord, NH 03301
Tel.: 603-271-2144

New Jersey State Library
Genealogy Section
185 West State Street
Trenton, NJ 08625-0520
Tel.: 609-292-6274

New Mexico State Library
Southwest Room
325 Don Gasper Avenue
Santa Fe, NM 87503
Tel.: 505-827-3805

New York State Library
Genealogy Section
Seventh Floor, Cultural Education Center
Empire State Plaza
Albany, NY 12230
Tel.: 518-474-5161

State Library of North Carolina
109 East Jones Street
Raleigh, NC 27601-2807
Tel.: 919-733-7222

North Dakota State Library
Liberty Memorial Building/Capitol Grounds
Bismarck, ND 58505
Tel.: 701-224-4622

State Library of Ohio
Genealogy Division
65 South Front Street
Columbus, OH 43266-0334
Tel.: 614-644-6966

Oklahoma Department of Libraries
200 N.E. Eighteenth Street
Oklahoma City, OK 73105-3298
Tel.: 405-521-2502

Oregon State Library
Winter and Court Streets, N.E.
Salem, OR 97310
Tel.: 503-378-4277

State Library of Pennsylvania
Forum Building
Walnut Street and Commonwealth Avenue
P.O. Box 1601
Harrisburg, PA 17105
Tel.: 717-787-4440

Rhode Island State Library
Office of the Secretary of State
337 Westminster Street
Providence, RI 02903
Tel.: 401-277-2353

South Carolina State Library
1500 Senate Street
P.O. Box 11469
Columbia, SC 29211
Tel.: 803-734-8666

South Dakota State Library
Memorial Building Branch
800 Governors drive
Pierre, SD 57501-2294
Tel.: 605-773-3131

Tennessee State Library and Archives
403 Seventh Avenue, North
Nashville, TN 37243-0312
Tel.: 615-741-2764

Texas State Library
1201 Brazos Street
P.O. Box 12927
Austin, TX 78711
Tel.: 512-463-5455

Utah State Library
2150 South 300 West
Salt Lake City, UT 84114
Tel.: 801-466-5888

Vermont Department of Libraries
Pavilion Office Building
109 State Street
Montpelier, VT 05609-0601
Tel.: 802-828-3268

Virginia State Library and Archives
Eleventh Street at Capitol Square
Richmond, VA 23219-3291
Tel.: 804-786-8929

Washington State Library
Washington/Northwest Collection
P.O. Box 9000
Olympia, WA 98504-0238
Tel.: 206-753-4024

West Virginia Division of Culture and History
The Cultural Center
1900 Kanawha Boulevard, East
Charleston, WV 25305-0300
Tel.: 304-558-0230

Wisconsin State Historical Society
816 State Street
Madison, WI 53706
Tel.: 608-264-6535

Wyoming State Library
Supreme Court and Library Building
3201 Capitol Avenue
Cheynne, WY 82002
Tel.: 307-777-7281

GENEALOGICAL RENTAL LIBRARIES

The following libraries circulate books (or microfilm) by mail for a fee. Contact them for a list of titles as well as costs and procedures for borrowing books. Most require membership for borrowing privileges.

Public Libraries and Genealogical Societies
AFRA Collection
Interlibrary Loan Dept.
Mid-Continent Public Library
15616 East 24 Highway
Independence, MO 64050
Tel.: 816-252-0950
Approximately three thousand circulating titles are available via interlibrary loan.

AFRA Collection
(Bound periodicals, tapes, films)
Alexander Mitchell Public Library
Interlibrary Dept.
519 South Kline Street
Aberdeen, SD 57401
Tel.: 605-622-7097
Approximately six hundred titles available.

Connecticut Historical Society
1 Elizabeth Street at Asylum Avenue
Hartford, CT 06105
Tel.: 203-236-5621
16,000-volume circulating collection

NGS Library Loan Service
4527 Seventeenth Street, North
Arlington, VA 22207
Tel.: 703-525-0050

New England Historic and Genealogical Society
101 Newbury Street
Boston, MA 02116-3087
Tel.: 617-536-5740
Circulating collection of ten thousand volumes, including family histories.

Private Companies and Collections American Genealogical Lending Library
P.O. Box 244
Bountiful, UT 84010
Tel.: 801-298-5358
Around 250,000 titles on microfilm/microfiche.

Genealogical Center Library
P.O. Box 71343
Atlanta, GA 30007-1343
7,000 books.

Genealogy Unlimited
Rental Library & Supplies
Route 8, Box 702-J
Tucson, AZ 85748

Heritage Researchers Library
P.O. Box 836
Terre Haute, IN 47808

Hoenstine Rental Library
414 Montgomery Street
P.O. Box 208
Hollidaysburg, PA 16648
814-695-0632
More than three thousand books, most for Pennsylvania.

Rent from Roberts
503 Locust St.
Mt. Vernon, IN 47620

Stagecoach Library for Genealogical Research
1840 South Wolcott Court
Denver, CO 80219
Tel.: 303-922-8856

Index

This index includes subject entries and selected bibliographic entries for authors and titles. Book titles appear in italics, as do foreign words. Repositories have been indexed only when their collection is unique or more extensive than that of other repositories.

F

Family
  Bible, 33, 64, 100
  category in Periodical Source Index,
    188
  collections, 68
  events, 66
  health history, 90
  histories, 18
  histories, unpublished, 156
  illness, hereditary, 90
  letters, 102
  resemblances, 195
  sources, 101
  traditions, 75, 192
Family History Dept. of the LDS Church,
  78
Family History Library Catalog®, 78
Family History Library (Salt Lake City),
  17, 20, 44, 76
  Ancestral File®, 52
  Family History Centers™, 78
  historical collection, 46
FamilySearch®, 78, 79
Farm Bureau, 44
Farm Credit Administration, 30
Farmers Home Administration, 30
Farms and ranches
  directories, 57
  family-owned, 44, 45
Farriers, 58
Federal
  agency reports, investigation of, 231
  buildings and grounds, 23
  census
    see Census, federal, 161
  employees, 169
Federal Extension Service, 30
Federation of Genealogical Societies Society
  Hall, 88
Federation of Women's Clubs Web site, 236
Feltner, Charles E. and Jeri Barton, 134
Filby, P. William, 12
Fingerprinting, 14
Fire-fighter pension records, 186
Fire insurance maps, 80
Fishing, 134
Five Civilized Tribes, 110, 113
  see also Indian Commission on,
    111, 113
Flood control, 31
Food Administration, 30
Foreign
  birth, marriage, and death records, 81
  emigration, records of, 82, 83
  relations, 21
Foreign Service Posts, 81
Foresters
  see also Organizations, fraternal

Catholic Order of, 95
Foundations, 38
France
  immigrants, 29
  Jews deported from, 99
  Quasi War with, 12, 14, 29
Franco-American Club, 75
Fraternities
  see Organizations, fraternal
Free black men, 10
Freebooter, 2
Freedman's Savings and Trust Company, 86
Freedmen's Bureau, 86, 87
Freedmen's Bureau of Refuges, Freedmen
  and abandoned land, 30
Freedmen's Savings and Trust Company, 87
Freedom of Information Act, 14, 217, 218
Freemasons
  see Masons
French Alien Registration, 13
Funeral
  directors, 150
  homes, 150
  memorial cards, 33
  record, 151

G

*Gale Directory of Publications and Broadcast
  Media*, 166, 167
Gaylord Music Library, 161
Gazetteers, 130
GEDCOM, 52, 78
Genealogical Resources in the New York
  Metropolitan Area, 229
Genealogical Society of Utah, 20
Genealogical society records, 88, 89
General Land Office, 23, 102
Genetics studies, 90, 91
Georgia, 74
German Alien Registrations, 14
Godfrey Memorial Library (Middletown,
  Conn.), 18, 38
Government
  document repositories, 230
  documents, unpublished, 237
  local, 38, 237
  publications, 231
Government Printing Office, 219, 230
Graduation programs, 50
Grand Army of the Republic, 92, 93
  Ladies of the, 93
Grange, National, 85
Grantee/grantor, 62
Grants land, 21, 102
Graphic material, 189
Graves, 42
Gravestones
  see also Tombstone
  WPA Index to Cemetery, 227

*Great Lakes Maritime History: Bibliography
  and Sources of Information*, 134, 136
Great Lakes Maritime Institute, 153
Gregory, Winifred, 164
Guardian, 140, 210
  apprentice's, 24
Guardianship, 25, 58, 94, 95, 200
  petition, 95
*Guide to Federal Records in the Federal
  Archives of the United States*, 23
*Guide to Local and Family History at
  The Newberry Library*, 124
*Guide to Research in Baltimore City and
  County*, 229
Guide to the Draper Manuscripts, 74
Guzik, Estelle, 229

H

Hamburg passenger lists, 82, 83
Hansen, James L., 165
Harbors, 31
Harper, Josephine, 74
Headstones
  see Tombstones
Health Service, 30
Heirlooms, 33
Heirs, 58
Hereditary
  illnesses, 90
  societies, 96, 97
Historical
  conditions and context, 31
  see also Lifestyle in period and place
    societies, 42
Historical Farm Award, 44
Historical Records Survey of the WPA,
  206, 237
Histories
  city, 207
  county, 207
  health, 115
  local, 164
*History and Bibliography of American
  Newspapers 1690-1820*, 164
Holocaust
  see also World War II
  records, 99
  victims, 161
Home sources, 75, 100, 190
Homeownership, 47
Homestead, 21, 102, 103
  declaration, 103
  locating, 130
  requirements, 102
Homestead Act of 1862, 102
Hospital records, 104, 105
Housing, public, 30
Howells, Cyndi, 118

Y